Judith Stephenson
Dept. Of Sociology

# Cross-Cultural Research Methods

*Comparative Studies in Behavioral Science:*

A WILEY SERIES

Robert T. Holt and John E. Turner, *Editors*
Department of Political Science
University of Minnesota

# Cross-Cultural Research Methods

**RICHARD W. BRISLIN**

*Culture Learning Institute*
*East-West Center*

**WALTER J. LONNER**

*Center for Cross-Cultural Research*
*Department of Psychology*
*Western Washington State College*

**ROBERT M. THORNDIKE**

*Department of Psychology*
*Western Washington State College*

*A Wiley-Interscience Publication*

**JOHN WILEY & SONS**

New York • London • Sydney • Toronto

Tables 9.1, 9.3, and 9.4 and the formulas on page 269 are reprinted by permission from Harry H. Harmon, *Modern Factor Analysis,* © 1960, 1967 by The University of Chicago Press.

*Library of Congress Cataloging in Publication Data:*

Brislin, Richard W                 1945-
  Cross-cultural research methods.

  (Comparative studies in behavioral sciences)
  Bibliography: p.
  1. Ethnopsychology—Methodology. 2. Social
sciences—Methodology. I. Lonner, Walter J., joint
author. II. Thorndike, Robert M., joint author.
III. Title. [DNLM: 1. Anthropology, Cultural.
2. Cross-cultural comparison. 3. Social behavior.
GN·400 B859c 1973]

GN273.B7            155.8'01'8         73-772
ISBN 0-471-10470-1

Printed in the United States of America

10 9 8 7 6 5 4 3 2 1

# Foreword

There are many, many good reasons why psychologists and their adherents should be interested in cross-cultural research. Hypotheses and hunches concerning socialized behavior derived from caged animals, captured college students, and patients or normal adults in Western society need to be tested and perhaps modified in cultures having different traditions and confronted with diverse environmental conditions. Those contributors to scholarly journals who write as if they had examined a representative sample of the world's population or who first describe what they have done in the past tense and then suggest they have established an eternal verity by suddenly switching to the present tense in the discussion sections of their papers would not perpetrate such illicit, sly generalizing if they were to imagine how persons in Asia, Africa, Central Australia, Latin America, or the Arctic regions might react to their methodological procedures. New phenomena are observed, new ideas are virtually inevitable the moment one plunges into a strange group without resisting the thrills from culture shock—and if you think I exaggerate you need only thumb through the rest of this book. Each society has its own somewhat unique problems and offers equally novel research opportunities. Then there are straight facts to be gathered, facts describing the differences between us and them or attempting to chart systematically the changes they are or are not undergoing in this merry miserable world. Such facts are valuable in their own right because facts are always patently needed and because now or later, we think they contribute to systematic theory.

Most psychologists are human beings and are able to find ethical or personal reasons to embark on jet planes to reach research sites. Developing nations actually seek, or can be made to realize that they should seek, psychologists to help solve some of their political or educational problems. Help means research. Few of us know or can acquire the languages spoken by peoples outside our conventional linguistic orbit; some of the translators and research assistants we employ eventually can be trained to succeed us in universities, governments, or private organizations. Here is only one of the quid-pro-quo's foreigners can offer hosts who provide research opportunities. Indeed, if the investigator's research is truly beneficial, he may lighten the cross Americans carry abroad as a result of the reputation of the C.I.A. and the bad manners of some of our predecessors who have ruthlessly interfered with people's lives by pushing their own research at all costs or who have failed to send back the promised report, reprint, or monograph.

Of course, whoever conducts cross-cultural research benefits over and beyond the additions to his bibliography. Unless he isolates himself in an enclave of compatriots, he becomes a little less ethnocentric. He is compelled to view the problems of his discipline and of his own society somewhat differently. He may possibly be able to feel like a citizen of the world without diminishing the meaningfully emotional components of his own patriotism.

The advantages of cross-cultural research in psychology—or any social science for that matter—are thus evident, *but* conducting cross-cultural research is not like stepping into a cozy laboratory or clinic. Much more than the tricky task of translating from one language to another confronts psychologists working in foreign countries. We have in this volume, really for the first time, a detailed, sophisticated exposition of the numerous salient problems arising when any method in the behavioral sciences is employed outside its area of origin. Forever after psychologists departing for the field can alert themselves to the difficulties they will face in planning and executing their research. In addition, the experimentalist and the clinician who are busy at home as well as students or the intellectually curious are here provided with solid bases for evaluating the cross-cultural studies they bring to their own attention. Bravo, thanks, we say to Professors Brislin and Lonner for offering this lucid, balanced guide through the jungle and to Professor Thorndike for patiently explaining how some of the more intricate statistical tools can facilitate the trek.

We are also grateful to the authors for a decision they made at the outset, wittingly or unwittingly. It would have been not only dull and boring but also undesirable and perhaps impossible to blueprint cross-cultural methodology without copious, relevant, and appealing examples. As a result the reader will find in every single chapter more than a catalog of do's and dont's. If fact, if I may discharge the conventional function of a foreword to a book, which is to preview and praise the contents, virtually every significant cross-cultural study having even remote psychological implications has been cogently summarized and in many instances intriguingly illustrated. Toward the end the authors fortunately stray so far from the purposes set forth in their first chapter that they provide us with provoking generalizations and sagacious suggestions concerning theory-building. Another bravo.

I must note one more praiseworthy misdemeanor that makes this book more valuable than the modest authors may have intended. The research they report has emerged, according to them, "within the last twenty-five years," though I think a careless or careful glance at their impressive list of references shows that most of it is less than a decade old. During this period the boundaries between psychology and the other social sciences have become thinner and thinner until it is frequently impossible to find them. The title of the present volume explicitly suggests that it is "concerned with psychology," but what do we find in its pages? Shockingly copious and refreshing references to the methods and discoveries of researchers who belong officially to other academic guilds, especially anthropology. It is pleasing to note here the Zeitgeist, since it has promoted a virtuous departure from an arbitrary convention that used to block interdisciplinary creativity.

Two serious caveats, which I cannot suppress. It should be obvious from what I have been saying, and it will be calmly demonstrated throughout this book, that cross-cultural research is incredibly exciting and rewarding. But investigation in exotic places is not all whiskey and curry. You may not get a visa to the country of your choice or, even if you do, you may not obtain permission to carry on research. You may get sick. You may even be lonesome. Your informants may not be punctual or they may never appear. Your well-laid plan formulated at home in the peaceful quiet of a library or an office may turn out to be unreal. And so on—on and on. Little wonder that most graduate students in psychology find it easier to obtain their union cards and their instructors to add to their fame, and occasionally their fortunes, by studying domesticated persons and animals within a short distance from their home ruts. Courage is needed to work cross-culturally; hence the rewards may be greater.

The synthesis of psychology and the other social sciences that must take into account the generalizations resulting from cross-cultural research is not close at hand. This book pushes us an appreciable distance forward, which is cause for grateful joy without doubt. Anyone toiling in the vineyard, however, must confront himself solipsistically: are not cross-cultural problems similar to or at any rate not qualitatively different from those existing when one person would comprehend another person within the same culture? Ostensibly we speak the same language, but do we? In this nonmetaphorical sense each of us is a culture, and therefore the unsolved problems so well illuminated by our three guides are also our own pathetic perplexities almost every moment of existence.

*Leonard W. Doob*

The last decade has witnessed the burgeoning of comparative studies in the behavioral sciences. Scholars in specific disciplines have come to realize that they share much with experts in other fields who face similar theoretical and methodological problems and whose research findings are often related. Moreover, specialists in a given geographic area have felt the need to look beyond the limited confines of their region and to seek new meaning in their research results by comparing them with studies that have been made elsewhere.

This series is designed to meet the needs of the growing cadre of scholars in comparative research. The emphasis is on cross-disciplinary studies, although works within the perspective of a single discipline are included. In its scope, the series includes books of theoretical and methodological interest, as well as studies that are based on empirical research. The books in the series are addressed to scholars in the various behavioral science disciplines, to graduate students, and to undergraduates in advanced standing.

*Robert T. Holt*
*John E. Turner*

*University of Minnesota*
*Minneapolis, Minnesota*

# Preface

In both 1954 and 1968, John M. W. Whiting wrote chapters on cross-cultural methodology for the first and second editions, respectively, of the *Handbook of Social Psychology*. Coverage was limited to the use of ethnographies or the data collection efforts of others, such as the Human Relations Area Files. The term "cross-cultural methods," then, came to have an anthropological connotation for many social scientists. In 1967 and 1971, however, there were symposia at the meetings of the American Psychological Association that dealt with other problems in cross-cultural methodology, especially those involved in the gathering of new data. These included attitude measurement, experimentation, analyzing rival explanations for data, and translation. We prefer the broader connotation and so have written chapters for this book covering many types of problems that arise whenever a researcher wants to compare behavior across cultures. These include the use of anthropological data files, but since this topic is covered so well elsewhere (e.g., Naroll and Cohen, 1970) we have presented an introductory rather than a detailed treatment. Our more involved discussions are on psychological topics (e.g., the four symposia topics mentioned above, testing, and theory construction) for which there are few cross-cultural sources available for methodological guidance. We hope that the book will be useful to all social scientists, even though our treatments will undoubtedly reflect our training in psychology.

A few words about the development of the book may be of interest. R. B. attended the University of Guam as an undergraduate because of his father's job assignment. He became interested in cross-cultural problems since he was a minority group member at the school among his Guamanian, Micronesian, and Filipino classmates. He went to the "mainland" for graduate school, but came back to do his dissertation on translation since University of Guam students speak and write English and one of ten other languages. W. L. essentially completed graduate school in Europe. He became so intrigued by cross-cultural research while at the University of Minnesota that he decided to immerse himself

xi

in it via cross-cultural topics and problems and ultimately a dissertation. R. B. and W. L. met in early 1970 and decided to join their efforts in writing a book designed to cover a wide range of methodological guidelines and topics for cross-cultural studies. They concur that a book like this could not be found during their dissertation projects, and that such a treatment of methodological issues would have been of considerable value.

During the very early stages of book preparation we asked a specialist, Robert M. Thorndike, to write two chapters on multivariate techniques. These would be aimed at an audience not wanting explanations in terms of matrix algebra and not wanting complex derivations. He confirmed that there were few clear, intuitive, non-mathematical treatments available, and so he agreed to write on factor analysis and other multivariate techniques. He did a great deal of special reading so as to make specific recommendations for cross-cultural research. We feel that he did an excellent job and are pleased to list his name on the title page.

Some of the ideas in Chapter 2 were developed during the summer of 1968. R. B. traveled to Northwestern University to work as a research assistant with Donald T. Campbell. One product was a paper on translation, jointly prepared by Campbell, R. B., V. Mary Stewart, and Oswald Werner. The paper has been circulated informally under the title, "Back-translation and other translation techniques for cross-cultural research." The involved schedules of the four authors have prevented a final published version. We would like to acknowledge the excellent work of Campbell, Stewart, and Werner, but remind the reader that interpretations in the present Chapter 2 are our responsibility.

The book is organized in two parts. Part One contains seven chapters dealing with substantive issues such as translation, experimentation, survey methods, and the use of psychological tests. This section covers methodological and problematic issues that one would encounter in most cross-cultural research. Part Two contains more technical material. Those persons contemplating the use of specific psychological tests or multivariate statistics would want to consult this section. The use of Part Two implies an understanding of Part One, and not vice versa.

Any book covering a wide range of topics such as this one does requires a great deal of library research, typing of readable drafts, and occasional advice from scholars regarding specific issues. Dennis Krueger was helpful in the early stages of library research, especially in tracking down obscure material. We wish to thank Mrs. Ann Drake of Western Washington State College's Bureau for Faculty Research, our chief typist, and Mrs. Jane Clark of the same office for their prompt and expert typing. Dean Herbert C. Taylor, Jr., of the Bureau for Faculty Research, kindly made many hours of Mrs. Drake's and Mrs. Clark's precious time available to us, and provided us with financial assistance. Thanks are also due Miss Candy Knaus of the Department of Psychology, Western Washington State College, for typing various sections of the manuscript. Special thanks go to Ann Brislin, who happily and courageously accepted the dubious distinction of being an unpaid research assistant. One of her numerous jobs was organizing and checking the accuracy of our extensive bibliography. A number of psychologists who are top cross-cultural methodologists were kind enough to honor our requests to read small sections of the manuscript, and their comments were always helpful and illuminating. They included Raoul Naroll, Harrison Gough, Leonard Doob, Harry Triandis, and George Guthrie. John W. Berry, Gustav Jahoda, and Philip E. Vernon were able to send us copies of hard-to-find material, and John L. M. Dawson made portions of his manuscripts, simultaneously being prepared, available to us. Lee J. Cronbach kindly sent advance copies of papers which were read at a 1971 conference on mental testing held in Istanbul, Turkey. Our greatest thanks, however, go to hundreds of cross-cultural researchers whose often innovative and pioneering work we have been privileged to review. Without these precedents as guidelines, a book on cross-cultural research methods would be shallow indeed. Of course, we take full responsibility for the use we have made of all the comments and material we received. R. B. finished his sections of the manuscript while a fellow, then a permanent staff member of the East-West Center, Culture Learning Institute. He would like to thank his colleagues for the encouragement and support that they so generously gave.

We wish to give special thanks to our chief reviewers, John Turner and Robert Holt, for their helpful comments. Finally, we are indebted to our editor, Gardner Spungin.

**Richard W. Brislin**
**Walter J. Lonner**

*June 1972*

# Contents

# PART ONE
# *Substantive Issues*

# CHAPTER ONE

## *Introduction*

Cross-cultural research has attracted a growing number of social scientists who are fascinated both by its advantages and disadvantages. The field itself is generally concerned with behavior as conditioned by living in a given country, culture, or environment, and its specific objective is to make comparisons of behavior between cultures. Of course, "making comparisons" implies that the underlying reasons for similarities and differences are sought. The advantages and disadvantages of cross-cultural psychology may become clear with this example. A certain psychologist is interested in the effects of parental child-rearing practices on the personalities of the children. Since he does research in his own culture, however, he may find that the range of parental behaviors available for study is limited. At this point he may look at *other* cultures that have more or less extreme practices (e.g., swaddling, severe independence training, and total nurturance by parents and other culture members). By studying these cultures he increases the range of his independent variable of interest, child-rearing practices, and its effects on his dependent variable of interest, the children's personalities. The researcher can then test hypotheses developed in his own country (e.g., greater levels of parental nurturance lead to corresponding levels of dependence), and/or modify his hypotheses to incorporate the new data. This procedure of starting in his own country and then gathering data in others increases the predictive range of the hypotheses and accounts for behavior in several cultures rather than just the researcher's own (Whiting, 1968).

If the procedure were as easy as that sketched above, there would be a vast number of cross-cultural studies. The problem however, is in planning and carrying out the investigation, that is, in the cross-cultural methodology. Assume that the researcher discovers that a certain culture-group in central Africa employs the "key" child-rearing practice for his theory. He has to face these and other problems in gathering and interpreting the necessary data:

1. gaining access to the culture;
2. obtaining samples of people equivalent to respondents from comparison studies in the researcher's own culture;
3. writing meaningful questions and translating them;
4. ascertaining that the questions written in one language are equivalent in meaning to those in another;
5. assuring that any additional tools of research (tests, equipment) are not merely a momentary and strange imposition on subjects;
6. interviewing people who may be much more hostile or courteous (both leading to biases) to researchers than respondents from Western countries;
7. developing reasons for the obtained data that are a function of all cultures under study rather than the researcher's own unicultural biases.

These are the challenges of cross-cultural psychology, and they have attracted behavioral scientists interested in solving them. Possible solutions to these and other problems constitute the largest portion of this book. Before dealing with them, however, we will attempt to explain in more detail what cross-cultural psychology is. A formal and widely accepted definition of "cross-cultural psychology" is not yet available, but we hope to *explain* what the term means in four ways:

1. by attempting a working definition which will undoubtedly be modified in the future;
2. by looking at four types of research which have been called "cross-cultural research";
3. by examining what a researcher can gain by engaging in cross-cultural research;
4. by content-analyzing 200 articles that have been submitted to the *Journal of Cross-Cultural Psychology*.

## A Working Definition of Cross-Cultural Psychology

In the minds of most social scientists, the term "cross-cultural psychology" is associated with the comparison of behavior between members of different cultural groups. The terms "culture" or "cultural groups" are very difficult to define. Choice of a definition is made more difficult because of sheer numbers; well over 150 definitions of culture have been reviewed by Kroeber and Kluckhohn (1952). There is some communality among definitions, however, and the reviewers found that the following "central idea is now formulated by most scientists. . .":

"Culture consists of patterns, explicit and implicit, of and for behavior acquired and transmitted by symbols, constituting the distinctive achievement of human groups, including their embodiments in artifacts; the essential core of culture consists of traditional (i.e., historically derived and selected) ideas and especially their attached values; culture systems may on the one hand, be considered as products of action, on the other as conditioning elements of further action" (Kroeber and Kluckhohn, 1952, p. 180).

Kroeber and Kluckhohn also speculate as to how this definition may change.

"The main respects in which, we suspect, the formula will be modified and enlarged in the future are as regards (1) the interrelations of cultural forms; and (2) variability and the individual" (Kroeber and Kluckhohn, 1952, p. 180).

If this speculation proves correct, psychology should make major contributions to cultural studies since the discipline is centrally concerned with the individual as a unit of analysis.

After reviewing a good number of cross-cultural studies in psychology, we are able to suggest a working definition which can be modified in the future: Cross-cultural psychology is the empirical study of members of various culture (as defined above) groups who have had different experiences that lead to predictable and significant differences in behavior. In the majority of such studies, the groups under study speak different languages and are governed by different political units.

## Types of Cross-Cultural Studies

The nature of cross-cultural psychology can be pinpointed even more by examining the types of studies that have been undertaken. This presentation closely follows the criteria suggested by Triandis (1969) to answer the question, "What makes a study cross-cultural?"

Certain studies have used concepts and theories developed in Western countries (most often the United States and European nations) and have investigated them in non-Western countries. These concepts include those from Piaget's developmental stages, Freudian positions, and Murray's needs. The investigations are often concerned with the antecedents and consequences of the behavior associated with the theories. The question is: Can behavior in non-Western cultures be predicted from these theories? The results will often indicate limits and shortcomings which, in turn, may lead to a better, more comprehensive theory. Chapter 6 covers several theories that have been investigated cross-culturally.

Other studies involve replication of Western-based experiments in other cultures, often with modifications to solve potential procedural difficulties. For instance, Western-based experimental studies of leadership, stereotyping, perception, learning, and conformity have been replicated in other cultures. Studies in this category differ from those in (1) above in that the theoretical position underlying the research is not as well developed. Chapter 2 on cross-cultural experimentation is concerned with the methodology of such studies.

The purpose of some studies is to investigate certain aspects of human behavior, but each experimenter in each culture has a hand in designing the procedures. Such procedures include the instrumentation, data gathering, and analysis. Studies of subjective culture (Triandis et al., 1972) are often of this type. When several researchers collaborate in the instrumentation, data gathering, and analysis, there is less likelihood that a Western-based framework will be artificially imposed in another culture. A disadvantage, however, is that adequate instrumentation (e.g., comparability of items) is hindered when individual researchers have the right to add or subtract items from the common pool. Chapters 2 and 3 on translation and survey methods cover these problem areas.

Test materials designed and standardized in one culture are often administered in another. These can be tests of intelligence, personality, interests, and so forth. The major problem is that since the test was designed in one research site, it may have no worth (and may give misleading data) in another. Chapter 5 describes the important issues in this area and Chapter 8 presents descriptions of many tests that are candidates for cross-cultural use. Chapters 9 and 10 cover multivariate methods for data analysis to be used when a large number of tests or instruments are administered cross-culturally.

## What Cross-Cultural Psychology Can Do

Gathering data in more than one culture has several advantages over the more common practice of gathering data in only one. The following reasons were suggested by Strodtbeck (1964) as to how researchers can profit by engaging in cross-cultural work. These reasons overlap each other and many studies will fall under more than one of the four categories.

1. The culture in which individuals live can be considered an experimental treatment. This fact implies that a researcher, by gathering data in another culture, can obtain experimental treatments (his independent variables) unavailable in his own culture. In investigating the development of conservation (i.e., the amount of pliable material is the same regardless of its shape) among children, Price-Williams, Gordon, and Ramirez (1969) gathered data from children in Tlaquepaque and San Marcos, Jalisco, Mexico. Some of the children were from families whose occupation was pottery making, and these children were accustomed to helping their fathers roll out and shape clay. These children acquired the conservation skill at an earlier age than children from non-pottery-making families. In addition, the children from pottery-making families acquired the skill faster than children from industrialized countries (e.g., the United States, Britain). The experience of the special group of children, then, served as an experimental variable that would be impossible to establish in a laboratory.

2. The differential incidence of a certain trait can be documented from

culture to culture. The best method for theory building is to find cultures that are high, medium, and low on a trait and then to discover the reasons for the difference. Durkheim's classic work on suicide is of this type. The concept "anomie" was suggested as the reason for differential suicide rates from country to country. Multi-nation public opinion surveys and the "Six Cultures" studies belong to this category In the latter (B. Whiting, 1963), a long interview schedule was completed by mothers in northern India, a Baptist community in the United States, a Gusii village in Kenya, an Indiana village in Mexico, a Barrio in the Philippines, and a village in Okinawa. The multiple sets of data allowed the researchers to suggest various reasons about, for instance, the interaction between mothers and their children.

3. Cross-cultural studies can indicate behavior patterns not present in the researchers' own country. Studies of this type are often concerned with how members of different cultural groups define their own experience. The work of both Triandis et al. (1972) and Feldman (1968) suggests that people in the United States and Greece have very different definitions of their "ingroup" and "outgroup." In the United States, the ingroup includes people from one's own country and the outgroup includes foreign tourists. In Greece, on the other hand, a person's outgroup includes countrymen with whom he is not closely associated.

In Feldman's experiments on helping behavior (e.g., people were asked to help an individual mail a letter), "when Athenians discriminated between a strange compatriot and foreigner, the Greek compatriot received worse treatment than the foreigner" (Feldman, 1968, p. 212). Discovering such differences as these is one of the most exciting aspects of cross-cultural research.

4. The cross-cultural researcher can also test hypotheses with existing sets of data or files of already-gathered information. This category has usually included only the comparison of anthropologists' ethnographies (Whiting, 1968), but there is no reason why other existing sets of data cannot be used. An example is Osgood's (1965) data comparing the meaning attributed to concepts by members of 25 cultures. One goal of the Triandis et al. (1972) work on subjective culture was to obtain large amounts of data on how people in different cultures categorize their experiences. Other researchers can use the files to test their own hypotheses. The data from the "Six Cultures" studies can also be used in this way.

## A Content Analysis Definition

The fourth explanatory method is to examine the published research, and we have done so by content-analyzing the first 200 articles submitted to the *Journal of Cross-Cultural Psychology*. The articles could be placed into one of fourteen categories, which were (from most-articles by category to least-articles by category): personality, experimental treatments, methodology, psychiatric disorders, education, literature surveys and theoretical papers, ethnic identification and modernization, development, need for achievement, industrial psychology, sociology/anthropology, psycholinquistics, sex differences, and peace and conflict. Some categories had more articles accepted for publication than others, a major reason being the methodological sophistication of the research tools used by the workers in the different areas. The results of our content analysis are summarized in Table 1.1.

Further defining information can be gleaned from an examination of the last two columns of Table 1.1. The forty papers in which the United States is listed as the target culture usually dealt with subcultural groups such as American Indians or so-called "hypenated" Americans (Japanese-, Chinese-, or Hawaiian-Americans). Outside the United States, India has been the most frequent target culture. This is because India is heavily populated, has serious population and other problems, has a subcultural caste system (which is itself attractive for cross-cultural problems of all kinds), and has a tradition of opening its doors to international sabbaticalists. African, Canadian-Indian, Australian Aborigine, and Israeli groups are often studied cross-culturally. The remaining target cultures are spread over at least 50 additional countries. It is about as surprising as the morning sunrise that the United States leads in the senior authorship of cross-cultural papers. Sixty-six percent (132) of the 200 manuscripts were authored or senior-authored by United States researchers, with Canadian (6.5%), Australian, Indian, and Great Britain (each with 4.5%) and Israeli (3%) senior authors accounting for another 23% of the materials received. The remaining 11% of the papers had senior authors from 13 other countries. Thus the 200 papers had senior authors from 19 countries, but at least a dozen other countries were represented by junior authors. Some of the more impressive papers published by JCCP, as well as by other journals which publish cross-cultural work, have been authored by three or more researchers, each representing a distinct cultural group. This trend toward collaboration will likely accelerate, since multiple-nation and enthusiastic coauthorship automatically serves as a check against ethnocentric biases of research strategy and data interpretation.

## Introduction to Cross-Cultural Methodology

The many methodological problems of the different types of cross-cultural research are covered in subsequent chapters on experimentation, testing, survey methods, and the like. Several problems, however, are common to all types of research and are consequently covered in this introductory chapter. These problems are:

1. The meaning of cross-cultural research, that is, determining whether research and research ideas carry the same meaning from culture to culture;

Table 1.1 Disposition Data, Research Categories, Target Cultures, and Country of Senior Author for 200 Submitted Manuscripts, *Journal of Cross-Cultural Psychology*

| N | % of total | % accepted within category | Category Description | Target Cultures | N | Country of Senior Author | N |
|---|---|---|---|---|---|---|---|
| 47 | 23.5 | 30 | General personality, including values, attitudes, stereotypes, roles, and so forth | United States<br>India<br>Multicultural<br>Denmark<br>Egypt<br>Ethiopia<br>Latin America<br>Hungary, Ireland, Japan, Germany, Italy, Lebanon, Nigeria, and Puerto Rico | 12<br>10<br>9<br>2<br>2<br>2<br>2<br>1 | United States<br>Canada<br>India<br>Hungary, Lebanon, and Nigeria | 33<br>6<br>5<br>1 |
| 24 | 12.0 | 58 | Experimental treatments, including child-rearing, cognition, perception, Piagetian research, social psychological concepts | Australian Aborigine, Africa, India<br>Multicultural, Japan, Zambia, West Indies<br>South America<br>Lebanon, Mexico, Philippines | 4<br>3<br>2<br>3<br>1 | United States<br>Australia<br>Great Britain<br>Africa<br>Japan, Lebanon | 12<br>5<br>3<br>2<br>1 |
| 21 | 10.5 | 28 | Methodological techniques and critiques; preliminary tryouts of new methods; norming or cross-validation of psychological tests | Multicultural, United States, Africa, and India<br>Mexico, Singapore, Canada, Israel, Spain, Switzerland, Turkey, Thailand, Uganda, and Germany | 5<br>2<br>1 | United States<br>India, Israel<br>Singapore, Africa, Uganda, Canada, and Turkey | 12<br>2<br>1 |

9

Table 1.1 (Cont.)

| N | % of total | % accepted within category | Category Description | Target Cultures | N | Country of Senior Author | N |
|---|---|---|---|---|---|---|---|
| 19 | 9.5 | 31 | Psychiatric disorders, mental health, clinical psychology applications | United States | 7 | United States | 13 |
| | | | | Canadian Indians | 3 | Canada | 2 |
| | | | | Malaysia and Southeast Asia | 4 | New Guinea, Malaysia, Egypt, Israel | 1 |
| | | | | Multicultural, New Guinea, Egypt, Philippines, Israel | 1 | | |
| 14 | 7.0 | 29 | Education, school-related behavior, school achievement | United States | 4 | United States | 12 |
| | | | | Lebanon, Yugoslavia, Thailand, India, Africa, Tanzania, Ghana, Japan, Ethiopia, and Mexico | 1 | Lebanon and Australia | 1 |
| 13 | 6.5 | 23 | Surveys, theoretical positions, reviews of research, speculative papers, all non-data based | Multicultural | 9 | United States | 8 |
| | | | | United States | 2 | Australia | 2 |
| | | | | Africa and Great Britain | 1 | Canada, Great Britain, and Japan | 1 |
| 12 | 6.0 | 67 | Ethnic identification, westernization, socialization, acculturation, modernization | Multicultural | 3 | United States | 6 |
| | | | | Japanese American, Australian Aborgine, Great Britain, Greek, Thailand, Chinese, United States Indian, Eskimo | 2 | Hong Kong | 2 |
| | | | | | 1 | Japan, Canada, Great Britain, and Australia | 1 |
| | | | | | | United States | 8 |

Table 1.1 (Cont.)

| N | % of total | % accepted within category | Category Description | Target Cultures | N | Country of Senior Author | N |
|---|---|---|---|---|---|---|---|
| 11 | 5.5 | 45 | Sociocultural factors in psychological development | United States<br>Mexico, Italy, Africa, India, Multicultural, Philippines, Israel | 4<br><br><br>1 | Great Britain<br>Israel | 2<br>1 |
| 9 | 4.5 | 55 | Need achievement and related concepts | United States and India<br>Philippines, Hawaiian-Americans, Aborigines, Ethiopia, and Multicultural | 2<br><br><br><br>1 | United States<br>India<br>Australia | 6<br>2<br>1 |
| 7 | 3.5 | 14 | Management and industrial psychology applications | Multicultural<br>Israel<br>Japan and Africa | 3<br>2<br>1 | United States<br>Israel<br>Great Britain | 4<br>2<br>1 |
| 7 | 3.5 | 29 | Sociology/anthropology, general | Multicultural<br>Historical<br>United States | 4<br>1<br>2 | United States | 7 |
| 7 | 3.5 | 14 | Psycholinguistics, semantics, bilingualism | United States<br>Finland, Mexico, Japan, Canada, and multicultural | 2<br><br>1 | United States<br>Finland, Japan,<br>Canada, Great Britain | 3<br><br>1 |
| 5 | 2.5 | 60 | Masculinity-femininity, sex differences | Norway, United States, Japan, Uganda and India | 1 | United States | 5 |
| 4 | 2.0 | 25 | Conflict, conflict resolution, peace | Multicultural<br>United States | 3<br>1 | United States<br>Sweden | 3<br>1 |

2. choosing appropriate topics for study;

3. discovering the problems specific to a given investigation;

4. experimenter and demand effects;

5. using the plausible rival hypothesis approach to rule out explanations other than the researcher's own interpretation of his data;

6. sampling respondents in different cultures;

7. using the emic-etic distinction as a general approach to solve cross-cultural problems.

*Meaning and Cross-cultural Research.* When we were in graduate school preparing for comprehensive exams, we would gather in groups and make up ridiculous questions in order to relieve tension. These were questions that would be on the comprehensive exams if everything went wrong for us. Regardless of field of preparation (e.g., clinical, social, and experimental psychology), one question was always suggested: "What does it all mean?" As we now rethink the issue, this question does not seem ridiculous for cross-cultural research. The *meaning* of every aspect of any investigation is important, and it is especially important for cross-cultural work since the researcher does not know the *meaning* that people of other cultures attach to our research process.

The Western-based researcher can approach potential subjects in his community, ask them questions, apply an experimental treatment, and then ask more questions. He generally knows the meaning of his procedures, since he himself is a member of that culture. In fact, methodologists write that research questions and procedures (unicultural) start with a self-examination by the investigator. With other cultures, however, the researcher does not have this knowledge from which he can build his investigation. He may not know, for instance, the meaning that other cultures attach to being interviewed. The respondents may assume that the interviewer is a tax collector, a dreaded government agent, or a friend of the chief. Or the researcher may not know the meaning that the respondents assign to his tests made for and standardized on Western samples. This latter point is especially important, since such tests have been used frequently in cross-cultural investigations. (Chapter 5 will be devoted to this issue.) For instance, Irvine (1970) suggests that intelligence testing should take into account aspects of mental functioning considered to be of central importance to other culture members (e.g., maintaining good relations with kin) that are not central to the mental functioning of Western residents, at least as defined by standard intelligence tests.

Fortunately, other cross-cultural researchers have faced these problems and have suggested solutions (e.g., Hudson, Barakat, and LaForge, 1959; Frijda and Jahoda, 1966). They have noted that certain problems seem common to all research but are especially acute in cross-cultural investigations because of the novel people, cultural practices, and languages involved (Nath, 1968).

*Choosing Appropriate Topics for Study.* Many cross-cultural problems will never plague the researcher if he chooses an appropriate topic for study in the first place. Choosing specific rather than general topics for investigation is a good start (Wesley and Karr, 1966). General or global issues should be avoided. Since little is known of the workings of another culture, variables such as social schemata, religious systems, and politics are difficult if not impossible to study. "These abstractions are so complex and multidimensional that they are of little use for cross-cultural research" (Whiting, 1954, p. 527). Campbell (1961) also comments on this problem.

"It goes without saying that a science cannot be built without intersubjective verifiability of observation. Psychological research on the accuracy and person-to-person agreement in independent reporting seems summarizable by the statement that the greater the direct accessibility of the stimuli to the sense receptors, the greater the intersubjective verifiability of the observation. The weaker or more intangible, indirect, or abstract the stimulus attribute, the more the observations are subject to distortion. It is quite conceivable that there are some aspects of culture, including its overall pattern or ethos, that are so abstract that intersubjective verifiability is lost" (Campbell, 1961, p. 340).

Some anthropologists have made suggestions for more refined research topics. "if a serious attempt were made to discover the leading conditions determining perceptual processes in native communities, much anthropological evidence could be given a more convincing basis than it is at present" (Bartlett, 1937, p. 410). A similar note of caution is given by Goldschmidt (1971) who uses the Greek concept of *aretê* to amplify the implicit enigma of studying profoundly subjective experience (see Chapter 6).

An example of specific, operationally defined research is that of Witkin (1967) who reports cross-cultural research relating such variables as perceptual style and severity of childhood discipline. His variables are usually objectively measured by such instruments as the Rod-and-Frame test or the Embedded Figures Test (see Chapter 8). Verifiable research is also possible in areas that can only be conceptually defined. In studying cultural stress, Naroll (1962) found that there is higher reliability in a stress trait such as drunken brawling than there is in the trait of deviant homicide. The former can be seen by the observer of a culture, while the latter is dependent upon the reports of others (Segall, 1965).

Choosing an appropriate topic for study includes the selection of cultures that manifest key differences for the testing of hypotheses. A good example is that of Berry (1966) who was interested in the relation between child-training practices (definable by observation) and perceptual style (as measured by well-documented psychological methods). He picked certain cultures because their members practiced widely divergent child-rearing methods. The Temne of

Africa are strict and demand obedience, leading to dependence among their children, while the Eskimos are lenient, encouraging independence. A "control" or comparison group of Scottish subjects was also tested. Berry predicted and found that subjects who had undergone the different child-training styles manifested corresponding dependent or independent perceptual styles.

In another exemplary study, Wober (1967) extended Western-based studies of perception by choosing a culture, the Ibo of Nigeria, whose members had been trained to value proprioceptive cues (reflexes involved in bodily movement) much more than Western subjects. Wober's study is also a good example of our concern with meaning. Western subjects value visual cues and do well on perceptual tests that emphasize this factor. It should be no surprise, then, that other-culture subjects who are not trained in visual emphasis do not do as well. Wober showed that the Ibo do better than Western subjects on a perceptual test demanding proprioceptive cues—these cues are meaningful to them but are less meaningful to Western subjects. In short, the important point to remember is that the researcher can manipulate and control variables by selecting specific cultures.

The opposite of careful selection is the "study" of a culture that happens to be available but not for scientific reasons. Some researchers, having worked with a certain psychological scale or test in a Western country, visit another country on a vacation or for a meeting. They then administer the scale to an easily available sample. Minimal contributions are usually made through this "sabbatical opportunism" research method. The researchers might have been *more likely* to complete a good study if they had chosen a scale or test for which responses in the visited culture would have been of interest.

*Discovering Problems Specific to a Given Investigation.* Any book on methodology can only present guidelines for research rather than cookbook solutions to specific problems. Cross-cultural problems often have to be discovered by the researcher and then solved. In questionnaire studies, for instance, people in some cultures respond well to pleasant, polite, and attentive interviewers, as do people in most Western societies. Subjects in other cultures, however, demand a more authoritarian interviewer if they are to give valid responses (Marsh, 1967). The investigator, then, has to vary his research style from culture to culture. Members of some cultures are unfamiliar with the materials in Western apparatus tests (Schwartz, 1963; Kellaghan, 1968) and thus perform less well than if familiar objects are used. Subjects in some cultures are unfamiliar with paper and pencils so that common Western testing practices have to be modified. Members of some cultures are overly courteous to researchers and are likely to give biased responses in the direction of maintaining a positive image (Jones, 1963). Gough (1970) points out that members of some cultures are not used to telling researchers about the relationship among objects. In

may not have the same effect because the key variable that caused the original effect may be inadvertently omitted or is less salient to members of the second culture.

Several examples can be given to show how researchers have thought about and have eliminated certain plausible rival hypotheses. In the Segall, Campbell, and Herskovits (1966) study of the influence of culture on visual perception, different administrators gave the optical illusion tests in different societies in the United States, Africa, and the Philippines. Since it was possible that some administrators would be more conscientious and/or more experienced in such testing, the rival hypothesis of different results due to sloppy administration was controlled by introducing systematic variation within the United States sample. Half of the tests were administered under extremely divergent procedures, and no differences were found in the magnitude of illusion. Similar variations were introduced to rule out differences in exposure time allowed the subjects.

In studying the amount of contact and intergroup interaction among ethnic groups on Guam and among religious groups in Vermont, Brislin (1968) was worried about a selection bias. Although the people in the Guam sample were assigned to places of greater or lesser opportunity for outgroup contact by chance, this was not true of the Vermont sample. Subjects in Vermont could choose which school they would attend, and hence they might choose a school because they wanted to interact with people from outgroups. Brislin then set up laboratory groups in which the amount of outgroup contact was experimentally controlled. Since the same relation of greater interaction with greater opportunity for contact was found in all three situations, he concluded that the hypothesis was sound.

If researchers have examined all alternative explanations for their data, they will be in a better positon to answer the questions that are raised about their study. Assume that a social scientist hears about the results of someone's research and writes, "Professor, your cross-cultural data are interesting, but I believe that sampling and translation problems can account for your results better than your preferred interpretation." The professor who has examined such methodological problems can then write back, "No, sampling and translation problems are not plausible alternatives. I have two sets of data proving the adequacy of the translation and showing that the samples in the different cultures are equivalent by several criteria." The necessity of gathering many sets of data is a major point made by Frey (1970) in a chapter written mainly for political scientists. He writes that readers of cross-cultural work will not be interested in the researcher's assurances that his data are sound, but they will be interested in seeing the empirical evidence.

Having many data points is, then, a good method of insuring that alternative hypotheses can be ruled out. Dennis (1966b) has long been interested interested in children's drawings (the Goodenough Draw-a-Man Test), and he recently published a summary article presenting data from forty culture groups. Dennis wanted to show that the factors of experience with representational forms of art and exposure to Western civilization would best account for the data which showed higher Goodenough scores in some cultures than in others. Other explanations may be: (1) heredity or biological factors; (2) differences in schooling; (3) urban children scoring higher than rural children; and (4) literacy and education of children's parents. With so many data points, however, Dennis was able to look at scores between and among the forty groups and to show that these four alternatives did not explain the data as well as his preferred hypothesis. Hudson et al. (1959) have also made the important point that opportunities for gathering many sets of reference points (data) must be built into the research plan so that the best interpretation of the results can be made.

Another way to rule out certain rival hypothesis is to determine which conditions of the study lead to "better" or "higher" performance in each of the cultures. That is, researchers should determine the conditions that make non-Western, perhaps preliterate, groups perform better than Western subjects. For instance, Segall, Campbell, and Herskovits (1966) determined that Western residents (the United States in this research) manifested more susceptibility to the Muller-Lyer illusion (below) than non-Western residents (most samples were from African nations). The latter, however, manifested *more* susceptibility to the

horizontal-vertical illusion (below) in line with the predictions. If the non-Western subjects had responded in the *same direction* to all stimuli, the researchers would not have been able to rule out the possibility that the subjects had misunderstood the instructions, were poorly motivated, were unfamiliar with the experimenter's asking questions, etc. Cole, Gay, and Glick (1968) studied the learning and the usage of mathematical concepts among the Kpelle of Liberia. They were able to find conditions that led to behavior inferior and equal to subjects from the United States. The conditions leading to good performance were those that allowed the Kpelle to use their own familiar measurement systems rather than the systems used in the West. To use some current vernacular, Cole et al. "had it both ways," that is, certain conditions led to results in one direction (United States better) and other conditions led to results in the opposite direction (Kpelle as good or better). By having both sets of data the researchers were able to answer the challenge that all their results may be caused by Kpelle unfamiliarity with Western measurement systems.

Reviewers of cross-cultural research often base their major criticisms on plausible rival hypotheses. In a review of child animism research, Jahoda (1958) examined relevant studies with regard to their samples, language used in testing, types of problems presented to the children, method of problem administration, and estimates of the investigator's personal influence. He was able to interpret and unify the seemingly contradictory literature by examining these several explanations of the data. The results of several studies were interpreted as being due to one or more of these problems. Jahoda was able to integrate the others (those that "passed" the plausible rival hypothesis test) into a meaningful framework.

*Sampling.* Plausible rival hypotheses can often be suggested by examining the sampling plan of a piece of research. Rival hypotheses due to sampling arise any time comparisons are made between one culture and another, since the differences found may be attributed to different selection methods or to different qualities of the samples (age, socioeconomic status) rather than to cultural differences (Lambert and Klineberg, 1967). In much research there is no sampling plan; an experimenter is likely to interview people who seem intelligent, talkative, cooperative, or who are readily available. Any of these factors may account for the data as well as the researcher's hypothesis. Sometimes random and stratified samples are attempted, but these are no panacea (Campbell, 1968), especially with non-Western cultures. In many cases the necessary information, such as a list of homes, streets, or even communities, will not exist (Wilson, 1958). Thus a probability or stratified sample cannot be drawn. Even if a census in each culture under study were to be taken and a probability sample attempted, problems of not-at-homes or differential refusal rates from country to country would plague interpretation.

Although they are rare, random samples have been drawn in cross-cultural research (Almond and Verba, 1963; see Frey, 1970). Even if the methodological problems discussed above are solved, the costs of such samples are great. To point out even more problems, the results of a cross-cultural survey on two random samples (cultures A and B) may be due to any of several aspects of the two cultures. The proposed cultural difference that the surveyors in cultures A and B hope to tap may be attitudes toward children, but the random samples may reflect several other differences. The members of Culture A may have a higher standard of living, may be more achievement oriented, or may have a more advanced system of government. Any of these factors can affect results on a questionnaire as much as attitudes toward child rearing. Plausible rival hypotheses are thus brought on by the random sample.

Another problem can be related by anecdote. One of the writers heard a talk given by a researcher about the attitude survey which he conducted in Africa. A member of the audience asked about the sample, and the reply was that the sample was drawn on a random basis. When pressed as to actual interviewing practice, however, the researcher admitted that a certain geographic area, in which people should have been interviewed under the sample plan, was not entered because of the dangerous travel conditions. Our interpretation is that comparing this "random" sample with that from another country would be dangerous at best. If a complete random sample is not feasible—and this is usually the case—the sample must be defined, such as all tribal leaders (based upon an operational definition) or nursing mothers, and so forth. Hyman et al. (1967) studied only experts (in their area of competence) in thirteen developing countries. The researchers felt that "a systematic and efficient control of error was required, and the survey approach commended itself."

The authors do not want to give the impression that random samples are worthless. Such samples assure that there is no systematic bias in the selection (e.g., cooperative people only interviewed), and generalization to those not in the sample is certainly important. If accurate counts of characteristics within a culture are desired (e.g., average age, income), random samples are necessary. For certain purposes, however, good research can be done by using non-random samples if the people to be studied are intelligently selected. Our purpose is to suggest how samples can be improved, and a good start is to use the plausible rival hypothesis approach.

The plausible rival hypotheses generated by either a random or non-random sample will have to be listed and ruled out one-by-one. Additional sets of data will have to be gathered so that sampling problems can be "controlled." As in many cross-cultural problems, the "solution" is to study how others have handled sampling. The only hard and fast guideline that can be given is the following: Gather many sets of data to support the goodness of the primary set.

In an excellent essay, Frey (1970) confessed that he should have gathered additional sets of data to complement those from his original sample. These additional sets would have illuminated the meaning of the primary set.

"One often overlooked and basic point is that the cross-cultural researcher must try to think through his intended analysis in some detail in order to develop revealing interrogative instruments (questionnaires and interview schedules). He must know the main direct controls he will apply in the analysis so that he can ensure, through his sample design, that he will have enough cases to permit those controls. . . . In my research, our study of the Turkish peasantry would, I feel, be more effective if we had obtained information from a few illuminating control groups from other sectors of the Turkish society. We did not adequately realize that we were not solely interested in variations *within* the peasantry, although such variations were of major importance to us. We were also interested in commenting on how peasants differed from other Turks. Focusing so completely on the peasants and excluding other groups has made the latter portion of the analysis much more difficult" (Frey, 1970, p. 236).

Two additional examples of how the sampling problem can be handled are given in Berrien (1967, p. 35). He quoted the research of Whitehill and Tazekawa who studied blue-collar workers in the United States and Japan. Their sampling problem was partially solved because the workers were selected from "specified equivalent industries" (p. 35). Similarly, Berrien himself has sampled workers from organizations "having equivalent objectives in two or more countries." Since the goals of the organization are the same, observed differences should reflect cultural values. The same assumption is made in cross-cultural studies of family life, that is, the family serves similar functions and thus a baseline for comparisons is available. Sampling problems can also be handled by taking advantage of naturally occurring levels of an independent variable. In certain areas of the world, members of the same culture have undergone different experiences. Dawson (1969b) sampled three groups of New Zealand Aborigines who were differentially urbanized. He thus had three levels of an independent variable (degree of urbanization) but with the same general cultural group as his base.

In another approach to sampling, the researchers take advantage of data from others or from their own pretest work. Lambert and Klineberg (1967), who were interested in children's attitude toward people from other countries, selected certain age groups for study after having examined the available literature on the topic. This literature indicated the important ages at which children's attitudes change. In addition, Lambert and Klineberg described their random samples carefully (age, sex, intelligence, socioeconomic level, etc.) so that subsequent researchers could pick different samples that might manifest theoretically relevant differences. In a study of the meaning of visual and verbal symbols, Osgood (1960) carefully pointed out aspects of his non-random samples that might lead to problems of interpretation. This practice helps others in the design of subsequent studies. Researchers should describe at least the following characteristics of their samples (Brislin and Baumgardner, 1971): age, sex, educational level, income, occupation, special training, place of residence in relation to other members of the culture. In short, the description should include all the characteristics of the subjects and environment which could potentially influence the results or their interpretations.

Pretest data will often help to pinpoint the best sample. Pearlin and Kohn (1966) were interested in sampling people from equivalent class positions in the United States and Italy. Their preliminary data showed that income and education were not suitable for manifesting similar class positions, but that occupational prestige was. They approached the sampling problem by minimizing the extremeness in the groups chosen to be interviewed, finally selecting members of the middle and working classes. They concluded that "Some intra-class variation is obscured by using only those two broad social class categories, but what is lost in precision is gained in increased cross-national comparability" (p. 468).

Sampling in cross-cultural research thus demands justification through one or more sets of empirical data. All samples should be carefully specified so that subsequent researchers can determine how their results (taken on their samples) relate to the original study.

*Understanding Cultural Variables: "Emic" Versus "Etic" Distinction.* Many social scientists, including the present writers, are concerned with the meaning of research procedures. One procedure is to administer an instrument questioned this practice and has proposed an alternative procedure. The problem is that every culture "should be understood in its own terms" (p. 122). Such description has been one goal of anthropology and is called the "emic" part of social science research.[2] Another goal, however, is to incorporate aspects of many cultures into a general hypothesis or theory, such as the influence of cultural art style on individual perception. Such theory building has been the goal of psychology (see Segall, 1965; Jahoda 1970a) and this goal is called the "etic" part of social science research. The problem for psychologists is that by administering cross-culturally a test standardized in one country (usually their own), they may be imposing an artificial etic and losing the emic or meaningful aspects of the other culture as practiced by *their* members.

Berry (1969) suggests the following revised research procedure:

1. Study only those aspects of behavior that are functionally equivalent between cultures. For instance, the goal of parents in different cultures is to raise their children to be competent and useful members of that culture. Parent to child behaviors (e.g., training in independence, language instruction) thus serve to help obtain the same goal (i.e., are functionally equivalent) in different cultures.

2. Descriptive categories derived from past research, perhaps in only one culture, can then be applied to the behavior in the other culture under investigation. This is the *imposed* etic.

3. The imposed descriptive categories must be adapted so that they explain the cultural practices of the other culture from their point of view. This is the emic description.

4. "Shared categories can then be used to build up new categories valid for both cultures (derived etic) and can be expanded to other cultures until a

---

[2] The emic-etic distinction is from linguistic terminology. Phon*etic* notation is meant to be a general system which can describe all sounds in all languages, while phon*emic* is meant to describe sounds that are meaningful in a given culture.

universal is established" (Berry, 1969, p. 125).

5. New instruments and research techniques can be devised and validated using the derived etic as a conceptual base. These instruments must, of course, be equivalent in meaning (including such issues as someone asking questions of someone else) to the members of the cultures under study. Chapter 2 is largely devoted to this important topic.

Since Berry's revised procedure is quite recent, no social scientists have followed his outline point-by-point. Researchers have, however, utilized similar types of thinking in their approach to cross-cultural problems. Cole, Gay, and Glick (1968) have reviewed attempts to analyze systems of thought that tie different aspects of culture together (emic principles). According to them, anthropologists and linguists

". . . take as a starting point the attempt to discover the coherence of ideas and behaviors within cultures as the basic datum for specifying the rules which tie together behaviors between cultures. Thus, for example, one does not compare 'myths' and 'scientific' thought directly, but one first makes an analysis of the formal structure that characterizes myth and science. It is these latter 'coherence' rules that are compared. . . . In our own work, we have, where design and opportunity arise, attempted to use this principle of intracultural comparison as a tool for gaining insight into cross-cultural comparisons" (Cole, Gay, and Glick, 1968, p. 189).

With regard to emic-etic distinctions, Wesley and Karr (1966), in a study of mother-child relations, gave several specific examples of the dangers of imposing an American-based etic without looking at the emic meaning behind German responses.

"If, for instance, a German and an American mother are both asked how they would punish misbehavior, both may give the same answer. However, the German mother may have interpreted 'misbehavior' to mean 'being ten minutes late for dinner,' the American mother perhaps as 'not coming at all.' The mothers might have given entirely different answers had the misbehavior been specified to mean 'ten minutes late for dinner' . . . . Mothers of two cultures may answer one and the same question with, for instance, 'moderate punishment.' By 'moderate punishment,' the mother of one culture may mean a verbal scolding, the mother in the other culture a physical punishment such as a slap in the face" (p. 260).

Gough (1970) likewise makes a distinction between the intent that social scientists from one country derive from a test item and the meaning that respondents from another country are likely to attach to the same item. Sometimes the item has to be changed to "get at" the same meaning in the other culture. Gough's test item example is from the California Psychological Inventory (CPI).

"Most personality assessment material has some sort of diagnostic rationale which may or may not be apparent from content, and which can be quite different from what content suggests. In translation it is this intent that must be maintained, not the content. Thus translators must know the infrapsychology of the tools they are converting and they must know the empirical connotations of an item as well as its linguistic and literal referents. The CPI abounds in items of this kind, i.e., those that need intuitive rather than linguistic conversion.

"Take for example the item 'Every family owes it to the city to keep its lawn mowed in summer and sidewalks shoveled in winter.' This assumes private ownership, single-family housing, cold winter climates, etc. The item functions all over the United States, because even in the South where it never snows people know about the poor snow-bound Swedes in Minnesota and answer accordingly. But in other cultures and settings the item is irrelevant and draws responses unrelated to the diagnostic function of the item in its original context. One therefore needs to search for relatively trivial yet visible methods for displaying an exaggerated form of allosocial behavior in the new culture. The French item 'The good citizen does not throw his garbage down the stairwell' is one outcome yielded by the intuitive approach" (personal communication).

The problem of meaning and the emic-etic distinction may become clear if we look from a very different angle. The most famous documentary film maker of the past 40 years was Robert Flaherty who made such features as *Nanook of the North, Moana of the South Seas*, and *Men of Aran*. His movies are accepted as stellar examples by his colleagues because they capture the essence of cultures from their members' point of view. A few quotes from his biography shows how he approached his work:

"As we always did afterward, we began by trying to explore the life of the people, to penetrate to the things that gave meaning for them. The best way to do this is to start with very simple, everyday things and let them lead you toward the feelings and beliefs which lie at the core of every people's life. We learned later that this is an absolutely necessary part of the process of getting close to our subjects . . ." (Griffith, 1953, p. 55).

As for distinguishing between emic and etic, Flaherty once had the same problem. He had come to Samoa after having finished *Nanook* in Northern Canada.

"Unfortunately we had come to Samoa with preconceived notions about the element of struggle necessary for a film. We did not have any scenario, but we had the idea that we were going to make just such another film as *Nanook*, with the drama of struggle to be found in the element of the sea" (Griffith, 1953, p. 61).

He changed his approach, of course, and made another fine film.

## Empirical Methods for Understanding Cultural Variables

Awareness of the emic-etic distinction is not sufficient for actual research since empirical methods are also needed. Nowak (1962), Przeworski and Teune (1966; 1970), and Berrien (1970) have described correlational methods designed to elicit the meaning of concepts in the cultures under study and at the same time to maintain the emic-etic distinction.[3] They suggest, after careful preliminary study, that a series of questions be written about some construct (e.g., parents' education of children) that will have the same meaning to both cultures under study. Przeworski and Teune call these questions the identical indicators. The questions begin to satisfy Berry's idea of proceeding from an imposed to a derived etic, since both cultures are studied until the researcher finds questions that tap the same meaning in each. The next step is to derive additional questions that will be different for each culture. The purpose of these culture-specific questions is to show aspects of each culture that are not meaningful to the other. The only condition is that the answers to the specific questions correlate with the identical indicators.

An example may help in understanding this important procedure. Assume that by preliminary work we find that the following set of identical indicators gives meaningful responses to samples in the United States and in an African community:

1. Does a mother protect her child?
2. Does a mother make sure that her child is in good health?
3. Does a father spend more time with his son or with his daughter?

These two specific questions may be meaningful to African respondents but not to residents of the United States:

1. Do parents teach their children basic skills in hunting and food preparation before all the village children are brought together and taught these skills?
2. Does a mother teach children about the elders of the village?

These two specific questions may be meaningful to the United States residents but not to African respondents:

1. Do parents teach their children basic reading skills before the children

---

[3] Although these writers do not use the terms, their goal of generating theories describing all cultures as well as understanding each culture separately is the same as that implied in the emic-etic distinction.

enter school?

2. Does a mother teach children about the leaders of the city, state, and country?

By intercorrelating the specific questions with the identical indicators, the researcher can determine whether the specific questions are eliciting functionally equivalent responses in the two societies. Such analysis is similar to the Hudson et al. (1959) suggestion that cross-cultural data analysis be done on an item-by-item basis so as to gain further insight into the meaning of summary scores based on several items.

The answers to the identical and specific questions give the following information:

1. meaning of the construct shared by both cultures;
2. further meaning of the construct held by members of one culture but not the other;
3. the derived etic which manifests those aspects that are common and specific to each culture as well as their interrelation.

Cross-cultural generalities can then be made which maintain the unique aspects of each culture.

The question remains: How do we find out identical indicators in the first place? One way is by studying the anthropological literature on the two cultures to be studied. Berry (1966) and Dawson (1967a,b) are just two of many psychologists who have started their investigations in this manner. In addition, Irvine (1968) points out that there is no substitute for first-hand contact with a society. His comment about participant observation refers to its status in psychology rather than in the other social sciences.

"To collect valid data the psychologist needs adequate and sympathetic training in understanding a society system that is alien, complex, and conceptually difficult. Participant observer research will acquire greater scientific status, it seems, as a result" (Irvine, 1968b, p. 3).

Berrien (1970) suggests close relations among researchers from both cultures under study. Discussion between the two investigators should result in sets of identical indicators for many issues. Wesley and Karr (1966) point out that both indentical indicators and questions specific to each culture can be suggested by people who have lived in both places.

## The Interpretation and Reporting of Data

Researchers have to be concerned with the meaning of all aspects of the research process, including the reporting of their data. This is a special problem in cross-cultural research since, if only one person interprets the data gathered in two cultures, his own biases may affect the implications he makes. Berrien (1967) reminds us that values found in one culture may not be universally understood. Lesser and Kandel (1968) found that while almost all school teachers in the United States are able to suggest how their behavior might influence their students, Danish teachers were unable to do so. The very thought of suggesting possible influences on their students was foreign to them. Lesser and Kandel were unable to suggest reasons for this finding. Data interpretation had to cease momentarily at this issue, picking up again at issues that were meaningful to both cultures. Of course, the fact that Lesser and Kandel were able to specify issues meaningful in one culture but not in another is in itself a contribution.

Researchers themselves cause another problem based on their ethnocentrism. They report data based on their own frames of reference in the jornals from their country. The alternative to this is Lesser and Kandel's suggestion (1968) that the researchers from each country independently analyze the data so estimates of *inter-interpreter* reliability can be made.

## Summary

Cross-cultural psychology can be explained by looking at the discipline from four angles. The first is to attempt a working definition. The definition we are employing is this: cross-cultural psychology is the empirical study of members of various culture (defined by Kroeber and Kluckhohn, 1952) groups that have had different experiences which lead to predictable differences in behavior. The second is to look at different types of cross-cultural studies. These are: applying concepts, theories, and tests developed in the United States and Europe, or replicating experiments from them, in non-Western countries; engaging in collaborative research with social scientists from other cultures. The third explanatory method is to examine the benefits of doing cross-cultural research. The advantages are: cultural experience can be considered to be a treatment impossible to achieve in a laboratory; differential incidence of traits can be documented to aid theory building; novel behavior patterns can be identified; researchers can take advantage of already collected data.

A fourth way is through an examination of the published literature, and we have done so through a content analysis of the *Journal of Cross-Cultural Psychology*, presented in Table 1.1. From this analysis it can be seen that certain topic areas have been more researched than others, certain countries have been overrepresented as data-collection sites, and that researchers from the United States lead in the number of published cross-cultural studies. These imbalances and their accompanying biases must change if cross-cultural psychology is to progress.

The following both summarize the major methodological points made in the chapter and provide procedural points for cross-cultural research:

1. While researchers may know the meaning (e.g., being asked questions and filling out interest blanks) of research procedures in their own country, they may not know how members of other cultures will react to such practices. Such information has to be learned either through participant observation, by working closely with members of all cultures under study, or through extensive pretesting.

2. Topics and cultures for study should be chosen on the basis of scientific, theoretical interest rather than on the basis of ease or a chance visit overseas. Topics should be operationally definable rather than general and abstract. The cultures under study should manifest key differences on some independent variable (e.g., strict or lenient child-rearing practices). Variables can be controlled through selection of cultures for study.

3. The plausible rival hypotheses that may threaten the validity of a study should be carefully considered and then listed. These rival hypotheses, often based on methodological difficulties, should be considered *in addition to* the author's preferred interpretation. Campbell's list of 15 possible threats (on pages 17-19) provides a good start to a complete analysis for any one study. The researcher should have opportunities for gathering data built into his design so that these alternative hypotheses can be ruled out. In other words, many stable reference points must be built into a research project so that valid interpretations of the results can be made.

4. The issue of sampling is probably best approached by means of the plausible rival hypotheses concept. Both random and non-random samples create certain alternative threats to the researcher's primary hypothesis. Random samples in two cultures may create problems because of the following: variables besides cultural differences (e.g., education, socioeconomic status) affecting results; differential completion or refusal rates creating interpretation problems; different interviewer practices in the two cultures. All samples should be defined very thoroughly so that future investigators can choose similar or different samples, depending on their purposes. In actual research, samples in different cultures have been chosen on the basis of these factors: groups from functionally equivalent organizations; key groups as shown by previous literature; groups with the same cultural background but who have undergone different experiences (e.g., people from one culture group who have been exposed to one of several forms of government).

5. Psychologists have the goal of incorporating the behavior of many cultures into one theory (etic approach), but they must also understand the behavior within each culture (emic approach). Research instruments should include items aimed at both etic and emic aspects, and researchers should always be aware of how other culture members are reacting to these instruments. Correlational

approaches for the analysis of questions applicable to all cultures and specific to each culture have been devised.

6. Researchers from the different cultures under study should analyze the resulting data separately and then compare their findings so that estimates of inter-interpreter reliability can be made.

# CHAPTER TWO

## Questionnaire Wording and Translation

Unless researchers present empirical evidence to support their claim that the different-language versions of the same instrument are equivalent, translation problems will always be plausible rival hypotheses for any obtained results. If people in a cross-cultural study perform more poorly on a test or have more "no opinion" answers to a questionnaire survey, the results may be taken as supporting a substantive theory. The results may, however, simply reflect poor understanding on the part of the subjects due to a poor translation of the test instructions or of the questions. We are dealing with an issue central to cross-cultural research; indeed, we can think of no problems that are more important.

Questionnaire wording (or the wording of any passage) and translation go hand in hand, since it is difficult for a bilingual to translate poorly written passages into another language. Cross-cultural investigators should be concerned with the communication of many aspects of their research, including the introduction of the research to potential subjects, instructions, questionnaires, and subject responses. All demand clear wording in one language and subsequent translation to another. Unfortunately, almost all the relevant translation research has been concerned with wording in and translation from the English language, and so we have to focus on this limited body of literature. Hopefully, however, this chapter will help rectify this by presenting guidelines applicable to writing clear and understandable passages in any language. We shall begin with a coverage of writing translatable English for any aspect of research. We then discuss questionnaire wording in particular, and this is followed by a treatment of the translation methods and the techniques for demonstrating original language-target language equivalence.

### Writing Translatable English

There have been three studies (see below) in which investigators have

32

examined the qualities of written English that translate both poorly and well. In these studies the "back translation" technique was used. Bilinguals were asked to translate a variety of English passages into a target language, and then other bilinguals (working independently) translated back to English. The two English versions were compared and differences in meaning noted. If the same types of errors were made over and over by different bilinguals, then the assumption was made that the original English wording caused the problem and not the translators themselves. Note that the investigator does not have to be able to read the target language, since he can read the two English versions and make inferences about the translation and make recommendations, perhaps, of how it may be improved.

The phrases that were regularly back-translated very well and very poorly were examined to see if inferences could be made about them. The investigators sought reasons that would explain why the phrases were successfully translated. The three research projects involved were: (1) Werner and Campbell's (1970) investigation of English to Navajo translations. Their passage was one of Kluckhohn and Strodtbeck's (1961) "stories" used to elicit value orientations. The story was about a man who had lost his livestock. (2) Sinaiko and Brislin's (1970) study of English to Vietnamese translations in which the passages were highly technical materials from a helicopter maintenance manual. (3) Brislin's (1972) study of translation between English and the Micronesian languages (Chamorro, Yapese, Trukese, etc.) used passages that dealt with five issues: religion, cultivating trees, how people choose friends, interaction among members of Micronesian groups, and the same Kluckhohn and Strodbeck story that Werner and Campbell used. The results of these studies were similar, and the combined information allows us to present a set of rules which will help others write translatable English. We hope that others will share their empirically based suggestions so that other useful rules can be formulated.

1. Use short, simple sentences of less than 16 words.

2. Employ the active rather than the passive voice.

3. Repeat nouns instead of using pronouns.

4. Avoid metaphors and colloquialisms. Such phrases are least likely to have equivalents in the target language.

5. Avoid the subjective mode, for example, verb forms with could or would.

6. Avoid adverbs and prepositions telling "where" or "when" (e.g., frequent, beyond, upper).

7. Avoid possessive forms where possible.

8. Use specific rather than general terms (e.g., the specific animal, such as cows, chickens, pigs, rather than the general term "livestock").

9. Avoid words which indicate vagueness regarding some event or thing (e.g., probably and frequently).

10. Avoid sentences with two different verbs if the verbs suggest different actions.

*Redundancy and Context.* In addition to these rules, we offer two more suggestions which should help a researcher write translatable English. One is providing redundancy, and the other is adding context for any difficult phrases. Redundancy helps in the construction of a questionnaire, since two phrases referring to the same concept allow the translator to be sure of the passage's meaning and permit the translation-checker to note errors when one of the phrases is different from the other. Campbell (1968) has written that every concept under investigation should be represented by at least two questions, differently worded if at all possible. If the two or more questions show similar results, a researcher may have more faith in his measuring instruments, and can also add more credence to his claim that the obtained results are not due to translation errors. If the study were of attitudes toward law enforcement, an example might be: "Do the law enforcement agents work effectively in this town? How well do the policemen do their jobs?" These redundant questions allow the translator to be more sure of the meaning when transforming the thoughts into another language. If he misses a word or idea in one phrase, he might obtain it from another. The redundancy also gives the eventual respondent a greater chance of understanding the purpose of the question. Note that if college freshmen followed this advice in writing papers for English Composition, they would receive the comment "wordy" next to their grades. This particular kind of wordiness, however, is good for cross-cultural research.

The popular semantic differential scales (Osgood, 1962; 1965) provide redundancy since they use a large number (sometimes as many as thirty) reference words. Some of the referent words (and their polar opposites) are similar, providing checks on each other. That is, responses to one pair of words can be compared with responses to a similar pair.

The concept of redundancy is derived in large part from the work of information theorists. George Miller, one of the most prominent proponents of information theory in psychology, points out the advantages of redundancy for all communication:

"It is reasonable to ask why we are so redundant. The answer lies in the fact that redundancy is an insurance against mistakes. The only way to catch an error is to repeat. Redundant information is an automatic mistake catcher built into all natural languages" (Miller, 1953, p. 8).

The principle of adding context to difficult terms is similar to the principle of redundancy, but comes largely from translation researchers themselves rather than from information theorists. For instance, Werner and Campbell (1970) point out that a word is translated least adequately when it is translated as a single item. Translation improves when a word is a part of a sentence, and is even better when the sentence is part of a paragraph. Longacre (1958) reports that long Bible passages are easier to translate than short ones, since the former provide more context for any one concept. Phillips (1959) noted that Malinowski's translation procedure included a careful addition of clarifying terms to provide more context.

Chapanis (1965), an applied psychologist interested in the interaction between man and machine, described context cues for improving understanding of human speech. "A word is much harder to understand if it is heard in isolation than if it is heard in a sentence" (p. 73). Also, in discussing the NATO alphabet, Chapanis said that it "is a specially selected one, full of context and redundancy for getting the maximum amount of information across" (p. 75).

This review provides a background for a set of rules Chapanis designed for a "language to be used under adverse conditions" (p. 75). The writers consider the translation process as an example of an adverse, difficult state of affairs. Chapanis' rules are helpful aids in writing the original language form which a researcher wants bilinguals to translate. These three of his five rules apply here:

"Use as small a vocabulary as possible and make sure that vocabulary is known to all the communicators."

"Use familiar rather than unfamiliar words." [Chapanis suggests the Thorndike-Lorge (1944) word count as a source.]

"Supply as much context for your words as possible. Put the difficult ones in a sentence if you can" (pp. 75-76).

Clearly, Chapanis' principles of maximum communication with human speech echo cross-cultural researchers' principles for maximum translatability.

*Other Factors Affecting Translation Quality.* Several researchers have written about other factors which might affect translation, although these suggestions are not supported by data to the extent that the context and redundancy principles are. Treisman (1965) observed that the difficulty of source language materials, in the form of information load, may affect translation. This point is of importance to cross-cultural researchers who wish to know how difficult their source language version can be before translation will be poor. Nida (1964) and Spilka (1968) made a similar observation, pointing out that familiar materials should be less difficult for translators and thus should be more easily translatable.

Examining these suggestions, Brislin (1970) was interested in determining if some content areas translate better than others, and if different levels of original-English difficulty affect translation. Three content areas, art (a step-by-step description of an artist's procedure), child-rearing (different cultural practices), and racial intelligence (opportunities of races, intelligence testing) were written at two levels of difficulty — easy and moderate—and translated or back-translated by 94 University of Guam bilingual students representing ten non-Indo-European languages, including Chamorro, Palauan, Tagalog, and

Korean. The easier of the difficulty levels (3rd grade English), written according to Werner and Campbell's (1970) previously presented five guidelines (the first 5 on p. 33) gave significantly better back-translations than the moderate level (7th grade English). This supported Treisman's conjecture. The racial intelligence essays gave better back-translations than the child-rearing essays, and both translated better than the art passages. Brislin surmised that one or both of the following reasons accounted for these results: (1) the student translators were more likely to have had experience with the subject matter of the racial intelligence and child-rearing passages, perhaps being more interested in them at the same time; (2) the art passages contained much more detail than the others and hence did not allow context and redundancy to ease translation. These data add another suggestion to the ten "writing translatable English" rules: Write essays that have concepts familiar to the translators, or secure translators familiar with the concepts, and avoid detailed description.

## Wording of Questions

The wording of questions for cross-cultural research is a more specific topic than the issue of writing translatable English. The rules for the latter should be used in all research. Special attention, however, has been given (especially by public opinion researchers) to the writing of questions that will, after translation, be asked of people in other cultures. The following guidelines, in combination with the previously presented rules, will allow a researcher to write his own questions which a bilingual can translate easily. In addition, they should be questions which respondents in the other culture will understand and be able to answer meaningfully.

Current knowledge about the correct wording of questionnaires is certainly imperfect. Little distinction has been made, for instance, between the following three problems, analyzed by Mitchell (1968). Instead, all are grouped into one error category so that sub-analyses are impossible:

1. topics about which the respondent has no opinion and is thus unable to give a meaningful, factual answer;
2. topics that are especially sensitive to members of certain cultures:
3. topics whose measurement demands greater sophistication in instrumentation.

The first two problems are discussed in the next chapter on survey research, and the last will be treated here. The basic problem in writing questions for cross-cultural research is that when the person who formulates the wording is not a member of all the cultures under study, he cannot say, "Oh, you know what I mean!" if he meets a blank stare from a respondent (Frey, 1970). Self-deceiving assurances that a set of questions is understandable will not be accepted by other social scientists.

*Specific Wording Problems.* Most students of a language besides their own can suggest words and concepts easily presented in one language but difficult to communicate in another. Public opinion researchers have shared some examples. The concepts "fair play" and "lonesomeness" are extremely difficult to render in German. "Husband" and "duty" cause problems when attempting translations to Japanese (Scheuch, 1968). Other wording problems are more complex, depending upon the entire frame of reference suggested by a given question.

"In the International Citizenship Survey by Almond and Verba [1963], one of the questions was: 'Here are some important problems facing the people of this country. Which one do you feel is most important to you?' One of the choices offered was 'spiritual and moral betterment.' The combination of this with 'a country's problem' in the context of a political interview seems plain silly in Europe. . . .

"In the same survey respondents were asked to choose from the following statements in order to describe their feelings when going to the polls:

1. 'I get a feeling of satisfaction.'
2. 'I do it only because it is my duty.'
3. 'I feel annoyed—it's a waste of time.'

"The implication of this ordinal scale, that a hedonistic component is a very meaningful dimension of political participation—'a feeling of satisfaction'—is in most European countries quite unwarranted; and in these countries joining the two statements 'I feel annoyed' and 'it's a waste of time' as equivalent expressions of displeasure is very problematical. To ask a Japanese respondent 'Where do you go on your vacation?' makes little sense since only the elite has the privilege of going on vacation" (Scheuch, 1968, p. 181).

Another example comes from a survey of political practices in Austria (Frey, 1970). The questions were formulated in the United States, and one asked how legislators make up their minds about their votes on a given issue. The question was meaningless to the Austrian legislators who have no real vote and instead act as decision-legitimizers.

*Wording Information from Decentering.* The first version of a question in the source language is likely to be changed before an adequate translation is possible. Certain words and concepts in one language, such as those mentioned above, will not have equivalents in another. The obvious response to this information is probably, "How do I know what and when to change?" The answer is to employ a translation decentering procedure.

Decentering refers to a translation process in which the source and the target language versions are equally important and open to modification during the translation procedure. One language does not contain content that must be translated without change into the other. That is, the researcher does not center on one of the languages. For instance, a standardized personality test might be modified after translation to and back from another language. Such modification might be based on knowledge of what terms will not translate well. Colloquial terms (such as "take advantage of" or "playing sick") might have to be changed. In decentering, both the source and the target versions contribute to the final set of questions, both being open to revision. Back-translation is the basis of decentering. Brislin's (1970) translation of the Marlowe-Crowne Social Desirability Scale (Crowne and Marlowe, 1964) provides an example of how the technique works. The original items from the scale went through the following successive translation procedure:

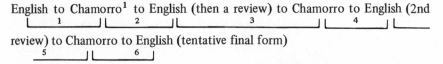

English to Chamorro[1] to English (then a review) to Chamorro to English (2nd review) to Chamorro to English (tentative final form)

For example, the item (number 18), "I don't find it particularly difficult to get along with loud-mouthed, obnoxious people" was translated, back-translated, and then reviewed. Reviews consisted of back-translation examination along with discussions between the investigator and the two bilinguals (steps 1 and 2 in the diagram). The terms "particularly" and "obnoxious" were not in the back-translation, and the bilinguals explained that there were no good Chamorro equivalents. The first back-translated version was then given to bilingual 3, and, after translation, to bilingual 4. Here, "get along with" was replaced in the back-translation by "talk with." In analyzing the change, the bilinguals felt that the Chamorro term for the latter would be more understandable to the projected subject population. This version was then translated (step 5) and back-translated (step 6). At this point there was word-for-word equivalence between the revised English and the back-translation. The final English version used in subsequent testing was, "It is not hard for me to talk with people who have a big mouth."

The decentering procedure determines the changes. The investigator does not decide himself but rather reads the back-translations to find the words and concepts that did not translate well. With the help of his bilinguals, he changes the English for a second try. Often this "change" will simply be the wording of the first back-translation. The sequence continues until there is equivalence between an English version (now different from the original version) and the back-translation. The different language versions are then ready for a pretest to determine if the questions are meaningful to the subject population. Other original items and their final "post-decentering" forms were as follows:

---

[1] Chamorro is the native language of Guam and the Marianas Islands.

Marlowe-Crowne

*Item No.*

| | | |
|---|---|---|
| 2 | original: | I never hesitate to go out of my way to help someone in trouble. |
| | revised: | I am never hesitant to find a way to help someone who has a problem. |
| 11 | original: | I like to gossip at times. |
| | revised: | I sometimes like to talk about other people's business. |
| 14 | original: | I can remember "playing sick" to get out of something. |
| | revised: | I can remember when I pretended to be sick so I wouldn't have to do anything. |
| 26 | original: | I have never been irked when people expressed ideas very different from my own. |
| | revised: | I am never irritated if people say something which is not the same as my thinking. |

*Application of the Context-Redundancy Principle.* The context-redundancy principle states that concepts should be surrounded by similar and contrasting ideas so that the purpose of the original concept will be clear. Realizing the value of this principle, agencies in other countries which do cross-cultural work are often irritated by questionnaires sent from the United States (Mitchell, 1968). These questions are often accompanied by instructions requiring the agency to preserve the exact original form. One agency now insists that the client must attach a paragraph explaining the purpose behind each question. The agency can then use the additional information to form a better question that will both retain the original purpose and be well suited to the target population.

Blanc (1956) suggests that rephrasing of questions during an interview seems unavoidable since respondents often say, "Will you repeat that?" Possible alternatives for each question could be included in an interview, the combination of which would provide enough context and redundancy for both the interviewer and respondent to be more precise regarding the meaning of each item. Using the context-redundancy principle implies that a great deal be known about the culture to be studied. Frey (1970) insists that unless researchers have an intimate knowledge of a culture, good questions cannot be written. This advice has been presented many times, but actual investment in gaining such knowledge is about as minimal as the quality of many questions used in current research.

*The Alternatives Provided Respondents.* Questions are only part of the cross-cultural instrument. The alternatives presented to respondents are also important and need greater attention than they have heretofore received. Since communication between interviewer and respondent is difficult, closed-ended questions that include more than three response alternatives (e.g., yes, no, and I don't know) should not be used. If his memory is taxed, the respondent might become frustrated and give the alternative he remembers rather than the one that reflects his opinion (Marwick, 1958). Where possible, the responses should be put into a familiar context. Cantril (1963) normally used the steps of a ladder to indicate different alternatives that respondents could give. Since ladders are unknown to the Zulus, he substituted a picture of a mountain with successive terraces that would be climbed while ascending. This was a much more familiar set of alternatives (Scheuch, 1968).

After the original English questions, alternative responses, or other materials have been prepared, they must be translated into another language. Of the several techniques, back-translation has been most researched and will be presented first, followed by other translation methods.

## Back-Translation

In suggesting methods for best translation results, Werner and Campbell (1970) recommended back-translation, since it gives an investigator a good deal of control over the questionnaire development stage of his research project. Imagine the following predicament: A researcher enters another culture and does not know the local language, but wants to ask questions of people in that culture. If he asks a bilingual to translate his questions for him, the researcher is ordinarily unable to judge the translator's competence, and is therefore unable to demonstrate the high quality of translation that good research demands. But with back-translation he has a check over the quality of both the questionnaire and the translators. The English-speaking researcher starts with an English language form that is likely to be translatable. Two bilinguals are them employed, one translating from the source to the target language, the second blindly translating back from the target to the source language.

An example will help in understanding this chain of events. The target language is Chamorro, described by Topping (1969) and investigated in Brislin's (1970) translation study. The original English is: "Can you go and get her book? I will use it at your home day after tomorrow." This might be translated into Chamorro as follows: "Kao sina un falague i leblo-na? Para bai hu usa gi gima-mu agupa'na." Roughly, some of the key individual English-Camorro equivalents are as follows:

| Kao | = a marker indicating a question |
| siña | = can, or be able to |

| falague | = go and get |
|---|---|
| -ña | = possessive indicating "his" or "her" |
| para bai | = marker indicating the future tense, first person |
| usa | = use; the "it" referring to the book is understood |
| -mu | = a possessive indicating "your" |
| agupa'ña | = day after tomorrow: "agupa" alone is tomorrow, and the "-ña" indicates "day before or day after." |

A second bilingual might hear or read the Chamorro and back-translate it as follows: "Will you be able to get his book? I'll use it in your home not tomorrow, but the next day."

Later in the chapter we will cover methods for determining the equivalence of material such as this. Note, however, that "his" and "her" were confused. This problem could be avoided by making the context of the original English clearer, indicating that a female owned the book. Specific knowledge of the languages involved makes it much easier to supply the needed context and redundancy in key places.

The investigator now has two versions in the original language which, if they are identical, suggest that the target version from the middle of the process is most likely equivalent to the source language forms. The word "suggest" is used, since several factors besides good translation can create seeming equivalence between source, target, and back-translated versions. The following are among such factors (Brislin, 1970):

1. Translators may have a shared set of rules for translating certain non-equivalent words and phrases (e.g., "amigo" and "friend" are not always equivalent).

2. Some back-translators may be able to make sense out of a poorly written target language version.

3. The bilingual translating from the source to the target may retain many of the grammatical forms of the source. This version would be easy to back-translate but worthless for the purpose of asking questions of target-language monolinguals, since its grammar is that of the source, not the target.

These problems are discussed in subsequent sections. For the present, however, suppose that the researcher finds errors in comparing the two source language versions. Knowledge of the errors gives the researcher some insight into the competence of his translators. If the two source language forms are not identical, he can confer with the two bilinguals, clearing up errors. He will often have to revise the original English to be sure of eventual identical items in the foreign and back-translated versions, the process known as decentering.

The following review discusses cross-cultural studies in which back-translation has been used, the few studies that have investigated translation itself, and other techniques that have been used in conjunction with back-translation.

Organization of the review centers around: (1) studies that have successfully used back-translation, (2) studies that have found back-translation a poor technique and worthy of criticism, (3) studies that have used back-translation but with little methodological comment, (4) back-translation employed with other techniques such as the use of bilinguals or a pretest, and (5) the evaluation of translation (especially back-translation) quality and equivalence.

*Research Reporting Successful Use of Back-Translation.* Fink (1963), Werner and Campbell (1970), Sinaiko (1963), and Brislin (1970) reported successful use of back-translation in relatively extensive detail. It will be instructive to examine their methodology for insights into the possible causes of their success. Fink's (1963) use of back-translation in a survey of Laos demonstrates the adaptability of the method. It was necessary that he translate from English to the Laotian language, but no interpreters competent in both languages could be found. Available were bilinguals who spoke either English and Thai or Thai and Lao. Fink therefore went through a successive translations procedure from English to Thai, to Lao, to Thai, to English. Sometimes the back-translated version was clearly different in meaning from the original version. Fink revised the original English and looked for problems in the three foreign language versions. In the Werner and Campbell (1970) research, Navajo subjects translated and back-translated several simple English passages, again with the original English open to revision. Sinaiko (1963) studied French and English in governmental work simulating multi-nation conferences. Skilled interpreters were used as subjects. Brislin (1970) had bilinguals translate a personality scale and/or set of performance instructions into Chamorro, Kusaien, and Palauan. Table 2.1 gives the original and back-translated versions of materials from these three studies, showing the types of changes that can be expected.

These successful uses of back-translation may be due to one of two reasons. (1) In the Fink (1963), Werner and Campbell (1970), and Brislin (1970) studies, the original English was open to revision. Some problems were solved by changing the English in anticipation of a good final translation. (2) In the Sinaiko (1963) study, the languages under study (French and English) had similar structures so that translation was probably easier than between English and the non-Indo-European languages investigated in the other studies. With these four studies as background, other research describing translation methodology will be summarized to examine whether either or both of the above reasons may account for good results using back-translation. A number of researchers (Jacobsen, 1954; OSCR, 1952; Hudson et al., 1959; Kluckhohn, 1960; Lambert and Klineberg, 1967; Gough et al., 1968; Kandel et al., 1968; Bass, 1968; and Triandis, Kilty, et al., 1968) reported successful back-translation of English prose passages. In all of these studies, the original English was open to revision after the first back-translation efforts. Gough et al. (1968) translated the

Table 2.1 Original and Back-Translated English From Three Research Projects Studying Translation from English to Navajo, French, or Chamorro

| Study | Original English | Back-Translation |
|-------|-----------------|------------------|
| Werner and Campbell (1970) | One time a man had a lot of livestock. Most of them died off in different ways. | One time a man's (stranger) livestock was existing (when) almost all of them died from different causes, it is said. |
| Sinaiko (1963) | flagrant<br>tottering<br>missiles<br>to allow discussion<br>his | blatant<br>vacillating<br>rockets<br>to permit debate<br>its |
| Brislin (1970 | I have almost never felt the urge to tell someone off. | I have never felt like scolding someone. |

Femininity Scale of the California Psychological Inventory into Korean. They reported that after the first translation, "Where the retranslated item was not fully equivalent to the original English, a new translation from English to Korean was made, and this new version checked once again" (p. 156).

Bass (1968) and Jacobsen (1954) translated into many European languages, finding success in all cases after revision of the English. Lambert and Klineberg (1967), Hudson et al. (1959), and Triandis et al. (1968), also with original language form open to revision, were successful with such divergent languages as Hebrew, Japanese, Arabic, and Greek. In the above studies, "success" in the use of the back-translation technique simply refers to the researchers' satisfaction with the results. More stringent criteria for translation equivalence will be discussed below.

The second possible reason for successful use of back-translation has to do with language structure. Several of the languages into which Jacobsen (1954) and Bass (1968) translated were Indo-European, thus similar in structure to the original English. These included Danish, French, German, Italian, and Spanish. In one of the few studies using a non-English source language, Stern et al. (1947) started with either French, German, or Italian questionnaires and translated them into the other languages, checking their work by back-translation. Fortunately for our assessment of the reasons for good back-translation, Bass' (1968) research program required translation into languages with structure similar and dissimilar to English. French was an example of the former and Hebrew the latter. Since revision of the English was made following translation into and back from both languages, the willingness to revise was most likely the more potent reason for back-translation success.

*Research Criticizing the Use of Back-Translation.* Phillips (1959), who supervised the translation of a sentence completion test into Thai and Nida (1964), who related the experiences of several people and their task of translating a humorous essay into several European languages, concluded that back-translation led to extremely poor results. However, in the Phillips study the conclusion that back-translation efforts were poor was made before the English was revised. In the Nida report the source was never open to revision. Such results, nevertheless, emphasize the gravity and importance of studying translation techniques and their products.

Other criticisms of back-translation include those by Gough (1968b) who commented that researchers often place too much faith in back-translation, thus relying on only one technique. The use of multiple methods, to be discussed below, may alleviate this problem. Similarly, Jacobsen et al. (1960) commented that the back-translation technique may produce a spurious sense of equivalence. The three criticisms of back-translation suggested earlier (p. 41) are also applicable here. Perhaps one reason for the existence of these problems is the lack of methodological comment in several studies that have used back-translation.

*Research Reporting Use of Back-Translation with Little Comment.* One of the most pressing problems of back-translation is the small literature reporting use of the technique. Furthermore, many researchers who mention its use have made few comments about their experiences that would be helpful to others. In earlier work Schachter (1954), Duijker (1955), and Ervin and Bower (1952) reported use of back-translation. Since they, too, did not comment on their experiences, it might be assumed that this technique gave successful translations. This assumption, however, cannot be accepted by the critical reader who demands careful specification of methodology. More recently, Almond and Verba (1963) and Cantril (1965) used but did not comment on the back-translation methodology. This omission in the two studies is especially distressing, since they were large-scale and potentially significant studies of attitudes in several cultures. The lack of an extensive methodology section makes it impossible for readers to judge the quality of the translated questionnaires.

In contrast with this lack of information, several excellent studies have reported the use of back-translation combined with other techniques. These other techniques will be described in the next section, both for their insights into the nature of translation for cross-cultural research and as an introduction to studies using some combination of translation techniques.

## Other Translation Techniques

*The Use of Bilinguals.* Translations can be compared for equivalence by having bilinguals take the test in both the original and translated forms (Schachter, 1954). Items that yield different responses could be studied and the problems examined. This technique has been used by Gough and DiPalma (1965), Triandis and Davis (1965), and Prince and Mombour (1967). In the Triandis and Davis study, samples of bilinguals took the questionnaire in the two languages with which they were familiar. Results for responses to each item were compared by matched *t*-tests, and the translations were reviewed when the *t*'s were significant. Prince and Mombour (1967) detailed their recommended procedure in five steps:

1. A careful translation should be done by the best person available. It is suggested that words with similar frequency of usage in the two languages be used.

2. The translation from step one should be tested on bilinguals. The researcher randomly assigns bilinguals to two groups. One group is asked the first half of the questions in language one, and the second half in language two; the order is reversed for the other group.

3. "The translation of items eliciting discrepant response frequencies should be held suspect and further attempts at translation should be made. Further trial runs should be made until comparable frequencies are obtained. Operational equivalence has then been achieved" (p. 236).

4. Discard test items if the procedure in step three continues to yield discrepant responses.

5. Carry out the survey "with reasonable assurance that differences found will not be spurious differences resulting from faulty translation of the instrument" (p. 237).

In this procedure item *frequencies* of groups equated by randomization are compared. Therefore, the charge that high original-translation reliability (a form of test-retest) could be obtained through respondent memory is not applicable.

At this juncture we would like to note that the bilingual technique can be used to study certain psycholinguistic hypotheses. For instance, the question of whether bilinguals have two personalities, one for each language, has been investigated by Ervin (1964). She administered the Thematic Apperception Test (see Chapter 5) to French-English bilinguals on two different occasions—the language of administration being English the first time, French the second time, or vice versa. All bilinguals had been raised in metropolitan France and were living in Washington, D.C., during the time of the study. Ervin had a number of specific hypotheses, including the prediction that women would show less of an achievement need using French because of the different role expectations in

France compared to the United States. This hypothesis was strongly supported. In her excellent plausible rival hypotheses analysis, Ervin suggested several possible reasons for her data, including the possibility that subjects told a story appropriate to the language they were using, or the stories reflected the content of the mass media in the two countries.

This is an exciting research area, but investigators must be especially careful that their translations are equivalent to the original language version of a test. If not, differences that might support the dual-personality hypothesis can be attributed to a faulty translation. Differences in individual test scores between languages are likely to be small, since they will be based on just a few of the items from the entire scale being used. Thus a faulty translation of any one item can cause a piece of research in this area to be held in disrepute.

*Pretest Techniques.* Pretesting is necessary even after careful translation, since nonsensical answers can occur in response to even the most carefully constructed questions. Two techniques have been suggested for cross-cultural research. The random-probe technique has been used in several studies (Schuman, 1966). An interviewer selects a random sample of items on a questionnaire and asks a probing question about each item. The sample that receives the probe about a given item is also randomly selected. The probe asked after a subject's answer is "What do you mean?" If a respondent's justification of the original answer is bizarre, then the intent of the question is not being conveyed. If the researcher examines the answers to this "meaning" probe given by all his respondents, he should have a good deal of insight into the quality of his questionnaire. In a similar procedure Mitchell (1966) reported that his interviewers rated his 27 questions used in Nigeria. The rating was to indicate how clear the question was to people. The rating thus measures how adequate the translation was in formulating a well-worded question. Ratings were high. Mitchell added that questions highest in rated clarity were highest in question reliability, as measured by two interviewers questioning the respondent (test-retest reliability). This supplementary test-retest reliability study provided added data in support of translation adequacy.

*Committee Approach.* We use the term "committee" to refer to the type of translation effort in which two or three people translate from the original to the target language and then compare results, often with another person. In this procedure, one envisions a group of people sitting around a table discussing the merits of each item. Barrioux (1948) reports that two translators worked on a French version of a test, and a third person chose what he thought was the best version of each item. All these opinions were then brought together to decide on an optimal translation. Sundberg (1956), discussing the German version of the MMPI, writes that two German students translated from the English, and then a

(1959) used the committee, back-translation, and pretest procedures in translating from English to Arabic. The weaknesses of one method were offset by the strengths of another. The use of more than one method, which is the essence of this issue, deserves elaboration since it is a special case of the use of multiple methods common to all branches of science.

The use of multiple methods in research is always more desirable than the use of only one. Teitelbaum (1967, p. 12) quotes von Békésy, Nobel Prize winner in Physiology and Medicine, as saying, "I never publish a finding until I have measured the phenomenon by at least five different methods. . . . I expect a fact determined this way to stand unchanged for about fifty years." In psychological field research, a good example of multiple methods is that of Sherif et al. (1961). The investigators studied the formation of and interaction among two boys' groups. Different methods, including observer ratings, subjects' reports, and an experimental criterion were used to assess the subjects' degree of friendly or hostile feelings. Webb et al. (1966) have presented an eloquent defense for the use of multiple measures and criteria in social science research.

Because of its obvious advantages, the multiple translation methodology of Hudson et al. (1959) was discussed above. Similar to the use of multiple methods is the use of multiple criteria for the assessment of dependent variables, advocated by many, including Campbell and Fiske (1959) and Dunnette (1963). For instance, in the area of work motivation, one dependent variable might be a person's rating of how satisfied he feels with his job. This one criterion, however, does not cover the entire content of work motivation (Vroom, 1964); it may be unreliable, and may be subject to response biases. A better procedure is the use of several dependent variables, such as individual ratings, supervisory ratings, absenteeism, amount of productivity, and the like.

## Evaluation of Translation Quality and Equivalence

To determine both translation quality and equivalence of source and target versions, researchers have dealt with: (1) comparisons of meaning, (2) ability to gain the same information from reading source and target versions, (3) responses to different-language versions, and (4) performance measures.

*The Development of Equivalence Measures.* Both Catford (1965) and Nida (1964) consider equivalence of meaning to be the most important aspect of translation. In most informal evaluations of translation, the emphasis on meaning guides conclusions regarding translation quality. In back-translation, Werner and Campbell (1970) and Fink (1963) reported the necessity of revising the source language version of a passage based on informal comparisons of the meanings of the source and back-translated versions. This procedure implies that the unit of translation quality may be a unit of meaning, a suggestion explicitly put forth by Treisman (1965). Using such a meaning criterion, Carroll (1966) asked raters to evaluate translations based on judgments of meaning. However, he did not actually devise a *unit* of translation quality that might be the unit of a translating quality *scale*. Both Niyekawa-Howard (1968) and Barik (1971) have evaluated translations by comparing source and target versions, carefully noting those places where meaning changed.

Other criteria designed to insure equivalent source-target meaning, have been suggested by Miller and Beebe-Center (1956), and by Macnamara (1967). Miller and Beebe-Center reasoned that if people could perform bodily movements after having heard either a source or target language instructions, and if the results of the bodily movement criterion were similar across all people, then the source and its translation must be equivalent. A performance criterion was used by Allport and Pettigrew (1957). In that study, Zulu subjects gave hand motions to indicate the presence or absence of the trapezoidal illusion. This suggestion is, of necessity, limited to the kinds of materials that can be examined through bodily movements. Both Miller and Beebe-Center (1956) and Macnamara (1967) suggested that people should give equivalent answers to questions written about a passage after seeing either the source or the target version of the passage. If answers are equivalent across people, then the source and its translation should be equivalent.

A major difficulty in assessing translation studies or translation evaluation methods is the lack of an ultimate criterion of translation quality, a problem noted by Spilka (1968). Nida (1964, p. 164) may have suggested such a criterion in his statement that one of the requirements of translation is to "produce a similar response" on the part of readers of a source and target version. As in behavioristic psychology, an observable, verifiable response may be the standard for an ultimate criterion of translation equivalence and quality.

With the above research as background, Brislin (1970) developed and tested five criteria to test the equivalence of source and target versions. These criteria might provide a researcher a repertoire for the different needs and limitations of the research at hand. Criteria 1, 3, and 4 were also tested in the Sinaiko and Brislin (1970) study.

1. Monolingual raters examine the original and back-translated forms of a passage, and write down errors that they feel would lead to differences in meaning if the two forms were administered. Different raters' judgments of these "meaning errors" can be compared in two ways. The first is the correlation between number of errors found by two or more raters over a large number of passages. The second is the percentage overlap in different raters finding *exactly* the same meaning errors. Two raters may each find seven errors in a passage, contributing to a high between-rater correlation, but one rater may find completely different errors than the other. Both the correlation and percentage overlap indices are necessary for an adequate description of criterion

one-meaning errors.

2. Bilingual raters look at the original and target versions and write down meaning errors as in criterion 1. These bilingual meaning errors can be compared with those meaning errors found by monolingual judges in procedure 1. This criterion is a more direct test of original-target language equivalence than that found in criterion 1 since criterion 1 tests the same language forms, and criterion 2 tests the different language forms.

3. Subjects should be able to answer questions about target language and back-translated passages. A questionnaire based on the content of the passage should yield similar responses from subjects if the versions are equivalent.

Criteria 4 and 5, both of which call for administration of test materials to subjects, presuppose a satisfactory back-translation according to criterion 1. As such, these two criteria are tests of how sensitive criterion 1 is to foreseeing and preventing problems in actual test administration.

4. If the passage in English asks for a performance of some sort, the subject may be requested to perform a task with the target language version as the instructions. If he can complete the task then the original and target versions are undoubtedly equivalent. Specifically, the original and foreign language versions are functionally (workably) equivalent. This is the "performance criterion."

5. An actual original language questionnaire and its target language translation are given to four groups of bilingual subjects equated by randomization. One group sees the original language version of the questions; a second group sees the target language version; a third sees the first-half original, second-half target; the fourth sees the first-half target, second-half original. If the versions are equal, then item frequencies should be the same, as should the total score for the entire questionnaire, across groups. In addition, the correlation between original and target language scores for groups three and four should be high. Since the four groups are equated by randomization, the versions of the questionnaire should elicit the same responses. This technique is an extension of the bilingual procedure outlined by Prince and Mombour (1967) and described previously.

Criteria 4 and 5 are suggested as "ultimate" criteria for translation since, following Nida (1964), it is assumed that if a source version and its translation elicit the same response or pattern of responses, the most important purpose of a passage is being conveyed. Responses are often the ultimate criteria for cross-cultural researchers who compare either performances to tasks or answers to questions across cultures.

All five of these criteria were applied to translations and back-translations, and all proved workable (Brislin, 1970). Especially important was the successful use of criteria 4 and 5, and their relation to criterion 1. That is, materials for administration were translated, back-translated and tested with the criterion 1 meaning error. After revision through decentering (as many as three rounds of source to target to source) the materials were administered. Subjects in the criterion 4 experiment were able to perform a picture-making task regardless of whether they received the original instructions or their translation. Subjects in the criterion 5 experiment had equivalent responses to the English questionnaire and its translation as shown by similar item frequencies and high split-half reliability coefficients for the groups seeing half the questions in each language.

Criteria 1, 3, and 4 were examined in the Sinaiko and Brislin (1970) research. Highly technical documents on helicopter maintenance were translated into Vietnamese. The following is an example of the maintenance instructions[2]:

"Lock collective pitch control stick in full down position and adjust droop compensator control tube to align center of bolt hole in aft arm of torque tube approximately level with top of support bracket. Due to shimming, manufacturer's tolerance, etc., variation of 0.250-inch from top of support bracket is possible and acceptable" (Sinaiko and Brislin, 1970, p. 57).

Three Vietnamese versions were prepared by three bilinguals, and these were subsequently back-translated. Counting the number of meaning errors (criterion 1) allowed an estimate of their relative quality. The translations were then labeled A, B, and C. Version A had more criterion 1 errors than B, and B more than C. Questions were then prepared (criterion 3) and Vietnamese mechanics were asked to answer them after reading only one of the three versions. A question about the above passage might be:

In what position should the collective pitch control stick be locked?

The mechanics were able to answer more questions correctly after reading A than B and more after reading B than C. For criterion 4, the Vietnamese mechanics performed an operational check on a helicopter using one of the three translations as instructions. Specialists in helicopters rated the quality of their work, and the results showed better performance using A, followed by B, and finally C.

This small body of research provides a test of the assumption that if the original and back-translation are equivalent by criterion 1, or by other formal or informal comparisons of meaning, a researcher can assume that the target language version is equal to both original language versions. This assumption may be spurious. Chance factors, a shared set of rules for translating and back-translating, or the uncanny ability of some back-translators to make sense out of gibberish, might account for original-back-translation equivalence. Without additional data obtained relevant to criteria 2 through 5 (especially 4 and 5), this inference is not acceptable. With further research, however, criterion

---

[2] The Sinaiko and Brislin (1970) study included an analysis of how the rules for writing translatable English are violated in documents of this sort.

1 may prove to be only the necessary test of translation adequacy. Specifically, many translations might be tested with criterion 1, and the results compared with the results of applying criteria 2 through 5. If the continued application of criteria 2 through 5 adds little correction to the verdict of translation adequacy derived from criterion 1 (if the same conclusions about translation equivalence are made), then the induction of foreign language equivalence from only criterion 1, along with a pretest, might be accepted for later translation efforts.

*Recommended Procedure.* We can summarize the work on translation equivalence by presenting our recommended procedure. Have several raters examine the original, target, and/or the back-translated versions for errors that lead to differences in meaning (meaning errors). If possible, have other raters answer questions after having read only one of the versions. To finally demonstrate translation adequacy, administer the materials to bilingual subjects, some who see the English version, some who see the translation, and some who see both. Responses should be similar across groups, as assessed by means, standard deviations, and correlation coefficients. Report experience using the different criteria for equivalence. Determine the verdict of translation adequacy derived from the meaning error standard and a simple pretest, and compare it with the verdict derived from the more formal and time-consuming administration to subjects. If the verdict is the same for many research projects, future research might only demand the simpler meaning error standard and pretest.

## Further Considerations

*Variations of Back-Translation Used to Solve Specific Problems.* The back-translation technique is adaptable and can be used to help solve specific cross-cultural methodological problems. Perhaps translations into more than one language are desired. If key bilinguals can be found, the following procedure can be established:

Original to target #1 to target #2 back to original. The key translator is the person fluent in target languages 1 and 2. He does not have to speak the original language. Both Fink (1963) and Brislin (1972) have used this multi-language back-translation procedure and have found it workable.

One of the shortcomings of back-translation is that much of the original language's structure might be retained in the translation. This would make a version easy to back-translate but useless and dangerous for cross-cultural research. The translation would not contain well-worded sentences that the target population will be able to understand. The back-translation variation used to overcome this problem was as follows (Brislin, 1972):

original, to target, to target rewrite, to original

The individuals performing the "rewrite" step were asked to think of a person they knew who spoke the target language but no other. They were then to rewrite the target version so that this person would be able to understand it easily because of its good grammar and clear presentation of ideas. Judged by the number of meaning errors (criterion 1) in the back-translation, this technique is usable.

*What Do Translators Do?* Bilinguals obviously engage in a great deal of thought while translating from one language to another. It is surprising, though, that few statements can be made about what they do. Only recently, a few studies have touched upon this issue.

When presented with technical terms for which there is not an exact equivalent in the target language, bilinguals make the original language simpler (Sinaiko and Brislin, 1970). When faced with the task of translating "by-pass valve" into Vietnamese, bilinguals changed the original English to "valve used to pass fluid in the way not normally used." They then could translate the latter into Vietnamese since equivalents existed for the simpler words. As another example, "tachometer" was changed to "rotation measuring device" and then translated. This has been called the "explain around" aspect of translation.

Bilinguals change general concepts to more specific examples of that concept. The word "livestock" was made more specific (e.g., "chickens." "cows") in almost two-thirds of the translations investigated in the Brislin (1972) study. Redundancy is omitted, many times by incorporating the redundant information into a previous phrase that has also covered the point to be made. The phrase "money is earned from selling fruit" was incorporated into the phrase, "Fruit sellers use their money to purchase necessities for their families." This finding does not suggest that the context-redundancy principle discussed earlier is wrong. Redundancy helps the translator understand the meaning of a passage. After the intial understanding, he may choose to omit the redundancy in his translation.

Translators omit grammatical forms present in one language but not in the other. Japanese has a grammatical form (the adversative passive) which implies "am not responsible for it." When translating from Japanese to English, bilinguals dropped this implication (Niyekawa-Howard, 1968). When translating from English to Japanese, this form was *added* whenever unpleasant events were described. Bilinguals sometimes change the original English so that it approaches wording with which they are familiar. In the Brislin (1972) study, all the translators had been exposed to basic Christian concepts since childhood. The phrase, "One way to make friends is to do nice things for another person" was back-translated in words very close to the Golden Rule ("Do unto others . . . ."). Passages about God's kindness were translated into wordings very close to the catechism teachings with which the bilinguals were familiar. Our recommendation is that further research should study the translator as an active agent rather than as a passive transmitter of words. Clinical psychologists have been interested in the ways and manner that skilled interpreters of complex personality profiles, like the MMPI, arrive at a final personality description (e.g., Kleinmuntz, 1969). Perhaps cross-cultural researchers interested in how translators make decisions can use some of the leads from these clinical studies.

## Summary

Although knowledge concerning translation for cross-cultural research is not perfect, more is known than would be implied from reading methodology sections of many articles. All too often researchers report that their English language scale was "translated and administered" to subjects in another culture. Such scanty information is not sufficient to rule out the plausible rival hypothesis of translation/instrumentation difficulties.

There are presently twelve guidelines for writing English that is likely to be translatable into another language. These deal with the grammar of English sentences as well as with the construction of entire paragraphs. The latter guidelines suggest adding context and redundancy to key ideas using concepts familiar to the translators (or vice versa), and avoiding detailed description. The wording of questionnaires has received special attention. To obtain an adequate translation, the original English will often have to be changed. The best original language wording can be determined by examining the various stages of the decentering process. A decentering sequence, based on the back-translation technique, might be:

original to target, to original, to target, to original

Original language terms that do not translate well will "filter out" and be replaced by terms which have equivalents in the target language.

After the original language version has been written, the researcher has a choice of three translation techniques. (1) In back-translation, one bilingual translates from the original to the target language, then a second bilingual blindly translates back to the original. The researcher does not have to speak the target language. He can compare the two original language versions and make inferences about the quality of the target. This technique has received more research attention than any other. Successful use presupposes a willingness to revise the original English. (2) Using the bilingual technique, the researcher asks bilinguals to take half the test in one language and the second half in the other language. When the data from many respondents are analyzed, consistency of responses can be determined. Analysis can also indicate those items that are answered (in a certain direction) more frequently in one language than in the other. (3) The committee approach is probably the weakest method. A group of bilinguals discusses each item or sentence and makes one translation. This technique does not control for shared misconceptions and possible reluctance to criticize the suggestions of another. It can, however, be profitably used in combination with the other techniques.

After a translation has been prepared by any method, it should be pretested. The literature provides many examples of a supposedly good translation that had to be revised because of specific problems discovered during a field test. Such examples point out the necessity of employing multiple methods in all cross-cultural research. The errors not caught by one method might be identified by another.

Cross-cultural researchers must demonstrate that their translations are equivalent to the original language versions. Five techniques have been developed: (1) comparisons of meaning between the original and back-translated forms; (2) comparisons of meaning, by bilinguals other than the translator, between the original and translated form; (3) answering questions written about the content of the original version; the questions should be answered correctly by people who have read only the target version; (4) comparing performance to instructions written in the original and in the target language; (5) administering both versions of a test or questionnaire to a sample of bilinguals. All five have been applied to translated materials and they have proved workable. Again, a pretest should follow the use of any of these equivalence criteria.

Limited information exists on what bilinguals actually do in translating from one language to another. This is an area in which research data are needed.

After obtaining his translation, prove adequate by any or several of the above criteria, the researcher is likely to gather data with it. He may use it as part of a public opinion survey (next chapter), or he may administer it as a test (Chapter 5). The successful completion of a survey or testing project presupposes a good translation.

# CHAPTER THREE

## Survey Methods

Cross-cultural researchers interested in any topic will find it useful to elicit and quantify the opinions, feelings, and intentions of subjects as part of their overall research strategy. This information may be the goal of the research, or it may be an important preliminary activity before valid testing or experimentation can be undertaken. The general term for this activity is "survey research," and even though such data collection may seem simple (after all, one person just asks questions of another!), this method has special problems.

The term "opinion survey" connotes a series of actions that are common in some countries but less so in others. If residents of the United States were asked to associate words with the term, they would probably say, "people knocking on doors," "asking embarrassing questions," "writing down answers," "market research," "political polls," and so forth. Frey has advanced a formal definition:

"I conceive of survey research as a method (or the products thereof) for systematically obtaining specific information from a relatively large number of individual sources, ordinarily through questioning" (Frey, 1970, pp. 175-176).

Of course, no good research is accomplished through a haphazard set of questions put to a convenient and available group of respondents. Rather, careful thought must be given to variables, hypotheses, controls, samples, opportunities for obtaining interesting findings, validity, reliability, coherent patterns, and so forth. This chapter reviews some major problem areas relevant to these goals and refers the reader to other sources for more detailed discussions of certain points. Moreover, survey methods discussed in this chapter should not be confused with the cross-cultural survey, another method discussed elsewhere in this book. We shall start our discussion with three somewhat mundane points which are often forgotten. Hopefully, these questions will introduce the difficulties involved in carrying out a good survey, the subtle controls necessary to solve various problems, and the need for sensitive perception of the survey as seen by individuals in other cultures. First, what are the uses of the survey in cross-cultural psychology? Second, is it right to assume that members of all cultures will answer any or all questions asked by a stranger? Third, is money available to finance large scale surveys?

## How the Survey is Used

A researcher rarely starts an investigation with a survey. Instead, he gathers data from his own observations and from case studies, then formulates specific hypotheses to be tested using the survey method. The uses of a survey, then, would be to document guesses and hunches obtained through less well-controlled methods. Converse (1964) also makes this point, reminding us that researchers will have little faith in a method until it can yield already established or widely supposed facts. Social scientists will be likely to accept surprising and non-commonsense findings only after confidence in a method has been established.

Surveys by one set of investigators have encouraged comment by others, and these comments should help increase the sophistication of the survey method. For instance, the Almond and Verba (1963) five-country study of political and civic attitudes, accomplished through interviews held with people randomly selected from national samples, has been constructively criticized by Frey (1970), Scheuch (1968), Mitchell (1968), and Riggs (1970). In fact, any large survey *will* receive intense comment by others who will insist that definitions, samples, questions, comparisons, controls, and so forth could have been better.

A third use of surveys would be to suggest hypotheses for experimental research. However, this potential link between methods has not been established, although there is every reason to suggest that it will. One possible reason that this link has not been established is that there have been few large scale surveys, perhaps less than twenty. Some experiments and surveys, however, have yielded complementary data even though the design of one did not influence the other. For instance, the results of Gillespie and Allport's (1955) survey measuring youth's outlook on the future fits in nicely with Meade's (1968) experiment on level of aspiration among Indian students. Both studies demonstrate specific cultural influences that affect people's thinking about what the future might bring.

## Answering Questions

It is easy for researchers to forget that residents of Western cultures, especially the United States, may be the only people who are willing to answer a wide-ranging set of questions. Scheuch (1968) reminds us that it is actually surprising that one person can interrupt another person in his home or on the street and ask such questions as:

1. Is resurrection possible?

2. Should social security funds be used to subsidize medical care for the elderly?

3. What constitutes a good weapons system for our country's defense?

4. Is there life on Mars?

It is even more surprising that those questioned will have an opinion on these issues. Unfortunately, they also have opinions (as one study has shown) on such non-existent issues as the "metallic metals act" (Payne, 1951), where American citizens gave firm opinions about a completely fictitious "news" item. One of the authors remembers a humorous segment on the "Candid Camera" TV show. Pedestrians were stopped and asked what they thought of the new television series, "Space Doctor." People had an opinion even though no such show existed. The respondents even had opinions to follow-up questions, such as, "What do you think of the nurse's wild hair-do?" People responded with answers that made some sense, for example, "Well, it fits in with the clothes they wear on the space ship." If Americans are not opinionated they are certainly opinion-oriented.

The ease of obtaining responses to questions in the United States tempts researchers to try the same technique elsewhere. Undoubtedly, however, people can ponder questions on topics like medicine for the elderly only in cultures where there is both leisure time and a value placed on thinking through problems to reach a solution. The members of some cultures must constantly struggle for survival. They solve a problem by remembering how it was solved in the past, and taking time to answer questions is unknown. The two biases contained in the above stories, "everybody can answer questions," and "I don't want to seem ignorant" are discussed below, along with others. Whether members of a particular culture can or will answer questions, it should be remembered, is an empirical question. Stycos (1960) reported very low refusal rates for surveys in the Carbibean, the Near and Middle East, and Italy. He had been warned by others that questioning would be impossible, especially since the survey dealt with sensitive issues like birth control and sexual relations. Stycos, however, was able to break down the barriers of fear and distrust (using techniques mentioned below) and he concluded that *greater* cooperation is possible in less-well-developed countries.

## Money

If the amount of printed space devoted to a topic is an indication of its importance, then the financing of surveys is a critical issue. Askenasy (1966), Bonilla (1964), Campbell (1968), and Frey (1970), all agree that large scale surveys requiring national samples (e.g., Almond and Verba, 1963) are very expensive and must be funded from the coffers of well-endowed organizations. Since treatments of this topic exist, there is no need to belabor the issue except to point out its importance.

## The Importance of a Basic Knowledge of Survey Methods

It seems strange, then, that so much effort has been put into developing guidelines for cross-cultural survey research if few surveys can be undertaken. It should be remembered, however, that survey methods can be adapted to many types of projects. Aspects of the method include sampling, interviewer-interviewee communication biases, data interpretation, and other matters. Many of these problems exist even when a large scale national sample is not the goal. Small scale surveys based on samples from smaller units than nations are possible, of course, and can yield important findings. One problem to be discussed concerns the selection of interviewers. This information should help in the design of other research as in, for instance, the selection of research assistants. As already mentioned, a researcher may want to gather certain information using survey methods before setting up a testing program or a series of experiments, and so will want to know the proper procedures.

## Interviewer Selection, Training, Assignment, and Verification

The interviewer, who is not necessarily the project director, obviously gathers the data when the survey method is used. How interviewers are selected, trained, assigned, and used is central to the successful completion of the research.

*Selection.* No researcher has manipulated the selection procedures used to hire interviewers to determine effects that various procedures have on the data actually gathered. That is, various groups of interviewers have not been differentially selected, put to work, and then compared. However, several investigators have given their impressions about good selection methods based on their experience. These suggestions should complement basic guides for unicultural surveys (e.g., Sheatsley, 1951).

Familiarity with a culture, the people to be interviewed, and proper channels of communication are necessary qualifications of the person who will be selecting the interviewers. Weiner (1964) considers it important that "the field researcher . . . live in the country for some months . . . to get a clear sense of personal relations before undertaking to hire anyone" (pp. 113-114). Armstrong (no date) and Frey (1970) agree that the following selection guidelines are valid, based on their experience in India and Turkey. These suggestions are undoubtedly oversimplified for widespread use, but they provide a good basic list that can be modified when better information is available. We present them as a start toward good guidelines, not as a final product:

1. Middle-class and middle-aged married women constitute a group from

which good interviewers have been selected.

2. Underemployed white-collar workers, from the middle-class and about 30 to 45 years of age, tend to inject their own biases into an interview.

3. Underemployed younger men and women, 20 to 30 years of age, have low motivation for the hard work demanded of an interviewer.

4. Underemployed postgraduates, graduates, and former social science students have low motivation, feel superior to the research, and shirk responsibility.

Bonilla summarizes observations of others (e.g., Wilson and Armstrong, 1963; Stycos, 1955) regarding selection for various groups.

"The principal idea is to weigh the alternatives seriously and patiently in terms of the specific research task and the availability of mobilizble talent. [A researcher should not] accept ready-made interviewer resources as best for one's own project without carefully examining the relevance of past experience, training, and performance" (Bonilla, 1964, p. 149).

In Turkey, Frey (1970) discovered that good interviewers could be selected from these groups: village headmen, teachers, and county prefects. These people had similar backgrounds to those who would be interviewed, and this is another selection standard. Girard (1963, p. 16) very bluntly asserts that "the interviewers must belong to the same racial groups amongst whom the survey is conducted." Going further, Girard states "that the status of the interviewers should be as close as possible to that of the persons interviewed so as to prevent the development of too marked a feeling of inferiority on the part of the latter." Hanna and Hanna (1966) make the same point based on their experience in Africa.

Finally, Hoffman's (1963) selection standards for his research in West Africa may prove helpful to others:

1. a high level of education, especially a command of English or French,
2. a command of the vernacular used among the people to be interviewed,
3. professional experience from past research or survey work,
4. ability to understand questionnaires in a limited amount of time, as demonstrated by an examination.

The one personality measure that has been used with modest success in predicting good interviewers is the dimension of "interpersonal sensitivity" (Cannell and Kahn, 1968). This concept includes human relations skills, empathy, and sensitivity to the needs of others. Obviously, finding candidates with only a few of the many above-mentioned qualifications will be a difficult task.

*Training.* After interviewers are selected they should undergo a series of training sessions, with the knowledge that termination during training may occur. Even poorly qualified candidates can be improved through properly designed training that meets the needs of a specific project. For instance, Marwick (1958, p. 150) bluntly asserts that "The first step taken to meet the problem of poorly qualified assistants was to give them as few opportunities as possible of using their own discretion." Training, then, would include instruction on how to handle all foreseeable problems. A knowledge test could be given at different times, and those with low grades terminated.

One organization in France, the Institut National de la Statistique et des Etudes Economiques (INSEE), has prepared a manual for its interviewer candidates in West Africa, and it has been reprinted in Wickert (1967). Several direct quotes from the manual should give its flavor and at the same time reaffirm our recommendation that others read the original document. Of course, this manual was written in response to a specific set of potential problems and would have to be modified for other surveys. Regarding the first contact between the interviewer and those to be interviewed, the manual reads as follows:

"Your chief concern on arriving at the village is to try to see the village chief (or the chief of the rural community) or his representative if he is not there. You will ask him whether he wants to call together the village or community council so that you can explain to them what you have come to do in their village. You will not insist; but if he thinks that it is not necessary, it is in general preferable that the maximum of people and especially the more important ones be personally advised of your arrival in order that they will not make false interpretations regarding your presence among them (you will establish your identity during the introduction)" (INSEE, 1967, p. 183).

On customs that might lead to reticence in answering questions:

"With respect to the customs of the country, you should be familiar with them since you have been recruited from that same region in order to know the local problems and anticipate any difficulties or special problems of the region in which you are going to work. You will have to explain very politely to the people that you understand very well why they might hold back information. You go on to say that it is in their best interests, in order to reduce the number of unhappy events that so often hit them, such as the deaths of newborns, that these questions that are addressed to them be answered as exactly as possible. If you think that one or several questions ought to be modified, note this in your record book and inform your supervisor whom you ordinarily will see at least once a week" (p. 182).

On carrying out the interview:

"During each interview only the people who live in the building of the particular family should be present. It would even be preferable to limit the numbers present during an interview to no more than two or three persons. However, perhaps, to limit numbers would be often difficult. Nevertheless take care that your questions are addressed to but one definite person at a time, and do your best (even if it is necessary to come back to a house that you have already visited), to obtain the responses from the specific knowledgeable individual (obviously you cannot question that individual if he is sick, or absent, or where there is a problem of small children). Do not take information from a child with respect to the members of a family or even of a servant about his master. However, in certain regions women will answer only in the presence of their husbands, or perhaps it is they who will respond in his place. You will have to make yourself conform to local customs. In some cases it might be advisable to go through the husband on both questions and answers.

"Under all circumstances politeness and respect are necessary. Even before coming into a compound, you always ask for permission to enter from the head of the family. Moreover, do not let people stand, but ask them to sit down in the shade and not in the sun. Once the questions have been asked, if you have no further need of them, let them take up their interrupted jobs after you have thanked them. Do your best, in brief, to create a friendly atmosphere in the interview. This will be the surest guarantee of the accuracy of the information that you obtain" (p. 185).

Frey (1970) outlined the training program he supervised in Turkey. It included lectures on the purpose of the research and on the nature of the survey instrument. If a trainee took a poor set of notes, he would likely be a poor interviewer. Unfortunately, for weeding-out purposes, a good set of notes did not necessarily indicate a good interviewer. The training also included a modelling procedure with trainees watching an experienced researcher complete the questionnaire with a respondent, handling some thorny issues. Trainees subsequently practiced on each other, and this interaction was followed by constructive feedback from the teaching staff. They then interviwed in turn a friend, an accessible stranger, and others in a full-fledged field test. Note that his technique is similar to the clinical practice of desensitization in which a patient *gradually* comes to grips with a feared object. A person afraid of snakes does not wrap one around his neck during the first therapy session. Rather, he thinks about snakes for brief moments during session 1, stands 30 feet from a caged snake during session 2, approaches to 15 feet during session 3, may tap on the cage during session 6, etc. Incidentally, watching a model approach the cage hastens the subject's willingness to do the same (Bandura, 1969). Obviously, Frey's modelling procedure during interviewer training has the goal of hastening the acquisition of necessary skills.

In another training program, the nature of scientific inquiry was stressed

(Stycos, 1960). Different forms of survey bias were made the object of ridicule through demonstration. For instance, the well-known possibility that respondents' answers are interpreted to fit the interviewer's point of view (Cannell and Kahn, 1968) could be covered. The purpose was to exaggerate poor interviewing practices so that the proper techniques would stay with the trainees. Training should also include preparation in the specific areas covered by the interview schedule. Weiner (1964) emphasized that in answering questions about politics, respondents in other countries may spend too much time on basic facts and may even lie if they feel that the interviewer is ignorant of the topic at hand. "A well-informed interviewer can gently call attention to an omission of fact or the commission of error and thereby diminish lying on the interviewee's part" (p. 125). In their advice on interviewing political elites, Hunt, Crane, and Wahlke (1964) reported that the respondents in their survey enjoyed being with a well-educated and conversant interviewer with whom they could have a two-way conversation covering issues both part of and not a part of the interview schedule.

*Usage and Verification.* A point often overlooked in survey research concerns the interviewer: after his work, he is a valuable source of information. Bonilla (1964) puts the case so well that he will be quoted at length:

"The interviewing of interviewers is one of the richest sources of insights (as to the significance and reliability of his findings) available to the researcher. Yet much too frequently, after the completion of a pretest phase or the first few days of interviewing, the practice of discussing in some detail each interviewer's work as he completes assignments has been discontinued. This not only involves a loss of useful supplementary data but is also demoralizing to interviewers at precisely the times when their motivation tends to flag, i.e., the point at which the interviewing process is becoming routine for them or when it is nearly ended. Interviewing is demanding work, particularly for the inexperienced who undertake such work in a hostile or difficult milieu. At the end of a day the good interviewer is brimming over with news of his own ingenuity in overcoming obstacles, of his perceptiveness in sensing refinements in the responses of interviewees. Even when the practical usefulness of such reports for the study begins to dwindle, efforts should be made to keep this channel of communication active. The interviewer is always apt to feel that he is the poorly rewarded work horse of a research team. Nothing is more calculated to alienate him entirely than boredom or indifference toward his individual field problems on the part of supervisors or study directors" (pp. 149-150).

In addition to interviewer usage, an important topic is interviewer verification. Verification refers to the follow-up procedures used to be sure that the interviewer has really completed the questionnaires that have been handed in.

This often takes the form of a call or visit to the respondents. Bonilla (1964) suggests that

" . . . interviewers are likely to view verification procedures as insultingly expressive of distrust. Too often the need for verification or the fact that such measures are being taken is played down or concealed until irregularities are uncovered. A much happier solution is to make explicit from the beginning the necessary and routine character of the steps taken to verify individual work and to carry on verification concurrently with interviewing, so that there is no room for thinking that verification is only a threatened control not really to be performed" (Bonilla, 1964, p. 150).

Verification can also be based on interviewer assignment. If respondents are randomly assigned to interviewers, data analysis can indicate a least two sources of contamination (Hyman, 1964). These suggestions are based on the assumption that since interviewers are randomly assigned a set of respondents, resultant differences between interviewers should be small. The first possible contamination would be the discovery of those items most affected by poor interviewer performance. For instance, of 8 interviewers, numbers 1, 3, and 6 may have received more "no opinion" answers on several items than the other 5 interviewers received. This may indicate that the three are asking the questions poorly or that the other five are asking them in such a way as to encourage replies when there is no opinion. Hopefully, response patterns to the other items could help decide which interpretation is correct. A second possible contamination, which is related to the first, is the problem of interviewers shirking their duty. If a certain interviewer continually obtains different patterns of responses than others, a second interviewer who is known to be reliable should verify the work of the first. In short, response patterns allow symptoms of interviewer failure to surface and permit opportunities for the project director to examine the problem carefully.

## The Linguistic Pretest

Hymes (1970), in describing the issues involving language usage in cross-cultural political science surveys, suggests that social scientists carry out a linguistic pretest before actual interviewing in any culture.[1] The purpose of the pretest would be to discover those aspects of the culture, involving communication between individuals, that might bias data. The information gathered would take the form of: who can be interviewed, how do people go about exchanging information, does the respondent also expect to ask questions, what forms of questioning are appropriate, etc. Such information would

[1] The concept was suggested to Hymes by Robert Holt.

contribute to the content of interviewer training sessions. The following examples reported by survey researchers suggest the type of information that a linguistic pretest would provide.

1. Hoffman (1963) reported that, in certain areas of West Africa, any visit from a stranger is a major event and people gather around to hear an explanation of what is going on.

2. Biesheuvel (1958) reported that some Africans have a difficult time understanding and interpreting pictures prepared in Western cultures. Subsequently Hudson (1960) presented empirical confirmation; his methods and results are reported in the chapter on experimentation. This research indicates that an interviewer cannot always show a picture or photograph to a respondent and expect him to comment on its content *as the interviewer perceives it*.

3. Marwick (1958, p. 155), also reporting on African survey research, reviewed the purpose of questioning and answering in the Cewas society. "When people meet, they ask each other a great many questions, and it may well be that the actual content of a person's answers is less important than his willingness to answer." The question-answer procedure is expressive (or consistent with social expectations) rather than intrinsically meaningful. Marwick also had to pay his respondents because they felt that answering his interview schedule was hard work. In addition, it was impolite to record a response without an exclamation, such as the Cewa equivalent of "really!" or "now, you don't say." In such a situation, the interviewer should be sure that he is not exclaiming selectively to the answers of his respondents. If the interviewer does over-react to certain items, the respondent may discover what the interviewer wants to hear and subsequently answer on the basis of this knowledge.

Another purpose of the linguistic pretest is to identify such biases. Often these are communication problems that exist between the interviewer and respondent. Several have been labelled and studied.

## Interviewer-Respondent Communication Problems

The survey problems collectively called "interviewer biases" are often based on communication problems between the interviewer and the respondent. That is, the interviewer may be asking questions that are perfectly clear to himself but that may be misunderstood by the respondent. Or, the respondent may be giving verbal responses that are misinterpreted by the interviewer. In either case the results summarized for all respondents are likely to be nonsense. Interviewing is communication, and effective communication must be two-way. The following section gives a list of potential communication biases that might affect the validity of data, together with references that discuss each in more detail.

1. *The rudeness bias.* In many surveys, the interviewer forgets that he is

interrupting others when he asks questions, and this may be perceived as rudeness by the respondents. Bonilla describes the interview as seen by the *other* person in the research.

"A total stranger appears, usually unannounced, and demands admission to the home. He proceeds to extract information about the family relationships of all who occupy the dwelling and then seeks to isolate one specific individual for more extended interrogation. He insists that the ensuing dialogue adhere to a rigid and unfamiliar pattern, frequently giving exact instructions as to the form in which he wants replies and sternly discouraging departures from his prescriptions. Though the subject matter and the phrasing of questions may seem to the respondent argumentative, embarrassing, gratuitously aggressive, or even dangerous, the uninvited visitor proceeds impassively, taking little note of the interviewee's distress or exasperation, all the while refusing to reciprocate by revealing his own sentiments regarding the matters under discussion" (Bonilla, 1964, p. 140).

Perceived rudeness on the respondent's part can be due to his lack of understanding. "What do they want with my time?" is probably a common thought. Jahoda (1968) points out that surveys in Africa have proved successful when interviewers introduced the questions by saying that answers will be useful for educational and/or medical services. In Italy, Stycos (1960) reported that linking his human fertility survey to the local doctor led to success. Respondents are familiar with these forms of Western civilization and can cooperate with research studying them. Our recommendation: if a survey does not deal with these issues, the project director should sincerely ask the area's medical and educational authorities if they would like some of their questions included in the survey. This gives the authorities valuable information, may result in improvement for the area, and allows the interviewer to introduce himself honestly. Survey researchers can often make friends by providing valued services.

2. *The "I-can-answer-any-question bias."* Respondents in the United States often have an answer for any question put to them. It is tempting to take such "information" as a reflection of real knowledge and to assume that members of other cultures can also answer questions with ease. Both conclusions are wrong. Converse (1964) deals with the first, presenting a sophisticated model for separating real from unheld information and opinions. The second can be handled by establishing rapport with respondents, reminding them that no one knows everything and that there will be questions that cannot be answered. Placing biographical items at the beginning of the questionnaire puts respondents at ease because they can answer them easily. Note how this is related to desensitization, mentioned earlier. These questions also allow the interviewer to establish rapport and trust during the time spent on these introductory matters.

For informational items, the interviewer should find out whether or not the respondents had the necessary facts at some time (Cannell and Kahn, 1968), and if they can reproduce the facts at the time of questioning. This can be accomplished by additional "probe" questions following the main inquiry.

3. *The courtesy bias.* Especially prevalent in the Oriental cultures, the courtesy bias refers to the respondent's orientation of giving the proper answer that he feels the interviewer wants. After all, isn't the purpose of a good host to entertain his guest and to cater to his needs? Mitchell writes:

"Some of the effects of the courtesy bias can be reduced by concealing the sponsorship of the study, by more effective training of interviewers, and by more careful wording of questions. With regard to wording, it is advisable to avoid the use of moral words that require either the respondent or the interviewer to pass judgment on the other. Above all, it is important to maximize the ease of giving a socially unacceptable answer, such as might be done through the standard practice of opening the question with 'Lots of people feel this way . . . and lots of people feel the other way. Which direction do you lean toward in . . . '" (Mitchell, 1968, p. 229).

4. *The sucker bias.* In some cultures, for example, Samoa (Keesing and Keesing, 1956), it is considered acceptable to deceive and to "put on" outsiders. Interviewers are likely to hear ridiculous answers, not given in a spirit of hostility but rather sport. The previous recommendation for careful interviewer preparation into the background of a culture can be repeated here. Interviewers can kindly point out discrepancies until the respondent discovers he no longer has a sucker. Genuine communication is then likely to occur.

5. *The hidden premises bias.* Respondents may attempt to discover who the interviewer is *really* representing and answer in line with this hidden premise (Frey, 1970). Respondents may decide that their visitor is representing the government. If they answer in a certain way, they might obtain free fertilizer (of which they have heard rumors) or a favor during the next tax-payment period. In a multiculture study, responses might be non-comparable if the sponsor of the survey is perceived as different from country to country. No general guidelines are available to help solve this problem. In some cultures the project director can seek help from the village leaders who might talk to potential respondents, preparing them for the actual interview.

6. *The reticent-loquacious bias.* Members of some cultures (e.g., Japanese, Chinese residing in Malaysia) are very reticent to start an interview and to talk long enough so that it can be completed. Members of other cultures (e.g., India) are happy to converse with others and may keep the interviewer so busy that his schedule is ruined. Mitchell (1968) reported that researchers who forget this bias could easily underweight the Chinese and overweight the Indian responses from any survey undertaken in Malaysia. Weiner (1964, p. 127) suggests ways of

dealing with the problem, giving special attention to interviews about political matters.

"... Where there is a cultural problem of reticence, the researcher must attempt to understand the reasons for it and devise a strategy for coping with it. Special attention may have to be paid to arranging for a formal introduction. Opening the conversation in the vernacular, although the interview may be conducted in English, may help establish rapport. There is also a private language of politics that the researcher will soon learn to use—the nicknames of politicians, abbreviations of political groups, land-revenue terms, bureaucratic titles, and an array of other facts known only to those relatively intimate with political life. In some cultures, one may proceed to political questions almost immediately, but in others one may expect to spend an hour engaged in light discussion while sipping tea before political questions can be raised. One may find too that two or three interviews with the same man must be planned in order to obtain information and an expression of attitudes that in other cultures can be gotten at during the first interview."

7. *The social desirability bias.* Many social scientists have recognized that respondents often answer questions to put themselves in a desirable light, flattering themselves by answering all questions as if they were fine and outstanding people. The seminal United States work in this area is that of Edwards (1957), while the basic cross-cultural references are Gordon (1968), Berrien (1968), Werner and Campell (1970), and Frey (1970). One way out of the problem is to force respondents to choose between or among statements equated for social desirability. Pretesting would determine statements rated equally as to how desirable it is for a person to hold a certain view in a given culture. For instance, the pretest raters might agree that the following statements would reflect equal desirability if a person could say that he performs the action involved. Each item would be part of scales meant to tap other dimensions (e.g., empathy and altruism).

*I always help old ladies across the street.*

*I stop to help people if they are stranded on the road.*

*I volunteer to collect money for charity at least once a year.*

Actual respondents, however, would choose the *one* that they felt best describes them. If cultures are to be compared, the alternatives available to respondents must be equated for social desirability across cultures.

8. *The status difference bias.* Although project directors should try to train interviewers who are similar to the respondents in the sample, this is clearly not always possible. Marwick (1958) had to use interviewers of higher status than the respondents (college students interviewing farmers and villagers in West Africa), and he reported the methods used to overcome the potential bias. The

interview was prefaced by a statement that urged frankness, assured respondents that no names would be used, and so forth. The first 15 statements were of the open-ended type so that articulate and reasonable answers would be given rather than automatic, socially desirable responses. Each topic of investigation was covered by five questions, but these were mixed into the interview rather than presented in succession. "This was done in order to prevent the informant from becoming cumulatively conscious of commenting on a particular policy or aspect of white administration" (pp. 153-154). Marwick mentioned that one of his interviewers recorded more hostile and anti-white responses than the other, and this may indicate that he had better rapport with his respondents.

9. *The racial difference bias.* Marwick (1958, p. 152) discovered that "Africans identify all Whites as members of the ruling caste of administrators, missionaries, and employees of labour." Hanna and Hanna (1966, p. 292) felt that this fact may radically affect interviewer results, and they carried out a small experiment to see if it would. In their own words: "Upon first arriving in Umuahia, we experimented with one assistant by having him pretest interviews with several ethnic groups. The results were convincing: he could not even begin to interview most of those potential respondents who were not members of his own ethnic group or faction." The conclusion is that a heterogeneous group of interviewers must be selected and trained so that the project director can match them to the people on the sample list. Hanna and Hanna (1966) make the very strong statement that no confidence can be placed in the results if this is not done. Similarly, Meade informs us that he always selects trainee assistants in India and Hong Kong from the same ethnic groups as those who will be in his experiments (Meade, 1968; 1970). After training, he stays as far away from the research as possible so as not to bias the results.

10. *The individual-group opinion bias.* In many cultures the interviewer has a difficult time obtaining individual responses since the person being questioned is constantly surrounded by others. Western-trained social scientists are accustomed to thinking that individual responses are more meaningful than group opinions, but both are important and "true" (Stycos, 1960). In his Caribbean surveys of family planning attitudes, Stycos found that individuals alone and the same individuals in groups gave conflicting answers. This finding is meaningful, however, since it shows the competing pressures that the individual faces.

## Needed Research

Both Bonilla (1964) and Mitchell (1968) emphasize that there is a great need for research on interviewer-respondent communication problems, more so than any other aspect of survey procedures. This is an excellent area of research for several reasons. Any well-documented findings would be of interest both to methodologists as well as to social scientists interested in cultural differences. If members of one group have difficulty communicating with another, this indicates cultural differences worth investigating so that the actual causes can be determined. There is also a good uni-cultural base for investigations. Rosenthal (1966), Orne (1962) and Hyman et al., (1954) have reviewed many possible communication biases that can affect research, with special emphasis on the United States. In a major review of the literature, Triandis, Malpass, and Davidson (1972) observed that the most successful cross-cultural investigations have been in topic areas previously subjected to extensive unicultural testing. Many of the "bugs" were removed before extending concepts and methods cross-culturally.

## Sampling Plans in Survey Research

We have discussed the sampling of individuals in the chapter introducing cross-cultural methodology and the sampling of cultures in Chapter 8, and the guidelines presented there are central to successful survey research. In addition, there are special problems when the survey researcher actually starts the hard work of carrying out his sampling plan, as opposed to talking about it on a theoretical level.

*Representativeness and Scope of Samples.* Depending upon the purpose of the research, the project director can emphasize representativeness or scope in the samples he selects from a population. Representativeness refers to research whose purpose is to document accurately the properties of the population. Description is the goal. Scope refers to research whose purpose is to analyze important aspects of a population. Inference is the goal. Two examples should help. Scheuch (1968) analyzed the difference between representativeness and scope in the Almond and Verba (1963) study.

" . . . if demonstrating between-nation differences was a chief purpose, representativeness of the sample was a main requirement; if demonstrating the effect of education on citizenship participation was a main goal, merely a normal representative sample would not do. Probably the authors did not fully realize the differences between the educational systems of the US and European countries, and consequently did not provide in their sample design for the small numbers of persons with a higher education in Western Europe. A disproportionate stratification would have extended the *scope of the sample* [emphasis ours] and might even have permitted a better gradation than the constantly employed split: primary education versus secondary education and more. Had they anticipated the different distributions of educational categories in the various countries, it might have been possible to show that 2% or so of adults in Western European countries with a university degree differ very, very significantly from persons with secondary education; of the samples actually used, even some of the presumed effects of higher education in general are of questionable significance" (Scheuch, 1968, p. 196).

Frey (1970) used Jewish people living in the United States as an example, posing the problem of whether they should be selected on a probability basis or whether they should be overselected.

"Are not the Jews a major minority group in the United States? Perhaps not, if the criterion is the proportionate size of the group, but certainly yes if the criterion is their contribution to various specified aspects of national life" (Frey, 1970, p. 240).

Obviously, sampling plans will depend on the questions that the survey researcher wishes to answer. Decisions have to be made regarding the following issues (Mitchell, 1968), especially since the costs resulting from different decisions will always be a major factor in survey planning:

1. Should a national sample be attempted, given the goals of a specific project, the adequacy of national lists, and the possibility of different response rates from country-to-country?
2. How many call-backs to not-at-home people should be attempted?
3. What replacement procedures should be used?
4. On what basis, if any, can respondents be self-selected? The answers to points 2, 3, and 4, should be included in the final description of the sample.
5. How good is the sampling frame? Are there different sets of information in existence to check the adequacy of the frame? This fifth point is so important that a section will be devoted to it.

*Adequacy of Sampling Lists.* The survey researcher, if he is to attempt any kind of systematic sample, must have a starting point. This may take the form of a list prepared by a government, professional survey agency, or university. Sometimes too much faith is placed in these lists. Mitchell (1968) tells two very disturbing stories.

The leading and most competent research agency in a large Asian city had prepared a listing of houses that were the basis for their random or stratified samples. About eight months after the list had been prepared, it was loaned to a university-affiliated group which checked its accuracy. It was found that about one of every four addresses on the list did not exist. Mitchell concluded the story with his opinion that the original agency must have known about their errors, but that this did not stop them from using the list as a basis for their work.

In Great Britain, the two major survey agencies do not use the same bases for choosing national samples. This may be why the two groups regularly make different predictions about election returns. An example: the two groups differ as to their definitions of socioeconomic status, making it difficult to compare one agency's middle- and lower-class worker response with the results from the other agency's sample.

Obviously, trouble exists when trying to make valid inferences with data like that in the two stories. Several sampling designs have been suggested that may help solve the above, and other, problems.

*Sampling Designs Aimed at Solving Specific Problems.* One problem is to determine differences (of any sort) that might be obtained by the various members of a research team. Estimates of the possible biases caused by human error can be made if the sampling plan is designed properly. Briefly, team members are assigned to carry out randomly designated tasks such as field direction, interviewing, and data analysis. Differences in the results from one member to another would pinpoint problem areas. This technique was mentioned earlier in the section on interviewer verification. Defining the socioeconomic status of respondents would be another example. Different members of a research team who are the supervisors of certain interviewers, may have different standards for defining socioeconomic status. These differences may seemingly be ironed out during preliminary planning, but faith alone never solved a methodological problem. If supervisors are randomly assigned a certain number of respondents, then the results their interviewers obtain can be compared for percentage of people at various S.E.S. levels, relation of S.E.S. to other responses, and so forth. Such a design allows the opportunity for replication, always a desirable goal.

The problem could well be the possibility of an early work termination. For example, government officials might ask researchers to leave half-way into their two-month time schedule (Hyman, 1964). Here, the design would involve scheduling half of the interviews, at random, during the first month and the other half during the second month. If termination occurs, the researchers still have the type of sample they desired, albeit smaller. Hyman relates the story of a very early usage of this type of research design. In 1937, P. C. Mahalanobis wanted to undertake surveys on a farming problem in India, but found that no competent research personnel were available. Some problems were solved in training, but since the problem was so potentially overwhelming, the director had to have an estimate of its effects.

"Research design was the magic helper that came to his rescue. Mahalanobis employed an indirect, logical solution that permitted him to estimate the magnitude of such errors in his findings, although he could not, in fact, curtail their occurrence. 'The method of *arranging* the field survey in the form of two separate but interpenetrating sub-samples in each zone was therefore adopted,' yielding two half samples to which two different sets of enumerators were assigned. By comparing the independent findings for these equivalent samples, Mahalanobis could see whether the results were affected by the particular field workers or were in good agreement no matter which field workers collected them. This highly sophisticated research design was pioneered long ago and regularly employed in a difficult and primitive setting, not in the more luxurious and easy setting of a modern survey in a Western country. Mahalanobis was more burdened with many problems, but as a result he had more, rather than less, need for a research design" (Hyman, 1964, p. 159).

Another major problem is the lack of a list for drawing samples. Researchers have never engaged in census work, market research, or public opinion surveys among the members of some cultures and thus have provided no listing which others can use. Scheuch (1968) has described variations of random walk plans, the purpose of which is to overcome the lack of a list. Assume that members of a village are to be sampled. One variation of the random walk design is to examine all the routes on which village residents walk, and then to sample houses from along the walk routes. No walk route would be duplicated from interviewer to interviewer. Another variation would be to interview at different places (3 dwelling units east, then 5 dwelling units north) from starting points at different localities in the village. The technique sounds promising but has not received wide-spread acceptance, perhaps because success depends upon interviewer honesty. It has also proved difficult for interviewers to follow the guidelines set down by their supervisors.

Bonilla (1964) has cautioned survey researchers about designs that sound fine but may be difficult to administer in the field. Pretesting is essential. "What may appear in the abstract to be a clear-cut and rigorous plan can prove a nightmare to apply . . . e.g., basic decisions will have to be made as to what a dwelling unit is" (p. 145). After any sampling design has been employed, imperfections discovered during field application should be noted. Marwick (1958) detailed the differences between the ideal and the real from his survey in Africa. For example, men who were engaged in physical labor had less chance of being interviewed than their numbers dictated. Interviews were held during the day and thus working-men would be away from their homes. In general, ease of contact made males more likely than females to be interviewed. Comparing his results with those of the government census office, Marwick found that his ratio was 115 males to 100 females, while the office recorded a ratio of 43 to 100. These biases could clearly affect interpretation of the data. This problem is somewhat related to certain "behavior settings" problems which Barker (1968) has enumerated (see Chapter 6).

Another problem of the difference-between-plan-and-reality sort is involved in the carrying out of a random sampling scheme. A researcher from Africa has told us that he has walked his feet off to reach the hut indicated by the sampling plan, only to discover that the potential respondent is not home or won't cooperate. Sweat and tears are necessary in such situations, and interviewers should be prepared for the possibilities of such frustrations. As indicated above, it is up to the project director to maintain morale so that bad experiences do not cause interviewers to quit.

*Interpretation of Survey Data.* Unbiased interpretation of data is just as important as unbiased sampling and interviewing. Once the survey has been completed the project director usually has a great amount of data that must be analyzed. Proper interpretation is essential since the inferences made will guide other researchers in future projects. The most basic rule is: Interpretation follows directly from the limitations imposed by the realities of data collection. For example, even though the analyst may want to interpret the results of a multiculture survey as representative of other cultures not in the original sample, he may not be justified in doing so. The project director is likely to have done research in nations whose governments have regularly admitted Western social scientists. India, Nigeria, and Thailand have been "overused" in this sense. "Hence we should be careful in our claims of 'maximizing diversity' and in our generalizations about 'developing societies'" (Frey, 1970, p. 202).

Even if a number of reasonably diverse and non-overly used cultures have been surveyed, differences in non-completion rates will plague interpretation. Non-completion rates are not randomly distributed across cultures but are substantive figures based on respondent accessibility and willingness to be interviewed. The Almond-Verba (1963) five-nation study constitutes the most frequently cited example of this problem. The non-completion rates for the five countries varied from 17 to 41 percent of the people originally scheduled for interviewing. Proper interpretation demands information on the type of people likely to be available and not available from country-to-country. Perhaps a sample of those not interviewed after three "call-backs" could be the subjects for a special sub-study. The project director could assign a special investigator to track these people down. Data might then become available from a group normally unrepresented in sample surveys.

The timing of data collection from country to country is very important. Scheuch suggests a plausible rival hypothesis based on time in his analysis of the Almond-Verba (1963) study.

". . . the authors observe that the frequency of political conversations in Germany is lower than that observed either in the USA or in the United Kingdom. They attribute this difference to differing 'political cultures.' An equally likely explanation would be (apart from the sampling problem in Britain) that the surveys were carried out at a time close to national elections both in Britain and in the USA, but halfway between elections in Germany. If I compare the 1959 data from Britain with the results for the same question in a nation-wide survey of ours just prior to the 1961 national election in Germany, the differences disappear" (Scheuch, 1968, p. 198).

Jahoda (1968) makes a similar point using the Human Relations Area Files (see Chapter 8) as an example. The information there may be too out-of-date to answer certain questions.

Finally, interpretation will be infinitely easier and clearer if opportunities for response validation have been built into the survey design. "I don't know" responses are difficult to interpret because they can mean many things: no opinion, lack of understanding, boredom, etc. In a survey of peasant attitudes, Frey (1970) validated the number of "don't know" replies against the number of trips respondents took to the city and to the number of relatives living there. He found the predicted relation which supported his hypothesis about opinion formation among peasants. Frey's design allowed clear interpretation based on data rather than a muddled discussion based on speculation.

## Summary

In opinion surveys, researchers ask questions of a large number of respondents, usually basing specific questions on a prepared interview schedule. Several seemingly mundane points are worth considering. The first concerns the uses of the survey method. The method is usually employed to document guesses and hunches obtained through less well controlled means, and the method often suggests hypotheses for even more rigid experimental methods. The second point is a reminder that not all people are accustomed to answering questions as are people from North America and Europe. Whether or not members of a given culture can answer questions is an empirical question to be answered during pretesting. The third point to be considered is the cost of surveys, which can be extremely large. This problem has received attention elsewhere (e.g., Askenasy, 1966; Campbell, 1968). Costs may preclude large scale surveys, but all investigators can profitably use elements of the method in modestly budgeted research.

Several survey practitioners have suggested guidelines for hiring interviewers, the people who will actually contact respondents and question them. Their combined advice yields this list:

1. The person selecting the interviewers should live in the culture under study to obtain a sense of personal relations among its members.

2. Middle-class and middle-aged married women are potential candidates while underemployed white-collar workers, underemployed young men and women, and underemployed students tend to be less desirable.

3. Interviewers selected from village headmen, teachers, and county prefects have proved successful.

4. The interviewer should belong to the same racial group as the people to be surveyed.

5. Command of the local vernacular, past experience, and the measurable personality dimension of "interpersonal sensitivity" may prove useful as selection standards.

After selection, interviewers should undergo a series of training sessions to sharpen their skills. The content of training, based on the experience of others, might include:

1. lectures on the content of the interview schedule and on the purpose of the research (incidentally, if a candidate takes a poor set of notes he will likely be a poor interviewer, but a good set of notes does not predict a good interviewer);

2. modelling sessions during which candidates watch an experienced interviewer handle difficult problems;

3. lectures and demonstrations making different types of survey bias the object of ridicule;

4. information on specific wording problems, and other practical issues, discovered during a linguistic pretest [this pretest is meant to indicate potential communication difficulties — for instance, in the Cewa (Africa) society, the willingness to answer a question is more important than the content of the answer];

5. practice on other candidates;

6. training in the specific content area under study;

7. a full scale field test with the possibility of candidate termination kept open;

8. the assurance that the survey director will verify the work of each interviewer (of course, the director will carry through his promise, having built the opportunities into his research design).

Interviewer biases, mentioned in point three directly above, are often based on communication problems between the interviewer and the respondent. The following biases have been identified:

1. *The rudeness bias.* Interviewers sometimes forget that they are taking up the time of the respondents, and this might be mistaken for rudeness.

2. *The "I-can-answer-any-question-bias."* Some respondents will give an answer to any question whether they have any knowledge or not. Reminding respondents that no one knows everything has proved successful in one cross-cultural survey (Tessler, 1971).

3. *The courtesy bias.* Especially prevalent in the Orient, people may decide that the interviewer wants a certain answer and that he should have it.

4. *The sucker bias.* Members of some cultures will "put a person on" and

give ridiculous answers in sport. An interviewer well-trained in the content area under study should be able to persuade the respondent that he is no sucker.

5. *The hidden premises bias.* Respondents may believe that the interviewer is "really" a tax agent or government official and answer accordingly.

6. *The reticence-loquaciousness bias.* While members of some cultures are very quiet and retiring during interviews, members of other cultures are so happy to converse that the interviewer's time schedule will be ruined. If proper controls are not developed, the former will be underrepresented and the latter overrepresented.

7. *The social-desirability bias.* Respondents often answer all questions to look good in the eyes of others, representing themselves as fine and outstanding people. Forcing a choice between statements equally weighted for social desirability may be a solution.

8. *The status-difference bias.* Marwick (1958) has identified definite trends in the pattern of responses obtained by different status interviewers. His student helpers were of higher status than the farmers to be surveyed. The major controls Marwick developed were: (1) The first section of the interview schedule contained questions that encouraged articulate rather than automatic responses; and (2) items on any one topic were mixed throughout the schedule so that respondents would be less aware that they were commenting in detail on that topic.

9. *The racial-difference bias.* When the interviewer does not belong to the same racial group as the respondents, extreme response biases can occur (Hanna and Hanna, 1966). The only suggested solution is to have an interviewer pool large and varied enough so that the problem does not occur.

10. *The individual-group opinion bias.* In some cultures, people are accustomed to giving answers in the presence of others and it may be impossible to isolate one person for questioning.

Depending upon the purpose of a given research project, the survey researcher may choose to emphasize representativeness or scope in the samples he selects from a population. Representativeness refers to research whose purpose is to document accurately certain properties (e.g., average income and opinions) of a population. Scope refers to research whose purpose is to analyze important aspects of a population and is usually the goal of research designed to build theory. For instance, Jewish people in the United States would receive less attention under a representative sampling plan than under a plan whose scope included business and economics. Regardless of the type of sample, some base for individual selection must be used. Sometimes lists are already available from local agencies, but there are several documented cases in which these lists were grossly inaccurate. Another problem is that samples are often chosen on different bases. This fact reinforces the point made earlier, in the first chapter, that sampling practices be carefully described so that other social scientists can interpret and profitably use any results. Sampling techniques are well enough developed so that they may be used to solve specific problems. If the research director is fearful of an early termination due to outside pressure, he can design the research so that one-half of randomly selected cases are involved in the first time period, one-half during the second. If early termination occurs, the first wave may have been completed so that the desired type of sample, albeit smaller, has been interviewed. Similar strategies can be used to solve the potential problems of doubtful interviewers and differing definitions of important variables (e.g., socioeconomic status). For any plan, pretesting is essential since a design that looks infallible on paper may be a nightmare in application.

Data interpretation follows directly from the limitations imposed by the realities of data collection. For example, claims of a representative sample of underdeveloped countries are unjustified when India, Nigeria, and Thailand are overrepresented. These countries have historically been open to social scientists and may be unrepresentative of other countries that have been less accessible. Other problems that should be spelled out during data interpretation are: between-culture differences in non-completion rates; timing of the data collection; number of "I don't know" responses. Especially in the latter case opportunities for validation built into the design will permit unmuddled interpretation.

# CHAPTER FOUR

## *The Conduct of Experiments*

In cross-cultural experiments the researcher manipulates a variable or variables to determine whether members of two or more cultures respond in a similar or different manner. The researcher exploits a situation, sometimes completely creating it himself and sometimes adding only a little to a naturally occurring set of events. This *creation, presentation,* and *manipulation* of variables contrasts with the correlational method of interrelating different variables that *already exist.* An example will make this distinction clear. A psychologist might be interested in studying whether the number of hours parents spend with their children in mutual play affects the children's personalities. The cross-cultural psychologist using the correlational approach could, for example, take a survey in six cultures. He could consult the chapter in this book on the wording of questionnaires, formulate his own questions, translate them, and then ask parents, "How many hours do you play with your children during each day?" The researcher may then want to construct a personality measure and administer it to the children of the parents just interviewed. He would then relate the two measures. Assuming that he gathers other data to rule out plausible rival hypotheses, such as differences in socioeconomic advancement or number of hours spent in school, the psychologist may be able to interrelate data suggesting the hypothesis that the amount of parent-child mutual play leads to distinctive personality traits, for example, independence or achievement need.

It would be more difficult, however, for the correlational psychologist to determine the causal direction within the observed relationship. One direction is that the amount of mutual play may affect children's personalities since the parents are able to guide desirable traits during the time spent with children. Almost as likely, however, the observed relationship may be explained by looking at the opposite direction: children with certain personality traits encourage their parents to play with them because the parents know they will have fun doing so. Even more complex, a third factor (probably missed in the

82

first plausible rival hypothesis analysis) may be affecting both of the original variables. For instance, the number of children in a family may dictate the amount of time that the parents can spend with each, and the relations among the children may affect the personality of each child.

If he is able to use the experimental method, the cross-cultural researcher can avoid many of these interpretative problems. The experimentalist would manipulate one (or more) variables in the six cultures to determine the effect of each variable on the other. Using the above example, an experiment could be designed in which some parents are encouraged to spend an extra two hours per day, for six months, playing with their children, while a control group of parents perform their usual daily routine. The extra play time would be the independent variable. Parents are randomly assigned to one group or another. Random assignment is infinitely better than the parent's own choice, since parents who *choose* to be in one of the groups are very likely different in many ways from parents who choose to be in the other. The dependent variable would again be the measure of personality. Assume that the extra two hours bring positive results. Again, a rival hypothesis analysis would be necessary, ruling out such threats as effects caused by *something* new happening, not the specific variable. The children might also discover that they are being studied and react so as to please the experimenter. Assuming that data have been gathered to rule out these threats, the experimenter is in a much better position to suggest a causal relation than is the correlational analyst.

A distinction can be made, solely for exposition, between two types of experiments. In some experiments, researchers present stimuli such as visual illusions, beakers of water, or photographs and ask subjects to respond to them. These involve no major manipulation and for this reason we call them "presentation experiments." In other experiments, researchers make a major change in some aspect of the subject's environment. The researchers may train people in different methods of leadership and then have the leaders interact with subjects. Or the researcher may train people to give the wrong answers on a simple task to determine whether a naive subject, in the presence of these trained "stooges," will also make a wrong response. Or the researcher may ask the subjects either to cooperate or to compete with one another in completing a task. These experiments are clearly different from the simple presentation experiments. We call them "major manipulation" studies. No implication is intended, of course, that one type is better than the other.

Now that these basic distinctions between the correlational and experimental approaches have been made, we shall present several critical issues that must be handled in a good cross-cultural experiment. These issues are based on the actual experience of several investigators. After a discussion of establishing experimental conditions, techniques of gathering good data are covered. These include assessing the independent variable, comparing experimental results with other data, and approaching experimentation when only correlational data are available. The advantages of a *series* of experiments to test one hypothesis are then discussed. Finally, an innovative cross-cultural experiment is discussed to point out how one researcher used the best elements of the experimental method.

## Establishing Experimental Conditions in Two or More Cultures

Before any consideration of methodological detail the researcher should choose a topic that is worth investigating for theoretical or practical reasons. With so many problems worthy of investigation, it is not useful to conduct a cross-cultural experiment only· because the researcher has some apparatus or procedures that he or others have previously used. As pointed out in Chapter 1, the "let's-see-what-happens-if" type of experiment should be avoided.

A few examples may prove helpful in understanding the special problems of cross-cultural experimentation. Kelly et al. (1970) were interested in bargaining behavior, where subjects have the choice of being threatening, honest, deceitful, or future oriented, in interacting with others. The nine investigators involved in the cooperative venture established identical experimental situations at eight laboratories in the United States and Europe. They kept the experiment simple so that all the researchers could carry out the procedures without special training. Its simplicity, in addition, afforded fewer opportunities to make mistakes. The investigators were especially interested in determining whether or not they could replicate each other's findings. They described their rationale for doing the study, mentioning the "fit" between experiment and cultural experience:

"A special argument can be made for the desirability of replication of bargaining experiments. These require the use of complex miniature social situations which subjects are likely to associate with their everyday social systems. Therefore, the results are particularly likely to reflect the different values, norms, and roles elicited by the experimental situation, rather than responses to its basic structural and motivational parameters"(Kelly et al., 1970. p. 413).

When an experiment is to be conducted in two or more cultures, the researcher has to decide exactly how much variation, if any, there is to be in procedures between or among cultures. Our example is based closely on the experience of Meade (1970). Assume that a researcher wishes to determine whether there are cultural differences in preference for a certain type of leadership between, for example, United States and Hong Kong subjects. He decides to employ different indigenous leaders, trained to manifest different leadership styles (e.g., authoritarian or democratic), who will interact in discussion groups composed of five people. These groups should perceive that their discussion sessions are interesting, and the researcher can contribute to this goal by providing relevant discussion topics. Here, however, is where the experimenter must make a decision. It would be difficult, if not impossible, to choose topics equally relevant to the groups in the United States and Hong Kong for obvious reasons: members of different cultures are concerned with different issues. Meade solved the problem by having the groups discuss slightly different issues which pretesting showed would enhance involvement. Groups in the United States discussed "improving the grading and examination systems," while Hong Kong groups discussed "abolition of intermediate examinations." Meade was more interested in equivalence of group involvement than in the exact equivalence of issues. Other, but certainly not all, cross-cultural psychologists would probably make a similar decision.

Greenfield (1966) gives us another example of the problem. Her experiment among the Wolof of Africa dealt with the Piagetian concept of conservation, and she studied it by pouring water from a large beaker into smaller glasses. She then asked the subjects if the amount of water was the same after pouring as it was before. She then wanted to ask another question often used with Western children, but was unable to do so.

"An interesting problem arose when it came to asking the unschooled [Wolof] children to justify their answers to this question. A previous experiment had shown that whereas the question, 'Why do you *think* or *say* that thus and such is true?' would meet with uncomprehending silence, the question, 'Why *is* thus and such true?' could often be answered quite easily. So the question asked of American children, 'Why do you *think* this glass has more (or equal) water?' was modified to, 'Why *does* this glass have more (or equal) water?' It would seem that the unschooled Wolof children are lacking in Western self-consciousness: they do not distinguish between their own thought or a statement about something and the thing itself" (Greenfield, 1966, p 233).

It is difficult to determine whether her modification made the American-Wolof comparisons invalid.

The problem of equivalence between experimental settings is by no means confined to discussions of cross-cultural psychology. In an excellent chapter on social psychological experimentation (with no explicit reference to cross-cultural problems), Aronson and Carlsmith (1968) have emphasized that no specific techniques can be provided to create and manipulate psychological variables.

". . .few experimental manipulations are identical; rather, the researcher must construct an experiment to fit his situation, borrowing only ideas and innovations from previous work. This is the case because, for the most part, social-psychological experiments depend so heavily on the special nature of the subculture in which they are presented that even those relatively standard procedures which do exist must be modified drastically so that they make sense in terms of the particular population the experimenter is working with. Thus it is useless to outline specific techniques for varying cohesiveness, self-esteem effort, commitment, conformity, aggression, guilt, or whatever" (Aronson and Carlsmith, 1968, pp. 39-40).

Methods for discovering techniques for successfully manipulating variables in another culture include anthropological reports, discussions with social scientists from other cultures, extensive pretesting, and long interviews with subjects after pretesting. These techniques have been discussed by others. In a review of cross-cultural research on child development, LeVine writes about anthropological reports:

"The more detailed the ethnogrphic acquaintance with the community, the more controls can be built into the [experimental] design to prevent contamination of the independent variables. Far from being an alternative to the systematic psychological study of children in exotic settings—as it has sometimes been presented—intensive ethnography is a prerequisite to systematic comparisons of individual differences" (LeVine, 1970, p. 569).

The technique of discussions with social scientists from other cultures has been used by Bronfenbrenner (1970), who has worked closely with Soviet colleagues in his studies of child-rearing practices in the United States and the Soviet Union. In a study of peer influence on a child's participation in prosocial versus antisocial behavior, Bronfenbrenner designed a test that told stories about different situations. One story was about a boy who found his teacher's key with the answers to an important test. The boy was then pressured to cheat by keeping the key. After using this test in the United States, Bronfenbrenner reported that he cooperated closely with Soviet colleagues to prepare a Russian language version. Minor variations were made to adapt it to the special nature of the Soviet cultural context, for instance, changing the United States day school to the Soviet boarding school. Regarding the pretest, we have spoken with several social scientists whose research is covered in other sections of this chapter. All agree that long hours of pretesting are necessary so that the independent variable, already clearly understood by the researcher himself, can be made meaningful to members of other cultures.

Assuming, for example, that the variable of need for achievement can be aroused in two cultures by using different techniques, the researcher must decide whether the different techniques will corrupt his experiment. There is no clear-cut solution to the issue, and the problem is now being debated by methodologists. In their discussion of a similar problem—whether or not subjects should receive different treatments to reach the same level of some independent variable—Aronson and Carlsmith (1968) mentioned that they were in disagreement. Furthermore, cross-cultural psychologists have obtained results that are a function of minor procedural differences. In research on cognitive conflict in the United States and Europe, Brehmer, Hammond, et al. (1970) had to admit that earlier findings reported in the Hammond, Bonaiuto, et al. (1968) study were due to differences in the sequence of problems subjects were supposed to solve. These sequence differences were originally thought to be minor, but the later research proved them to be of central importance.

As with many cross-cultural problems, the "approach" to a solution is the gathering of more data. Specifically, a researcher should have information on how his independent manipulation is perceived in the cultures under study.

## Assessing the Independent Variable

In all experiments a variable is manipulated, such as (1) high versus low aggression, (2) high versus low motivation to learn, and (3) high versus low association among words to be learned. The effects of these variables are then measured. An additional step is possible. When a researcher says, "I measured the success of the independent variable's manipulation," he means that another measure has been added to his design. This measure usually comes either shortly after the independent manipulation itself or after the experiment is over. This measure assesses whether subjects become (1) differentially aggressive, (2) differentially motivated to learn, or (3) differentially aware of the association among the words to be learned. The added measure is important if the experiment is conducted in two or more cultures. If the manipulation "takes" in one culture but not another, the results may be meaningless.

A good example of this type of measurement is from Sinha's (1968) study conducted in India. He was interested in studying the need for achievement, a theoretical concept developed in the United States (see Chapter 6). He wanted to instill a competitive or a cooperative drive in Indian subjects, who were members of work groups, and he did this through different sets of instruction. In an attempt to assess the competitive versus cooperative manipulation, he first administered the projective Thematic Apperception Test (described in Chapter 5) to determine how many achievement themes subjects gave. As predicted, the competitively-oriented subjects gave more. Sinha then counted the number of times subjects assisted each other during the time they worked together. The cooperation-oriented subjects were higher on this measure. With these additional sets of data, Sinha could confidently say that his subjects reacted appropriately to the manipulation. This information also provided insight into the meaning of the independent manipulation among subjects from a culture in which the basic concepts under study were *not* developed.

Methodologists, not writing for cross-cultural psychology in particular, have recently commented on assessing the experimental manipulation. Wuebben (1968) has prepared a most thorough treatment, and he is especially concerned that the assessment of the manipulation might corrupt the later dependent variable measure. If the two measures are taken in the reverse order (dependent variable followed by manipulation assessment), the second score might be affected by the first in this case also. Wuebben suggests some designs that are worthy of careful study. The basis of these designs is that some subjects at random are assessed on one measure but not the other (so that the influence of one on the other can be estimated). This demands that more subjects be used, but at the same time such a procedure leads to better data.

## Comparing Experimental Results with Other Data

At times, the results of an experiment can be compared with other cross-cultural findings, allowing further insights into both sets of data. Barrett and Bass (1970) have reviewed cross-cultural studies of superior-subordinate relations, many coming from the Management Research Center.[1] One study (Barrett and Franke, 1969) was based on "Exercise Communication," in which managers from seven countries (Belgium, Denmark, India, Italy, Norway, the United Kingdom, and the United States) sent messages in a one-way or a two-way communication pattern. In one-way communication the receiver cannot question the sender, although he can in two-way communication. The subjects' feelings about two patterns were measured at the end of the exercise. The results were compared with data gathered independently by Haire, Ghiselli, and Porter (1966). They measured the propensity of managers to share information and objectives, interviewing managers from a number of countries, including the seven listed above. This concept was defined by responses to a scale measuring autocratic and democratic attitudes. The correlation between preference as a receiver for one-way communication and the share-information measure was $r = .82$. This high correlation indicated that one-way communication was related to an autocratic style and that two-way communication was related to a democratic style.

Additional information on the two forms of communication comes from another study, this one dealing with "Exercise Supervise" (Ryterband and Barrett, 1970). This study dealt with acceptance of coercive supervision among managers from the seven countries, and this measure correlated $r = .89$ with preference for one-way communication. The important point to note is that these different types of data which were gathered by different people fall into a coherent pattern. The converging results demonstrate the validity of the concepts involved in these studies.

## Correlational Studies that Approach Experimentation

As pointed out earlier, experimentation involves control over the conditions

---

[1] Dr. Bernard Bass has kindly invited readers to contact him for further information on the many studies undertaken by his Center. His address is: Management Research Center, Graduate School of Management, University of Rochester, New York 14627.

of the research. This means that a researcher can present certain stimuli or perhaps manipulate a variable to determine its effects on another variable. At times, a researcher can "approach" experimentation if he is able to take advantage of several variables in the natural world and "pretend," in his data analysis, that he has control over them. An example will help.

Brewer (1968) was interested in the determinants of social distance among members of 30 African tribal groups. She studied three variables that occurred naturally within the pattern of relations among the groups: (1) perceived similarity between tribes; (2) physical distance between tribes; and (3) educational-economic advancement of tribes. All three variables were dichotomized into high versus low groups. For each of the 30 tribes, Brewer analyzed the feelings of a specific tribe toward eight outgroups (other tribes) which represented each of the eight combinations of the three variables. Figure 4.1 presents the basis for the data analysis. The dependent variable was social distance between a given tribe and the other eight, defined by four questions (e.g., "Would you willingly agree to share a meal with . . .?") that scaled with adequate reliability. The data were then reduced through the analysis of variance technique (Winer, 1962). Correlation coefficients were also computed to complement the analysis of variance. Both analyses determined that all three variables led to significant results, but perceived similarity was by far the most powerful determinant of social distance. Brewer also measured the effects of familiarity (acquaintance) between groups, defined by (a) number of members of one group who live with the other group, and (b) number of members of one

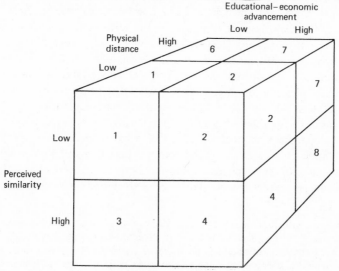

Figure 4-1. Determinants of social distance: the eight blocks represent relations between each tribe and eight others. Note that block No. 5 is "hidden" below block No. 6.

group who are familiar with the language of the other group. The results indicated that greater amounts of familiarity led to less social distance. As in all research, of course, readers will have more faith if others find the same results. In a completely independent but contemporary study, Brislin (1968), working with Pacific Island groups, measured the degree of people's contact with outgroups and then familiarity with the languages of outgroups. As predicted, a positive relationship between these measures and degree of friendship choice was found. In a later study, Brislin (1971) also documented the strong influence of perceived similarity on intergroup relations.

In strict terms, the Brewer study is correlational, but it is similar to an experiment for several reasons. First, the researcher was able to find data points for all combinations of the three conditions (see Figure 4.1). Second, the data were analyzed to discover which of the three variables was the strongest determinant of social attraction. Third, it was possible to discover interactions among the three variables. The interaction Brewer found was that for highly similar outgroups, there were no social distance differences for tribes high or low on the educational-economic measure. But for low similarity outgroups, high advanced outgroups were held at less social distance than low advanced outgroups. These three qualities are always part of real experiments, and attempts can be made to incorporate them into correlational studies.[2]

## A Series of Experiments to Investigate Hypotheses: Perception

The soundness of any hypothesis is judged on the basis of many experiments rather than three or four. There are a few problem areas in cross-cultural psychology that have been of central focus in a series of experiments. Examples are achievement motivation (reviewed by LeVine, 1970), cognition (Goodnow, 1969), perception, and conformity. We will examine the latter two as examples of cross-cultural hypothesis testing. The perception studies constitute an example of "presentation experiments," while the conformity studies are an example of what we have called "major manipulation experiments."

The following hypothesis has attracted much attention: Perception of objects is partly determined by specific, identifiable experiences. This hypothesis is especially amenable to cross-cultural investigation since different peoples have obviously had different experiences, and these experiences should be reflected in responses to perceptual stimuli. To be properly tested, this hypothesis would

---

[2] The Brewer (1968) study incidentally, is a good "preview" of a large cross-cultural study to be published in several years. It has been described by Campbell and LeVine (1961). Brewer was a research associate with the project for several years. The forthcoming study will examine social distance and ethnocentrism using more potential determinants, tribes, analyses of competing theories, and so forth. The literature review, prepared as part of the study, has been published (LeVine and Campbell, 1972).

have to be the basis of studies that

1. use different perceptual tests,
2. are undertaken in different cultures,
3. are designed by various investigators,
4. employ subjects from various age groups (who naturally have had different perceptual experiences as a function of age),
5. employ subjects who have received training that might affect perception.

This general hypothesis can also be the basis for more specific predictions. For example, members of culture A and culture B should differ in their responses to a specified perceptual test. Table 4.1 summarizes some of the studies that have tested the hypothesis in these various ways. Looking at so many studies, of course, gives a picture of how well the general hypothesis has been supported in addition to how well more specific predictions from the general hypothesis have fared. The following discussion expands on the outline presented in Table 4.1.

*Visual Illusions.* The work on cross-cultural perception is divided into three areas. Visual illusions were first investigated cross-culturally by Rivers (1901), and the largest study is that of Segall, Campbell, and Herskovits (1966). The researchers in the latter study were centrally concerned with two illusions, and they suggested environmental counterparts for them. In the Mueller-Lyer illusion (Figure 4.2*a*), the horizontal line with the "arrowheads" forming an obtuse angle is judged by those in Western cultures as being longer than the line with the arrowheads forming an acute angle. The environmental counterpart is the familiar Western depiction of corners and distance (Figure 4.2*b*). The prediction resulting from this analysis is that members of cultures who do not live in "carpentered environments" will perceive *less* illusion than Western residents. Non-Westerners are not as likely to make the correction for "distance" and thus report that the top line in Figure 4.2*a* is longer. Most studies have supported this prediction. Jahoda and Stacey's (1970) study which used artists as subjects also provided support. The artists, who had undergone long training in depicting perspectives on paper, were less susceptible to the illusion than non-artists. The major plausible rival hypothesis is that the amount of pigmentation in the retina is correlated with susceptibility to this illusion (Jahoda, 1971).

The horizontal-vertical illusion (Figure 4.2*c*) has a flat plain or plowed field as its environmental counterpart (Figure 4.2*d*). The vertical line represents the plain or furrow extending away from the observer. In viewing such a situation, the observer knows that the distance represented by the vertical line is actually longer than it looks to him. Residents of cultures who live in open plains or flat land suitable for farming would have more experience with such perceptual situations than Western residents. The latter are familiar with their vistas being interrupted by smog, mountains, and buildings. The prediction (from Segall et

Table 4.1 Evidence for the Hypothesis that Perception is Determined by Experience

| | Perceptual Tests | | |
|---|---|---|---|
| | Visual Illusions | Three-Dimensional Perception | Field Dependence vs. Independence |
| Different cultures and different experimenters: | "Carpentered world" and the Mueller-Lyer Illusion<br><br>Supportive:<br>Segall, Campbell, Herskovits (1966): 15 cultures in U.S.A., Africa, Australia<br>Dawson (1967 a,b);West Africa<br>Berry (1968): Eskimos and Temne of Africa<br>Jahoda (1966): Ghana<br>Problematic or equivocal:<br>Jahoda and Stacey (1970): Ghana<br>Davis and Carlson (1970): Uganda<br><br>"Open terrain" and the horizontal-vertical illusion<br><br>Supportive:<br>Segall et al. (1966)<br>Jahoda and Stacey (1970)<br>Problematic or equivocal:<br>Berry (1968)<br>Dawson (1967 a,b)<br>Jahoda (1966)<br>Deregowski (1967): West Africa | Experience with Western methods of depiction<br><br>Supportive:<br>Hudson (1960, 1967): Groups in Africa and Europe<br>Deregowski (1968a, 1968b): Central Africa<br>Guthrie, Brislin, and Sinaiko (1970): Vietnamese | Socialization affects perceptual style as measured by the rod-frame and/or the embedded figures test.<br><br>Supportive:<br>Witkin (1967): U.S.A. Europe, Africa<br>Wober (1966, 1967): Africa<br>Berry (1966): Eskimos and Temne of Africa<br>MacArthur (1967): Eskimo<br>Dawson (1967a, b): Africa |

Table 4.1  (Cont.)

| | Perceptual Tests | | |
| | Visual Illusions | Three-Dimensional Perception | Field Dependence vs. Independence |
| --- | --- | --- | --- |
| | Size constancy and the Ponzo illusion<br><br>Supportive:<br>Leibowitz et al. (1969): Pacific Islanders<br>Leibowitz and Pick (1972):  West Africa | | |
| Different age groups | Ponzo illusion and size constancy<br><br>Supportive:<br>Leibowitz and Judisch (1967): U.S.A.<br>Vrislin and Leibowitz (1971): Pacific Islanders | | |
| Effects of training | Mueller-Lyer and "carpentered world"<br><br>Supportive:<br>Jahoda and Stacey (1970): artists | Training programs can overcome lack of three dimensional perception<br><br>Supportive:<br>Dawson (1967a): Temne of Africa<br>Guthrie, Brislin, and Sinaiko (1970): Vietnamese | Special training can affect perceptual style<br><br>Supportive:<br>Gruen's (1955) data from U.S.A. dancers, interpreted by Wober (1967) |

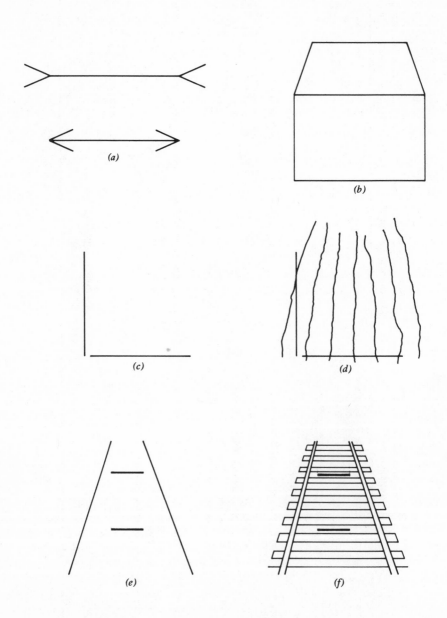

Figure 4-2. Three visual illusions and their environmental counterparts.

al., 1966) is that specifiable groups in Africa, living in flat, open terrain, will perceive *more* illusion than Western residents. The researchers found positive (but not perfect) support from their data. Other studies, however, have not supported the prediction and hence other factors must be examined to explain the illusion.

Leibowitz, Brislin, Perlmutter, and Hennessy (1969) suggested that the Ponzo illusion (Figure 4.2e) may be explained in terms of size constancy. The converging lines indicate distance, and observers may "correct" for distance by saying that the top line is longer. An experiment was designed using both figures similar to those pictured in 4.2e and 4.2f. Western observers reported a large illusion when the environmental cues of the railroad tracks were added to the basic figure, but Pacific Islanders (who had never left their island, even for a holiday) saw the same amount in both figures. The Islanders had never seen railroad tracks, and other instances of converging lines in the distance were absent from their experience. Studies of children from both the United States and Pacific Islands indicate that the magnitude of the illusion increases with age, just as competence in size constancy judgments increases with age (Brislin and Leibowitz, 1970). Leibowitz and Pick (1972) have replicated the basic cross-cultural findings in Africa, again testing subjects with different perceptual experiences.

*Three-Dimensional Perception.* Residents of Western cultures are accustomed to interpreting pictures like that shown in Figure 8.6 (see p.233).They recognize that the converging lines, the relative size of the animals and the tree, and the super-imposition of lines indicating the relative position of the hills all depict distance, or nearness-farness. These cues, however, are not understood universally. Hudson (1960, 1967) has designed six pictures (see Chapter 8, p. 233) and has validated them as a test of the ability to perceive (i.e., infer) three dimensions from two-dimensional drawings. Most of his subjects were drawn from various African tribes, and they performed less well on the test than Western subjects. Further, African residents who have had contact with the Western culture because of their occupation (e.g., manservants in the city) do better than their counterparts who have not had this contact. Deregowski (1968a; 1968b) has replicated this work, and has added an analysis of the exact reasons behind the African observers'difficulty. Guthrie et al. (1970) found that, as predicted, Vietnamese technicians performed less well on the test than technicians from the United States engaged in the same mechanical specialty.

Dawson (1967a) found that a training program undertaken with African laborers increased three-dimensional perception. An experimental group received training that encouraged practice in drawing while a control group received no training. The trained group performed with fewer errors on a post-test.

*Field Dependence and Independence.* Witkin (1967) has discussed the possibilities of employing his concept of perceptual style, originally developed in Western countries, in cross-cultural studies. The distinction he employs is field dependence versus independence. Dawson (1967a) described the distinction:

"Witkin et al. [1962] have defined the field dependent person as one who orientates himself by reference to the environment, has a greater need to function as a member of a group, has lower performance on measures of field dependence, whilst individual perception tends to be global. Females tend to be more global and field dependent whilst males tend to be more analytical and field independent. Witkin has found that relevant variables relating to the development of field dependence include harsh parental discipline, strict control, conformity, authority, and the age and extent of psychological differentiation which the developing child achieves from his mother. Mothers of field dependent sons tend to be dominating, emotional, and anxious, whilst the father is generally passive and an inadequate role model" (Dawson, 1967a, p. 117).

The field-independent person, on the other hand, "is able to perceive items as distinct from the organized field of which they are a part" (Witkin, 1967, p. 239). The variables encouraging development of field independence are the opposite of those (listed above) encouraging field dependence.

Several tests are available to measure this perceptual distinction. Figure 4.3*a* pictures an item from the embedded figures test (see also Chapter 8). The test taker is asked to find the smaller figure in the more complex drawing. Figure 4.3*b* presents the rod-and-frame test in which a subject adjusts the slanted rod to an upright position while he and/or the frame are tilted. The field-independent person is able to break up the complex embedded figure and is able to adjust the rod independently of the frame or the cues from his own body position. Perceptual style is supposed to be determined by experience, and this proposition has been empirically tested. Witkin (1967) has reviewed studies undertaken in the United States, four European countries, Israel, and Hong Kong, and these studies have consistently found the sex distinction to be valid. Berry (1966) and MacArthur (1967) have investigated Eskimo groups. There was a prediction of *no* sex differences in these studies because women are not treated as dependent in these groups. Their data were supportive of hypothesis, demonstrating social and environmental influences on perceptual style.

Dawson (1967a, b) investigated two African tribes, the Temne and Mende, who differ in severity of socialization practices, the Temne being much stricter. As predicted, the Temne were more field-dependent on several tests. Wober (1966; 1967) found that tribesmen from southern Nigeria performed more independently on the rod-and-frame test in the tilted-body condition than did subjects from the United States. They performed in a dependent style, however, on the embedded figures test. Wober predicted these results, noting that the

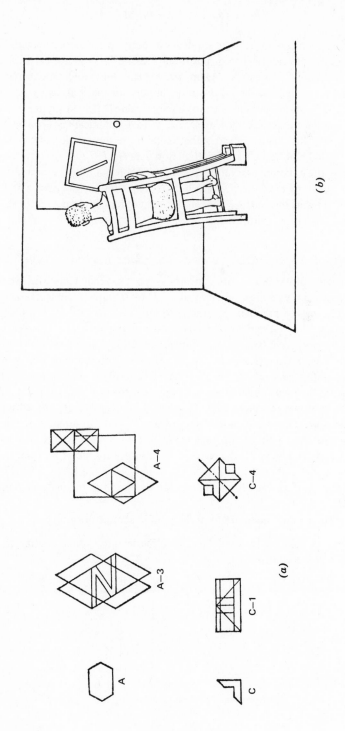

**Figure 4-3.** Examples from (*a*) the embedded figures test and (*b*) the rod-and-frame test.

West African subjects were accustomed to using proprioceptive cues (e.g., hunting and dance activities) as in the tilted rod-and-frame, but not visual cues, as in the embedded figures test. Again, the explanation based on experience is supported by the data. Wober also found support for his analysis by reviewing Gruen's (1955) data gathered from highly trained United States dancers. Although the data have not been presented so that statistical tests can be made, the direction of the means indicates that dancers are more field-independent in the body tilt rod-and-frame situation than non-dancers.

Gathering the experimental information as in Table 4.1 allows one to discover work that needs to be done. Obviously, the major research need is a series of studies on the *development* of perception, employing children at different age levels from a variety of cultures.

## Cross-Cultural Studies Employing a Major Manipulation: Conformity

Many cross-cultural studies of conformity have extended the work of Asch (1952) who employed college students in the United States as subjects. He asked an individual, in the presence of others, to judge which of three lines was the same length as the comparision line, as shown in Figure 4.4. Unknown to the subjects, however, Asch had trained confederates to give wrong answers on some of the line-judging tasks. The naive subject answered after hearing others testify that line 2 is the same as line A. He thus has a conflict—should he accept the evidence from his own senses or should he accept the evidence from the group? Accepting one's own judgment (line 3) is called "independence," accepting the group judgment (line 2) is called "conformity," and choosing in the wrong direction, opposite to the group judgment (line 1) is called "anticonformity" (Hollander and Willis, 1967). A review of the conformity literature from studies carried out in the United States can be found in Kiesler and Kiesler (1969). The following review of cross-cultural studies is an extension of the material outlined in Table 4.2.

Cross-cultural studies seem useful to help understand conformity if

1. different tasks were used in the experiments, some central to the maintenance of the culture,

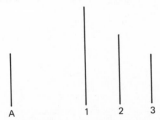

**Figure 4-4.** The Asch Line-Judging Task.

Table 4.2  Cross-Cultural Studies of Conformity

| | Types of Tasks | |
| --- | --- | --- |
| | Judging Length of Lines | Discussing Opinions and Attitudes |
| Different experimenters in diverse cultures | Data-gathering efforts from many cultures to add to U.S.A. information (Asch, 1952; Kiesler and Kiesler, 1969) | Meade and Bernard, 1973: U.S.A. and Hong Kong; Zajonc and Wahi, 1961: India |
| | Milgram, 1961: France, Norway Kahn, 1965: Pakistan Whittaker and Meade, 1967: Brazil Lebanon, Rhodesia, Hong Kong; Timaeus, 1968: Germany Frager, 1970: Japan | |
| Cultures with strong expectations for conformity or independence | Berry, 1967: Eskimos, Temne of Africa | |

2. different experimenters did the research,
3. different cultures were studied, including
4. cultures that have clear and strong demands for independence or conformity.

The percentage or pro-majority errors, or estimates of conformity, is about 33% in Asch-type studies carried out in the United States. A similar percentage has been found, with subjects of the same age, in replications in Pakistan (Khan, 1965), and in Brazil, Lebanon, and Hong Kong (Whittaker and Meade, 1967). Asch (in Whittaker and Meade, 1967) has written that no generalizations should be made about non-laboratory conformity from these results. Data in a study by Timaeus (1968) remind us to heed this warning, as he found that German subjects conform less than United States subjects. The great fault in these studies is that no measurement was made of what the experimental situation means from culture to culture. Or, in more technical language, the effectiveness or meaning of the independent manipulation was not assessed. The Asch situation may be a cue for arousing social approval needs in culture A, rugged individualism in culture B (Germany, perhaps?), and disgust with human experimentation in culture C. We are unable to choose among these alternative explanations since no data exist. We know of one conformity study that had to be rejected for publication because the authors had no data on the meaning of the independent variable. They were unable to impugn a reviewer's observation that the large differences between cultures may have been due to coercion rather than to conformity.

This weakness was not as evident in studies by Milgram (1961) and Berry (1967). Milgram found less conformity among French than Norwegian subjects, and gathered evidence to show that the French have norms that allow people to assert their individuality. Berry's study was specifically concerned with societies whose members *should* perform differently on the Asch task. The Eskimo culture stresses independence since each family unit provides for its own survival needs. The Temne of Africa, however, stress conformity since survival needs are satisfied by cooperative group activities such as planting, harvesting, and storage of food. As predicted, the Temne were much more conforming, demonstrating that a prediction on a laboratory task can be made by observing means of satisfying life's goals. These findings are in line with the results grathered from the Mashona of Rhodesia by Whittaker and Meade (1967), the only culture they studied that had a higher "conformity score" than the United States. This tribe also has a strong norm insisting on conformity.

Frager (1970) and Meade and Barnard (1973) have observed anticonformity, the process in which subjects are incorrect in the judgment but at the same time away from the group judgment. Frager's study analyzed Japanese college students on the Asch task, and one's impression after reading the article could easily be that the subjects were tired of being studied and wanted to ruin an experiment. Frager observed, in his plausible rival hypothesis analysis, that the results may have been due to the presence of a Western experimenter working with Japenese subjects. The same results occurred, however, when the study was replicated with a Japanese experimenter. Additional information was not available to give much insight into the reasons for anticonformity, a phenomenon never observed among members of Western cultures performing the Asch task. Meade and Barnard studied groups in the United States and Hong Kong and found anticonformity when subjects gave their opinion on an issue, discussed it (stooges disagreed with the subject), and gave their opinion again. Many subjects, more in the United States than in Hong Kong, went even further in the direction opposite to that of the group. Again, the process is not well understood.

Zajonc and Wahi (1961) investigated the instrumental value of conformity among students from India studying in America. They found that Indians with a high need for achievement were likely to conform to American opinions if they felt that holding the opinion was useful "in getting ahead." In addition, they found that high need-achievers resolved conflict between American and Indian norms by choosing the former. Low need-achievers choose the Indian norm. This study is valuable in showing why different types of people do and do not conform.

In summary, the cross-cultural conformity literature constitutes a mixed blessing. We know that members of several cultures conform equally on the Asch task and that others conform more. We can suggest that the latter people behave as they do because of the strong demands present in their society. One Temne subject told Berry: "When Temne people choose a thing, we must all agree with the decison—this is what we call cooperation" (Berry, 1967, p. 417). The literature on anticonformity, however, is not well understood and the only cross-cultural contribution is that the phenomenon has been observed. The picture would be more clear if data were available showing how members of other cultures were thinking as they performed the experimental tasks. The biggest research need is for more studies that deal with conformity to opinions and beliefs as opposed to line judgments. These opinion studies might be concerned with issues central to the maintenance of the societies in which they are carried out.

## A Series of Experiments in Two Cultures

The major cross-cultural studies to date have involved data gathered from many cultures, as in the Segall, Campbell, and Herskovits (1966) study of perception or the Dennis (1966b) study using the Goodenough Draw-A-Man Test (see Chapter 8). The cultures represent different levels of an independent variable, such as degree of contact with Western methods of drawing. Their responses to the same dependent variable, such as drawing ability, are then gathered. A functional relation between the two variables is often suggested. Another technique is to design a series of experiments and to carry them out in two cultures. This "in-depth" research undertaken in two cultures results in a pattern of findings. The series of findings can be interpreted more reliably than a single finding (Campbell, 1961), such as the discovery that the members of culture A do better on memory task X than members of culture B. There may be a dozen reasons for this difference, for example, education, child rearing, and linguistic differences, but probably not so many competing explanations for the results of many studies done in cultures A and B.

Michael Cole and John Gay were involved in such a research project. They were interested in determining what aspects of the Kpelle culture (West Africa) lead to poor performance in mathematics as taught in school. Further, they wanted to suggest which aspect of normal Kpelle mathematical behavior might be incorporated into a school curriculum so that better and higher quality learning would be possible. Summaries of their research can be found in Gay and Cole (1967) and Cole, Gay, and Glick (1968). Another major research project completed by these investigators is reported in Cole, Gay, Glick, and Sharp (1971).

The researchers set up different experiments to investigate matematical behavior, comparing groups of illiterate children, school children, and adults from the Kpelle society with children and adults from the United States. The concepts studied in their experiments and a sampling of results are as follows:

1. *Geometric concept formation.* Kpelle children did as well as children from the United States if they had seen the geometric shape in school.

2. *Logic identification.* Kpelle subjects were better than their counterparts in the United States at learning disjunctive concepts (e.g., John *or* Mary will go). The Kpelle linguistic structure is less ambiguous for the expression of disjunction than is English. Conjunctive concepts were learned at an equal rate in both the Kpelle society and in the United States.

3. *Volume measurement.* Kpelle subjects were better at estimating amounts of rice, a familiar commodity in Africa.

4. *Time estimation.* Only small differences between the Kpelle and subjects from the United States were found, indicating that reports of the Kpelle "primitive sense of time" are false.

5. *Length of distance in armspans.* Kpelle subjects were more accurate than subjects from the United States. Armspans are a familiar measuring device for the Kpelle, and "the culturally sanctioned measure leads to consistent measurements" (Cole, Gay, and Glick 1968, p. 182).

6. *Judging number of dots presented for short intervals.* Using a tachistoscope, different numbers of dots were presented either randomly

scattered or in patterns. Kpelle subjects did not take advantage of the pattern arrangements as did the subjects from the United States.

7. *Verbal mediation and learning.* Kpelle children are able to employ verbal labels that generalize a series of specific instances. They learn this skill at about the same age as American children.

These diverse results can be explained in terms of cultural familiarity with the specific mathematical issue (e.g., volume or distance measurement devices). The number of rival explanations is few because the results are consistent. The authors explained the reasoning involved, using one of the studies as an example:

". . . in the experiment on learning which involved various types of logical connectives the American groups found the conjunctive problem harder than the disjunctive problem, while the Kpelle groups experienced about equal difficulty with the two types of problems. This finding corresponds to what we know about an aspect of the two cultures (in this case, their languages). However, it has an added virtue in that the importance of the result rests on the relation between performances within each culture. Whereas it is easy to generate hypotheses about the factors causing a difference between two behaviors compared across cultures, the number of hypotheses concerning why, within a single situation within each culture, the relationship between two behaviors should be reversed is considerably smaller. Consequently, we have greater confidence that we are dealing with a reliable cultural [in this case, linguistically determined] difference" (Cole, Gay, and Glick, 1968, p. 189)

In the future, a series of studies investigating psychological processes in two or more cultures will replace the one-shot study so common today.

Our reviews of the perception, conformity, and Cole-Gay research are examples of how cross-cultural literature can be organized. From such literature reviews, key studies can be formulated. Some researchers, though, are more interested in breakthrough studies than in well-researched areas. They are not likely to gain quite as much from previous literature.

We should like at this juncture to review a study which was quite original in its scope and execution. At the same time it is a good example of a methodologically sophisticated cross-cultural experiment, and it also provides an introduction to unobtrusive measures.

## An Innovative Cross-Cultural Experiment

Feldman (1968) was interested in discovering the determinants of helping behavior in three cities (Boston, Paris, and Athens), but no previous cross-cultural studies of this topic had been reported. Feldman had to be innovative, but this did not mean that his study could not be based on well-founded experimental principles. Note how the desirable aspects of experimentation, discussed previously, were part of his design.

Feldman studied the previous non-experimental literature on helping behavior in the three cities, including anthropological, sociological, questionnaire, and tourist reports. Feldman was specifically interested in the amount of help the people offer to foreigners and to compatriots, that is, to visitors versus fellow citizens. The concept is best defined by looking at different types of helping behavior, thus allowing a pattern of findings to emerge. He set up experiments in which a person asked another to perform one of five helpful behaviors. The same experiments were carried out in Paris, Athens, and Boston:

1. Stopping a person and asking him to give directions.

2. Asking help in mailing a letter.

3. Determining whether a person falsely claims money. (The experimenter asked a subject if he had dropped some money. Actually, it belonged to the experimenter.)

4. Determining whether a cashier accepts an overpayment for merchandise. (This study was carried out in pastry shops.)

5. Discovering (as everyone often wonders) whether taxicab drivers overcharge people.

The social context of the encounter was varied. The context between the foreigner or compatriot help-seeker and the setting could be (a) casual or (b) occupational, and (c) there could be an opportunity to cheat the help-seeker and (d) the help-seeker could ask for a monetary or non-monetary favor. Both help-seekers and subjects were randomly assigned to conditions. Careful procedures were used to assure an absence of experimenter bias in subject selection. In three of the experiments, every fourth oncoming pedestrian in busy sections of each city was chosen. In a fourth experiment (overpayment in pastry shops) Feldman was able to randomly sample sites, since good lists were available of all pastry shops in the three cities. Interviews were held with a sample of subjects to see if certain manipulations were perceived in the desired way. For instance, information was gathered to determine whether subjects perceived the help-seeker as a foreigner or as a compatriot. This technique, of course, is designed to check the manipulation of the independent variable. In the falsely claiming money experiment, the check fit the social situation very well. After the subject walked away from the experimenter who had asked about the lost money, another experimenter ran after the subject and asked, "Hey, is that guy giving money away?" Answers were recorded to determine how the subject perceived the first interaction.

In general, when differences between help granted to foreigners and compatriots did occur, the compatriots received more assistance in Paris and Boston, while the foreigner received more help in Athens. The Athens findings (e.g., 93% of the subjects did not help a compatriot mail a letter) are very supportive of the Triandis, Vassiliou, and Nassiakou (1968) findings about the Greek definition of the ingroup and outgroup. The Greek ingroup includes family, friends, and tourists, but not other Greeks whom a person doesn't know. This concept is different from the definition of the ingroup in the United States, which includes family, friends, and other Americans but which excludes tourists.

The dependent variables that Feldman used belong to the class recently labeled "unobtrusive measures." The most widely read exposition defending their use was prepared by Webb et al. (1966), and a recent collection of studies using such measures has appeared (Bickman and Henchy, 1972) which also contains excellent original material by the editors. We define unobtrusives broadly, including behavioral measures that a subject emits naturally, not knowing that he is part of a research project. Feldman's measures of helping behavior are good examples since subjects either refused or helped others in a normal, everyday context, unaware that they were being studied. Our favorite example was related to us by Bochner (1971). Either a white or an Aborigine girl, equated on variables such as age, personal grooming, and so forth, entered a randomly assigned butcher shop in Sydney, Australia. She put down a coin and asked for bones for her dog. Taken over several stores, the white girl received more bones. In addition, a dog expert blindly examined all bones, and the data showed that the white girl had been given higher quality bones.

The recent development of unobtrusive measures has arisen from shortcomings with verbal measures, such as the ten possible biases that can be problems when questionnaires are used (pp. 68–72). Unfortunately, unobtrusives are not the answer to all cross-cultural problems, especially since the exact reasons underlying subjects' responses are not available. But they do alleviate subject-demand characteristics (Orne, 1962), and this is a major point in their favor. This leads us to one further recommendation regarding the setting for cross-cultural experimentation. Assume that we have set up a laboratory and are ready to test a subject unfamiliar with laboratory procedures. Not only is the confrontation with a radically new experience likely to produce distortions and constant errors in a subject's reaction, the appearance of a foreign investigator can be even more upsetting to him. Wherever possible, all experimentation should be conducted within a setting which will not be out of the ordinary for the subject. Many, if not the majority, of psychological investigations are conducted within the artifical confines of a laboratory, a situation in which the subject never finds himself during his normal, everyday routine. This, as Orne (1962) points out, has produced an excessive amount of error, most of which has been either ignored or denied by experimenters. It is important, then that cross-cultural researchers do not go astray and make the same mistakes. Sir Frederick Bartlett made the same point in 1937, but for the most part traditional psychology has continued to ignore his sage advice.

## Summary

In experimental methods a researcher creates, presents, and manipulates an independent variable, such as hours of mother-child contact, and examines its effects on a dependent variable, such as the personality of children. The manipulation of the independent variables makes the experimental method different from the correlational approach. In the latter, a researcher would question mothers about contact with their children and would then correlate this measure with the results of a personality scale. The cause-effect relation is much easier to interpret in the experimental method, since mothers do not choose to be in one group or another as they do in the correlational example. If mothers choose to spend a given amount of time with their children, the reasons behind the choice will give the analyst an unmanageable number of plausible rival hypotheses.

Regarding types of experiments, a distinction can be made between "presentation" and "major manipulation" studies. In the former, the experimenter presents stimuli such as visual illusion tasks or photographs and then asks subjects to respond. In the latter, the researcher makes a major change in an aspect of the subject's environment, sometimes by training confederates to perform in a certain manner while interacting with the subject.

The experimental method demands attention to several key issues. The first regards the establishment of experimental conditions in the two or more cultures under study. Since this issue is now under debate, our suggestions are tentative.

1. Keep experimental situations as simple as possible so that colleagues in other cultures can run the study without special training. Simplicity also affords less chance for errors.

2. The researcher should equate the desired psychological state within subjects rather than the exact experimental stimuli. If subjects in the United States and Hong Kong are to discuss interesting topics, the level of interest is more important than the exact topics. Consequently, the subjects in the two cultures may discuss different topics.

3. Methods for successful manipulation of variables can be discovered in anthropological reports, discussions with social scientists from other cultures, extensive pretesting, and interviews with subjects after pretesting. We feel that this last technique can be especially fruitful, as Aronson and Carlsmith (1968) have also suggested.

4. If there is one *sine qua non* of experimentation, it is that the meaning of the independent variable must be assessed among subjects from the cultures under study. Assume that aggression is being studied in two cultures and that the independent variable is aggressive drive while the dependent variable is the tendency to hurt another. The experimental design should include an additional measure to determine whether the same level of aggressive drive was achieved

among subjects from the two cultures. If the aggressive drive is not the same, responses to the dependent variable will be difficult to interpret.

5. When possible, the results of experiments should be compared with other cross-cultural findings, thus allowing further insights into both sets of data. In a series of studies on communication styles, Barrett and Franke (1969) found that managers from certain countries preferred a one-way communication style in which the receiver of messages could not question the sender. This information was compared with other sets of data which showed that one-way preference was related to autocratic attitudes and to the acceptance of coercive supervision. The different sets of data fell into a coherent pattern, demonstrating the validity of the concepts under study.

6. Some correlational studies have qualities like those found in experiments, and they can be analyzed as if they were so. These special studies have data for all combinations of the independent variables under investigation and can thus be analyzed for interactions and for a demonstration of which independent variable has the strongest effect on the dependent variable.

*The Benefits of a Series of Experiments.* The soundness of any hypothesis is judged on the basis of many experiments rather than three or four. If the same hypothesis can be supported by (1) various experimenters who (2) employ different variables in (3) diverse cultures, then there is a good reason to consider the findings sound. An example of such a hypothesis can be found in the psychological literature: perception of objects is partly determined by specific, identifiable experiences. In addition to the three facets mentioned directly above, research in this area has employed (4) subjects from various age groups and (5) subjects who have received special training that might affect perception. When organized around such facets, needed research can be identified. The literature in this area was reviewed, and the conclusion was that studies of perceptual development are especially needed. These would examine children at different age levels from a variety of cultures Children at different ages have naturally had different perceptual experiences that should lead to different performance when compared to adults.

A similar review of the conformity literature (i.e., a group of individuals pressure a single subject to adopt an incorrect judgment) also shows a major area of needed research. Studies should be done which investigate conformity to opinions and beliefs as opposed to more neutral tasks such as judging the length of lines. These opinion studies might be concerned with issues central to the maintenance of the societies in which they are carried out. The major methodological weakness of many conformity studies is that the meaning of the independent variable was not assessed. That is, data were not available showing how subjects from other cultures were thinking as they performed the experimental tasks. What might have been a cue to accept the judgment of others in one culture might have been a cue to rugged individualism in another. Without the additional data, valid cross-cultural comparisions were difficult to make.

*A Series of Experiments in Two cultures.* If members of culture A do better on a task than members of culture B, there are a great many plausible rival hypotheses to plague data interpretation. A better experimental procedure is to gather data using many tests and procedures, chosen because members of culture A should score higher on some and members of culture B higher on others. Gay and Cole (1967; also see Cole, et al., 1971) carried out such a series of experiments on mathematical learning among children from the United States and among the Kpelle of West Africa. Their results included the findings that the Kpelle were better at learning disjunctive concepts and at estimating the volume of rice. Subjects from the United States were better judging the number of dots presented for brief intervals. The groups were equal in time estimation and geometric concept formation. The resulting pattern was easy to interpret in light of known cultural experiences and cultural differences.

Feldman (1968) likewise completed a series of small experiments in an investigation of helping behavior. He was very careful in his selection of situations in which helping might be manifested, his selection of subjects, and in his assessment of the independent variable's meaning in the three cultures. His excellent study is a model from which others can learn good experimental design. The dependent variables he used belong to the class called "unobtrusive measures," which quantify behaviors that a subject emits naturally, not knowing that he is part of an experiment. The use of such measures can alleviate subject-demand characteristics, or the "I-am-being-studied-how-should-I-act?" phenomenon.

# CHAPTER FIVE

## Cross-Cultural Use of Psychological Tests

During the first three or four decades of this century, many psychologists were captivated by the fascinating prospects and promises of "culture-free" and "culture-fair" tests. Stimulated largely by the nature-nurture controversy, such tests were deemed necessary to help find universals in mental functions. The quick successes (or fresh approaches) that such tests presented had a brief intoxicating effect, but contemporary psychologists are now correcting the legacy of errors inherited from this very forgivable passion. Researchers are retreating and regrouping, virtually unanimously agreeing that a test unequivocably fair to all people in all cultures is a distant hope. But soft terms die hard, and this psychological shorthand has achieved functional autonomy. Recent modifiers such as "culture-reducing," "culture-leveling," or "culturally equivalent" are hopeful signs, but research by scores of psychologists has failed to build an impenetrable case for a *lingua franca* among psychological tests.

Frijda and Jahoda (1966) theorize that a "culture-fair" test could be achieved in at least two contrasting ways. The first is "to construct tests equally unfamiliar to all," which is a virtual impossibility since tests are designed within particular originating cultures. The second would be to devise "culturally 'appropriate' tests or tasks, whereby a particular psychological dimension is assessed by means of a medium familiar to the members of each culture" (p. 117). Wober (1969) asks whether or not all claimed "cross-cultural" research to date (tests as well as other investigations) should be reexamined to see if such research has been more truly "centri-cultural."

Major United States textbooks (it is not ethnocentric to read "World" textbooks) on psychological testing (Anastasi, 1968; Brown 1970; Cronbach, 1970; Freeman, 1962; Horrocks, 1964) typically devote ten or twenty pages to cultural (or socioeconomic, ethnic, and racial) factors, and the message given by them all is consistently the same: culture fairness has run its course or never really existed. Because of the lessons learned from this defunct research, those psychologists who identify with cross-cultural research are now much more

109

cautious when using tests. In this chapter we shall survey these cautions, and give what hopefully will be an overview of the pitfalls to avoid in adapting, constructing, administering, and interpreting tests in or for a culture different from one's own.

To a majority of researchers in the area, cross-cultural testing usually encompasses two general domains: (1) the measurement of intelligence, that is, the search for culture-common or culture-relevant factors of intelligence, and the resolution or explanation of any found differences, and (2) culture-personality study, usually using familiar devices such as the Rorschach or the Thematic Apperception Test, two major projective techniques on which many cultural anthropologists have teethed. Recently, objective paper-and-pencil personality tests have been enjoying increasing cross-cultural use. These and projectives will be discussed later.

Implicit in all cross-cultural testing is either theory support, construction and modification, or simply pragmatic personnel selection and classification. Most cross-cultural studies in psychology have dealt either with the measurement of intelligence or the study of personality, with the latter encompassing a vast number of constructs. Obviously, the study of any construct may at least be attempted cross-culturally, and perhaps all of them have been studied to some degree. The measurement and utilization of intelligence, however, quite appropriately deserves primacy within any culture, for the wealth of any nation—developed, developing, or "primitive"—is the ability of its people. Once properly identified as having requisite abilities for differential placement, each person can then conceivably contribute more to the health, well-being, and productivity of his country.

The fascinating cross-cultural study of personality has, for psychologists, often been preempted by intellectual assessment, but personality study will certainly become increasingly important in the domain of cross-cultural intelligence testing. For example, it will explain further why certain cultural conditions shape personality as they do, and why these factors must be considered in the appraisal of intelligence. Such important areas as field-dependence—field-independence research (cf. Witkin et al., 1962; Berry, 1966; Dawson, 1972), internal versus external locus of control studies (Rotter, 1966), attitudes, cultural motivational strategies, and other aspects of personality research must not be divorced from the measurement of mental abilities. For example, a country cannot long survive on only a fashionable personality; but one with an unexciting personality or colorless "national character" which mines and exploits its mental and creative potential has a better chance for survival and growth. It is axiomatic that the great nations have become great, industrial, and prosperous because mental energies were tapped.

How can existing tests best be extended to other cultures? A few years ago, during the filming of a Hollywood movie, the script called for the sound of heavy rain hitting a tin roof. Sound effects specialists tried several things—buckets of rice poured onto sheet metal and snare drums, static from the radio, spraying the side of a building with a pressure hose, and others. Nothing produced the desired sound, except real rain hitting a real tin roof, which some smart young thing suggested be recorded and dubbed in the sound track. This story, perhaps apocryphal, is analogous to the use of psychological testing by means of imported tests. If the aim is to assess the mental ability of people in a culture that has yet to develop its own testing scheme or system, it is necessary to assess what is important in and for that culture. This implies not imposing or projecting one's own psychological values onto other cultures. This may be considered the cardinal principle of cross-cultural testing, and will be the prevailing theme of this chapter. It makes little sense to go through various technical contortions in adapting an American or British test so that it "fits" the target culture. The mere existence of a famous test, such as one in the Wechsler series or the Stanford-Binet, does not mean that it must be used, or that somehow it automatically qualifies. It will become quite clear, in fact, that many such adaptive efforts have been dismal failures. Moreover, we can take the pragmatic position (e.g., Biesheuvel, 1972) which suggests that if an ability test is to be used only within a culture (i.e., no cross-cultural comparisons are being attempted), we need only have a test which will spread individuals over a reasonable range of scores. Or, we can adopt a few guidelines from Piagetian researchers who must *not* rely upon standardized tests since they are interested in what the subject does rather than what he seems to know (see Chapter 8 for examples of Piagetian testing).

For various reasons, researchers may want to take a highly conservative position and work out a quasi Latin-Square design when extending home-grown tests to other cultures. The shape of such a design might be like this: to be perfectly sure that different test administration conditions cancel out, test $A_B$, developed in culture A and used in culture B, as well as a test likewise developed in culture B, should be administered to four groups: (1) $A_B$ $B_B$; (2) $B_B$ $A_B$; (3) $A_A$ $B_A$; and (4) $B_A$ $A_A$. Groups (1) and (2) would be administration conditions in culture B, and groups (3) and (4) the conditions for culture A, with a counterbalanced order of administration. Triandis and his associates (1972) recommend this procedure, and essentially satisfy it through the various techniques of measuring subjective culture that they have developed.

The current trend is not, however, to place tests claiming to have appropriate culture-fair features into categories of accept or reject. Rather, it is the use to which the test scores are put (e.g., selection or industrial placement) and not the internal item by item fairness features or the scores alone that are important. A good theoretical example of such use is given by Thorndike (1971). He argues that fairness may be developed by setting levels of test performance that will qualify applicants or students from diverse cultural groups in proportion to the percentage of those in the groups who reach a specified level of criterion performance. Thus, neither mean test scores nor mean criterion values alone would be used as indicators of "superior" or "inferior" performance. Different regression lines for each group as the lines relate to the same levels of criterion performance across groups would be instrumental in guiding one's use of the word "fairness."

Since languages vary as much as any human variable, so-called nonverbal tests have been used cross-culturally much more than verbal tests. The rationale is that if language and all verbal symbols can be eliminated, and that if the resulting nonverbal stimuli can be cleansed of any cultural favoritism, then the resultant distillation would be a pool of "culture-common" stimuli, the use of which will allow true cross-cultural comparisons. However, it is probably wrong to assume the nonverbal stimuli are less variable (i.e., more "culture-fair") than verbal stimuli. More will be said of this later.

In introducing his Culture Fair Intelligence Test, Cattell (1940) upbraided psychologists for "years of neglect in regard to the real foundations of intelligence testing." He added that this "represents the cost of precipitate, incontinent, and complacent multiplication of intelligence tests without sound research and theory concerning the nature of intelligence" (p. 162). He then listed "common objects" and "common processes" which together could serve as a possible nucleus for finding the "greatest common knowledge" among diverse cultures, upon which to build a matrix of items for intelligence tests. Granted the appropriateness of his first "common object," the human body and its parts, all the others (e.g., trees, four-legged animals, parents and children) do not have constant, equivalent, or identical meaning in all cultures. His common processes (e.g., breathing, mating, sleeping, birth and death, running and jumping), though truly culture-common, are nevertheless best represented by the virtually invariant human form involved in them. Puristically, his other common objects are not really universal and their processes are manifestly different from human processes. For example, trees do not eat, sleep, or jump. We would thus be left with a potential item pool consisting of one universally common object (the human form) depicted in widely varying processes. The point is that Cattell's admonitions, correct as they may have been, seem less convincing when one considers the less-than-ubiquitous objects and processes which may be used in devising test items. Rulon and Schweiker's (1953) Semantic Test of Intelligence, one of many attempts to eliminate the need to use only verbal stimuli, was an approach to test construction incorporating many common objects and common processes of the type Cattell envisioned, although these test developers were apparently not using Cattell's comments as a guide. This test was designed for use with illiterates in the United States.

Cattell's work in cross-cultural testing, and the work of Penrose and Raven (1937), Raven (1960), the extensive field work with the Porteus Maze Test (cf.

Porteus, 1950, 1965), and others, particularly in developing countries, were a few of the additional pioneering attempts to devise tests free of cultural, or at least verbal, influences. These efforts and a large number of studies that have attempted to export, import, or develop new tests, have given us a considerable accumulation of information related to cross-cultural testing problems and cautions. Under the general heading of test-related problems in cross-cultural research, Ortar (1963), Wesley and Karr (1966), Gordon and Kikuchi (1966), Gordon (1968), Berrien (1968), Schwartz (1963), Irvine (1965), Biesheuvel (1949), Anderson (1967), Vernon (1969), and others have surveyed certain studies, or conducted their own, and discussed and summarized the problems of test adaptation, administration, and norming. A recent international conference on mental testing (Cronbach and Drenth, 1972) was directly concerned with these problems. Bernardoni's (1964) mythical development of a culture fair test for the Ugh, No, and Oo-La-La cultures (paralleling United States "majority" and "minority" groups, and serene South Sea Island Cultures) humorously discusses diverse cultural motivations in taking tests. Further, at least one American psychologist (as reported in *Psychology Today*, August, 1970) has proposed a test which would pinpoint a critical issue in sub- and cross-cultural testing. Professor Robert Williams has dubbed this the BITCH [Black Intelligence Test Counter-balanced for Honkies (Whites)] Test which shows that white Americans can be made to look pretty stupid when pitted against norms developed in the Black-American subculture.

In projective testing, problems are not so much related to adaptation and administration as they are to interpretation of potentially limitless data. Later in this chapter, projective techniques will be discussed separately, if only to distinguish them from paper-and-pencil and other types of tests. Non-projective personality tests are subject to at least the same kinds of limitations as intelligence or ability tests, and pose certain special problems. A synthesis of general cross-cultural testing cautions follows, and later a closer look at some of the more widely used, as well as some of the more recent and promising tests, will be presented.

Definitions of tests (cf. Anastasi, 1968; Cronbach, 1970) include or imply the following elements (see Ortar, 1963, for an extended discussion):

1. a stimulus, or stimuli,
2. stimulus and administration standardization (objectivity),
3. response elicitation,
4. behavioral representativeness of sampled responses,
5. the existence of either measureable constructs or comparable criteria, and
6. suitable measurements and evaluation scales (norms).

## Stimuli, Verbal and Nonverbal

Assuming that the (usually American or British) test must be translated, and that norms comparable to those used in its *originating* culture will be used, translation is the single most important part of the adaptation process (in this context, verbal is distinguished from nonverbal "translation"). General translation problems and procedures were discussed in detail in Chapter 2, but specific, idiosyncratic problems are inherent in any verbal device, and even nonverbal tests are not absolutely free from translation problems (for example, with written or spoken instructions). Moreover, straight and simple literal translations will not do; the problem of equivalence must be solved [see, for example, Przeworski and Teune's (1970) book in this series].

The goal should be translation for equivalence, a dual process, and a major problem is that equivalence can be established only through a common external criterion, which itself may be elusive. In the introductory chapter we presented Gough's example of this type of equivalence (which he is temporarily calling intuitive, as opposed to linguistic, translation). The United States phrase "Every family owes it to the city to keep its lawn mowed in the summer and sidewalks shoveled in winter" has its intuitive French equivalent in the French item "The good citizen does not throw his garbage down the stairwell." There must be a matching of empirical connotations, item by item, culture by culture. Countless other examples can be given, and the reader may wish to exercise his imagination by formulating plausible translation equivalents of this type for many cultures for such common test items as "When is Washington's birthday?" "What do we celebrate on the 4th of July?" and "Name four men who have been presidents of the United States since 1900." Robertson and Batcheldor (1956) give a detailed discussion of these kinds of cultural adaptations in their British study using the Wechsler Adult Intelligence Scale.

The reader should completely understand Chapter 2 on translation before launching a test translation project. Nontesters too will benefit from a solid discussion with a psychologist familiar with tests and their internal components. It is too easy to ascribe incorrect, "face valid" meanings to individual items, for many of them are, upon examination, quite removed from what they *appear* designated to measure. The item "I like to take long walks in the woods," may intuitively suggest a certain personality type, while scoring it against appropriate external criteria could reveal a less face-valid type. For example, the above item may serve as one of several critical items which have successfully "predicted" extroversion better than they have predicted introversion. All other internal aspects of the test (format, instructions, recording of answers) should not be divorced from external conditions which may affect reliability, nor should the spoken or written directions and the role of the examiner, for example, how he is perceived and the possible ways he may influence the examinee (see Rosenthal, 1966, and below).

Most of the more frequently used or long-established American and British tests, whether of intelligence, academic achievement, personality, interests, values, or any other general area, have been translated, usually into many different languages. The Stanford Binet and the Wechsler series, for example, can probably be found in many more translated forms than the *Reader's Digest* (which boasts 13 translations). The test publisher, the copyright holder, or both, can provide researchers with bibliographies, at least, and quite likely the translated test itself. It is nearly a certainty that any Western test more than three years old has been translated or adapted for at least one non-western culture. It may take a dozen letters and some neat bibliographic detective work, considering the plethora of tests, to find what currently exists. Once in hand, however, a previously translated test by no means constitutes a license to apply it without first carefully considering its validity and reliability for its current cross-cultural use. In reporting an effort to find an optimal translation of a personality scale for the measurement of anxiety, Spreen (1961) wrote:

"Whereas [the validity of a translated test] obviously can be achieved by submitting [it] to the usual validation and reliability studies used on new tests, the possibility for cross-cultural comparisons diminishes the more changes [sic] are necessary for revalidation" (p. 1).

This means that unless successive approximations toward increasingly satisfactory cross-validation and reliability have been done, and unless such data are reasonably current, adapted translations may be faulty. Work with European versions of the translated Strong Vocational Interest Blanks is a case in point (cf. Lonner, 1968; Meijman, 1969). An apparently acceptable, but experimental, German adaptation of the men's form was used as the basis for adapting the similar women's form, but without much attention being given to cross-validating the latter. Further, the German version was the link between the original United States form in updating a rather old French adaptation of the 1937 SVIB. Validity must suffer in such a procedure, and only tenacious cross-validation can be the remedy. Making a utilitarian (lazy?) assumption that current and respectable validity across two or three cultures is acceptable for several others can lead one unknowingly to meaningless data. Without proven validity, the net result can be a gradual erosion of possibilities for any clear cross-cultural comparisons.

Contrary to what intuition may tell us, nonverbal, manipulative, and performance tests demand at least as much attention during adaptation as do verbal tests (see Werner and Campbell, 1970). Since verbal tests assume *familiarty* with the presented stimuli (words, sentences, numbers), and nonverbal tests (matrices, formboards, mazes) assume *unfamiliarity* with the stimuli, the former may actually have an initial edge in terms of understandability.

Ortar (1963) has arranged most test-related stimuli hierarchically, with the first two being most culture bound and, hence, most complex to adapt:

1. Pictures or models
2. Abstract performance materials
3. Abstract paper-and-pencil tests
4. Language materials
5. Number materials

The assumption that nonverbal stimuli have more nearly identical cross-cultural meaning is groundless. Ortar writes:

". . . This [assumption] ignores the fact that whereas the practice of using language as a means of communication is characteristic of all advanced cultures, the practice of using visual means to represent various kinds of subject-matters is not equally prevalent among all such cultures" (p. 221).

And further, ". . . only if the medium is perceived by the subject precisely as envisaged by the author, can the response be expected to refer to the identical subject matter" (p. 220). Lovegrove (1968) similarly writes,

"In industrial societies visual perception is the predominant means of communication. Pictures and diagrams are part-and-parcel of everyday living as is spatial thinking an essential feature of problem solving in a technological culture. This is not the case with African populations. Indeed tests with high diagrammatic or spatial content instead of favoring Africans present them with considerable difficulty. The simplicity of the African visual environment characterised by a comparative lack of clear lines of demarcation between figure and ground and by expanse and distance appear to have contributed towards the African's visual perception being holistic rather than analytic" (p. 785).

The works of Berry (1966), Hudson (1960), Witkin (1962, 1967), Wober (1966, 1967), Dawson (1967) and others, and earlier the work of Beveridge (1939) have opened a new and quite important area of research in perception-as-a-function-of-culture. Their work will be discussed later when specific tests, or types of tests, are presented, and other culture-perception material is presented in Chapter 4.

The use of nonverbal measures changes the nature of the translation (adaptation) problem but does not eliminate it. Anderson (1967), in discussing the problems of comparing nonverbal stimuli, used figures from the Welsh Figure Preference Test (see Figure 5.1) as an example of cultural differences in responding to them, and rightly states that one figure (Figure 5.1a)

". . . a biology student in any [Western] society could clearly and unambiguously interpret . . . [but that] Figure 5.1b, on the other hand, has no clearly understood meaning to [a Westerner] —yet an American Indian might well interpret it in terms of the pictographic symbol for 'mountain'"(p. 127).

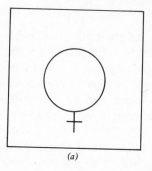
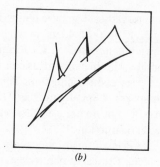

(a)                                                                                        (b)

**Figure 5-1.** Two figures from the Welsh Figure Preference Test.

The Ojibwa tribe's symbol for mountain is actually quite similar to to the Welsh drawing.

## Test Administration (Objectivity) and Response Elicitation

Most principles and procedures of administering tests to peoples unfamiliar with them have come from researchers who have concentrated on African cultures. Schwartz (1961), Price-Williams (1962), Cryns (1962), Brimble (1963), Irvine (1965), Silvey (1963), and MacArthur, Irvine, and Brimble (1964) are important examples. However, Vernon (1969) is a major guide in this area, since he has outlined many of the essential cautions, noting most of the above research in his own African and other cross-cultural work. Halfway around the globe, Hicks (1969), McElwain and Kearney (1970), and Ord (1970) have also attended to test administration problems, with special reference to their experiences in testing Papua and New Guinea and Australian Aborigine subjects.

The principles listed below are largely the result of pooling the writings of all those cited above, especially Vernon, Hicks, McElwain and Kearney, and Ord. If some of our own thoughts concerning administration procedures give the following list an aura of over-cautiousness with potential research subjects, it is because we were guided by the tired adage, "Always teach to the child (here, research subjects) of lowest ability; that way everyone will understand."

1. Be in polite control of the testing situation, and show skill, smoothness, and confidence at all times. Awkward or poorly prepared test handling may confuse the subject, who may interpret movements as part of the test.

2. All aspects of the testing procedure should be aimed at eliciting the expected response. Nothing, including the handling of pencils and papers and the recording of responses, should be taken for granted. Treat the preliminaries as a teaching situation, departing as little as possible from the teaching methods to which each examinee is accustomed. If possible, have the examinee point to the

response rather than have him write it.

3. If test booklets must be used (group administration), minimize the constraints imposed on the examinees in working from the first page to the last. Consider the benefits of using one page per item, or group of items, collecting each page upon completion. This would eliminate the need for the examinee to turn pages. "Spiral omnibus" (heterogenerously arranged items) tests should normally not be used. Rather, each separate test should be preceded by its own special instructions.

4. Printed instructions on the test booklet or answer sheets should be avoided. Critical junctures (starting, stopping, and turning pages) should be controlled by the examiner. Do not, however, assume that oral instructions are without problems. Individual examiners will vary in voice, clarity, and manner, and the examinees' dependence on the examiner may increase rather than reduce constraints. In New Guinea, Hicks (1969) found that the most difficult arithmetical questions were those which used the most words—not necessarily because of weaker numerical ability but because of inability to understand some of the questions asked.

5. The test should be explained through the use of visual aids, paralleling as closely as possible the exact operation to be performed. Blackboards can be used with those who are familiar with them, but only for material that they will understand when using this medium. For figural and any unfamiliar material, mock-ups, large diagrams done to scale, or other means of explanation or instruction should be used, and these should be oral. Such instructions must take into account idiosyncrasies of local speech and expression.

6. Preliminary to the actual test, supervised practice should be allowed and encouraged, and clear feedback to each examinee should be given. Variations in both basic tasks and individual items or groups of similar items should be considered as units and practiced separately. The regular teachers of the examinees might well be used as helpers or administrators, especially since the examiner may not know when to proceed with the assurance that the goals of the practice session have been met. Cultural values (e.g., unwillingness to ask questions, to admit confusion, or to outdo their peers) may give false assurance to proceed. Coaching may not add a great deal. In using the Raven Progressive Matrices with African secondary school children, Silvey (1963) found that scores increased by an average of fifteen percent after one trial attempt, by seven percent after an explained example of each type of problem, and by twenty-two percent for subjects who were given both explanation and practice. Lloyd and Pidgeon (1961) found that European, African, and Indian children showed similar gains in pure practice effects, while Indian children showed little gain from coaching. Certain Indian cultural values were given as possible reasons for this difference.

7. Different motivational influences should be considered as means to increase cooperation. Labov (1970) sat on the floor with young subjects and ate potato chips with them to create a pleasant atmosphere. Changes in the routine of school, or testing in a room or building different from the one associated with the routine may be exciting. The "specialness" of the experience supervised by a foreigner should be emphasized. On the other hand, too much of an exciting change of pace could lead to inattentiveness. Be observant of any changes in the motivation or attention of subjects, and take a break when fatigue or stress is suspected.

8. Be wary of what messages are being transmitted nonverbally. Subjects of a different language are adept at in gauging the gestures and tones of the voice of the examiner to seek cues indicating approval of their actions. Similarly, if an interpreter is used, carefully watch his gestures or tone of voice which may be influencing the subjects. Also, make certain that the interpreter understands exactly what he is to do. He may be quick to please the tester or quick to say that he readily understands the test and his duties during testing when he actually does not.

9. When testing subjects individually, it may be wise to leave the doors of the testing room open so that the subject does not feel closeted, or so that he will be in visual contact with his peers. Perhaps permit or even encourage other subjects to look in on the testing through doors and windows. This may both soothe the subject being tested and reduce the anxieties of those onlookers who are yet to be tested. If it will cause no interference, two testers operating at the same time may want to conduct the administration in the same room so that those being tested can see one another. Also, it should be insured that the first person being tested carries back a favorable report to those who are waiting their turn.

10. To the extent that the items allow, familiar items or those closest to immediate experience, should be given first, followed by more unusual, unfamiliar, or abstract items. The items should be suited to the examinee's environment, and this must be determined by experiment or tryout. Items suspected of not being understood are better off discarded or replaced. All test material other than what is being used at the moment should be out of the subject's visual field. The task at hand should be easily reached by the subject, for example, he should not have a low chair or he should not have to squat.

11. Some children may be skilled in picking up "postures of response assent" (eye or head movements, or general body tension) conveyed by the examiner. Aborigine children, especially females, are apparently skilled in "playing the game" of selecting the correct response not through an analysis of the test item but by cueing on the responses of the tester.

12. After practice, instructions, and the test are given, consider administering the test again as soon as practicable, throwing out first efforts. Or at least first

efforts can be compared with retests and examined for noteworthy differences. A second or even third testing may develop confidence and give more accurate results. Another tactic to consider is to allow all subjects to reach an asymptote, test a final time, and measure results from the asymptotic base.

13. Test content should be examined and cleansed of any items that are superfluous or potentially impossible to understand without a great deal of instruction. Certain spatial relations-type items or inferred three-dimensional items may be of this order. The overall test variety and number of items should be just enough to get the essence of what is being measured. Avoid frills unless they are truly of experimental interest.

14. Speeded tests should be avoided unless speed is a critical factor in what is being measured (e.g., assembly and miniature work sample tests, and clerical tests). Take into account the cultural valuation of time and speed. If speeded tests must be used, the subject may have to be constantly motivated to work as quickly as he can. Power and speed tests in combination, however, give added information. Knapp (1960) found, for example, that speed tests following power tests resulted in higher scores for samples of both Mexican and American subjects.

15. Never discuss a subject's performance with others in his presence, even in a language the subject does not understand. Gestures and tones of voice can communicate performance.

16. The particular sexual codes of the culture should be understood and eliminated as a negative factor in testing. For example, if the subject is an adolescent female and the examiner is a prohibited male, testing may be impossible.

17. A friendly touch or pat on the head by an adult stranger may not be interpreted as encouragement or friendliness, and should therefore be avoided.

18. People being tested may have a variety of names (baptismal, tribal, secret, or nickname), and it would be helpful to find the proper name for the foreign examiner to use. Nicknames derived from English may be derogatory, and should be used with caution.

19. Rewarding children with sweets or small gifts may be appropriate, although some testers suggest avoiding this because it has not always made a difference in attitude or cooperation. However, adults who are brought away from their work for testing may have to make up time lost on the job. Therefore, paying adults the prevailing rate for time away from their jobs would be a good practice.

Biesheuvel (1949) has extensively discussed test adaptation and administration problems, and cites examples and cautions similar to those above. His comments concerning attitudes toward the test situation, temperamental factors, and the effects of schooling are important to summarize here. For example, he writes:

"For a number of reasons it is virtually impossible to equate motivation in different cultural groups. The competitive spirit is not as strong in non-European groups, where it is one of the chief cultural manifestations. The non-European will therefore not be greatly concerned about doing well in order to beat his fellows, unless of course he has acquired the European outlook. Doing well in the test for its own sake is likely to occur only when the purpose of testing and its full implications are appreciated. The uneducated non-European has very little notion of what it is all about, and those who are educated know only too well from past experience that conclusions unfavourable to their racial or cultural group are likely to be drawn from the findings. This produces attitudes varying from outright hostility and refusal to do the tests, to going through the motions without making much effort, or to an uneasiness which by its inhibiting effect impairs the efficiency of thought. . . . Such a constitutional factor [of many non-European groups to work continuously at high speed] may also play a part in determining capacity for sustained effort, although physical condition, incentives, and motivation generally account for the major differences in drive" (p. 69).

Lastly, Biesheuvel suggests that ". . .regardless of test medium, the groups to be compared should have an equivalent amount of schooling from equally well-trained teachers" (p. 70).

Biesheuvel then cites an earlier study by Dent (1937) documenting the superiority of the school-going groups over the non-school-going groups, and at the same time showing that these differences could not be due to environmental or progressive parental attitudes only. But such control group procedures are impracticable if not impossible, for, as Biesheuvel concludes,

"The extensive control of the educational factor which appears to be desirable cannot, however, be achieved, unless the two races to be compared share a common culture or one has thoroughly assimilated the culture and enjoys equality of opportunity within it . . . and that these conditions cannot be satisfied in the majority of inter-racial intelligence test studies" (p. 71).

All the above cautions and potential problems in test administration may leave the reader stunned to the point that he may be afraid to move a finger or utter a word, lest something go wrong. However, one may never encounter *all* these problems or even a majority of them in any given project. Test administration conditions will vary by culture; some conditions will pose few problems, others may present numerous obstacles. If the above points are used as guides, the experienced tester should, by checking them against the particular requirements or constraints of his project, confidently proceed with the assumption that nothing will go wrong.

## Behavioral Representativeness of Sampled Responses

The type of behavior to be sampled and compared cross-culturally through tests must be carefully examined. By Western definitions, intelligence, achievement, and ability tests are designed to measure *maximum* performance, while other instruments are designed to measure *typical* performance. This latter category includes personality, interest, attitude, and values questionnaires and inventories. In competitive Western cultures, tests of maximum performance are reflections of the culture, and the test construction is predicated on such competition. Intelligence and achievement tests, especially when they are obviously being used for selection and placement, are classic examples. To coax or coach individuals from non-competitive (in the Western sense) cultures into performing "maximally" may result in an unrepresentative sample of maximum behavior on that culture's terms. In other words, a tested sample of maximum behavior in the West is culturally isomorphic, while sampling such behavior using Western-type tests in non-Western countries may be culturally irrelevant or inappropriate. With differential test-taking motivation, an American group of college-bound high school students taking, for example, the CEEB (College Entrance Examination Boards), will be expected to score higher than a group of non-college bound (or even college-bound, depending on the competition) Korean students taking an equivalent test, even if all other factors, save for motivation, appear to be equivalent.

The construct, "intelligence," is worthy of close attention, and since this time-honored kingpin of all psychological constructs is, like all others, man-made, it warrants even closer attention when viewed cross-culturally. Conceptions of and the underlying logic of other constructs, when couched in cross-cultural terms, may closely parallel some of the more recent modes of analysis and reasoning involving the construct of intelligence. Other common family names in Western psychology, for example, "anxiety," "introversion," "dominance," "hyperactive," and many more may require a shift in logical analysis before we can assume such psychological shorthand to be valid for all cultures.

It is beyond the scope of this book to wrestle with the various conceptions of human intelligence. However, researchers may want to be familiar with such positions as Cattell's fluid ($G_f$) and crystallized ($G_c$) intelligence (Cattell, 1963), Guilford's "three-faces" theory (Guilford, 1967; Guilford & Hoepfner, 1971), Spearman's "g" (Spearman, 1904, which incidentally, has historically received more attention cross-culturally than any of its bedfellows), "Experience-Produced Drives" (Hayes, 1962), Thurstone's Primary Mental Abilities (Thurstone, 1938), Guttman's Facet Theory (Guttman, 1965), and others. Most of these theoretical positions are nicely summarized in McReynolds (1968). There is another conception of intelligence which, though not necessarily singled out here as our nomination as the "best," will nevertheless help illustrate the critical need to keep psychological constructs in focus and in context in cross-cultural research. This illustrative model is Hebb's (1949) distinction between Intelligence A (genotypic) which, it is said, cannot be measured or observed, and Intelligence B (phenotypic), which is the product of nature (genetic equipment) and nurture. Intelligence B may be considered a trait or characteristic that exists to the extent that environmental conditions permit. To Intelligences A and B has been added Intelligence C (Vernon, 1955), which is no more, and no less, than a tested measure of Intelligence B, the stream of intelligence, and a possible inference to Intelligence A, the wellsprings. Further, genetic equipment and physiologic equipment are not synonymous. In his impressive study and discussion of the interaction between intelligence and culture, Vernon (1969) makes two additional points about Intelligence B that are important for our immediate purposes:

1. It is not static or fixed for life. A child's intelligence may rise or fall if his environment, education, or personality are altered.

2. We must discard the idea that Intelligence B is a kind of universal faculty, a trait that is the same (apart from variations in amount) in all cultural groups.

Vernon's work is replete with evidence favoring his and Hebb's stances and, of course, the positions of others. Slightly more recent work by Irvine (1970) graphically displays that the construct, Intelligence X (not necessarily to be alphabetized with A, B, and C), is one "used to label scores from intelligence tests used in non-Western cultures and adapted from Western tests in the knowledge that such scores carry with them variance from indigenous thought systems" (p. 24). Irvine further notes the

". . .contention that the values of non-Western societies with a considerable oral tradition for the transmission of skills will prescribe the criteria for intelligent acts. Such acts may require a completely different use of knowledge from that of the individually competitive, industrial West. The precise relationship of this kind of intelligent act to the kind of act that is recognized as intelligent in Western societies is as yet unknown" (p. 24).

A most useful example of the probable fallibility of blindly importing Western constructs is given by Irvine (1969a, 1970). Drawing from the work of anthropologists and sociologists in Africa, Irvine supports the position that the control of kin relationships through the spirit world, in which ancestors play a crucial role, affects intelligent acts quite unlike systems of causation in Western societies. The anthropological evidence is that knowledge of the environment is based upon a "categorization of objects and people that is directly related to their capacity for influencing the acts and fortunes of others" (p. 26). The Mashona of Central Africa were chosen by Irvine to illustrate this dimension of intelligence.

Consider a correlation model for Western theories (the shaded area in Figure 5.2), where $R_{11}$ represents intercorrelations of a battery of ability and attainment tests (e.g., verbal, numerical, abstract reasoning) used to predict "capacity to perform cognitive tasks that are highly valued in societies stressing technology, individualism, and competition," and where $R_{22}$ represents intercorrelations of tests such as those used by Guilford (1966) in his structure of intellect model (e.g., divergent production, evaluation) or by Thurstone's (1938) primary abilities (e.g., word fluency, spatial abilities, and perceptual speed). $R_{21}$ and $R_{12}$ would represent intercorrelations of these types of tests.

To this familiar four cell matrix add tests of the $R_{33}$ kind and their intercorrelations (unshaded areas of Figure 5.2) with the $R_{11}$ and $R_{22}$ type. Among Mashona, the $R_{33}$ kind of test would be based upon their beliefs as the basis of intelligent acts *unlike* Western intelligent acts. Using rules and observances of the Mashona (compiled in Shona dictionary form by missionaries and ethnographers), Irvine has used such predominant beliefs as: (a) A woman must not sit on a hearthstone; her husband might die; (b) do not express admiration for natural objects (e.g., as a tree or its fruit); you might develop an antipathy to marriage; and (c) do not destroy the eggs of a crow; you may cause no rain to fall in your area. Such statements have been classified in terms of "the knowledge required before the statement can be understood; and second, the consequence of nonobservance of the rule, i.e., whether the possible causal effects are on kin (statement a), or on oneself (statement b), or on natural phenomena (statement c)." Table 5.1 shows the analysis of 113 such statements. The most common kind of knowledge is of natural objects and animals, or objects with sexual or social connotations, of personal habits and symptoms, and of utensils and utilities. Note the lack of emphasis on time, an important

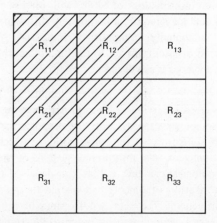

**Figure 5-2.** An intercorrelation matrix which would accommodate "Non-Western-type" factors (the unshaded cells).

behavioral factor in Western societies.

Intelligent Shona acts are thus of a conforming kind, with "primary reference to the affective climatė of one's own relationships with the spiritual force of the living and ancestral spirits of the kin group" (Irvine, 1969a, p. 99).

It is Irvine's contention that the hypothetical $R_{33}$ dimension would have to measure the mode of thought that "perceives events and uses knowledge in a complex field of personal relationships whose organization is essentially affective" (p. 99). Of particular importance would be the $R_{13}$ and $R_{23}$ parts of the matrix to determine the relationship of skills peculiar to the African (in this example) or those skills peculiar to other cultural groups with those imported by educational or other means. Irvine's hypothetical model suggests the following generalization: it may be that intelligent behavior as measured by school-type tests is little related to intelligence behavior in the village ($R_{13}$), but that certain underlying processes of the type Guilford's model, for example, includes [such as memory, evaluation, and discrimination], would be common across all behaviors, regardless of the mode of thinking, for one cultural group ($R_{23}$). Irvine concludes that

"...to conceive of intelligence as a statistical construct with the same meaning in other cultures that impose rules of behavior by means of a value system that is only partially related to that of Western societies, could mislead further efforts to clarify the roles of language, ecology, and affect on cognition within and across cultures, if only because it would tend to inhibit the sampling of behavioral domains that are irrelevant in the construction of "intelligence" tests in western societies, but are extremely relevant in the observed behavior of traditional, and predominantly oral, societies" (1970, pp.28-29).

Table 5.1    Analysis of 113 Mashona Observances and Omens[a]

| Consequence of Action on | Knowledge Required | | | | | |
|---|---|---|---|---|---|---|
| | Natural Objects, Animals, | Kin, Sex, Social | Personal Habits, Symptoms | Utilities | Seasons, time | Total |
| Self | 22 | 19 | 15 | 7 | 0 | 63 |
| Kin and community | 14 | 9 | 3 | 7 | 1 | 34 |
| Natural phenomenon | 5 | 1 | 1 | 1 | 2 | 10 |
| Natural objects, animals | 1 | 2 | 1 | 2 | 0 | 6 |
| Totals | 42 | 31 | 20 | 17 | 3 | 113 |

[a]From Irvine, S. H. (1970, p. 27).

Cross-cultural psychology will likely find that many different "types" of intelligence or intelligent acts are quite functional, and that they can lead to perfectly acceptable solutions to problems *without* necessarily inferring that a certain pet theory of intelligence "explains" observed intelligent behavior. If a certain type of thinking appears odd, do not dismiss its importance. Remember that at one time the Volkswagen looked odd on American streets.

Possible difficulties could arise even when dealing with seemingly unimpeachable visual processes, and data from cross-cultural research on perception (discussed below) can be useful in constructing "simple" items requiring only rudimentary visual discrimination. For example, in constructing an intelligence test for use in secondary schools in Nigeria, Taylor and Bradshaw (1965) included an item in a classification subtest which required the candidate to "find the picture which does not belong" (see Figure 5.3). Not knowing the rules of the game, subjects unfamiliar with tests could opt for the size constancy of the presented alternatives as the criterion, justifiably picking the relatively small horse as the "wrong picture." Other plausible reasons could lead to a wrong answer; for example, of the five representations only the dog does no carrying (in most cultures). The same kind of "illogical" analysis may penalize a creative Westerner, but at least the West has a cultural expectation for "typical" responses. We may not know a priori what is an expected or acceptable answer in many cultures. Taylor and Bradshaw presented no item analysis, so we cannot pursue this example further in terms of unexpected cognition in selecting alternatives. But this example should reinforce the dictum that nothing on the part of the examinee's perception of such items should be taken for granted. A recent study reinforces this conclusion. Guthrie, Brislin, and Sinaiko (1970) investigated the differences that scale irregularities (such as those in Figure 5.3) can cause. In a study of Vietnamese and United States mechanics, they showed that those items with constancy differences were a major factor in obtained scores, causing the Vietnamese to score lower on a tool-knowledge test. Further, those Vietnamese who *could* deal with the constancy differences tended to do better in a mechanics' training course than their counterparts who had constancy problems.

**Figure 5-3.** An example of a constancy problem among pictorial test items.

## The Importance of Either Measurable Constructs or Comparable Criteria

Cross-cultural use of tests of typical performance, generally under the broad umbrella of personality tests, require the same administrative cautions as others, but their use, construction, and especially their interpretation demand special care. In the United States and other Western nations it is quick, impressive (usually for the client), and reasonably productive to "slip somebody a test," to use clinical argot, as an expedient means to assess and to play the parlor game, "Let's see how *they* do on *our* test," often with each player using his own set of rules and scoring system or norms. It is a double indictment for psychological ethnocentrism that so much attention has been given to validation within the test-originating culture and so little thought to cross-cultural cross-validation, although the current trend is more promising.

Personality tests can be classified as either criterion-oriented (criterion keyed, empirical or "atheoretical") or construct-oriented (theory-related or rational). Gordon and Kikuchi (1966) questioned the validity of using criterion-oriented tests in cross-cultural research, arguing that internationally varying criteria may result in uninterpretable results cross-culturally. Translating and applying an instrument used to measure truly culture-bound criteria in a culture other than the one for which it was intended may lead to scores quite unrelated to the "same" criteria in the target culture. This obviously means that tests may be translatable and understandable in other cultures, while norms may not be. There is ample evidence that even if criteria (for example, those used to "key" the Strong Vocational Interest Blank or the Minnesota Multiphasic Personality Inventory) are meaningful in other cultures, norms must be based on all the subtle characteristics of individual cultural groups and their particular range of human variation. Our point is that many personality tests may have to be revalidated in other cultures and that it can *never* be assumed *prima facie* that any given set of one-culture norms are cross-culturally valid.

If criteria are essentially culture-bound, the mandate would then be to use construct-related tests. This is essentially Gordon and Kikuchi's position: "...the items in such tests represent samplings from a universe of items that help define the constructs, and test results are interpreted in terms of the constructs rather than the particular items that happen to be used" (p. 180). Further, they recommend that before a test is translated there should be reason to believe that the construct, measured by the items in the original test, is meaningful (exists) in the target or second culture, and that the joy of easily translatable items is not sufficient reason to assume that the construct exists in the second culture.

In his response to Gordon and Kikuchi, Berrien (1968) argued that criterion-developed tests and construct-oriented tests are "aspects of a common problem which cannot be handled by accepting one approach and rejecting the other" (p. 4), and that the distinction involves "the way in which a construct is viewed cross-culturally."

Using a hypothetical range of behavior indicative of some construct, represented by Figure 5.4, Berrien suggests that if there is item overlap (A-C in culture X and B-D in culture Y, for example), it would be possible to link the two cultures together through the overlap in the B-C range. In this example, the issue is the operational definition of the construct, that is, "whether one looks at it from the standpoint of the criterion, or the test items which sample the universe of behaviors defining the construct" (p. 4). The differential distribution of the same construct among cultures, and the Gordon and Kikuchi recommendation that both sets of items in the two forms should reflect the same level or strength of the construct *within* each culture, to be accomplished by including as many identical items as possible in both forms by the test, is a central issue. Berrien approached this issue by suggesting that,

"In the first place, the vast majority of criterion-developed tests for aptitudes and achievements have not proven to be highly predictive even when the criteria have been clearly defined and factorially simple. This is not to say validity coefficients have not been useful when combined with selection ratios and expectancy tables for certain purposes. However, the predictive success of those few criterion-developed personality tests as a class has been even more disappointing. Nevertheless the continued use of both types of tests can be justified largely on the grounds of construct validity [Cronbach and Meehl, 1955]. It therefore appears that the distinction which Gordon and Kikuchi draw between the two kinds of problems above actually involves *the way in which is construct is conceived cross-culturally*" (p.4).

Berrien's solution of both overlap and extended limits lies in recognizing the bicultural or multicultural limits of the construct, particularly if one is to interpret the findings "in terms of the construct rather than the specific items that happen to be used." The solution would require that "all items (insofar as they are understandable) used in all forms be administered to all samples. Such a procedure would probably result in some items being nondiscriminating in

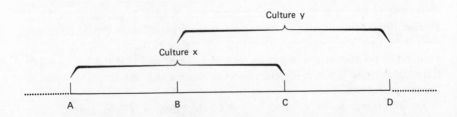

**Figure 5-4.** A hypothetical overlap between two cultures on a psychological construct.

culture X that would be highly discriminating in Y, and vice versa" (p. 5). Berrien noted also that this is the case in employing intelligence tests over large age ranges that represent different age subcultures.

Gordon's (1968) response to Berrien contains counterarguments and counter-proposals, and this three-part exchange is a valuable series which goes beyond the construct-criterion discussion. Consideration is also given to item selection and other matters of critical importance to those planning to use questionnaire-type personality measures. It should be noted that this exchange contained a discussion of the meaning and intercorrelation of Berrien's (1964) Edwards Personal Preference Schedule study and Kikuchi and Gordon's (1966) Survey of Interpersonal Values study, both of which concentrated on Japanese adaptations and translations of the respective instruments. In a later study of Japanese and American values through the use of the Survey of Personal Values (Kikuchi and Gordon, 1970), cross-cultural comparisons of values were made only after determining that the Japanese translation also carried the constructs implied in the instrument. Through "factorial structure, reliabilities, relationships with other [Japanese] personality measures, and group differences" (p. 185), evidence was claimed regarding the possibility of comparing the constructs cross-culturally. These comparisons of different types of data are necessary for cross-cultural understanding, a point made in the introductory chapter.

Berrien (1967) earlier suggested that

"the way out of this dilemma [of items measuring psychological variables in culture A but inappropriate for culture B] is to ensure by both rational and empirical means that the construct is meaningful in the cultures under examination. This can be done by determining whether the measures of the constructs vary in relation to some other independent variable(s) as hypothe-sized from some theory. Ideally, such a theory should specify fundamental behavioral dimensions whose definitions are culture-free" (pp. 40-41).

Berrien's position is flexible and open-ended, unlike the position taken by some who tend to treat constructs and criteria as completely different entities. Criteria and their guiding construct(s) can help define each other. For instance, an American who has taken the MMPI may meet all the designated criteria (behavioral signs and clinical appraisal) to be correctly psychometrically classified as paranoid. Since the "nomological network" and its systematic inferences that are used to help define the construct, paranoid, include the criterion (observable) values attributed to it (i.e., MMPI responses identical to MMPI responses of "known" paranoids), is it not possible that the same criterion values can be reached in other cultures? If so, then it is also possible that the same underlying construct (i.e., the cultural meaning of the diagnosis) can be concomitantly measured elsewhere. Part of this criterion-construct issue may be due to an apparent reticence by many to admit that much of the Western world, at least, is an amorphous blend of more similarities than differences. John Wayne and Donald Duck will eventually reach even the heart of the Amazon jungle. If criteria are becoming increasingly interchangeable, then the interchangeability of theory-related constructs cannot be far behind.

## Empirical Approaches to Cross-Validation

Obviously, the ideal cross-cultural personality test would be one whose items have universal applicability and whose diagnostic or descriptive scales have common international referents. Construct and criterion would indeed be synonymous.

Harrison Gough, the creator of the California Psychological Inventory, maintains that the CPI items were written in "folk language" which tap "folk concepts." These concepts, Gough writes,

". . .occur in everyday social living and, in fact arise from social interaction and are aspects and attributes of interpersonal behavior that are to be found in all cultures and societies, and that possess a direct and integral relationship to all forms of social interaction" (1968, p. 67).

Much of Gough's recent work has been on the cross-cultural validation of the CPI. For instance, the socialization scale of the CPI successfully diagnoses delinquency in the United States. Gough (1965) has shown that the translated scale makes the same known-groups differentiation in several other cultures. See Chapter 8 for other CPI examples. Gough has also been a key innovator and theorizer with respect to translation and validation problems encountered in the cross-cultural adaptation of tests, questionnaires, and inventories. His work in this area is among the best available.

Brislin's (1970) approach to the cross-cultural use of personality and "standardized" tests involves decentering, the process of revising the original English to attain an adequate translation. He suggests that an English scale be translated, back-translated, and edited to alleviate problems, such as phrases that have no ready equivalent in the target language. The edited English verson, now likely to be more easily translatable, becomes the first step in the procedure, which is repeated several more times. The process ends when the back-translation and first-step version are identical by some quantifiable standard, as discussed in the translation chapter. Brislin wanted the Marlowe-Crowne (Crowne and Marlowe, 1964) social desirability scale translated into Chamorro, and obtained equivalent first-step and back-translation after three translations. The original and decentered (revised) English were then different. For instance, the original item 4, "I have never intensely disliked anyone" became "I have never really disliked someone" in the third back-translation. The original item 16, "I am always willing to admit it when I make a mistake" became "I will always admit when I am wrong."

To test the equivalence of the revised English and the Chamorro translation, 80 bilinguals received either the English ($N$ = 20), Chamarro ($N$ = 20), or combined English-Chamorro ($N$ = 40) scales. Similar means and variances, and high split-half correlation coefficients ($r \geqslant .85$) indicated adequate reliability of the revised English and of the translation, and equivalence of the different language versions. To test the equivalence of the original and revised English, 80 American college students received either the original ($N$ = 20), revised ($N$ = 20), or combined original-revised ($N$ = 40) English scales. Means, variances, and split-half correlation coefficients ($r \geqslant .85$) indicated the equivalence of the original and revised English. The means, incidentally, were quite comparable to the standards reported by Crowne and Marlowe (1964) for similar populations. It seems, then, that a "standardized statesider" scale can be revised to make translation possible, and if the revision can be demonstrated as equivalent to the original, then past research using the original can be used in making cross-cultural comparisons and arguments. Demonstrating equivalences of original and revised English, and translation of the revision, can assure good cross-cultural data. At the same time, the previous studies that have used the test with samples in the United States can be profitably compared with the new cross-cultural data. There will probably be instances in which certain items must be revised so much (to achieve good translation) that they will no longer be comparable to the original. The above technique can identify those items. Such extreme action may be needed in 10 items of a 40-item test. Perhaps the remaining 30 items can be linked to past single-country literature again for comparison purposes.

Glatt (1969) also gathered data to evaluate a test adapted for other cultures, in this case the MMPI which was mentioned above. The test was translated into German, Spanish, and French and administered to bilinguals who took the test both in English and in one of the other three languages. The translations were evaluated by studying mean scale score differences between English and other-language versions, correlations between scale scores, diagnoses by clinicians based on blind analyses of both versions, and clinicians' judgments as to personality "change" as represented by the two tests. The results showed that certain scales (pathology, deviance, and peculiarity) were likely to manifest more abnormality in the translations than in the English, and that one of the translations was not very good. Both Brislin (1970) and Glatt (1969), however, have not taken the next step of cross-validating their translations in the other cultures. That is, they do not know whether their tests differentiate people in the other cultures in the same way as the tests do in the original culture. Glatt emphasizes this problem, indicating that people are using scoring keys developed in the United States rather than doing the necessary work to develop their own in the other culture. Furthermore, it is now generally recognized in the United

States that the MMPI "diagnostic" scales (i.e., hysteria, psychopathic deviate) do not parallel the old Kraepelinian psychiatric nosology which the MMPI researchers originally used as a model, but this is a problem of minor importance in view of current MMPI use. (See Chapter 8 for additional comments concerning the MMPI.)

## Projective Techniques

The term *projection* is attributed to Sigmund Freud, and his most famous account of projection as an ego defense mechanism is discussed in the case of the paranoid Dr. Schreber (Freud, 1911). Freud used the term as early as 1895, and it was a central concept in his single anthropological sortie, especially with regard to the development of taboos (Freud, 1913). Jung also used the concept of projection in a word association technique used to identify unconscious conflicts, which he called complexes. It was psychoanalytic theory and holism (the emphasis on studying behavior in full context, or macroscopically, rather than its small components, or microscopically) that stimulated the cultural anthropological use of projective techniques.

To guide us in this section we shall use Lindzey's (1961) definition of a projective technique:

"...a projective technique is an instrument that is considered especially sensitive to covert or unconscious aspects of behavior, it permits or encourages a wide variety of subject responses, is highly multidimensional, and it evokes unusually rich or profuse response data with a minimum of subject awareness concerning the purpose of the test. Further, it is very often true that the stimulus material presented by the projective test is ambiguous, interpreters of the test depend upon holistic analysis, the test evokes fantasy responses, and there are no correct or incorrect responses to the test" (1961, p. 45).

Buros' (1970) major compendium of personality tests and reviews includes nearly 100 old, new, dying, or dead tests classified as projectives. A major text devoted to projective techniques (Rabin, 1968) discusses at least 50 instruments in terms of their validity, reliability, and overall usefulness. At least one writer (Kaplan, 1961) notes that more than 150 studies done in 75 societies have used projective techniques, and his figures were estimated more than a decade ago; surely by now the number of studies has at least doubled. Presenting these figures here is not intended to startle the rugged empiricist or to delight the dedicated ideographer; merely listing non-projective tests would fill a small dictionary. These figures do, however, suggest that to discuss the value and potential of projective techniques in cross-cultural research requires a special book. There is such a book, and the reader is directed to Lindzey's (1961) *Projective Techniques and Cross-Cultural Research.* To attempt here a coverage of projective techniques as broad as Lindzey's would be pretentious and redundant, and space obviously would not permit it. We shall merely discuss projectives generally and give a summary of Lindzey's findings and implicit recommendations, as well as the views of others who have surveyed projectives as cross-cultural tools. We shall also present a summary of perhaps the most significant recent advance in projective testing, the Holtzman Inkblot Technique.

A quarter century ago the noted anthropologist Hallowell, probably the leading figure in stimulating the anthropological use of projectives, considered it paradoxical that anthropologists have historically been interested in the bones of extinct people and in talking with people and recording their languages. Commentating about the period between 1915-1945, he observed that only in the last 30 years, however, have ". . .some anthropologists. . .begun to look their erstwhile informants in the eye and to think about them as *people*" (Hallowell, 1945, p. 195). Then, as now, the projective device, long a strong arm of the psychoanalyst and clinical psychologist, allowed anthropologists to give measurable dimensions to the characteristics of cultures holistically, in full context, with little concern for studying individual personalities as a clinician would do.

If the famous Rorschach Inkblot Test[1] was not the maid of honor in the unsettled marriage of anthropology, the study of man, and psychology, the study of people, it was certainly the ringbearer. Herman Rorschach himself recommended that his test, which first appeared in 1921, was well suited for cross-cultural research, and the first such use of his test was probably done in 1921 by the master himself (see Rorschach, 1942). Bleuler and Bleuler's (1935) comparison of some unspecified Europeans and 29 Moroccans may have signalled the start of a psychology-anthropology rapprochement via projectives, aided and abetted by the first reported cross-cultural use of the Thematic Apperception Test (Henry, 1947), in which Hopi and Navajo children were the subjects. Following these initial studies using the two chief projective devices, the Rorschach and the TAT, came an increasing number of studies using them and many other projectives, and also a parade of new adaptations of existing techniques used for cross-cultural research.

Lindzey explained the considerable preference for projective techniques in culture and personality study when he wrote

"For various reasons, projective techniques have appeared to many observers to offer more possibility for cross-cultural application than most other personality instruments, which often display a heavy dependence upon a given language and specific cultural content or experience. Consequently, as the empirical study of various problems concerned with the relation between cultural variables on the one hand and personality variables on the other has

[1] See Sundberg (1961) and Lubin, Wallis, and Paine (1971) for evidence that overall use of the Rorschach in the United States is declining slightly, being replaced by other tests.

expanded, there have been increasing demands upon projective techniques to fill the need for an instrument that can make meaningful statements concerning personalities from a variety of cultures" (1961, p. 9).

Rabin (1968), following Lindzey, gives a five-fold classification of projective techniques:

1. Association techniques (word association, Rorschach).
2. Construction techniques (TAT, the Blacky Pictures) in which the subject "constructs" a story once presented with the stimulus.
3. Completion techniques (sentence completion, Rosenzweig Picture-Frustration Study).
4. Choice or ordering techniques (Szondi, Picture Arrangement).
5. Expressive techniques (psychodrama, painting).

The use of projective techniques demands the same cautious approaches required in the use of other tests, discussed earlier. They may, in fact, require certain special cautions, especially in interpretation. Moreover, the so-called "ambiguous" stimuli of projective techniques, which are often assumed to be their major advantage for cross-cultural research, may be as culture-bound as the stimuli which many paper-and-pencil tests present to the subject. Perhaps the ink-blot stands alone among projectives as a more or less genuinely ambiguous stimulus, all other techniques bearing traces of the culture in which they originated.

It was pointed out earlier that visual stimuli, which so many projectives present to subjects, are at least as equally culture-bound as verbal stimuli. The Walt Disney-like appearance of the Blacky Pictures, the American middle-class context of the Rosenzweig Picture Frustration Study, the grossly outdated and macabre "mug shots" of the Szondi Test, and the famous TAT cards, many of which carry the somberness and character of movies, novels, and newsreels of the United States in the 1930's and 1940's, are but a few examples of the material with which the cross-cultural projective tester will be working, adapting, and attempting to extract sufficiently valid data. And it may take more than merely substituting a polar bear cub and his family for the family of dogs used in the psychoanalytically oriented Blacky Pictures (for use with Eskimos, presumably), or changing the color of skin in the P-F Study pictures, or the photographs used in the Szondi (for use with nonwhites). Riess, Schwartz, and Cottingham (1950), for example, found that substituting Negro skin color for white skin color in the TAT card does not facilitate the response of Negro subjects, noting that it may in fact impede it. Also, Hudson (1960) and others have found that members of some cultures have difficulty interpreting three-dimensional cues in Western-made pictures. Several of the above-mentioned tests have been devised with the tacit assumption that three-dimensional cues are easily interpreted from their two dimensional counterparts in a drawing or photograph. Cross-culturally, this is definitely a very risky assumption.

Many investigators have created special adaptations of the TAT or CAT (Children's Apperception Test) cards for use with particular groups. Thompson (1949a, 1949b) modified the TAT for use with Negroes (which Riess et al., and others, have usually found wanting). Among other attempted TAT adaptations are: for American Indians (Alexander and Anderson, 1957; Henry, 1947; Pastor, 1970); for South African natives (Lee, 1953; Sherwood, 1957); and for Pacific Islanders (Lessa and Spiegelman, 1954). Modified versions have been used with studies investigating achievement, affiliation, dominance, group cohesiveness, national character, personnel selection, and more. Perhaps the only card of the TAT series not requiring adaptation is the one blank card.

Missing Lindzey's review by only months was de Ridder's (1961) comprehensive study of the personality of urban South Africans, in which a specially adapted TAT was the central instrument used. It is not known why de Ridder apparently did not consult Sherwood's (1957) detailed monograph which was addressed specifically to the design of modified TAT pictures for use in South Africa, giving 14 criteria to use as guides in modifying pictures so as to insure their appropriateness in a cultural context. These guides can certainly be a primary source to be used in adapting the TAT for use in virtually any culture. Again, we want to restate our belief that a search for guiding material will almost certainly be beneficial.

Preston (1964), in an extensive monograph discussing the results of using a variety of tests with Eskimos, notes that the "construction" technique of the unadapted TAT was the hardest test in the battery for her subjects, probably because it required more "verbal fluency" than the other tests used. The Eskimos were not able to produce "complete" stories, and themes given by them were "prevailingly 'unhappy' situations or feelings" (p. 398). Preston speculates that the TAT elicited such incomplete or depressing stories either because of Eskimo attitudes toward the white race (since the cards depict Caucasians), their "depressive" tendencies which she found in Rorschach protocols for the same group, or the fatalism characteristic of surviving precariously in an Arctic environment.

Lindzey (1961) reviewed numerous anthropological or ethnological accounts, treatises, and research reports dealing with projective techniques [cf. Abel, 1948; Adcock and Ritchie, 1958; Henry, 1955 (which includes comments by Caudill, Fiske, Honigmann, Nadel, Spindler, and Spiro); Lantz, 1948; Mensh and Henry, 1953]. He summarized the various points of criticism attributable to these studies, noting that many were unwarranted or overgeneralized. Many criticisms, however, can correctly be called "on target." Further, Lindzey reviewed a large number of studies in which (usually) one of about 25 projective devices was central to each study, and has provided us with a list of their "modal flaws." These criticisms and flaws are summarized below by category.

## On Target Criticisms

1. One must never be content to collect projective data alone. Other data, supportive of projective technique findings and relevant dimensions within the culture, should be maximized.

2. Since projective techniques rest upon subtle language differences, every caution must be used in interpreting responses and in exerting "control over the conditions under which the verbal responses are elicited" (p. 190). Variations due to linguistic differences must be separated from personality differences.

3. By using projective techniques one ordinarily omits some procedure he might otherwise have employed. The problem is one of considering many alternatives, and not relying on one procedure or another to the exclusion of equally useful or corroborating techniques.

4. However valid projective techniques may be for Western countries (or, in general, for cultures different from those for which a technique was developed), it is *"a task for the future to demonstrate that they possess cross-cultural validity" (p. 191).*

## Modal Flaws

1. Few studies attempted to "protect the interpreter. . .from knowledge concerning the culture being appraised." This refers to the contamination issue mentioned earlier, and of those attempting "to provide some degree of protection against contamination, only a small number were successful." Further, no study provided "a compelling demonstration of the independent merit of the inferences derived from projective technique protocols when compared to inferences secured from other vantages" (pp. 296-297).

2. The general tendency of investigators was to "rely upon subjective impression when relating projective technique data and inferences derived from traditional ethnographic sources" (p. 297).

3. Characterizing most studies was the "failure to provide a full description of the circumstances under which the test is administered" (p. 297).

4. There has been a tendency to fail "to explore the possible contribution of non-personality factors" to the findings (p. 298). This would include situational and chance factors, alternative hypotheses, or other parameters such as age, education, and sex.

5. The examiner's influence upon test performance was usually not accounted for. True, the work of Rosenthal (1966) and others, which documents the importance of experimenter effects, was not extant for any of these studies, but in all of them there was a casual attitude toward documenting the role of the examiner, where attributed personality differences could have been due to characteristics of the examiner, including age, sex, cultural background, or training.

6. Common to many studies has been the "failure to select for comparison, groups sufficiently well matched on parameters of known relevance" (p. 299) so that other factors contributing to differences or variation could be ruled out.

7. The mechanical application of elaborate scoring systems and actuary-based interpretive generalizations developed from studying Westerners have been used too often to the exclusion of subtle cues, culturally contextual information, or "clinical judgments." In other words, norms and scoring systems were assumed to be valid elsewhere, and actuarial approaches were blindly adopted.

8. A tendency to fail to integrate "findings derived from projective techniques" and "data derived from traditional anthropological techniques" (p. 300) has resulted in a continued isolation of two groups of data, neither of which confirms or refutes the other.

9. Wide cultural variation between individuals has led to the "tendency to take group averages and treat them as descriptive of the group as a whole" (p. 300). This is especially important when tests, notably the Rorschach, yield such wide response variation, not only of personality measured by one investigator, but also between researchers working with similar groups.

10. A discouraging element is that there is "relatively little evidence of cumulation of sophistication and wisdom." Lindzey notes that more recent studies "are little superior to those reported a decade or more ago" (p. 301).

These, then, are some important points to consider when using projective techniques cross-culturally. More recently, Spain (1972) has extended the list of cautions and criticisms and pitfalls to avoid when attempting to use projectives in psychological anthropology. Lindzey's fourth and last "on-target" criticism (above) is one with which other writers have been concerned. In an earlier essay reviewing the use of projective tests cross-culturally, Kaplan (1961) admits to a personal impression that "the projective test is a useful if not necessary technique and that further explorations of this method are warranted," but concludes that

"My judgements about the cross-cultural use of projective tests have been vary harsh. I have looked for the positive values in these tests and found them very scant. I have looked at the difficulties in their use and found them to be enormous, and have concluded that, as these tests are being used and interpreted at present, only a modicum of validity and value can be obtained from them" (p. 252).

Frey, a political scientist with a remarkable ability to "see through" the issues (especially with respect to the stimulus equivalence value of projectives), similarly concludes that

"Their validity in widely variant non-Western cultures is even more uncertain. Effective cross-cultural usage of techniques like the Rorschach depends utterly upon within-cultural validation of a complex, far from intuitive scheme for interpreting the extremely remote stimuli and responses that are involved. Taking all these facts into consideration, it does not seem that the projective test is any master key to cross-cultural equivalence. For certain purposes it is an extremely useful tool, a valuable addition to the researcher's kit. But it is not, as has been claimed, a unique answer to our interrogative problems in cross-cultural research" (Frey, 1970, p. 266).

Perhaps no other research tools in psychology divide psychologists more than do projective techniques. This "split" is perpetually mirrored in the epistemological strife between the "soft-headed clinikers" and the "rugged empiricists." (For an excellent discussion of the issues here and a catalog of the adjectives which each use to describe the other, see Meehl's classic 1954 monograph.) The writers have witnessed a number of times (during symposia, for example) attacks and counterattacks, with projectives and empiricism the weapons, and "science" the battleground. As is true with psychological tests in general, projectives are probably neither as bad as their most vitriolic opponents nor as good as their most dedicated followers claim. In the vast expanse between these extremes lies the complex jungle of variables and issues needing resolution before concrete validation can be claimed.

One would like to believe that Lindzey's thorough review of projectives would have been the primary reference for studies employing them after the appearance of the book in 1961. Otherwise, it would be logical to assume that we would see a continuation of studies containing many of the flaws Lindzey has summarized. While no exhaustive search for cross-cultural projective test research was initiated to determine the influence (or availability) of Lindzey's book, it is true that of six studies between 1963 and 1967, only two reference Lindzey. They were Melikian (1964), who used 10 TAT cards with Arab university students and determined that the cards had equal stimulus value to both Arab and American students, and Georgas and Vassiliou (1967) who collected Rorschach norms representative of the greater Athens area through testing 200 Athenian adults. The four studies not citing Lindzey (whether or not the authors knew of its existence) are not given here since to do so would make it appear that we are serving summonses for errors of omission. The point to be made is strictly the methodological imperative that sources are available in book form, journal articles, or by personally corresponding with an expert in the area about to be researched.

The most notable recent advance in projective techniques has been the emergence of the Holtzman Inkblot Technique (Holtzman, Thorpe, Swartz, and Herron, 1961). Owing to "an impressive number of carefully designed validity studies which yielded negative results" which led to the realization of "inherent weaknesses" in the Rorschach (Holtzman, 1968, p. 137), the HIT was developed, retaining the meaningless or ambiguous nature of inkblots. A number of features make it attractive for exploratory cross-cultural research. It consists of two parallel forms, A and B, each containing 45 inkbolts, and two practice blots which are common to both forms, while the Rorschach has 10 inkblots. In addition, the HIT differs from the Rorschach in the following ways:

1. The blots are "richer and more varied in color, form, and shading."
2. Varying the degree of symmetry or balance among the blots provides a "new stimulus dimension for analysis."
3. Only one response per card rather than an unlimited number holds more constant the number of responses.
4. A brief, simple, and standardized inquiry immediately follows each response.
5. The parallel forms, which have been carefully etched, permit test-retest designs and studies of changes within individuals.
6. Standardized percentile norms for various populations, including foreign groups, are provided for 22 scores.
7. Group methods of administration, including films or slides, and computer scoring make it useful for both large scale screening and individual diagnosis and assessment.

The HIT thus has all the features of the Rorschach, including most of the scoring categories, plus many of its own features (such as anxiety, pathognomic verbalization, space, and hostility), and can thus be considered a careful attempt to meet the standards of psychometric instruments. Cronbach (1970) notes that "the test construction and standardization was carried out with a degree of attention to technical detail no other personality test can match" (p. 637). Although HIT and Rorschach scores have much the same meaning, the HIT offers more promise in the validation of inkblot hypotheses, and the standardized method of administration is, from a cross-cultural standpoint, a most welcome characteristic.

## A Summary of Cross-Cultural Testing Problems

It would satisfy tradition at this juncture to summarize or briefly review the ground we have covered. Since what has thus far been presented in this chapter *is* a summary of work by many people, we shall depart from tradition.

Assume that you have cleared customs, have unpacked your bags, have had at least three exotic meals, and that you are now "at home." Further, assume that your cross-cultural project will depend to some extent upon the use of "tests." A final assumption is that the sampling problems have been, or will be, solved, perhaps by having followed the suggestions presented in other chapters of this book. The following checklist should help guide you in the proper selection and use of a psychological test.

## The Selection of the Stimuli (Tests)

1. Is it your aim to measure maximum performance or typical performance? The former may be more critical in terms of placement or selection, while the latter may be descriptive only. If the stimuli to be presented are nonverbal, is their justification to assume that subjects will attach to them the same intentional meaning as do you or the test developer? In other words, can culturally or panculturally relevant meaning be ascribed to the "ambiguous" or otherwise familiar stimuli to be presented? What previous evidence is there to support the appropriateness of the selected tests?

2. If there are few or no precedents in the use of stimuli presented, what anthropological or ethnographic evidence can be advanced to defend the selection you have made? Of course, you will probably have the opportunity to consult with an indigenous confidant, hopefully a behavioral scientist, regarding the project. He and other members of the culture will be valuable judges and sources of information concerning the selection of tests, or the modification of any parts of the tests.

3. If the stimuli are verbal, the translation problem looms as large as any other, and beyond that problem, the understandability of the test by the subjects. Is there a reasonable doubt that the best available translation is faulty? If so, do not use it. Rather, with appropriate help, painstakingly do your own translating, determining before final application that you are comfortably "on target." If the translation is at least minimally adequate, can you be assured that items will be understood as intended? A detailed interrogation concerning each item should be made, determining in each case its cultural relevance. Follow any one or a combination of the translation procedures outlined elsewhere in this book. Learn from the mistakes of others. Assume that any translation, even yours, has flaws that can be discovered only after application and detailed analysis.

## Administration and Response Elicitation

1. Considering the type of test, ages of examinees, their general ability and motivational level, and their language familiarity, as well as all environmental conditions, ask yourself, "What is the best possible way to administer the test to this particular group?" Use the "minimax" principle, minimizing the potential deficiencies in administration while maximizing the gain (desired response elicitation). Take nothing for granted.

2. Review all the principles listed earlier, and in checklist fashion query yourself and your administrative assistants, as well as teachers or others within the culture, concerning possible problem areas.

3. Remember the probable uniqueness to examinees of the entire testing situation, and the probable impact (both positive and negative) you will make on

them.

4. If because of administration difficulties there is a reasonable doubt that administration, and hence measurement, fell short of minimum expectations, do not use the results.

## Behavioral Representativeness of Sampled Responses

1. Any good test should have content validity, that is, it should represent the behavior considered important. The process of content validation involves checking test items against a conceptual framework with which the examinees are supposed to be familiar, or under which they can be logically classified (as in personality measurement). Obviously, for example, a chemistry test should contain items at an appropriate level of chemistry knowledge.

2. Cross-culturally, the content validation procedure would have to depend on anthropological or ethnographic evidence which would support the notation of behavioral representativeness offered by the test.

3. Unless the tests being used make a reasonable claim of culture-fairness, or unless they are experimental and contain unknown quantities, determine their appropriateness before they are administered. After administration, an examination of the responses should be made to verify their appropriateness.

4. The cultural range of the behavior being measured should be estimated. A restricted range of behavior may justify a different testing approach than the approach used to measure a broader range of behavior. For example, environmental conditions may allow little opportunity for the development of extreme individual differences.

## The Existence of a Measureable Construct

1. Rembember that psychological constructs are man-made and are customarily linked to some theoretical position. The attribution to members of culture X the constructs formulated in culture Y must be done through cross-validation. Only then can it be claimed that the constructs have mutual cultural relevance. Culturally appropriate and valid operational definitions of the constructs should be given.

2. When it can clearly be accomplished, criterion-oriented validation must be distinguished from construct-oriented validation. Unjustifiably interchanging one type of validity for the other can lead to a mixing of validation concepts and, hence, specious cross-cultural comparisons.

## Suitable Measurement and Evaluation Scales (Norms)

1. Related to the above comments, norms gathered for one culture should ordinarily not be used to evaluate people in other cultures. While measurement

itself can be assumed to be culturally unbiased, norms and scales most likely carry unicultural biases.

2. Where multi-national norms are used, determine whether the comparisons are based on the same or similar parameters (e.g., age, sex, and level of education) for each person or group in each culture being studied. If, for example, multinational norms have been developed, these can serve as anchor points. Lacking such norms, inferences about any culture for which norms are not available can be rife with errors to unknown degrees.

## Projective Techniques

1. It is clear that projective techniques are at least as difficult to adapt for cross-cultural use as other types of tests. In the interpretation realm, they demand special cautions, due to their open-ended nature.

2. Four general guidelines can be used as minimum methodological requirements when using projectives:

(a) Projective data should be supported by information based on other techniques. When a projective is employed, the researcher should justify why he did not use a more direct test. Since cross-cultural validation has been neglected, this should be a goal for all future research.

(b) Many studies have been contaminated because the person interpreting the responses to the projective stimuli knew the name of the culture and was familiar with it. Blind interpretation is necessary.

(c) The entire set of circumstances surrounding test administration must be described since subtle variation can have major effects. This would include descriptions of the setting, as well as the age, sex, and other descriptions of the respondents as recommended elsewhere in this book.

(d) Avoid the very common practice of taking a group average and then using it to describe the group as a whole. Ranges and variances must be reported.

3. Caveats given by previous researchers (Kaplan, 1961; Lindzey, 1961) who have surveyed projectives as they have been employed by cross-cultural researchers should be thoroughly reviewed.

4. A new direction in projective testing, the Holtzman Inkblot Technique, may make it desirable for cross-cultural use. Its parallel forms, practice inkblots, rich variety of stimuli, variations in inkblot symmetry and balance, one response per card, standardized inquiry following each response, and possible computer scoring, may signal a respectable advance in this area.

This chapter has been devoted to general issues and problems in cross-cultural testing. For discussions of specific cross-culturally useful psychological tests and other measuring devices, see Chapter 8.

# CHAPTER SIX

## Some Research Orientations and Frames of Reference

### Introduction

Cross-cultural researchers in psychology usually either aim right for the jugular vein of a theory to see if the theory can survive rigorous tests in other cultures, or they simply add important data to a common pool of knowledge about a theoretical stance. The former can be considered tests of universality, while data gathered in the latter approach are from a national or cultural ("local") level, with researchers fully aware from the outset that theory application and extension, and not a theoretical inquisition, are the goals. Thus, any theoretical position can be frontally attacked [as many researchers have done with Piaget's conservation principle (see below)]. Or, in the latter approach, we can see new wine in old bottles (applying McClelland's theory of achievement motivation to other cultures for example). These two common approaches are, however, really part of the same enterprise, and it may be difficult to distinguish one from the other. Furthermore, they may occur simultaneously or serendipitously.

Any theoretical orientation, or any construct, axiom, postulate, or corollary in the social and behavioral sciences can be investigated cross-culturally. A comprehensive text in psychology can be opened to any page at random and there before your eyes (and your imagination) will leap a series of hypotheses perhaps worthy of attention cross-culturally. We put this supposition to a quick, easily replicable test. From a leading (United States, of course) 900-page introductory psychology text (the specific one is immaterial) were culled some 30 pages which dealt with measurement and statistics (truly "culture-free" material), and some 40 pages which had even the most casual mention of "culture." Then the text was opened at random to 10 of the remaining pages, and the key material on each was noted: Adlerian concepts, autokinetic movement, success and failure, anxiety reactions, sleep, short term memory, stereotypes, color perception, discrimination and generalization, and the Wechsler Adult Intelligence Scale. All these topics were discussed by Americans

143

for Americans and perhaps other Westerners, when in fact all of them very likely have an unknown number of cultural permutations. Actually, most of these 10 topics have been studied cross-culturally, but no such research was cited in the text. This is an unfortunate but forgiveable series of omissions, and the authors of an American text cannot be faulted for this. To rewrite the text so as to account for all known permutations of the topics cross-culturally would require 75,912 pages.

Cross-culturists would like to see textbooks rewritten to accommodate the world and not only the neighborhood. This is the most exciting aspect of cross-cultural psychology. But one's motives should be a bit more serious than merely taking potshots at theory and old shibboleths. No theory is puncture proof. Actually, since a theory is never a fact and since it stands in opposition to a fact, the most astute theoreticians are likely to be the ones who are most hospitable toward the impact that cross-cultural research can have on broadening the bases of understanding in all the behavioral sciences.

The "random page" tactic mentioned above can lead to the demise or drastic overhaul of something heretofore "known," and the then somewhat less credible book is abruptly closed. While not discouraging such a hit-and-run approach, our aim in this chapter is to encourage a more concerted effort to "think cross-culturally," and to actively create research strategies, but within solid frameworks. Also, one should leave as much to benefit the culture studied as he takes home for self-benefit. At the very least he should modestly advise the appropriate people in the investigated cultures of his findings and the interpretations he makes from them.

To "think cross-culturally" is a term easy to defend, difficult to define, and even harder to do. It is hard enough to try and understand—to think about—one's own limited sociocultural environment and to order everything in neat perspective But surely thinking cross-culturally involves at least a systematic sifting through the widest possible range of alternative approaches to observe or measure phenomena, eliminating them one by one until a satisfactory methodological focus is reached. Later, through research, the chosen approach will hopefully be confirmed as appropriate and sound when possible rival hypotheses are themselves dismissed one by one. The similarities or differences between country X and country Y on some configuration of a dependent-independent variable interchange may be impressive to the point of euphoria, but the picture may be incomplete or untrue. Regression artifacts, accidential correlations, improperly used samples, and open-ended "can't lose" procedures of experimentation and data interpretation are but a few examples of what may, with equal plausibility, have led to astounding findings. A challenging and perhaps paradoxical element in cross-cultural work is that it virtually demands "stereophonic" (pancultural) thinking, and most of us have not had a need to go beyond "high fidelity" (ethnocentric) thought. Clinicians have often said that to understand and treat schizophrenia effectively one must begin by experiencing firsthand the world of the schizophrenic. This paradox may have its cross-cultural analog in the fact that most of us have been calibrated for only one culture, and thus have little hope of ever fully grasping any two worlds equally well simultaneously. Those few behavioral scientists who are bilingual or multilingual, who can rightly claim dual ethnicity, and who are also cross-cultural researchers, are exceptions. Harry Triandis, Henri Tajfel, F. L. K. Hsu, and others who know equally well the subtleties of more than one culture are examples of the few. A researcher in cross-cultural psychology who falls short of these qualifications must compensate by using an unusual amount of methodological rigor in his own investigations and in reading the efforts of others. Of necessity he must share most cultural experiences vicariously, through data and through thorough explanations of data by others. He must *also* be tolerant of but not acquiescent to methodological shortcomings that are not easily solvable.

A motto of cross-cultural researchers should be the slogan attributed to the late student of individual differences, Donald G. Patterson: "A difference, to be a difference, must make a difference." By this statement Patterson surely meant that merely a significant t-ratio, F-ratio, or chi-square is not enough; some important social or behavioral consequence must lie beyond sterile statistical findings. Levels of significance, or lack of them, do nothing, but people who interpret them can do anything. The point to be made is that "thinking cross-culturally" also involves a rather scrupulous look at both alleged differences and alleged similarities. "Similar" conformity scores, for example, for Brazilians and Swedes, do not necessarily mean that Brazilians and Swedes have equal amounts of conformity in terms of what conformity means—and what its consequences are—in their respective cultures. Likewise "different" scores on the same attribute or measure may be just that—different *scores*, where in reality the attribute may be phenomenologically identical in each culture's terms. The Greek concept of *aretê* may be helpful here. A definition of *aretê* has been given by Goldschmidt (1971). It is

". . . the qualities a person should ideally possess, according to the consensus of his community. Every normal community has a set of ideas of human conduct we may call its aretê. If we are to understand the *workings of society* we must take cognizance of this phenomenon as it is one of the most important aspects of institutionalized behavior, though not always given overt expression. If we are to understand the *character of any particular society,* we must know what elements of human behavior enter into its aretê, what its particular ideals are. For the central point is that every people has ideals but the nature of these ideals varies from one culture to another. If we want to understand the *character of an individual's behavior,* whether normal or pathological, we must know the context of values in which he has grown up, for his behavior is meaningful only as set against the arete of his culture" (p. 58).

Cross-cultural researchers often hear variations of this comment: "I can understand it when you find similarities between cultures, since similarities are rather expected. But, how do you account for non-biographical or genetic differences? Isn't it hard to explain them convincingly?" The answer is "yes," but also that any real differences—statistical differences that make behavorial differences—must be clearly the result of cultural conditioning. The world is a laboratory, and nature herself has designed the different treatments. These treatments are called cultures. It is not the researcher's fault that the behavior of the human species is uncannily spread over countless variables, but it is the researcher's mandate to try to work in this vast jungle of error with the aim of determining whether a difference is really a similarity or a similarity is really a difference. We do not yet have a magnificent table of standard scores for every conditionable human characteristic so that every culture can be judged according to some common, unequivocal reference point. Until we do, the most difficult problem of all in cross-cultural research will be the satisfactory and accurate interpretation of data.

In the social and behavioral sciences there has been a nagging controversy over the use and misuse of variants of the cherished significance test. A collection of excellent essays on this topic is well worth reviewing (Morrison and Henkel, 1970). It is both easy and tempting to overinterpret data (e.g., the meaning of "levels of significance"), either through a blinding love affair with a theoretical predilection using "cute" and "clever" designs or through ad hoc analyses. Holt (1971) writes that he has

"the uncomfortable feeling that all of us have at one time or another found our empirical research to yield findings incompatible with our initial theoretical hunches and then provided an ad hoc explanation for our findings, neatly supported by footnotes to some appropriate theoretical statements. The clever and industrious investigator can build a career on sophisticated analytical routines and on ad hoc explanations of findings that appear in retrospect to be good examples of an 'integrated' research program, but which in fact have only been an easier way of escaping the requirements of a *modus tollens* impact on a theory, never once effectively refuting or corroborating a single aspect of his theoretical network" (pp. 138-139).

Holt's comment is one of his reactions to a provocative thesis relating to a "methodological paradox" that exists between the social and behavioral sciences and the "hard" sciences such as physics (Meehl, 1967). This paradox is alarmingly appropriate for most psychological researchers to consider, and it is even more necessary that cross-cultural researchers consider it. Meehl reminds us that there is a fundamental difference between physics and the behavioral sciences in the way measurements are used. Research designs in physics are designed to measure *point values* among variables, while research in the social sciences is designed to test *probable differences* [e.g., the magnitude of a *directional* (one-tailed) difference between means]. Thus the paradox is that in the social sciences increasing the number of observations *increases* the chance that significant relationships between variables will be found, while in physics the *opposite* is true.

Consider the typical correlation coefficient. Since every psychological variable is probably related in some way with every other variable, the probability of any one correlation coefficient being exactly zero is much smaller than its being greater or less than zero. Now since one needs only to increase the size of the sample(s) to increase the probability that even very small correlations will be significant, the "increased precision" of measurement weakens the strength of the hurdle that must be passed to either support or refute a theory empirically. Meehl asserts that methods of increasing precision (improved instrumentation, better experimental design, increasing sample sizes, and the like) will "yield a probability approaching 1/2 of corroborating our substantive theory by a significance test, *even if the theory is totally without merit*" (p. 111).

The point to be emphasized here is that "everything in the brain is connected with everything else" and that the larger the sample the more likely will statistically significant differences among variables be found. Meehl tells how he and a colleague demonstrated this by generating a mammoth intercorrelation matrix for 55,000 Minnesota high school seniors. A correlation matrix of 45 miscellaneous variables (number of siblings, club membership, mother's occupation, and the like) revealed statistically significant relationships in 91% of the pairwise associations. The huge sample was the greatest contributor to this inflated picture, of course. But "accidental" correlations can and do occur among variables even when much smaller samples are involved. This is especially true in social, personality, and cross-cultural arenas where theories are not yet sufficiently developed to enable the researcher to make point-predictions. To approximate the stability and accuracy of point-predictions in measurement, sample size is increased bringing with it a number of significant differences or associations. Some of these are not artifacts, some are spurious. Sorting them with objectivity, or being able to sort them at all, may be a difficult task.

Of course, "innocent" and higher and higher levels of significance, or decreasing the probability of committing a Type I error (rejecting the null hypothesis when it is true), and ad hoc explanations are not the only means at our disposal to feel comfortably safe in data interpretation. As Pelto (1970) suggests, the anthropological researcher often differs from the deliriously empirical psychological researcher in that the former will usually try to gain more than just statistical support for his findings. For example, personal observations, anecdotal evidence, descriptions of logical relationships, and other contextual information may give added credibility to statistically significant findings. Similarly, Lykken (1968), a psychologist who used the same brush as Meehl (1967) in painting his colorful critique of the use and interpretation of levels of statistical significance, writes:

"The value of any research can be determined, not from statistical results, but only by skilled, subjective evaluation of the coherence and reasonableness of the theory, the degree of experimental control employed, the sophistication of the measuring techniques, the scientific or practical importance of the phenomena studied, and so on" (pp. 158-159).

These suggestions reinforce our recommendation to use multiple methods in the same study, a point made elsewhere in this book.

## Selected Major Research Guides

This chapter is designed to give an overview of (1) general orientations and useful aids for data collection; (2) different ways to break the world of cultures into manageable units for the purposes of making comparisons cross-culturally, and (3) specific and rather well-integrated frames of reference which will continue to be of major importance to cross-cultural psychology.

A brief introduction to the Human Relations Area Files and related compendia is given first, since they constitute massive repositories of known information and scientific data on hundreds of human groups, from small tribes to entire societies. Approaches to identifying units of measurement, including the "cultunit" and "behavior settings," are presented next, followed by a reiteration of the "emic-etic" distinction, which was discussed earlier in this book, and cultural "theorics." A significant part of the chapter is devoted to four specific frames of reference:

1. the Piagetian influence as an example of research strategy in the cognitive and developmental domain;
2. "cultural thematics" as best represented by McClelland's work on achievement motivation;
3. Dawson's "bio-social" psychology, which is an explicitly cross-cultural theory based upon quite recent data from diverse cultures;
4. measures of modernism, or various ways to investigate individuals and cultures as they advance to higher levels of industrialization or Westernization.

*The Human Relations Area Files (HRAF).* The materials and publications associated with HRAF form the largest compilation of cultural data in the world. These data are the result of ethnographic, first-hand observational reports by anthropologists, missionaries, and so forth. The system, originally called the Cross-Cultural Survey, was started in 1937 at Yale University's Institute of Human Relations, under the general leadership of George P. Murdock. Currently, the nonprofit HRAF is sponsored and controlled by 23 universities, all but two of which are in the United States.[1] Additionally, there are associate member institutions throughout the world, and since 1958 they have been receiving microfilmed files of the accumulating material. HRAF also has its own press which publishes, among other things, the results of selected scholarly research and, in addition to the documents listed below, the quarterly journal, *Behavior Science Notes,* now in its sixth year. *Behavior Science Notes* publishes information about the files and HRAF's member institutions, as well as substantive research articles.

The files are primarily an indexing tool and are designed for use in general research, studies of specific areas and cultures and, of course, cross-cultural and comparative research. Two publications are basic for the proper use of the files. These are *Outline of World Cultures* (Murdock, 1969) and *Outline of Cultural Materials* (Murdock et al., 1967).

*Outline of World Cultures (OWC).* This is an alphanumeric system of classification which organizes the known tribal cultures of the world into units (including extinct and historical peoples), and which is continually being revised. It is the universe from which cultures are selected for inclusion in the files. While most of the files are relatively inactive, it is the intent of HRAF to provide and maintain a cross-cultural sample of more than 200 of the better-described cultures. These cultures are selected on the basis of maximum geographic dispersal, and the availability and reliability of the literature pertaining to each.

*Outline of Cultural Materials (OCM).* This is a system of classification, also alphanumeric, of the subject areas on which the files are based. Analysts process the materials, which are basically descriptive, from a variety of sources, but primarily from documents resulting from field observation. Currently, information is codified into more than 700 categories (e.g., kinship, alcoholism, murder, and farming). Most of the categories are cross-referenced to related categories. Codes also include name and discipline of the author of the source of material,

[1] HRAF member institutions are: University of Chicago, University of Colorado, Cornell University, Ecole Pratique des Hautes Etudes, Paris, Harvard University, University of Hawaii, University of Illinois, Indiana University, State University of Iowa, Kyoto University, University of Michigan, State University of New York at Buffalo, University of North Carolina, University of Oklahoma, University of Pennsylvania, University of Pittsburgh, Princeton University, Smithsonian Institution, University of Southern California, Southern Illinois University, University of Utah, University of Washington, and Yale University. Detailed free information about HRAF's entire operation can be obtained from the member institutions or by writing the Human Relations Area Files, Inc., P.O. Box 2054, Yale Station, Connecticut 06520.

dates when collected and published, OWC indices, and name of society. Each page of each source is copied many times for each file; one copy is filed under each index category. Thus the Files enable a researcher to look up a topic quickly.

A publication related to the above HRAF-sponsored publications is the *Ethnographic Atlas*, which contains coded and cross-referenced information concerning nearly 1300 of the world's cultures. These coded materials have appeared from the inaugural issue (1962) onwards in *Ethnology: An International Journal of Cultural and Social Anthropology*. For each culture the code defines such features as population and demographic characteristics, and social, political, and economic structures. Major bibliographic references are cited for each addition to the list. One volume of *Ethnology* (1967, Vol. 6, No. 2) serves as the key summary of and guide to the *Ethnographic Atlas*.

Because many people have pointed out the need to develop a system to correlate the *Ethnographic Atlas* codes with the codes used in the *Outline of World Cultures*, O'Leary (1969) has prepared a concordance of the two systems. This includes four separate listings for ease in cross-referencing: (1) alphabetical by society; (2) by OWC codes; (3) by EA code, and (4) by EA serial number.

*The World Ethnographic Sample (WES).* By 1961 Murdock's WES contained a selection of 565 tribes to be used as a quasi-universe from which can be drawn quota samples. Sixty culture areas, 10 each from the six major regions—Africa, Circum-Mediterranean, East-Eurasia, Insular Pacific, North America and South America—are classified in it. The ten areas usually include (1) the most populous society in the area; (2) the best-described culture in each of the cultural sub-areas; (3) one example of each basic type of subsistence technology present: (a) farming, (b) herding, (c) fishing, (d) foraging; (4) one example of each major rule of descent present: (a) bilateral, (b) patrilineal, (c) matrilineal, and (d) double; and (5) one example from each linguistic stock or major linguistic sub-family present. (See also Moore, 1961; Naroll, 1970).

As an example of its use, one may wish to reduce the cultural similarity of sample neighbors by taking a random sample from WES, taking one society from each of its sixty culture areas.

*HRAF in Practice.* A researcher using HRAF will receive ample assistance from those in attendance at the member or associate member institutions. However, a brief example here may be helpful in preparing for an HRAF-based project. Suppose that a researcher wished to learn all that he could from the files about child-rearing practices among the Lummi Indians of North America. The preliminary steps (paraphrased from HRAF's *Research Guide* (Ca. 1969) are to:

1. Consult OWC to find the code for the Lummi (which is NR 15; the Klallam and Puyallup Indians also share this code number).

2. Check the OWC file and related documents to see if materials have been processed for the Lummi.

3. Check category 111 of the Lummi file. Category 111 (a constant for all cultures on file) gives bibliographic citations for each source processed for the Lummi, together with brief descriptions of the contents of the sources, information about the author, the evaluation of the source by the HRAF staff, the date of the citation, the analyst's name, and other information of perhaps decreasing importance to mention here.

4. Check the index and table of contents of OCM for child-rearing practices and related practices that may be helpful. All the file slips in the Lummi file for each of the relevant categories in OCM should be studied.

5. Read the definitions of the relevant categories in OCM. The index and table of contents are not as indicative of category coverage as are category definitions and what is included in it.

6. Check additional OCM categories to which each of the categories is cross-referenced (e.g., kinship, sibling relationships, mother-father roles, and so forth).

7. Check categories adjacent to all those above.

8. Check to see if guides to those files have been prepared.

9. Consult three other categories—identification, cultural summary, and methodology—for further information concerning the Lummi.

After this, the *Ethnographic Atlas* can be consulted for further information. In it, for example, the Lummi alone are assigned EA code Nb15.

HRAF's *Research Guide* can further be paraphrased here to give examples of the four levels of difficulty of questions that can be asked of the file:

*Simplest.* Do the Lummi have child-rearing practices? One OCM category alone can answer this question.

*Simple.* Do the Lummi depend on the extended family in child-rearing? Cross-referencing to other categories may be necessary here.

*Harder.* What is the nature of Lummi child-rearing practices? This is the initial question asked, and in effect requires the researcher to follow the steps outlined above.

*Hardest.* What values do Lummi parents hope to instill in their children? This type of question must be rephrased, perhaps in a number of ways, depending on what the researcher means by "values," or in what particular value he is interested. For examples: "Do the Lummi stress dependency, or obedience to authority?" Dependency, obedience, and authority could serve as key words in initiating a cross-referencing search.

The primary purpose of HRAF or any system of cataloging cultures is of course to provide researchers with accurate data on the "universe" of cultures, from which samples can be drawn. An ideal sample of cultures would perhaps be drawn in a way similar to the stratified random sampling technique that Wechsler and his colleagues used in selecting individuals to serve as members of norm groups in developing his series of individual intelligence tests for the United States. Wechsler's goal was to make certain that every individual had, like any good sampling technique, a theoretically equal chance of being selected. The country was stratified, according to census and other demographic data, into a number of different categories, and samples from these categories were then drawn in direct proportion to their actual frequencies. For example, if white, male farm laborers accounted for 1/200 of the total population, and if the total standardization sample required 2000 subjects, then 10 white, male farm laborers should be in the sample. That each person in each strata has an equal chance of being selected is not unlike placing each and every person in one, and only one, of a number of boxes of varying sizes and then taking random samples from each box according to its size.

Taking samples of entire cultures, and then sampling within them, is a much more complex job than getting a standardization sample of individuals; one individual has no variance, while one culture has unknown variance. Cultural samples and subsequent individual sampling within them would of course be identical to the Wechsler procedure *if* the world could be parceled out in various chunks of known size and composition. Many researchers have devoted a good share of their professional lives to the delineation and description of such "parcels." Add to this cultural complexity the massive problem of maintaning files so that usable data will be available upon which frames of reference, or research hypotheses, can be based, and one can see why HRAF or any such system should be only a starting place.

Naroll (1970a) gives an example which is important to consider when using the *Outline of World Cultures* in a way paralleling Wechsler's sampling procedures or the sampling methods employed by those who need a sample truly representative of the universe—for example, the Gallup or Roper political polls:

"The sample survey man would prefer a list of inhabitants of the city he studies. But he can make out very well with a list of its buildings. Some of the buildings on such a list have many residents; some have few; others have none at all. But if he takes a probability sample of the city's buildings, he can then count the number of residents in the buildings in his sample and weight his findings accordingly. Similarly, some of the categories in Murdock's *Outline of World Cultures* list or refer to many tribes, some list or refer to only one or two, a few refer to only a part of a tribe, and many refer to no contemporary society at all but to something else again entirely—to an entire region, or to historical or archaeological or even paleontological and ethological data. Such listings are analogous to uninhabited buildings in a conventional sample survey" (p. 895).

It is widely but mistakenly believed that files such as HRAF are virtually synonymous with the cross-cultural survey method of research, and that this method has been identified primarily with anthropological research. Perhaps as many as one-third of HRAF-based studies were done by psychologists, and this proportion will likely increase as more psychologists come to depend on it as a primary starting point. It is not well known that the method is used in generalizing about *variables* as they exist at an individual level. Moreover, the method is actually a study of ethnographies and not of living people; this is, as Naroll says, a way of looking at people "through a glass, darkly." Naroll (1970b, p. 1228) emphasizes that

"The task of the cross-cultural survey then is to sort out the general (but not universally invariable) from the particular among human affairs. . . .. But its strongest point so far has been its use in studying functional relations between varying traits in human societies or cultures."

Naroll's comment may sound contradictory to what was said above about traits, but note that traits among human *societies* or *cultures* and not among individuals in them is at the center of the cross-cultural survey method. The traditional anthropological approach is at the group level, whereas psychological approaches are usually concerned with the individual.

The two references by Naroll (1970a, 1970b) are excellent in all respects, and both should be thoroughly reviewed prior to initiating a project which may require the use of samples of cultures. One is a comprehensive discussion of cross-cultural sampling as it has been approached in survey-type research, the other with just how valuable the survey method has been. In the latter, Naroll has listed eleven problems of the cross-cultural survey method. The following is a summary of these points:

1. *Sampling.* Including representativeness, merits of different types, the problem of "nonresponding" tribes.

2. *Societal unit definition.* What is a tribe or society, and what are we counting in statistical summaries of tribal comparisons?

3. *Data accuracy.* What errors of fact or reporting are in cross-cultural codings? When ethnographic accounts have been translated, how accurate are they? Some files are hopelessly outdated for research on some questions. Jahoda (1968) warns of this same problem.

[2] At the Royal Anthropological Institute in 1889, Tylor read a paper which pioneered the cross-cultural method. He showed "adhesions" (correlations) between certain traits. Francis Galton pointed out that traits often spread by diffusion, either by borrowing or by migration. Thus the "problem." For example, if two societies have common origins or have extensively shared traits but are now distinguishable (and sampled) as separate societies, they are not truly independent. If these two societies are considered independent, then correlations between traits that they share will be spuriously high because of a diffusion artifact. Naroll (1970c) has summarized about ten proposed solutions to Galton's Problem. Smith and Crano (1971) propose yet another solution using a combination of factor analysis to identify marker variables across cultures (such as the presence or absence of agriculture) and various correlational procedures to examine the extent of functionally shared traits.

4. *Conceptualization, classification, and coding.* In view of cultural varia-tions, which systems of behavioral representation, taxonomies and the coding of materials should be used?

5. *Galton's Problem.* Do cross-cultural correlations reflect functional as-sociations or cultural diffusions?

6. *Causal analysis of correlations.* This is the problem of discerning causal direction among correlated variables and how to deal with the unmeasured unknown. [See, for example, Guthrie (1971) below, for an analysis of this problem.]

7. *Paucity of relevant data.* How can hypotheses be tested or problems analyzed if no accurate data or statistics for key cultures are available?

8. *The "combing," "dredging," or "mudsticking" problem.* How to deal with, for example, the 50 of 1,000 correlations that are expected by chance to be significant at $p < .05$, even if the correlations result from meaningless data? (Recall "Meehl's Paradox," mentioned earlier).

9. *The general problem of statistical significance.* This is the problem of freak relationships, and tests of significance related to random and non-random samples.

10. *Regional variations.* Do "worldwide" results truly reflect world-wide tendencies, or instead merely the "regional" situation?

11. *Deviant case analysis.* Why are there exceptions when the association in question is conspicuously absent?

The use of cultural or ethnographic surveys has been of central importance to scores of cross-cultural studies. A number of the more popular studies can be found in Ford (1967). Whiting and Child's (1953) *Child Training and Personality* can be used as a quick example of certain of the above problems associated with improper use of ethnographic surveys at both the sampling level and the interpretive level.

Whiting and Child studied personality patterns among primitive cultures by operationalizing many Freudian concepts. They sampled 75 primitive societies as being the 75 for which the necessary ethnographic data were available. Naroll (1970a) has pointed out that Whiting and Child did not say exactly what they meant by "available." It is evident, Naroll concludes, that Whiting and Child "opportunistically searched for suitable reports and stopped looking when they had found 75," and that "had they continued to search, they might have found at least 75 more societies with suitable data" (p. 905). The Whiting and Child study produced numerous data on antecedents (e.g., oral or anal frustrations) which seemed later to account for deviant adult consequences (e.g., conflict or various illnesses) in line with Freudian theory.

Recently, Guthrie (1971) reanalyzed the Whiting and Child data, using the "off-diagonal" approach suggested by Campbell and Fiske (1959). In their splendid paper, Campbell and Fiske maintain that proper trait validation should contain two processes. One is *convergent validation* (which would include high correlations between independent measurement procedures measuring the "same" trait). The other is *discriminant validation* (where, for example, too high correlations between measures can invalidate the measures with which they are supposed to differ). These processes would involve the use of a multitrait-multi-method matrix which displays the intercorrelations of several traits which have all been measured by each of several methods. The matrix would enable one to analyze validity data resulting from (1) several traits and one method, (2) one trait and several methods, and (3) several traits and several methods. Thus triangulation (convergence) as well as discrimination between measures of different traits can help pinpoint true sources of variance, relatively useless validity coefficients, overlap of "operationalized" traits, redundancy of methods, and so forth, —all of which enhance confidence in the accurate measurement of traits.

We now return to the central point. Guthrie used the Whiting and Child data to calculate a matrix of 666 correlations (the state of computer technology in 1953 precluded such calculation) between all ratings of childhood training practices and subsequent treatment customs (antecedent and consequent variables). He did this maintaining that "only by examining the matrix of correlations [for any set of variables] can one be sure that he is measuring one trait alone and not many others equally as well, and also that his validity index is not inflated by methods of data collection common to both test and criterion."

Guthrie (1971) has shown that many off-diagonal relationships which were not predicted from theory were higher than those which theory would suggest be examined, and that

"This suggests that off-diagonal values should be examined in research using this design in order to be sure that non-predicted correlations are not higher than those called for by theory. When the latter are higher one should suspect either the theory or uncontrolled method variance. The temptation, of course, when one finds a significant relationship which was not predicted, is to offer an interpretation for the new finding. A more parsimomious conclusion, however, is that shared method variance is present rather than true variance in the variables to which the indices refer. Paraphrasing Campbell and Fiske (1959), the correlation or systematic variance among scores can be due to measurement features as well as to trait content" (p. 322).

*Other Cultural Samples and Ethnographic Information.* A number of sampling procedures for use in cross-cultural surveys are readily available. The better ones are called probability samples. Several of them are summarized below. More complete discussions can be found in Naroll (1970a, pp.903-915).

*The HRAF Quality Control Sample.* HRAF experts followed rigid specifications in composing two lists, or levels, of societies based on the comprehensiveness of ethnographic literature (HRAF, 1967). "Level B" specifications were: (a) at least 1200 pages of cultural data; (b) overlapping coverage by at least more than one reporter; (c) at least one formal monograph; (d) no serious challenge to the accuracy of the ethnographic account; (e) well-rounded coverage of demographic, political, and life cycle information; (f) reports done while each culture was still functioning economically and politically; and (g) some record that each culture was available for one hundred years before basic field work was done. "Level A" specifications called for (a) an additional 1000 pages of ethnographic data; (b) involvement of at least two professional anthropologists, one of whom must have spent at least twelve months in the area and have had a working knowledge of the native language.

The resulting 204 societies (58 Level A and 146 Level B) were classified into sixty cultural areas, following Murdock's *Ethnographic Atlas* and the principles underlying the World Ethnographic Sample. Efforts were made to follow principles of inclusion and exclusion by level in each of the sixty areas, so that randomizing assigned levels within the strata would be possible. Thus the Quality Control Sample is a subset of HRAF as a whole.

*Permanent Ethnographic Probability Sample (PEPS).* In 1963 a committee of six—P. J. Bohannan, F. L. K. Hsu, D. T. Campbell, R. Naroll, R. D. Schwartz, and R. C. Snyder—initiated work on a world-wide ethnographic probability sample. Rigid bibliographic requirements eliminated the inclusion of many tribes, and other work was eliminated because the field worker failed to meet high standards pertaining to his length of stay in each area or his knowledge of the language. The result is a list of tribes which have been described in readily identifiable and accessible ethnographies (see Naroll et al., 1970).

*Naroll's War, Stress, and Culture Sample.*   This sample combined subsamples of Naroll's Overland Diffusion Arcs and the WES subsample. The diffusion arc subsample was designed as a forty-five strata probability sample. Each strata consisted of a strip of the earth's surface 300 nautical miles on either side of the arc and 800 nautical miles long. Detailed procedures led to the final result of taking a probability sample of a bibliographically defined universe.

Because the final diffusion arc procedure resulted in the selection of a large proportion of the tribes in the WES, the WES (whatever its biases) was used to save sampling time at little apparent cost in bias. Naroll notes, however, that "WES is suitable as a quasi-universe only for studies whose bibliographic requirements are so strict that a large proportion—perhaps two-thirds—of the tribes fail to meet them." It is important also to note that Naroll (1970a) recommends, "If a sampler needs to draw on primitive tribes with especially rich coverage, then, he can save much time and expense by checking those in WES and ignoring the others" (p. 909), even though WES is not a probability sample.

*The Societal Research Archives System (SRAS).*  SRAS is an energetic effort to create a computer-based retrieval and research facility. It, like HRAF, uses bibliographic sources and data as well as codes. Under the auspices of the University of Pittsburgh's Cross-Cultural Cumulative Coding Center ($C^5$), it is still in the development stage. Inquiries about SRAS should be sent in care of Douglas R. White, who has primary responsibility for all of its programs.

We shall summarize White's (1970) discussion of the steps, and implicity, the rationale necessary when using SRAS:

1. *Sampling and integrating data from different sources.* This is the problem of drawing a representative sample of data from the two thousand societies, coding the relevant data.

2. *Data quality control.* This is an attempt to reduce systematic error from (a) differences in the quantity of material from perhaps overrepresented societies in a sample; (b) differences in the quality of material where one feature may be better described and another not described at all; (c) differences in coding techniques; (d) differences in ethnographers' techniques (e.g., better knowledge of the language) leading to source error; (e) differences due to actual versus verbal behavior which produces origin error (e.g., informants' reports versus actual case-incidence reports).

3. *Structural controls for comparability of societal units.* An attempt is made here to control for the diversity of cultural conditions, so that units and terms used to describe them are made more comparable for generalizing from culture to culture.

4. *Distributional analysis.* This is the familiar "Galton's Problem"–the problem of diffusion or historical relations producing common constellations of social forms.

5. *Mapping data of results.* Computer programming allows the mapping, for distributional and historical analysis, of trait distributions or of trait co-occurrences and clusters.

6. *Culling out likely functional associations.* Screening out "those correlations which have possible functional significance barring those which are the result of selection bias," and a number of possible errors. [This is analogous to the results of *A Cross-Cultural Summary* (Textor, 1967)].

7. *Third factor controls.* A matrix of 36 million correlations stored on tape will allow researchers to ask if any third variable, X, might intervene or be correlated with the correlation found between A and B.

8. *Reformulation of study designs.* Once correlational procedures have led to the provisional acceptance of certain hypotheses, this "feedback" system will allow the researcher to construct a hypothetico-deductive model in which additional hypotheses can be tested. This would be a storage facility which would articulate previous SRAS results with new formulations.

## The Identification of Social and Behavioral Units

All psychological research using samples of subjects for inferential purposes must address the problems of representativeness (within universes) and comparability (across universes). Those conducting animal studies which include, for example, samples of every $n$th rat from strain $A_1$ (control) and every $n$th rat from strain $A_2$ (experimental) are in rather enviable positions with regard to making comparisons. The control of variability is clear if anthropomorphizing is not. Human studies using, for example, samples of American college females versus American college males (two samples from the same universe differing only with respect to sex) are much less "clean" than the above animal study, primarily because the subjects are from the species *homo variabilis*. Adding limitless subtleties of cultural diversity magnificently compounds the problem of cross-cultural comparability. Generally, as one moves up from simple to more complex species or structures, sampling from them for purposes of comparative analysis becomes increasingly complex. Moreover, this complexity exists at both the individual level and the societal level. It is probably easier to discern the reasons for aggression between neighboring primitive tribes $A_1$ and $A_2$ in New Guinea (a cultural analog of rat species $A_1$ and $A_2$) than it is to discern why industrial societies A and W, which are separated by language, history, political systems, economic systems, and so forth, have a long-standing mutual aggression pact. The New Guinea tribes no doubt are much less variable both in terms of their origins and individual differences, and in terms of cultural complexity.

This simply means that sampling people and, subsequently, their behavior is an extremely important aspect in the development of cross-cultural frames of reference. In addition to what the reader already knows about sampling and what further information is presented elsewhere in this book on the topic, there are two abstractions related to sampling which merit attention in the development of frames of reference for cross-cultural purposes. One is at the societal (people) level, the other is at the behavioral settings level. A third abstraction, the emic-etic distinction, can serve as a conceptual liaison between the other two. Also discussed are cultural typologies (Goodenough, 1970), otherwise known as "theorics" (Naroll, 1971)—a quite useful anthropological concept.

*Naroll's Cultunit.* Articulated with the cross-cultural survey method of research, which looks at variables at the societal level, the cultunit is a recent solution to the problem of defining discrete cultural units (societies or tribes) so that probability sampling within them can lead to less ambiguous assessment of treatment (culture) effects. Naroll (1964, 1970d) discusses at length the development of the culture-bearing unit—the cultunit—and its ethnographic precursers. The reader is directed to these basic sources in which Naroll has much more comprehensively presented these concepts than is possible in the following summary.

Naroll (1970d) has listed 10 criteria for defining whole societies:

1. Distribution of particular traits being studied (inclusiveness within one society or the need to sample in societies).
2. Territorial contiguity between cultures.
3. Political organization.
4. Language.
5. Ecological adjustment (types of subsistence economy, generally).
6. Local community structure.
7. Widest relevant social unit.
8. Native name (but some people have no name for themselves, some are not sure what to call themselves, and some have two or more defining names).
9. Common folklore or history.
10. Ethnographers' units (various units used in the past, with no consistent pattern).

The basic difficulty in the possibility of using all or most of these criteria preliminary to making comparisons is that societal unit definitions in the past have been vague and inconsistent. The cultunit makes use of the "clearest" three of these ten criteria—invariably (1) language, (2) territorial contiguity and, whenever there is sufficient authoritative political structure, (3) political organization. Various problems with the other seven criteria precluded their use in the final definition of the cultunit. Thus, the cultunit is defined as *people who are domestic speakers of a common distinct language and who belong either to the same state or the same contact group.*

Naroll (1970d, p. 733) has proposed the use of four cultunit types:

1. *Hopi type.* People who belong to no state but who speak a common distinct language and who are all interconnected by successive contact links.
2. *Flathead type.* People who belong to a state all of whose members speak a common distinct language.
3. *Aztec type.* People who belong to a state in which unintelligible dialects occur and who are domestic speakers of a dialect intelligible to speakers of the lingua franca of the state, that is, the dialect in which state officials usually transact their business.
4. *Aymaran type.* People who belong to a state in which unintelligible dialects occur and who are domestic speakers of a dialect not intelligible to speakers of the lingua franca of the state.

Two things must be remembered when using the above types: (1) no two people belong to the same cultunit unless they speak the same language at home, and (2) no two people belong to the same cultunit unless they are in contact.

The cultunit is offered as a means to aid the researcher in solving sampling and counting problems in cross-cultural surveys. Naroll makes no pretense that the cultunit is "simple and elegant," preferring rather to call it "complex and cumbersome." But it is superior to any other precisely defined concept of the culture-bearing unit. When applied properly, the investigator may find the cultunit helpful to:

1. Arrange the sample by cultunit type(s).
2. Summarize relevant data.
3. Cite relevant sources.
4. Discuss specific problems of particular cultunits in notes at the end.

As previously stated, the cultunit is a concept which has been designed to be a servant to the cross-cultural survey method of research, that is, the total society level. We shall now give an example of the second abstraction to use in the development of frames of reference—this one at the level of individual behavior within specific settings.

*Behavior Settings as Units for Cross-Cultural Comparisons.* The individual is the smallest unit with which a cross-cultural researcher will have to concern himself. Nevertheless, he is an intact, self-contained unit, and embodies many if not most of the characteristics of the culture in which he functions. Allowing for individual variations within groups or societies, it is generally the system, in which an individual is a subsystem, that shapes individual behavior. When a sample mean is calculated, the mean is that one hypothetical individual who has all the characteristics of "averageness" for that sample. When means for two samples are computed and compared, we are comparing individual "averageness" within systems, the differences (or similarities) of averageness being attributed to how the system has shaped the behavior of individuals within each system.

This is quite obvious, and is a gross simplification of what much of cross-cultural comparative research attempts to do. The naive observer will perhaps be especially impressed with cross-cultural differences (so-called "Whopper variables") rather than similarities, because of cultural tunnel vision or simple fascination with the "unusual." "Do the Turks really do that?" say the British. "Do Finns actually think that. . .?" say the Americans. And so on. Viewed from a systems standpoint, there is no good reason why the Turks should not do that, or why the Finns actually think that. . .or why the British and Americans are so surprised. When understood at a behavioral level within a system, there are no mysteries to be found in cross-cultural research.

What are psychologically significant and scientifically adequate parts of a culture? Roger Barker, a current spokesman for the Lewinian tradition, has spent many years attempting to answer his own question within the constraints of *behavior settings* and *behavior setting claims,* and in general, within the constraints of ecological psychology (see Barker and Wright, 1955; Barker, 1968). Barker (1971, p. 17) lists the following characteristics of behavior settings.

1. Behavior settings involve ongoing patterns of extra-individual behavior

whose identity and functioning are independent of the participation of particular persons.

2. A behavior setting has a circumjacent soma of physical objects: of walls, doors, fences, chairs, dishes, typewriters, ad infinitum, arranged in a characteristic spatial pattern, at a particular temporal and physical locus.

3. Behavior settings are homeostatic systems; they normally persist, often for years, at a relatively stable, characteristic level.

Further, behavior settings are phenomenal, preperceptual, and ecological; individuals within them do not have to be aware of them per se. A behavior setting contains opportunities where inhabitants can satisfy personal motives, and where they can achieve multiple satisfactions.

A behavior setting claim is "all the forces acting upon individual members of a setting to enter and participate in its operation in particular ways." Individual opportunities and obligations are subsumed under this concept. The behavior of an individual is *claimed* by the nature of the setting; the behavior of a Ford Motor Company riveter is claimed by job demands, and under times of austere employment the demands on him are greater than in times of full employment. The behavior of the Eskimo male, who must do many and varied jobs (apparently with pride), is a function of the demands made on him by his behavior setting. The behavior setting and the claims made by it comprise a human ecological system. Dawson makes similar distinctions within his biosocial theory (discussed below).

*The Interdependence of a Hierarchy of Units.* In his writings, Barker suggests that for comparative purposes the world can be divided into a number of units: *People as units.* As they enter a usual sampling design, individual people *qua people* may be inadequate units for the study of behavior systems. This does not mean that behavior cannot be described and differentiated cross-culturally. It only means that *cultural sources of behavior cannot be explicated simply by studying individuals.*

*Towns, Villages, and Similar Loci as Units.* Small units such as towns and villages allow the researcher to deal with manageable numbers of solutions and sources of information. He is also able to see the people in situ. The problem here is whether or not these loci represent anything but themselves as systems. But if they are microcosms of larger systems (the cultures or societies in which they exist, as in the cross-cultural survey method), the value of the research done at this level is increased. At worst, we will have comparisons of two ecological systems.

*Tesserae as Units.* Barker has confined the study of systems (usually towns, which are microcosms of the countries of which they are a part) to selected *tesserae*—small "pieces" within systems—for the same reason that entire cultural behavioral systems in general are too unwieldy. Thus, a town would be isomorphic to the country, and tesserae would be isomorphic to the town.

Any systematic unit can be marked off in grids of space and time, and complex happenings within system samples demarcated by these two coordinates can be documented. Tesserae, which are created by the researcher because he is ignorant of the system,

". . .are common, well-tested ways of sampling aggregations of related phenomena. A beaker of pond water, a quadrate of the earth's surface, a ten-minute moving picture of a beehive, and a five-minute observation on a playground provide in some respects less fragmentary pieces of functioning systems than individual, isolated amoeba, plants, bees or children. They provide *some* of the normal contexts within which the individuals live" (Barker and Barker, 1961, p. 463).

*Behavior Settings as Units.* Some characteristics of behavior settings were given above. Complete details of them can be found in Barker and Wright (1955) and Barker (1968). Behavior settings have common features across cultures, but they vary within them. For comparative purposes it is useful, for example, to list the 10 or 20 behavior settings most common within each culture, and then to analyze the claims that these settings have on individuals. The essential feature of behavior settings is to make possible cross-cultural comparisons by counting equivalent parts.

*An Example of Multi-Unit Analysis.* Barker and his colleagues compared American and British children as they existed as a function of town, tesserae, behavior settings, and the claims that each made on their lives. The 10 behavior settings of Midwest and Yoredale in which the residents spend the greatest amount of time, together with the person hours spent in each setting are (from Barker and Barker, 1961, p. 464):

### Midwest (United States)

| Variety Name | Particular Name | Hours/Yr. |
| --- | --- | --- |
| Streets and sidewalks | Variously named streets | 77,544 |
| Grocery stores | Kane's Grocery | 24,780 |
| Drug stores | Clifford's Drug Store | 20,855 |
| Restaurants | Gwyn Cafe | 17,000 |
| Restaurants | Pearl Cafe | 16,821 |
| Banks | Midwest State Bank | 14,719 |
| School classes | 7th Grade | 14,705 |
| Department stores | Cabell's Department Store | 13,911 |
| Drug stores | Denton's Drug Store | 13,871 |
| Post Office | Midwest Post Office | 13,602 |

### Yoredale (British)

| Variety Name | Particular Name | Hours/Yr. |
|---|---|---|
| Streets and sidewalks | Variously named streets | 300,000 |
| Markets | Yoredale Market Day | 44,000 |
| Railroad station | Yoredale RR Station | 29,585 |
| Milk depot | Express Dairy | 28,830 |
| Cinemas | Supreme Cinema | 28,704 |
| Garages | Marble's Garage | 27,565 |
| School classes | Upper Juniors | 26,694 |
| Builders | Church, Builder, and Funeral Director | 26,325 |
| School classes | Lower Juniors | 26,082 |
| Cinemas | Castle Cinema | 22,880 |

As one example of the relationship between settings and claims, consider the following number of parts for Midwest and Yoredale:

| | Number of Settings | Number of Persons |
|---|---|---|
| Midwest | 579 | 715 |
| Yoredale | 494 | 1300 |
| Ratio: Midwest/Yoredale | 1.18 | 0.55 |

"According to the theory of behavior setting claim gradients," Barker writes, "Midwest behavior settings bring stronger pressures on citizens to enter and participate in them than do Yoredale settings."

These and other data too comprehensive to include here mean that "the relatively undermanned settings of Midwest 'claim' more of the citizen's time, more of his energy, and elicit from him greater versatility of behavior than the Yoredale settings with a greater number of inhabitants."

Finally, consider the following important comment by Barker (1971, p. 30):

"We judge that these differences in the participation, responsibility, importance, and breadth of social contacts of Midwest and Yoredale residents are neither capricious nor the consequence of the individual choices, *but that they are a necessary consequence of the behavior setting arrangement with-in the ecological environments of the two towns.* [Italics ours.] People in Midwest *have* to participate to a greater degree than in Yoredale. We predict that Englishmen imported to Midwest would *have* to participate also, and that this would occur immediately with no learning period involved."

Earlier it was suggested that the same conformity scores for Brazilian and Swedish samples may actually constitute a difference. Ecological psychology, with its use of the differential impact on groups and individuals that behavior settings and claim gradients have on people from different ecological systems, can be used as a means to discern the "true" meanings of "similar" or "different" scores when comparisons are made. Some validity across systems may be represented by the same scores, but the different behavioral systems demand a need for different interpretations because of the existence of different criteria.

## Emics, Etics, and Theorics

The emic-etic distinction was briefly presented earlier in this book. We consider it important at this time to develop these concepts more fully and to present a third and similar concept—theorics.

Cultural anthropologists and, more recently, psychologists have found it convenient to borrow the terms emic and etic from a psycholinguist (Pike, 1966). The study of phon*emics* examines sounds used in one particular language, while an examination of phon*etics* will allow the linguist to attempt generalizations to all languages. However, a sufficiently large number of phonemic investigations are necessary before universal phonetic regularities can be validly inferred.

Berry (1969) is the first cross-cultural *psychologist* to present formally the concepts of emics and etics as recommended orientations in cross-cultural research. His analysis of the problem was stimulated largely as a result of numerous treatises by anthropologists of similar relevant topics. For example, Goldschmidt (1966) proposed that comparisons between societies or cultures should be made only to the extent that the comparisons address possible solutions to recurrent problems of mutual significance to the cultures in question. Goldschmidt maintains that social problems and solutions to them are recurrent, not inconsistent institutions. Berry characterizes the distinctions as follows:

| Emic Approach | Etic Approach |
| --- | --- |
| Studies behavior from within the system | Studies behavior from a position outside the system |
| Examines only one culture | Examines many cultures, comparing them |
| Structure discovered by the analyst | Structure created by the analyst |
| Criteria are relative to internal characteristics | Criteria are considered absolute or universal |

Berry recapitulates some of the ways that adjectival modifiers clarify the way in which these terms are used. For instance:

1. An *assumed etic* presupposes that certain behavior in a system external to our own can be understood by using an emic framework.

2. An *imposed emic* assumes that aspects of one's own behavioral system can

be found in other systems. Done haphazardly, this is the cardinal sin in cross-cultural research.

3. Both of the above may lead to an *imposed etic* approach, which would doom an analysis if imposed blindly. This would lead only to an anecdotal study ("how well can they do on our tests"), telling us little about the internal relationships among numerous variables.

Finally, Berry explains in the following way how a *derived etic*, which will allow valid comparisons, can be achieved:

"If, however, we enter into the system knowing that our point of entry (be it etic or emic) is only a poor approximation to what we wish to have, then the first major hurdle is passed. Modification of our external categories must then be made in the direction of the system under study, until we eventually achieve a truly emic description of behaviour within that culture. That is, an emic description can be made by progressively altering the imposed etic until it matches a purely emic point of view; if this can be done without entirely destroying or losing all of the etic character of the entry categories, then we can proceed to the next step. If some of the etic is left, we can now note the categories or concepts which are shared by the behaviour system we knew previously and the one we have just come to understand emically. We can now set up a derived etic which is valid for making comparisons between two behaviour settings and we have essentially resolved the problem of obtaining a descriptive framework valid for comparing behaviour across behaviour settings. This new derived etic can then be transported to another behaviour setting (this time as an imposed etic), be modified emically, and then form the basis of a new derived etic which is valid in three behaviour settings. When all systems which may be compared (limited by the initial functional equivalence requirement) have been included, then we have achieved a *universal* for that particular behaviour" (1969, p. 124).

Psychologists and other social scientists are considerably behind cultural anthropologists in documenting etic categories which will allow comparisons between two or more cultural systems. For instance, anthropologists have for many years been analyzing emic kinship systems in terms of eight etic concepts that have been available since Kroeber (1909) or even earlier. The key concepts constitute an inventory, or checklist, against which any kinship term system can be compared. [See Tyler (1969) for a variety of papers on this topic, and for an introduction to componential analysis, the statistical technique that has been used to study kinship systems.]

Just as political scientists do not have an etic inventory which will allow valid comparisons across political systems, psychologists do not have an inventory which could serve as a basis for an etic analysis of psychological constructs, although work with the construct of intelligence is promising (see Chapter 5).

In the development of kinship theory, anthropologists have identified four kin term systems that are related to social structure (Naroll, 1970b, pp. 1238-1240), and these revolve around the eight etic concepts which may be used to study any kinship system in as exhaustive a fashion as currently possible. The concept of *theorics,* advanced by Goodenough (1970) as *typologies* and introduced by Naroll (1971) as theorics now enters the picture. Theorics are typologies of systems (such as the four kinship systems) which should be distinguished from etics and emics since the latter were used in the development of theorics. The sequence of development went from a series of emics, to etic categories, to theorics.

Naroll (1971) writes that

*"Theoric* concepts are those used by social scientists to *explain* variations in human behavior. Among the variations to be explained are the variations in *emic* systems. If we assume that a science of human behavior is possible, we must assume that much of the variation in *emic* systems is functionally related as effect to cause to variations in other aspects of human affairs. Consequently, if we do not understand the range of variation of *emic* systems, we cannot be said to have defined our theoretical problems adequately. Development of an *etic* system is the most parsimonious way to define and describe the range of variation of *emic* systems. But there is no reason to suppose that the *etic* categories are likely to be otherwise powerful in explanatory theory construction" (p. 7).

Theoric categories in cross-cultural work would be the precise operational definitions of its variables. The validity of a theoric category is proportional to how much the skilled investigator can learn through the use of the category as part of his overall research design. The message from anthropologists may be that an urgent task for cross-cultural psychology is to develop a standard set of theoretically suitable theoric categories and terms.

Perhaps the closest that cross-cultural psychology has come to an integration of concepts like theorics is represented by "cultural thematics," a term that McClelland has used to explain "emic" variations in needs, aspirations, and so forth. The work on cultural factors affecting perception and susceptibility to illusions represents other widely studied phenomena. If we are interpreting the notion of theorics correctly, and if we were to extend its use to the considerable research on need achievement, perception, or illusions, then it may be possible to develop several theoric categories for each (e.g., African type, Indian type, Eskimo type, and so forth), the use of which in comparative studies immediately explains it. The same may be possible in all areas of cross-cultural psychology, wherein the sufficiently described categories in each could be useful in explaining emic variations in the same domains.

Thus we have at least these three orientations for explicit cross-cultural use. Consider the importance that cultunits, behavior settings, and the emic-etic-theorics distinction can have in making, or making possible, cross-cultural comparisons. Suppose that we draw samples of Canadian and Tanzanian female nurdwinders, subject them to various types of supervisors, and conclude that the Canadian females wind more nurds under male supervision. So what? Are we certain, a priori, for example,

1. That females, to an extent equivalent in both countries, usually wind nurds?
2. That nurdwinders in each country, male or female, are usually supervised when winding nurds?
3. That supervisors of nurdwinders are usually male and/or female, or can be either?
4. That ratios of males to females in both countries are equivalent?
5. That nurds have similar behavioral, economic, and ecological meaning in both countries?
6. That either or both countries care about the experiment in the first place?
7. That nurds exist?

Are we in fact comparing incomparables, like comparing eggs with tobacco? It is perfectly clear that to make valid cross-cultural comparisons we must make a sizeable shift of reasoning so that meaningful comparisons are possible, not by using levels of transplanted unicultural phenomena, but by using levels of in situ cultural phenomena that can be functionally equated between cultures. Only by using sampling methods like the cultunit, and by documenting exhaustively the cross-cultural equivalence of dependent and independent variables can we hope to find differences that *make* differences and similarities that make sense.

With this introduction to a number of critical methodological considerations, we now proceed to summaries of four important frames of reference. To varying extents, all of the preceding introductory concepts can be discerned either explicitly or implicitly on the following pages.

## Intellectual Development a la Piaget

The developmental psychology of the Swiss psychologist, Jean Piaget, has reached unquestioned stature as one of the chief movements in child psychology. For half a century Piaget and his students and colleagues, notably Barbel Inhelder, have been documenting how the intellect grows. It is a rather difficult theory to fully grasp, and space precludes our going into it in any detail. To probe deeply the intricacies of the theory would require the reading of a seemingly endless amount of material. Piaget has authored or coauthored about fifty books and a hundred or more articles. Several recent books (e.g., Phillips, 1969; Ginsburg and Opper, 1969) have presented the theory in summary form, any one of which contain references to the major works of Piaget and to detailed explanations of the theory by others (e.g., Flavell, 1963; Furth, 1969).

The theory traces the development of intelligence from birth through the mid-teens (and implicitly adulthood), and is divided into four major periods: (1) sensorimotor (0-24 months); (2) pre-operational thought (2-6 or 7 years); (3) concrete operations (7-11); and (4) formal operations (12-15 years). These are in turn subdivided into subperiods and stages which follow the same *sequence* of development even though individual differences in *rate* are certain to occur.

Cross-cultural psychology is endowed with a liberal number of studies and some recent surveys of Piagetian research. Piaget has welcomed such research and Jerome Bruner, another eminent expert in cognitive growth, has actively promoted the cross-cultural examination of intellectual development. Jahoda (1958) has summarized cross-cultural work with Piaget's formulations on animism, casualty, and moral judgment; a section in Price-Williams (1969) includes studies by Greenfield, Goodnow, and Price-Williams; Georgie-Hyde (1970) has detailed an extensive study on the conservation of number and quantity; and Dasen (1972) has summarized Piagetian research done in non-Western cultures. Since 1969, Dasen and his colleague, Dr. Gavin Seagrim, have maintained an irregularly appearing *Inventory of Cross-Cultural Piagetian Research.*[3]

As Dasen (1972) points out, cross-cultural Piagetian research has primarily focused on the concrete operations period (7-11 years), largely abandoning the earlier and later periods. The emphasis on this period seems quite defensible, since if non-genetic factors are to influence the development of intelligence, they will likely do so during these "middle years" when the earlier period of formal education intervenes, rather than during the earlier or later periods. It is true, of course, that factors such as malnutrition or severe sensory deprivation during the sensorimotor period can have a marked influence on later development (cf. Werner and Muralidharan, 1970). We may expect to see a rapid increase in cross-cultural work concentrating on this infantile period of intellectual development, since research concerned with the concrete operations period is bound to reach a point of diminishing returns, and more will need to be known about factors affecting earlier development.

The principle of conservation has far and away been the most widely studied of all Piagetian concepts. Without conservation, it is said, can there be no rational thought. Conservation essentially means that despite irrelevant changes, such as merely rearranging the physical or observable properties of objects or quantity, the properties remain invariant. For our purposes here, rational

[3]To close followers of Piagetian research, Drs. Dasen and Seagrim will make copies of these inventories available upon request. The mimeographed inventories include abstracts of recently completed and ongoing research. They also welcome the receipt of new references of include in future issues. Use this address: Australian National University, Department of Psychology, P.O. Box 4, Canberra A.C.T. 2600, Australia.

thought involves the conservation of number, weight, length, substance, continuous and discontinuous quantities, and volume.

Two brief examples will explain the basic nature of conservation experiments. In the *conservation of substance,* the child is given two identical balls of clay or some other malleable substance. He is asked whether there is the same amount of clay in each. If he thinks not, he is told to make the balls equal by adding or taking away clay. While the child watches, *E* molds one of the balls into a sausage shape. The child is then asked if the untouched ball and the sausage have equal amounts. If the child is consistent in maintaining that they do have equal amounts, then he has conserved substance. In the *conservation of weight,* the same two balls of clay are placed on a balance so the child sees that they are the same weight. One ball is then transformed into a sausage shape, and the child is asked to judge whether or not the objects will, when again placed on the two sides of the balance, weight the same. If after a series of such changes in shape the child continues to recognize that they weigh the same, conservation of weight is established.

Each of the several conservations follow a sequence of development, but, as noted earlier, rates may vary. Generally, Genevan children conserve weight and substance by age 4, and continuous quantities by age 6 or 7. Thus it is the rate (Genevan versus non-Genevan) and not the sequence of development that has been studied cross-culturally. It must also be emphasized that "pure" Piagetian research does not use typical standardized psychological tests as dependent variables in the various experiments. Rather, they are largely manipulative-type tests which allow the researcher to observe how the individual is approaching the solution. Georgie-Hyde (1970) gives an excellent description and account of the use of many of these tests, and Heron (1971) points out, using Zambian data, the dangers of using locally constructed psychometric devices to measure Piagetian concepts. A recent book has been devoted to testing and measurement problems within the Piagetian framework (Green, Ford, and Flamer, 1971).

Also, a *Concept Assessment Kit—Conservation* has recently been developed (Goldschmid and Bentler, 1968). The kit contains three scales. Two of them are parallel forms and are designed to measure six conservation tasks, while a third scale measures slightly different dimensions of conservation. This standardized instrument has recently been used in an energetic multi-researcher, multination project using as subjects boys and girls in six different cultures (Goldschmid, Bentler, et al., 1973). In that study the kit demonstrated high reliability in indicating specific environmental factors affecting conservation acquisition.

Combining curves not unlike typical S-shaped learning curves that Dasen (1972) and others have presented and curves suggested by Bayley (1955), a number of possibilities concerning the rate of intellectual growth exist.

As Figure 6.1 shows, groups of children within cultures can develop according to rates a, b, or c, and cross-culturally, with ages held constant, groups can

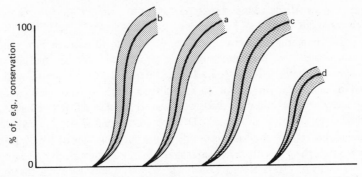

**Figure 6-1.** Ages held constant cross-culturally, or increasing ages within one culture. a = the Genevan rate of development; b = somewhat ahead of the Genevan rate; c = somewhat behind the Genevan rate; d = non-conservers, or those starting at a, b, or c who fail to reach the concrete operational conservation period.

develop at the same rate as Genevan children (a), they can be advanced (b), or they can lag behind (c). Moreover, individual variation (the shaded areas) can be expected to increase both intra- and cross-culturally in both the rate and age of achieving conservation. Curve d depicts those who may start at a, b, or c, but who never reach the concrete operational stage.

The rationale and experimental techniques used in studying intellectual development cross-culturally have taken many forms. A dozen of these are presented below, together with both brief examples of specific techniques within each and the basic, or expected, findings.

1. *Studying two or more ethnic groups who are either living separately or together, but who share the same general cultural milieu.* Studying the conservation of number and quantity among Arab, Somali, Indian, and European children living in Aden, Georgie-Hyde (1970) found (1) that these children performed in ways analyzable in conventional Genevan fashion, (2) that Piaget's "stages" were generally operative among these samples, (3) that characteristic responses were qualitatively similar to Piaget's norms, (4) that sex was not an important variable, and (5) that the variance between the groups increased with age, confirming the progression of stages.

2. *Two or more groups of subjects from the same tribal stock or ethnic background, one of which is living traditionally, the other of which as been acculturated in varying degrees by living in a neighboring "European" community. The groups are sometimes called High and Low contact groups.* Part of de Lacey's (1970) study showed that high contact Australian Aborigine children performed better than low contact Aborigine children on a test of classificatory ability developed by Inhelder and Piaget.

3. *Unschooled versus schooled rural children (or urban versus rural*

*children), non-Western.* Greenfield (1966) found that among the Wolof, bush schooled children reached conservation by ages 11-13, while only half of the bush unschooled children did so.

4. *Sex effects within homogeneous groups.* Among other results, Za'rour (1971) found that Lebanese males conserved number and liquid at greater percentages than Lebanese females at all ages studied (5-9). The greater freedom for play and exploration that Lebanese males have suggested as the reason for the difference, although other, non-Lebanese, studies have found no sex differences.

5. *Language effects, including bilingualism.* De Lacy (1970) graded low and high contact Aborigines on a 17-item "index of contact" scale. Those items related to the extent of language used at home by each group received double weighting. He found striking differences in the ability to classify objects according to category (see 2 above). These differences may be partly due to language, since the low contact group used English at School and the vernacular at home, while the high contact group used English both at school and at home.

6. *Genetic factors, where full-blood groups are compared with mixed-blood groups, and all other factors are held constant.* De Lemos (1966, 1969a,b) studied Aboriginal children living in the same environment. Some of the children were full-blood Aborigines, while others were known to have European ancestry. Many conservation differences favored the part-blood children, but Dasen (1970) found no such differences when the study was replicated with a different sample of the same Aboriginal children, using the same tests.

7. *Malnutrition, that is, brain damage or neurological deficit as a result of it.* As Dasen (1972) has pointed out, no cross-cultural study specifically assessing the effects that malnutrition has on Piagetian tasks has been done, but cross-cultural studies by, for example, Werner and Muralidharan (1970), have documented that malnutrition has a marked effect on intellectual as well as other development (e.g., head circumference and visual-motor development).

8. *Variable physical or social stimulation, including differential child-rearing practices.* Many authors (see Dasen, 1972) have postulated that cultural traditions of deprivation of physical or social stimulation (e.g., the Indian swaddling of babies for many months) may have accounted for failures of some cultural groups to reach the operational stage, but no study has definitively proven that such deprivation affects rate or the eventual attainment of operational thought. No cross-cultural Piagetian studies using child-rearing practices as the independent variable have yet been noted.

9. *Age (Normative studies).* Price-Williams (1961) studied five groups of illiterate children from the West African Tiv tribe on the conservation of continuous and discontinuous quantities. Even though he had difficulty in establishing exact ages (5-8 years), Price-Williams asserts that conservation was reached by the Tiv at approximately the same ages that Western children reach it.

10. *The effects of "magical" thinking (versus implied comparisons with empirical thought).* Greenfield (1966) found that when she poured the water (conservation of continuous quantity), unschooled Wolof children explained the change in terms attributing magical qualities to $E$ (Greenfield), and conservation was low. When $S$s poured the water, conservation went up. *But* they claimed that the water they poured was not the same as when she poured it (though in fact it was).

11. *Perceptual-environmental-experiential.*     Several studies, (e.g., Vernon, 1969; Bruner, Olver, and Greenfield, 1966; Goodnow, 1969) have shown how experimental and general ecological factors affecting development can affect the rate of achieving conservation. Goodnow gives an example of a Chinese boy asserting that sometimes rice comes in bags stacked horizontally and other times it comes vertically, but that all the bags observed contain the same amount of rice. Having carried them, he knew; other children without such experience may be deceived by the shape of the bag. Price-Williams, Gordon, and Ramirez (1969) hypothesized and confirmed that children of Mexican pottery makers would show conservation earlier than non-potters' children. The children of potters were "speeded up" in the development of conservation (and other stages as well) simply because they experienced from an early age onwards both the playing with bits of clay and how much clay it would take to fit molds for baking.

12. *Subjects from automated versus subjects from manual cultures.* In a sense, all "Genevan" versus "non-Western" studies have addressed the possible differential rates of growth that manual cultures may impose on children as opposed to the stimulation of the normative automated cultures. Thus, we should expect all "Western" children to conform to Genevan data. Furby (1971) has suggested a theoretical framework to use in these and other investigations dealing with this dichotomy. Table 6.1 summarizes this theoretical framework, postulating what kind of Piagetian performance we should expect as a function of type of reasoning and type of environment.

In summary, cross-cultural research within the Piagetian framework has thus far confirmed that the stages of development and their sequence as postulated by the Genevan school can be identified everywhere. On the other hand, such research has *not* confirmed and sometimes has even refuted the notions or propositions that (1) all normal individuals in all cultures pass through all stages, and with regard to every form of cognitive task. Appropriate environmental support or stimulation appear to be necessary for the achievement of certain levels of development; (2) the ages for reaching stages conform to the Genevan norm; and (3) the order of development is invariant, for example, reaching conservation of quantity before weight, and weight before volume.

Finally, in an earlier, unpublished section of his 1972 Summary of Piagetian research, Dasen wrote

Table 6.1   Summary of Theoretical Framework

| Type of Reasoning | Perceptual Flexibility | |
| | High (Manual Environment) | Low (Automated Environment) |
| --- | --- | --- |
| Empirical (Western) | No difficulty with conservation of identity or perceptual flexibility | No difficulty with conservation of identity |
| | Should perform better than any other group | Difficulty with perceptual flexibility |
| | | Should perform better with screen[a] present |
| Magical (non-Western) | No difficulty with perceptual flexibility | Difficulty with both conservation of identity and perceptual flexibility |
| | Difficulty with conservation of identity | Should show the poorest performance but schooling can help by teaching empirical reasoning |
| | Schooling can help by replacing magical thinking with empirical thinking | |

[a]In some conservation experiments, a screen is used to temporarily hide from view *E*'s rearranging objects or liquids.

"We are faced with the usual and quite obvious conclusion: operational development does not depend on any one single factor alone, but on a complex interaction of a number of these factors. Cross-cultural research has already helped to clarify, to some extent, their relative importance, but if further rapid progress is to be made, research in this area will have to change from the mainly piecemeal 'safari'-type to the planned and coordinated use of cultural and ethnic differences. While these cannot be manipulated as in the laboratory, they can be selected more carefully, and cross-cultural research can become more precise. In this respect, an active interdisciplinary collaboration between psychology, anthropology, sociology and the medical sciences would be an enormous advantage."

## Achievement Motivation

This psychological construct probably outranks both Freudian and Piagetian concepts in sheer numbers of cross-cultural investigations if one takes into account its relative youth. Alternately called the achievement motive, need achievement, or simply *n* Ach, achievement motivation means "a competition with a standard of excellence." In a broader view, Atkinson and Feather's book of readings supports their position that

"The theory asserts that a person's motive to achieve (*n* Achievement), his motive to avoid failure, and his expectation of success in some venture strongly influence the character of his motivation as it is expressed in level of aspiration, preference for risk, willingness to put forth effort and to persist in an activity" (Atkinson and Feather, 1966, p. v).

We will give only a very basic orientation to the theory of need achievement as postulated and perpetuated primarily by David C. McClelland. In addition to the numerous references found on the following pages, the reader is directed to these fairly recent publications: Atkinson (1958), Heckhausen (1967), LeVine's (1970) review of childhood influences on *n* Ach, Birney's (1968) summary of research on the achievement motive, and the hundreds of cumulative references that are found in them.

Cross-culturally and otherwise, one may view *n* Ach as consisting of psychological *antecedents* at the individual level and economic *consequences* at the national level. Examples of the antecedents have been documented by McClelland, Atkinson, Clark and Lowell (1953), Winterbottom (1958), and Rosen and D'Andrade (1959), among others, and the most numerous examples of the consequences can be found in McClelland (1961). Carrying this one step further, recent projects have attempted to stimulate this cause-effect relationship by teaching achievement motivation to individuals in developing countries in the hope that those countries will reap the economic benefits. A large project of this kind is mentioned below.

Between the seminal work by McClelland and his colleagues and the more recent applications (covering about a 25-year interval), can be found hundreds of studies which give this area of research a solid and very impressive superstructure. The research cited below is but a small fraction of what is available on *n* Ach, and we beg forgiveness for any serious and unintentional errors of omission.

*The Basis of the Theory.* Achievement motivation is related to economic growth. When McClelland and his colleagues were laying the groundwork to verify this cause-effect relationship, a sociological treatise by Max Weber (1904) and a psychological dissertation by Winterbottom (1953) gave further substance to their formulations. Weber hypothesized that the Protestant Ethic resulted in the rise of modern capitalism, and Winterbottom explained simply how this was done: the Protestant Ethic encourages middle-class parents to instill independence and mastery of activities in their sons, and the resultant high level of *n* Ach embodies the spirit of modern capitalism.

Intensive studies of ancient civilizations are given as evidence that this spirit, or *n* Ach, has been around a long time. For example, in Anthenian Greece the level of *n* Ach was at a peak during the period of growth prior to the climax of its economic development. HRAF studies of primitive tribes confirmed the hypothesis that high *n* Ach leads to economic activity of an advanced type. Also, significant correlations between, for example, achievement imagery appearing in children's stories in 1925 and units of electrical output in 1950 have given more substance to the theory. (It should be noted that units of electrical power were rather ingeniously used as a marker variable, since they are constant throughout the world, whatever their source.) In this type of analysis, children's stories have been scored for themes of *n* Ach with the assumption that the adults who wrote them apparently passed on the attitudes, aspirations, and values that they unconsciously considered most important (see McClelland, 1961, for details).

Numerous ways of measuring achievement themes have been attempted. Pictorial material, especially certain cards from Murray's Thematic Apperception Test, are perhaps the most common (see Chapter 5). Experimental procedures designed to arouse the achievement motive, after which fantasy stories are written, are other popular procedures. Ring-tossing and block-stacking by children, under various conditions of parental supervision or contact (where the parent's influence is observed and recorded), is yet another method, and even the analysis of "doodles" has proven successful. Folk tales and dreams have also been analyzed for their achievement themes (see LeVine, 1966). Most of the commonly used measurement techniques show reasonably high interscorer reliability (the TAT being a major exception), and the objective computer has been told how to score *n* Ach themes.

More recently, Lynn (1969) has prepared a questionnaire to measure achievement motivation, with the hope that it will have higher reliability than existing methods. Items designed to tap achievement attitudes were answered by various British samples, and then factor analyzed. Not unexpectedly, Lynn contends that a single achievement factor emerged, which is uncorrelated with Eysenck's factors of neuroticism and introversion-extraversion and with all but two of Cattell's 16 personality factors (see Chapter 8). Lynn also shows that scores on his questionnaire differentiate various criterion groups of "known" high achievers. The questionnaire has also been given to samples from several other cultures [Melikian, Ginsberg, Cuceloglu, and Lynn (1971); Iwawaki and Lynn (1972)]. The scores appear to have some consistency across cultures, but detailed cross-validation and standardization are necessary before it can be put to general use.

There are currently available a number of questionnaire-type "achievement motivation" instruments. Such devices probably do not measure spontaneous interest in achieving as measured by the "thought-sampling technique" offered by certain projectives and McClelland's pioneering instruments. Rather, ample evidence says that such scales do not measure achievement motivation but achievement values. What they are measuring, in effect, is the extent to which an individual is identifying with a conformist Protestant Ethic (McClelland, 1970).

*Cross-Cultural Studies of the Origin of n Ach.* Two American studies suggestive of the origins of achievement motivation in the United States will set the stage for a discussion of cross-cultural extensions. In the earlier Winterbottom (1953) study, the importance of the mother's tendency to encourage independence and mastery in children who are high in need achievement was emphasized. Rosen and D'Andrade (1959) studied the role of both parents in infusing high *n* Ach, and they concluded that fathers and mothers both play an important role in providing achievement and independence training, with the fathers apparently contributing much more to the latter, and the mothers stressing achievement training. The mothers were seen as having high aspirations for their sons, and the fathers were not dominant. Mother dominance appears to permit the growth of achievement motivation, since by dominating she is "imposing her standards," while a dominating father may crush his son by "imposing himself."

Cross-cultural studies of children and parents paralleling American methodology are numerous. Rosen (1962) studied the relationship of family structure to socialization and achievement motivation in Brazil. Using a TAT measure, observations, interviews, and questionnaires, the *n* Ach of Brizilian boys was compared with the *n* Ach of a roughly matched sample of boys from the Northeastern United States. Breaking the samples into five social classes, Rosen found linear negative relations of social class with mean age of both achievement training and independence training in both countries. The distribution of achievement scores for both groups was similar, but social class accounted for smaller proportions of the variance for the Brazilians because in all social classes their mean levels of achievement motivation were so much lower. The lower Brazilian level was attributed to the traditional Brazilian family—authoritarian fathers, and mothers who are less likely than mothers in the United States to train sons in self-reliance, autonomy, and achievement. However, Rosen mentioned that poverty, a rigid social system, marriage instability, and disease are other Brazilian factors which could possibly account for the differences. Parenthetically, in a somewhat post hoc confirmation that the TAT is an acceptable method of measuring achievement motivation in Brazil, Angelini (1966) found no difference in the average achievement scores for Brazilian and United States male university students.

Several studies have assessed the role that fathers play in influencing the achievement motivation of children. Bradburn (1963) hypothesized that Turkish males would have low *n* Ach because of the extreme dominance of the father in traditional Turkish families. He also hypothesized that Turkish males who for some reason were not dominated by their fathers should have higher need achievement. Testing the first hypothesis, he compared Turks attending a middle management school at the University of Istanbul with American junior executives participating in a similar program at Harvard University. The Americans showed much higher preoccupation with achievement. Furthermore, Turkish men who had lived apart from their fathers before age 14 had higher achievement scores than men who had lived with their fathers after age 14—a finding that confirmed the second hypothesis.

In Trinidad, Mischel (1961) found that Negro children preferred immediate small reinforcement (a one-cent candy bar) as opposed to the preference of East Indian children for delayed larger reinforcement (a ten-cent candy bar) to be given several days after the immediate reinforcement was available, but refused. Both were rewards for completing a questionnaire. The preference for the immediate reward was even more profound for many of the children, especially the Negroes, who were without fathers. Significantly more children who chose delayed reinforcement had fathers present, and those children also showed more concern with achievement.

In a study comparing *n* Ach of Northern (Boston area) and Southern United States male and female Negroes, many differences were found, including a linkage between father absence and low *n* Ach (Nuttall, 1964). Also, a negative correlation between *n* Ach and authoritarian child-training practices was found.

While one may expect lower need achievement among boys from fatherless homes in "non-father dominated" cultures, the higher achievement themes found for low-father-contact Turkish males is interpreted to be a result of the release from father dominance. McClelland (1961) notes that cultures high in *n* Ach tend to have an abundance of travelling males (fathers as sailors, for example), and that this should be especially true in authoritarian cultures where other factors, such as "mothers with high standards of excellance," are present. McClelland offers an educated guess that

"It is an ironic twist of history to think that seafaring peoples who acquired slaves from subject nations in the triumph of their success may have caused their own undoing by increasing *n* Achievement of those they had conquered and decreasing their own by shifting the balance of which fathers were away from home the most" (1961, p. 405).

Many cross-cultural studies using older subjects have appeared. In one study, for example, Tedeschi and Kian (1962) used four TAT cards to measure achievement themes among 30 American and 30 Persian students in both relaxed and "aroused" conditions (false Harvard "norms"). Between groups there were no significant differences in either condition on the strength of *n* Ach, but among Persians the aroused condition produced greater achievement themes than did the relaxed condition. The Persian students may have been more willing than the Americans to compare themselves with the fictitious Harvard norms. Reboussin and Goldstein (1966) compared Navajo students attending the Haskell Institute with white United States college students, testing the hypothesis that the Navajo are lower on *n* Ach. It was found that Navajos were *greater* than whites on *n* Ach, but a selective feature may have been operating in favor of the Haskell Institute students, since so many more whites than Navajo attend college or advanced institutes.

Among more recent studies, Sloggett, Gallimore, and Kubany (1970), using 12 ethnically ambiguous TAT cards, compared fantasy need achievement among three Hawaiian groups of differing ethnicity. Finding no significant differences on *n* Ach between high and low achieving indigenous Hawaiians, the authors challenged the notion that low *n* Ach accounts for low academic achievement among Hawaiian children. In another Hawaii-based study, Kubany, Gallimore, and Buell (1970) have cautioned against importing to other cultures (imposing an etic) the Western notion that "intrinsic" motivation to do well is sufficient to measure *n* Ach, especially among subjects from cultures that attach great importance to group acceptance. Using "public" (extrinsic factors) and "private" (intrinsic factors) methods to measure achievement-oriented behavior, they found that Filipino high school boys performed much better when they were observed than when they were privately performing the same task and receiving the same rewards (predesignated scores for "shooting down" airplanes in a flight simulator).

Interested in power, affiliation, and achievement motivation as they relate to occupational aspiration of American Negroes, Littig (1971) studied two groups of college students. One group was attending a middle-class Negro college, while the other was attending a predominently working-class Negro college. Among other findings, Littig concluded that

"Both achievement motivation and power motivation demonstrated a correlation with aspiration to traditionally closed occupations among the working class Negro groups. Strong achievement motivation was moderately related to aspiration to closed occupations in this group and strong power motivation was highly related to traditionally closed occupations in this group" (p. 85).

*National Consequences.* One of the obvious benefits that developing contries gain from so much research on achievement motivation is how to motivate and train individuals in its acquisition, or how to exploit the achievement motivation that exists. A massive project of this kind was attempted for India, Southern Italy, and Tunisia (McClelland and Winter, 1969). For Indians, the researchers tried to overcome childhood training and to move the achievement motive up the hierarchy of needs through a ten-day training course. They tried to teach the entrepreneurs many things, among which were the practice of "achievement thinking" and the setting of personal goals. The project has been discontinued, but apparently not without some success, and the reader may want to consult the text describing it and the many formidable obstacles with which the researchers had to grapple.

The reader may also want to consult research reported by an Indian psychologist who studied *n* Ach among agricultural and business entrepreneurs in and around Delhi (Singh, 1969, 1970). Singh tested the hypothesis that individuals with high *n* Ach are more susceptible to changes in economic opportunities than their counterparts with low *n* Ach. He found differences on measures of *n* Ach among four levels of agricultural entrepreneurs, among eight levels of business entrepreneurs, and between agricultural and business entrepreneurs. The unsurprising finding that business entrepreneurs were higher than agricultural entrepreneurs on *n* Ach was ascribed to two possible reasons: (1) business entrepreneurs are exposed to relatively more business opportunities, or (2) most of the business entrepreneurs had higher motivation levels initially, and migrated from rural and urban areas.

The consequences accruing to a nation with high *n* Ach may not all be positive or healthy. Through the use of a lag model, and making the assumption that the later values of adults are a function of the books they read as children, Rudin (1968) hypothesized that "psychogenic" death rates in 1950 would be related to the *n* Ach scores derived from children's literature in 1925. Making rank-order intercorrelations of death rates in 16 of the 22 countries for whom children's literature was scored and available, Rudin found an "agressive death" cluster (homicide, suicide, and cirrhosis of the liver) to be associated with a 1925 high power motive, and an "inhibitive death" cluster (ulcers and hypertension) significantly related to high achievement motives. He also found that film attendance correlated + .55 with *n* Ach, − .05 with *n* Power, and that book publication correlated −.48 with *n* Ach, + .02 with *n* power.

Barrett and Franke (1970), however, criticized Rudin on both methodological and theoretical grounds. They increased the number of countries studied, and they expanded the time span to include 1925 versus 1950, and 1950 versus 1965 comparisons. They found "psychogenic" deaths to have social, economic, and medical expalnations, and not psychological motive explanations. The only stable relation found was between suicide and ulcers. Durkheimian status integration was positively correlated with homicide and negatively correlated with deaths from suicide and ulcers. Other correlations (e.g., wine consumption with cirrhosis, and zinc consumption with hypertension) were clearly not related to the psychological motives studied by McClelland.

Achievement motivation as a sweeping, imaginative theory has not gone uncriticized. For example, Inkeles (1971) has summarized some major reservations about McClelland's general methodology and conclusions. Specifically, he points to these possible deficiencies:

1. Specific child-rearing environments and techniques that produce high need

achievement in contemporary individuals have been difficult to isolate.

2. No evidence has been presented to establish that those from schools which used textbooks rich in achievement imagery were, as individuals, strong in need achievement, and thus later more often became entrepreneurs.

3. There has been a "failure to specify the social conditions under which high need for achievement might or might not result in entrepreneurial behavior [and] in entrepreneurship that was effective in bringing about significant economic change on a society-wide basis (p. 274)."

4. Most critical, says Inkeles, is the question:

"How far is the more frequent achievement imagery found in certain times and places a reflection of changed social conditions rather than a cause of them? After all, the children do not themselves write their textbooks. It is therefore logical to assume that certain social changes that had already occurred must have stimulated adults to produce textbooks with more achievement imagery. In that case achievement imagery becomes more the product than the cause of social change. And we are left wondering why men with a propensity to heightened achievement imagery were writing textbooks instead of organizing businesses" (1971, p. 273).

Nevertheless, research on achievement motivation and related constructs is expected to continue at an accelerated pace. Surely the "cultural thematics" approach that it represents will lead to a succession of refinements in complicated methodology. The many findings of McClelland and his associates have built a strong keystone for similar imaginative cross-cultural work.

## Dawson's Bio-social Psychology

In his inaugural lecture from the chair of psychology of the University of Hong Kong, Dawson (1969a) explained his conceptual system which has been designed to study the psychological effects of bio-social adaptation to biological environments. His opening statement was:

"Bio-Social psychology is concerned with the way in which adaptation to different biological environments results in the development of particular habits of perceptual inference, cognitive processes, and psychological skills, which are thought to be adaptive for these environments. In addition it is considered that adaptation to different biological environments will result in the formation of related adaptive social systems, which in turn will influence the development of psychological skills needed for survival. While bio-social research deals mainly with subsistence environments, bio-social research problems also arise in modern societies in terms of overcrowding, isolation, proverty, and ecological factors" (p.1).

This statement abridges a point of view which has generated considerable research. It also summarizes a psychosocial ecological perspective which seemingly has endless research potential. Several psychologists have formulated human ecological hypotheses. For example, Barker's work, mentioned earlier (Barker, 1968, 1971), is concerned with environment and behavior, and a recent text is devoted to issues in this area (Proshansky, Ittelson, and Rivlin, 1970). Likewise, Murphy (1947) and Wohlwill (1966, 1970) have made attempts to systematize the interactions between ecology and behavior. Anthropologists such as Rappaport (1967) and Vayda (1969) have made similar attempts to develop comprehensive holistic systems. These so-called organismic positions are popular among nearly all behavioral scientists for, as Hall and Lindzey (1970) have reminded us, "Who believes that there are isolated events, insulated processes, detached functions? . . .We are all organismic psychologists whatever else we may be" (p. 330).

How does Dawson's system differ from other holistic systems? Why is it perhaps of more value to cross-cultural psychologists? The major and perhaps only reason is that it is designed explicitly for cross-cultural research, while most of the others are unspecified, general, and eclectic, but they, too, can certainly fit a cross-cultural mold. Further, some of the others are formal and integrated theories of personality while Dawson and his colleagues seem to be more interested in the global aspects of biological and social man-in-transition from subsistence to modern societies. Dawson's position will be fully explained in his forthcoming book on human ecology and behavior (personal communication). A specific large-scale application of the theory is described in his other forthcoming book dealing with psychological effects of bio-social change in West Africa (personal communication).

Dawson asserts that one of the most important aspects of his theory concerns a group survival theme: how a culture functions as a biological adaptation mechanism which permits, by socialization and norm enforcement, the transmission of necessary skills and attitudes, which in turn insure the perpetuation of that culture. The importance of the system to cross-cultural psychology chiefly involves the established finding that different biological environments produce different methods of bio-social adaptation. For example, the work of Barry, Child, and Bacon (1959) strongly supports bio-social theory. Barry et al. studied 104 societies and successfully predicted that (1) societies with hunting and fishing economies would have low food accumulation and that "adults should be individualistic, assertive, and venturesome," and (2) societies with agricultural economies would have high food accumulation and that "adults should tend to be conscientious, compliant and conservative." They also successfully predicted that in each type of subsistence society the appropriate child-training and socialization practices insuring the survival of the society were emphasized and maintained.

Using relevant data from Barry et al. and also data collected by Dawson in

West Africa, Berry (1966) performed and published the first cross-culture and cross-ecology empirical support of Dawson's system. Berry extended the subsistence/socialization network by successfully predicting that different ecologies stimulate in different ways the development of visual inference habits (see below).

At its current stage of development, Dawson's system concerns the biological and social environments (socialization processes) and how they interact to affect biological and social change. To demonstrate cross-culturally these causes and effects, Dawson, like Berry, has essentially been forced to dwell upon polarized extremes of both biological and social environments; there is seldom a glimpse of the "average" human condition, except to the extent that "average" is defined within the polarized extremes. However, this is an advantage. It is these limited, smaller, and more homogeneous extreme environments in which the bio-social design is more useful for the study of a variety of psychological processess. Larger and diverse Western-type environments do not allow effective control and manipulation of the relevant biological and social variables and their covariation. Melting pots introduce too many competing and contaminating variables.

Table 6.2 depicts the variables within the system. The system involves the relationship between the two independent variables—the biological and socio-cultural environment—and the numerous psychological, physiological, and ecological dependent variables. The following brief explanation of the system as shown in Table 6.2 is given (Dawson, personal communication):

"The postulated relationship between adaptation to the biological environment and the development of adaptive socio-cultural systems is indicated [in Table 6.2] by the arrow going from the top left to the top top right. The closeness of the relationship between the biological and social independent variables is further considered to depend on both the extent of 'extremeness' of the biological environment, (e.g., jungle, snow or desert), while with increasing technological sophistication, the closeness of the relationship would tend to diminish. Thus a closer relationship would be expected between a more extreme desert, snow or jungle-type environment, and the form of adaptive socio-cultural system developed. It is further assumed that as man obtains increasing mastery over his environment through technological skills, his biological environment will be further transformed through cultural adaptations. These effects are indicated by the dotted arrows shown going back from the socio-cultural environment to the biological environment."

Consider a brief example of part of this bio-social interaction. Hamburg (1965) gives evidence that high population density is associated with increases in adrenal function and aggressive behavior, and a decrease in gonadal function. As depicted in Table 6.2, there would be an interacting effect between physical

Table 6.2  The Bio-Social Psychological System[a]

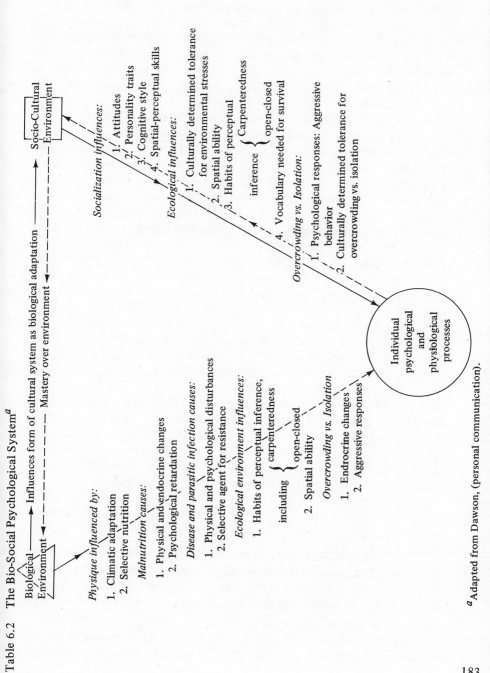

[a] Adapted from Dawson, (personal communication).

183

overcrowding and increased social pressures. Hence, the theory postulates that people from group-oriented agricultural societies would have "a higher cultrually determined threshold level to stresses from physical overcrowding than, for example, individuals from isolated snow or hunting environments. Thus the more individually-oriented Eskimo and Arunta hunters would be expected to have a lower threshold level to physical overcrowding (personal communication)."

The *biological environment,* a term which Dawson uses ecologically, includes physical factors such as climate, food resources, altitude, and the like, and the relationship of living organisms to it. Environments ". . .are classified from *moderate environment* with fewer problems of human adaptation to an *extreme environment* where human adaptive responses must also be extreme to ensure survival" (Dawson, 1969a, p. 2). In dealing with environmental extremes, such as the harshness of West African jungles, Dawson uses the term *biological deficiency* to account for abnormal aspects of environmental variables, such as disease, malnutrition, poverty, overcrowding, and isolation, which are more likely to occur under extreme environmental conditions. Kwashiorkor, a protein deficiency disease, has often been the focus of studies, in extreme environments of assorted physical and psychological retardation, and the interaction of sex and socialization in the development and maintenance of cognitive style (see below).

Included among the most frequently cited cross-cultural studies are those dealing with the effects that extreme biological environments have on visual inference habits. These classic studies fit Dawson's position nicely; indeed, it is obvious that they significantly influenced him in the development of his bio-social framework. Elsewhere in this book some of these studies have been discussed. They include the work of Berry (1966) and Dawson himself (1967a, 1967b), who showed that Eskimos living in the stark, infinite horizon of the North develop different perceptual styles than Africans (Temne) living in "rounded," "horizonless" jungles. The Arctic environment apparently influences the development of field independence in the Eskimo, while a differentiated jungle causes African tribesmen to be field-dependent. Further, Berry and Dawson offer evidence that child-rearing practices in these different subsistence environments lead to the development of skills which are best suited for individual and group survival in those environments. Dawson writes:

"These Temne-Eskimo studies have thus provided evidence to support the bio-social hypotheses in that both societies have developed social organization which is biologically adaptive for their environments, which has in turn encouraged the appropriate psychological skills needed for survival. The Temne have harsh socialization and strict social sanctions, which ensure the development of a high degree of conformity and group orientation needed for the growing and accumulation of the basic crop, rice. With their extremely permissive social system and socialization the Eskimo have encouraged the development of individual independence and high spatial ability needed to hunt and locate the group spatially in their snow environment" (1969a, p. 6).

In a more recent analysis of the role of culture and ecology in the development of perceptual skills, Berry (1971) extended the network to include eight subsistence-level samples, each of which was placed in either a traditional or transitional ecology dimension. Although the influences of education tended to result in certain perceptual superiorities of the transitional groups undergoing westernization, Berry showed that

"... visual skills are developed to a degree predictable from an analysis of the ecological demands facing the group, and the cultural aids developed by them. Further it is apparent that there are relationships between the ecological and psychological variables which are more than dichotomous ones; they appear to covary in a systematic way ... and can be demonstrated to be adaptive to the ecological demands placed on the group" (p. 335).

The "carpentered" versus "non-carpentered" environment hypothesis, which suggests that the different environments lead to differential susceptibility to illusions, is another example of ecological factors affecting perception and perhaps life styles. These studies (e.g., Segall, Campbell, and Herskovits, 1966) have been discussed elsewhere in this book.

Considerable data, then, gathered from extreme environments show that different socialization-sex interaction leads to skills necessary for survival. Witkin's (1962) theory that normal males have a more field-independent cognitive style and greater spatial ability, and that normal females are field dependent and have less spatial ability, has been given support by several, but not all, cross-cultural ecological studies. A series of studies by Dawson (1967a, 1967b) in West Africa on a Kwashiorkor endocrine dysfunction showed that the dysfunction led to a more global field-dependent perceptual style on the part of the male, compared with a control group without the dysfunction. Another aspect of Witkin's theory, that maternal dominance results in greater field dependence in the male, also received support. Sons whose fathers had a larger number of wives were found to be more field dependent because of decreased contact with the father and increased maternal contact and dominance. (See also, for example, Dershowitz, 1966.)

A number of studies (e.g., Hubbert, 1915; McNemar and Stone, 1932; Tyron, 1931) have shown that sex-based cognitive style (e.g., spatial skills) exists in rats as well as people. Building upon these earlier investigations, Dawson (1972) studied the effects of hormone-induced sex reversals in rats. He investigated the effects of estrogen on male rats, and the effects of testosterone on female rats, to determine whether alterations in spatial learning occurred after their administration. This animal study (one of the rare and welcome experimental animal studies done for the purpose of investigating human cultural variables) has its corollary in disease- or nutrition-based circumstances, like Kwashiorkor, that are found in underdeveloped cultures, and the interaction that these circumstances have with sex-based socialization practices and roles. Dawson's estrogen-induced male rats showed a significant change toward the female spatial learning mean after the second try on the Tolman maze, while no significant changes were found for the testosterone-injected females. The reason for the sex difference appears to be that the females developed a response disposition, while the males showed a greater degree of spatial or place learning. This coincides with the rather consistent finding that males, more than females, develop (are reinforced for) spatial learning. A recurring finding in nearly all cultures is that dominant males—the hunters, food gatherers, and builders—are reinforced in the development of the types of skills, including spatial ability, which foster male dominance. Another factor in these studies, which would initially favor the male but which would also lead to a greater decrement in learning on the part of the male after the injection of estrogen, is that the criteria used were highly loaded spatially and were thus more sensitive to male changes. Perhaps both male rats and male humans have a great deal to lose when such criteria are used, while the testosterone-induced female can neither simply nor quickly gain "male" ability. Thus, a major criticism of this and similar investigations is that the criterion measures are male-oriented. Dawson concedes this point, and he notes that better criterion measures (sex-free?) are needed for both rats and humans.

The essence of this study, and its implications for cross-cultural psychology, is stated by Dawson:

"... it is considered that for the male the brain is probably programmed neonatally by androgens which facilitates the development of a masculine cognitive style through social learning. Similarly it is considered that for the female the programming of the brain neonatally by oestrogens facilitates the development of a feminine cognitive style through social learning. While it is considered that the differentiation of masculine and feminine cognitive styles is facilitated neonatally by the appropriate sex hormones, it is also postulated that these cognitive styles can be reversed by opposite sex hormones, particularly in infancy. In addition, it is considered that both masculine and feminine cognitive styles which are normally reinforced by same sex social learning influences, can be reversed by opposite sex socialization influences, particularly in cases of sex hormone dysfunction in infancy, or where the level of same sex hormones may be low" (1972a, p. 35).

*The T-M Scale of Attitude Change.* As we have seen, much of Dawson's work concerns the interaction of the biological and social environments leading to biological and social change. This is especially important where modern technological influences in education, housing, and medicine are transforming subsistence, or underdeveloped societies. Such social change involves biological change, and Dawson believes that controlled bio-social experiments should consider both these variables. To study these relationships, Dawson has developed a Traditional-Modern Social Environment Scale, and he envisions the development of a Biological Development Scale. In his comprehensive West African study, Dawson (1967c) also employed a large number of other psychological tests and scales, essentially at all times paying due caution to the methodological pitfalls that plague researchers using tests in non-Western cultures.

The Traditional-Modern Scale (the T-M Scale) has been designed to measure attitudes and attitude change as people move from traditional to more Western or modern environments. Variations in socialization pressures and the presence or absence of authority systems result in varying degrees of susceptibility to attitude change in the traditional or modern direction. The independent variables Dawson used to investigate attitude change include the nature and degree of modern contact, the nature of cultural authority systems and socialization systems, and the degree of culturally determined tolerance for cognitive inconsistency in belief systems.

Dawson's T-M consistency theory of attitude change has been developed from similar theories, such as Heider's (1958) balance theory, Festinger's (1957) cognitive dissonance theory, and Osgood and Tannenbaum's (1955) congruity theory. It is held that the T-M model of attitude change is an advance over its predecessors because the method of measurement it employs relies on real-life field studies with high external validity, while the others may have depended too much upon artificial laboratory conditions to investigate attitude change.

Basic to T-M theory is the premise that cognitive inconsistencies resulting from exposure to rapid social change must be resolved by compromise attitudes. It is considered that the resolution of traditional-modern conflict is less likely to occur with more highly valued, high affect traditional attitudes, while adaptive compromises are more likely to occur for less important attitudes.

The initial development of the scale is fully explained in Dawson (1967c) in the context of an investigation of attitude change in Sierra Leone. Scales have also been constructed for use with Australian Aborigines and Chinese (Dawson, 1969b; 1971). The scales are always constructed so that they include traditional and modern attitudinal statements that are culturally appropriate. Wisely avoided are attempts to translate a common scale for use in a variety of cultures.

T-M scales consist of 18 to 30 or more minor, culturally meaningful subscales (called concepts), each of which is subdivided into four major subscales. The concept of male dominance (traditional higher status of the male over the female), for example, is measured by having subjects react to its major subscale items:

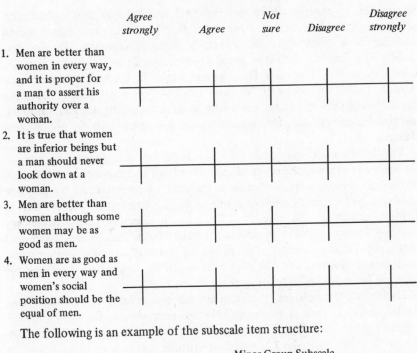

The following is an example of the subscale item structure:

| | Minor Group Subscale | | | | | | | | | | | | | | | | | |
|---|---|---|---|---|---|---|---|---|---|---|---|---|---|---|---|---|---|---|
| | A | B | C | D | E | F | G | H | I | J | K | L | M | N | O | P | Q | R |
| **Major Subscales** | | | | | | | | | | | | | | | | | | |
| Traditional | 1 | 1 | 1 | 1 | 1 | 1 | 1 | 1 | 1 | 1 | 1 | 1 | 1 | 1 | 1 | 1 | 1 | 1 |
| Semi-traditional | 2 | 2 | 2 | 2 | 2 | 2 | 2 | 2 | 2 | 2 | 2 | 2 | 2 | 2 | 2 | 2 | 2 | 2 |
| Semi-Western | 3 | 3 | 3 | 3 | 3 | 3 | 3 | 3 | 3 | 3 | 3 | 3 | 3 | 3 | 3 | 3 | 3 | 3 |
| Modern | 4 | 4 | 4 | 4 | 4 | 4 | 4 | 4 | 4 | 4 | 4 | 4 | 4 | 4 | 4 | 4 | 4 | 4 |

Each of the 18 (in this example) T-M minor subscales (A to R) has four items comprising the major subscales: (1) Traditional, (2) Semi-traditional, (3) Semi-Western, and (4) Modern; these four subscales, in turn, have 18 items. The response scales are transformed to scores ranging from 5 (Agree strongly) to 1 (Disagree strongly), and are then summed. This gives four major subscale scores across the 18 minor subscales. Another score, the Range of Variation (RV) is obtained by subtracting the Traditional subscale score from the Modern. RV is high when the modern is higher than the traditional and low when the traditional is higher than the modern.

The scale, then, is scored in two directions, *down* each of the 18 minor subscales and *across* the four 18-item major subscales. The minor subscales are scaled by having the four items rank-ordered from traditional to modern by judges from both the traditional culture and a modern, European culture. This involves the calculation of item means for each of the four items so that both item content and position can be altered to insure that the means do not vary from 1, 2, 3, and 4, respectively.

Thus, the four major subscales for 18 minor subscales can theoretically range from scores of 18 (maximum traditional) to 90 (maximum modern). A maximum RV of either +72 (90 − 18) or −72 (18 − 90) is possible, but such extremes are very unlikely.

Figure 6.2 displays what may hypothetically result from the scaling of the attitudes of two groups, one from an urban metropolis and the other from a traditional rural village.

The few studies reported to date have yielded considerable data, and Dawson and his colleagues have investigated numerous other variables (such as father's occupation, birth order, and parental attitudes) and their correlation with T-M Scales. They have also been successful in demonstrating the internal validity of the scales by measuring attitudinal conflict and correlating the degree of conflict with GSR measures in laboratory settings. In one such study (Dawson et al. 1971), it was found that for Chinese subjects the more "important" (highly valued and traditional) concepts elicited a significantly higher level of GSR arousal in response to attitude change. Peer-group pressures resulted in a greater change in a traditional direction for more important Confucian concepts (e.g., humility and respect for the aged), while attitudes toward concepts unimportant to the Chinese (e.g., ghosts and lightning) changed in a modern direction. A similar study (Dawson et al., 1972b) using peer-group pressures to affect attitude change among Hong Kong Chinese showed significant correlations between GSR and high attitude conflict (resistance to change).

A final example of what the T-M Scales have recurringly measured relates to somewhat of a reinstatement of certain traditional attitudes after the apparent

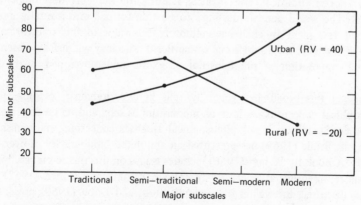

**Figure 6.2.** Hypothetical T-M score profiles for urban and rural samples.

transition from traditional to modern attitudes. Dawson found that after Sierra Leone subjects had become "modernized," especially through university training and increased contact with the Western world, they reaffirmed certain aspects of traditional culture. This corroborated findings by Jahoda (1961). Jahoda sumizes that "After passing through a temporary phase of inferiority [the Sierra Leone subjects] return to an enlightened appreciation of things African."

Thus Dawson's developing bio-social theory certainly merits close attention, since it is a frame of reference for cross-cultural psychology—the only one of its kind to be concerned exclusively and cross-culturally with both the biological and social aspects of man as interdependent phenomena. It intentionally dovetails well-documented cultural anthropology findings and recent cross--cultural psychological investigations. Through a comprehensive network of interrelated variables the system enables the researcher to study small homogeneous societies in detail. A promising method to measure many of the theory's major points has been developed, while a second measuring device (to measure biological environments) is under construction.

## Measures of Modernism

Modernization (or Westernization) and its measurement represents an interface between various disciplines. Sociologists, anthropologists, and political and economic theorists have attempted definitions of modernism and the "modern man," outlining at the same time the consequences of modernization. These theorists have recently been joined by psychologists, who more often than other social scientists attempt to measure rather than define modernism and its opposite, traditionalism.

The study of how modernization occurs and how it can be promoted and even accelerated will undoubtedly receive a great deal of attention in the future. The economic, political, and medical reasons for inducing development are obvious. The world appears destined to be transformed into a totally modern one, and few seem to challenge militantly the value of this transformation, although there are no doubt some romanticists who may whimsically resent the eventual evaporation of pre-industrial or exotic underdeveloped areas of the world.

Work in this broad area generally falls in two domains: sociological and philosophical conceptualizations of modernism as one, and its measurement as the other. Sociological and philosophical treatises concerning modernism are numerous. Brode (1969) has presented an annotated bibliography of over 2500 sources. A book by Weiner (1966) includes essays on this theme prepared by 25 scholars representing a variety of disciplines. Peshkin and Cohen (1967) have further discussed the values of modernization, and Doob (1960) presented a major treatment of the impact and consequences of the modernization of Africa.

An entire issue of the *Journal of Social Issues* has been devoted to the topic (see Gusfield, 1968). The interested reader is directed to those sources.

The following researchers have developed scales or techniques to measure modernism: Smith and Inkeles (1966), Kahl (1968), Doob (1967), Guthrie (1970), Stephenson (1968), and Dawson (cf. 1967c).[4] With the exception of Dawson's Traditional-Modern Scale, which was discussed earlier as part of his bio-social framework, we shall briefly summarize these methods. First, however, it may be helpful to outline some of the characteristics of the modern man. Kimmel and Perlman (1970) have written that research in this area has described an "ideal" modern man as one who

".. . believes he can control his environment; follows the mass media; is politically and intellectually oriented; is not closely tied to his relatives; has an equalitarian view of family life; values change, and punctuality; and prefers urban life. He is open to new experiences and people, and respects education and science" (p. 121).

More compreheisively, Inkeles (1966) has suggested that among the more important characteristics of the modern man are the following:

1. A readiness for new experience and an openness to change.
2. A disposition to form or hold opinions over a large number of problems and issues that arise not only in his immediate environment but also out of it. His orientation in the opinion realm is more democratic.
3. An orientation toward the present and future rather than toward the past.
4. An involvement in planning and organizing as a way of handling life.
5. A belief that he can dominate his environment for personal advancement, rather than being dominated by it.
6. A confidence that people and institutions can be counted on to meet their obligations and responsibilities.
7. An awareness of the dignity of others and a disposition to respect them.
8. A faith in science and technology, even if it is a primitive faith.
9. A belief that rewards should be according to contributions and not by whim or special properties unrelated to his contributions.

With this brief backdrop, we now turn to the various measures.

*The Smith-Inkeles Overall Modernity (OM) Scale.* Smith and Inkeles (1966) initiated the development of their scale by locating 33 modernism themes or issues (including the 9 most salient themes given above) that have appeared in the literature. To measure these themes, a long series of questionnaire-interview

---

[4] Dennis (1966) suggests that Goodenough Draw-a-Man Test scores, rather than being indices of intelligence, can be used to measure modernization as the degree of exposure to Western art forms.

items of either the fixed-alternative or open-ended type were prepared. So that the items would not be susceptible to acquiesence response set, the researchers avoided an agree-disagree format. They also attempted to avoid social desirability response set by balancing the desirability of the alternatives associated with each item. Pretesting of the large initial pool of items over a two-year period led to a final selection of items that tentatively satisfied several criteria, including that they (1) measured the identified themes, (2) overlapped in their measurements, (3) dealt with pancultural human situations which were identifiable by men of little or no formal education, (4) were easily translatable, and (5) elicited a good distribution of response in each country being investigated.

They then applied these items to samples of "common men" representing the traditional, base-line culture in Argentina, Chile, Israel, India, Pakistan, and Nigeria. Ages ranged from 18 to 32. $N$'s ranged from 700 to 1300, for a total $N$ of 5500. Before each four-hour inverview, which was conducted by educated native language interviewers whose social origins were the same as the interviewees, extensive translation, retranslation, and pretesting were done in each country. Thus, 5500 interviews in six countries resulted in data from the responses to 159 items measuring attitudes, values and opinions, self-reported behavior, and verbal fluency. The 119 items measuring attitudes, opinions, and values comprised the first, or Long Form of the OM Scale. Examples of these items are:

*Would you treat a stranger with: trust/caution/distrust?*

*Limiting size of family is: necessary/wrong*

The adequacy of these items as measures of modernism was checked by examining both their theoretical and empirical bases. The theoretical check was essentially a subjective one, in which the researchers compared their conceptions of modernism with numerous other conceptions found in the literature, while the empirical check involved an examination of modernity scores as they related to social indices which are "generally acknowledged to be associated with modernity."

The final modernity score for individuals was the average response to the 119 items, each of which were dichotomozed as close to the median as possible into "modern" or "traditional" poles. The Long Form yielded essentially the same psychometric characteristics in all countries (means, medians, ranges, and standard deviations approximately equal), and reliability coefficients ranging from .73 to .87.

At this point, Smith and Inkeles were confident that these data gave evidence that the 119 items tapped a consistent, underlying dimension of psychological modernity, and proceeded to develop a series of successively shorter forms of the original measure while retaining sufficient reliability and validity.

Short Form 1 was compiled by first selecting for each country the 50 items which correlated highest with the total Long Form score. Then any of these items which were common to at least four of the six countries were selected. This resulted in a 38-item form.

Since Short Form 1 was judged to have items not truly representative of the underlying 33 themes of modernity, Short Form 2 was derived by selecting the *single* item which best represented each theme in all countries, regardless of the magnitude of their correlations with the total Long Form score. In case of ties, the investigators judged which item was the more relevant. This form has higher item-to-scale correlations with the previous forms, and their reliability coefficients remain about the same (.68 to .81). The authors claim that this form will probably be the most useful and cross-culturally applicable of all the forms they developed.

Short Form 3 was derived by the criterion group method. Smith and Inkeles identified in the literature the three most powerful determinants of individual modernity: education, urban experience, and occupation (especially industrial experience). After obtaining measures for these three independent variables (e.g., years of education) for individuals in each country, they correlated each of the 119 Long Form items with each of the variables. Then for each country the top 50 items (average correlations with the three variables) were selected. The six 50-item lists were then compared, and all items common to at least four of the six countries were found. Thirty-four items survived this test.

Yet another form was derived by using procedures similar to those in constructing Short Form 2. This was done by finding the one item from each of the 33 theme areas that best represented that theme in terms of its correlation with the criterion variables identified for use with Short Form 3. This resulting Short Form 4 correlates .81 or above with Form 3 and .77 or above with the Long Form.

Finally, two additional and even shorter forms were constructed. The content of the 12 items which appeared on all four of the short forms was examined for overlap. Two items were judged to be redundant or superfluous, and Short Form 5 consists of ten items. It correlated from .62 to .79 with the Long Form, and reliabilities dropped only slightly, averaging about .70. Short Form 6 contains 14 items: the ten attitudinal-type items of Form 5 plus two items representing the 23 original information items and two items representing the 17 measures of self-reported behavior. It is only this form which uses items representing all original 159 items, before they were pruned to include only attitude- and value-type items.

An individual answering in the modern direction on Short Form 5 has the following characteristics:

1. He has an active interest in public issues.

2. He wants higher education for his children.
3. He approves of new agricultural techniques.
4. He prefers candidates who have special education.
5. He believes that hard work is important for the country's future.
6. He approves of science.
7. He approves of restricting family size.
8. He is interested in world news.
9. He believes he can understand the thinking of people who come from distant places.
10. He is willing to acknowledge that man can be good without being religious.

Thus, Smith and Inkeles have built a strong case for the development of a series of modernity measures. They "consider it notable in the highest degree that ... 119 attitude questions and some 40 related informational and behavioral items should show such extraordinarily similar structure in six such diverse countries—and even more than that number of cultural groups" (1966, p. 377). Further details about the causes and consequences of modernization—in the context of the six-nation study—can be found in Inkeles (1969a).

*Kahl's Scales.* Kahl (1968) developed two modernism questionnaires, one long and one short, for use in Brazil and Mexico. He followed some of the initial procedures that Smith and Inkeles used (for example, surveying modernism literature and conducting interviews in each country prior to scale construction), and then got involved in various factor analytic procedures which lead to independent but similar scales for both Brazil and Mexico. In his monograph, he related the various factors to fertility ideals, education, occupation, and political values.

Perhaps more than any of the other measures of modernism, Kahl's may be of primary value because of the criticism they have generated. For example, Guthrie et al. (1970), whose technique of measuring modernism is summarized below, point out that the majority of Kahl's statements "are such that one has to disagree to offer a modern statement ... and that Kahl's results are distorted by the fact that one appears modern by disagreeing with a statement." An additional shortcoming concerns the structure of Kahl's items. Consider these two items:

*Making plans only brings unhappiness, because plans are hard to fulfill.*
*People in a big city are cold and impersonal; it is hard to make new friends.*

Both of these items actually contain two ideas. We cannot be sure to which part the individual's response refers. Roughly two-thirds of Kahl's items are of this two-part variety. Perhaps that type of item could be made into a single idea by constructing them according to "if-then" propositional and impersonal statements (with apologies to the *intent* of Kahl's items), such as statements

*If making plans only brings unhappiness, then they are hard to fullfill.*

*If people in the big city are cold and impersonal, then it is hard to make new friends.*

*Guthrie's Traditional–Modern Interview Schedule.* For the purpose of examining modernization in the Rural Philippines, Guthrie et al. (1970) developed a 118-item interview schedule. It consisted of four parts:

1. *Demographic Data.* (age, education, occupation, family size). 30 items.

2. *Perception and Anticipation of Change.* Twenty questions were designed to access impressions concerning the conditions of the community at present and as they were five or ten years ago. The same questions were rephrased to determine how they expected things to be in ten years. Domains included income, housing, politics, interpersonal patterns, and chances of success. 40 questions.

3. *Traditional and Modern Attitudes–I.* Ten questions asked the respondent to choose between two solutions to a social problem. The alternatives were designed to be equally attractive and reasonable. One alternative was a justification for traditional behavior, the other for modern behavior. Example:

*All of a man's chickens died. Should he:*
a. *quit growing chickens?* (traditional)
b. *have some of the dead ones examined by a government bureau man?* (modern)

Twenty questions consisted of pairs of attitudes representing a traditional and a modern point of view on the same issue. These were presented as pairs of statements which were considered "fair statements of modern and traditional points of view." Example:

a. *success depends on hard work.*
b. *success depends on luck.*

In eliciting responses, the researchers capitalized on a popular local form of entertainment with which all respondents were familiar. This game, which both on radio and in social gatherings is traditional in the area, follows a debate format. Whoever offers the best presentation of puns and plays on words is the winner. Total, 30 items.

4. *Traditional and Modern Attitudes–II.* Items drawn primarily from Smith and Inkeles' (1966) OM Scale posed questions (e.g., what is the ideal size family for people who marry now?) and offered two to five alternatives representing modern or traditional solutions, points of view, or responses. 18 items.

Subjects were drawn from four similar communities, at distances of approximately 50, 100, 200, and 400 kilometers from Manila.[5] Within each community 18 men and 18 women between the ages of 20 and 55 were selected from three social levels: the educated, landowning *big people*, *little people* of the *poblacion* or town, who worked at semi-skilled and unskilled jobs, and *little people* of the *barrio*, a cluster of houses occupied by those who till the nearby land and generally earn little more than a subsistence. Thus, the researchers addressed the problems of *proximity* to modern influences, *sex* of respondent, and *social class level*. A total of 432 subjects, 108 from each of the four communities, were selected.

The resulting data were subjected to various forms of analysis, primarily factor analysis and chi square. While numerous differences and factors were found between subjects as a function of item groupings, the overall results showed that social class was the only one of the three independent variables which was a major source of difference in outlook. There were virtually no sex differences, few differences associated with proximity to big city influences, but there were frequent differences between little people and big people, the latter usually expressing more modern attitudes. The majority of little people also responded in modern directions, but those with money did so more often.

Guthrie and his associates suggested that rural Filipinos with modern attitudes avoid conflict by their optimism. They expect more jobs, invest in education, and have high occupational aspirations. They emphasize hard work and in the face of exposure to mass media and material goods they tolerate discrepancies between the ideal and the real.

Numerous other analyses and explanations are presented as a result of this study, but we cannot go into them here. Our purpose is primarily to summarize the method of measuring modernism in this specific Filipino context. The scale consists of a mixture of items borrowed from historical precedents, typical psychological scale construction techniques, thoughtful and insightful rationale based on local customs, and sound hunches. Guthrie and his colleagues, unlike those who have constructed other measures, had no explicit plans during the development of their scale to make it cross-culturally invariant. But because of its length, and its coordination with theoretical conceptions of modernity, and because the researchers based its construction on the better aspects of prior modernism scales, we are left with the impression that the Guthrie scale should hold up well if extended to other cultures.

*Doob's Scales.* In presenting for general use the scales he developed for

---

[5] Staggering the distance from major urban centers, and thus the degree of contact with Westernization or modernization influences, is a common approach in studying the "marginal man." For a methodological example using marginality and other factors as dependant variables in cultural adjustment, see Berry (1970).

measuring modernism in Africa, Doob (1967) refreshingly admits that while constructing them he had "striven to be as unoriginal as possible." Asserting that researchers "ought not to feel as if we are borrowing a colleague's toothbrush whenever we include his items on our own schedule" (p. 414) either he borrowed items already existing, with or without modification, or he constructed new ones. By doing so he took advantage of the successes of others and avoided many of their mistakes.

There are eight 10-item scales, each designed to measure a particular feature of modernism. The scales are:

I. *Temporal orientation.* A future rather than a past or present emphasis.

II. *Government.* A belief that the present government has important functions to perform for its citizens.

III. *Confidence and optimism.* A feeling that life is pleasant and that people control their own destiny.

IV. *Patriotism.* Strong national feelings and attachment.

V. *Science and determinism.* "Correct" knowledge and a conviction that phenomena are scientifically intelligible.

VI. *Conception of people.* A non-paranoid, generous, and trusting conception of human nature and one's fellow men.

VII. *Politics and leaders.* Approval of one's leaders and their policies.

VIII. *Tribalism.* A tendency to discredit or de-emphasize traditional values and practice.

The 10 items on each schedule are presented as statements. The first item on each schedule is from Scale I, the second from Scale II, and so on. This order is repeated seven additional times until the last, or eightieth, item is reached. Responses are usually recorded by using a 3- to 5-point Likert-type format.

In practice, the direction of the rating is usually based upon what local African leaders *appear* to consider desirable in terms of their definition of modernism or modernization. Then, as he did for 14 samples in Eastern Africa, Doob simply sums the sample's responses to items and establishes cutoff points in terms of percentages answering in the modern direction. For example, one may define a group's response to an item as "strongly modern" if 75% or more of the sample responds according to the predetermined, local conception of modernization. On the contrary, 25% or fewer of the group responding in the modern direction on the item can be called "non-modern."

Doob's interviewing schedules can also be used as questionnaires. They have the advantages of offering researchers common instruments for limitless comparisons, they are short, and the *criteria* of modernism are neither static nor imposed (though the *concept* may be), since modernism is defined idigenously. This latter feature has obvious within-culture value, but in the absence of external, empirically derived criteria, which themselves may vary, the diverse variable judgments of modernity across cultures may make the scores incomparable to any unknown degree. Thus, while Doob may hope that modernity has some or many pancultural features (which is undoubtedly the case—see below), his scales at this point yield primarily "local" meaning, which was precisely his intention.

*Stephenson's Method and a Modernism Measurement Debate.* This example of a measure of modernism is important not so much for its usefulness, but for the debate that it generated concerning what modernism is, its cultural meaningfulness or its "universality," and how it should be measured.

Critical of previous measures of modernism, especially Smith and Inkeles' OM Scale, Stephenson (1968) redefined modernization in terms of how cultures independently define it according to their norms. Under attack was the assumption that modernism has uniform characteristics throughout the world. Stephenson then proceeded to develop a measure which would not "impose" norms of modernism on a culture.

In a small, rural Appalachian community, extensive interviews with residents led to the selection of fifty statements "taken directly from field notes in which the community itself defined traditionism and modernism." Each statement was coded to indicate which of seven "value areas" it represented: time, achievement, work, education, person-versus-object orientation, religion, and sex-role orientation. Then, seven "expert" judges who were familiar with the cultural area rated the statements as modern, traditional, or ambiguous. The two items from each of the seven areas which received the highest interrater judgment as representing modernism, as well as a final "last minute" insertion, formed a 15-item instrument.

With instrument in hand, interviewers applied it to 130 respondents. Following this, they constructed a six-item Guttman scale by employing scalogram analysis, a type of item analysis. Even though items representing the value area of work did not meet the predetermined scalogram criteria for final inclusion, Stephenson maintained that this procedure resulted in a culture-specific measure of modernism, and that currently such a scale (or procedure) is the only workable type. He argued that other attempts may be "meaningless" unless local criteria are the basis for measurement.

The issue, then, is essentially the same issue which was discussed in Chapter 5 on the cross-cultural use of psychological tests: Should cross-cultural measurement rely on construct-related or criterion-related instruments? Inkeles' (1969b) comments on Stephenson's assertions and methodology are incisive and to-the-point. Inkeles' chief complaint is that "imposing" theoretical constructs of modernism violates nothing, and in fact may be as good or better than using indigenous criteria. Indigenous criteria are fine, but limiting simply because quite salient features of (pancultural modernism) constructs cannot be rated as traditional or modern by local residents unless the residents are made aware of their existence.

In a comparison between an indigenous India scale of modernity (much like Stephenson's) and the Long Form of the OM Scale, Singh and Inkeles (1968) found a correlation of .56. The two forms are by no means identical, but they appear to be tapping similar dimensions. Also, correlations of the two methods with objective criteria of modernization suggest that the "transcultural measure derived from sociological theory predicts 'modern' social characteristics more accurately than does the indigenous measure constructed on the basis of advice from local informants!"

Stephenson's (1969) reply to Inkeles' criticism was chiefly an admission that he probably overstated the case for his indigenous device. But he is safely correct, and Inkeles implicitly agrees, that neither method is best in an absolute sense; the various methods summarized in this section support such a position. The reason for desiring a scale to measure modernism will depend upon its uses. Moreover, there may be a certain amount of folly in using any of the current methods, since Gusfield (1967), for example, is critical of the assumption that the traditional-modern continuum is linear. He lists seven fallacies that are frequently overlooked by those who discuss these paired opposites:

1. Developing societies have been static societies.
2. Traditional culture is a consistent body of norms and values.
3. Traditional culture is a homogeneous social structure.
4. Old traditions are always displaced by new ideas.
5. Traditional and modern forms are always in conflict.
6. Traditionism and modernism are mutually exclusive systems.
7. Modernization processes weaken traditions.

Those who refine existing measures of modernism or who develop new techniques are going to have to grapple with the issues Gusfield raised and with a confusing array of constructs and social science jargon. Terms such as modernism, moderization, urbanization, and westernization have often been used interchangeably. Rhetorically, they may have some redeeming value, but they are far from being operational definitions. Specifically, a distinction between modernism and westernization will have to be drawn. Is a nation modern when it is westernized? And what are the criteria for reaching a westernized state? Highways? Supermarkets? No more visitors from the National Geographic Society?

Much research in this area obviously has dealt with a "traditional-modern" continuum as if everyone knows what it is, and that traditional societies are all traveling at different rates up the same long hill toward the pinnacle. Unlike true dichotomies (like male-female), the traditional-modern distinction may be a convenient artifact designed by researchers so that meaning can be given to their measures. The modal cross-cultural study in this and most other areas of research uses questionnaires, interviews, or some type of instrument which, upon analysis, lead to a sorting of people into tidy categories. Even the most rough instrument can yield data which can potentially force people into categories of convenience, and not necessarily into categories that reflect reality.

As some researchers who have developed measures of modernism have implied, modernism may be an indigenous state of mind which does not yield to an external directive. In his work in the Philippines, Guthrie found that Filipino peasants can move back and forth at their whim along this assumed continuum, depending upon real or imagined implied payoffs. As noted earlier in this chapter, Dawson and others have found that after a satisfactory level of modernism has been reached, Africans desire to return to certain cherished traditional systems. Others have documented the fact that modern medicine and witchcraft can exist side by side. This suggests that science, that paragon of modernism, does not necessarily mean splitting atoms or developing new enzymes. Moreover, what is modern today must by definition be traditionalism tomorrow.

We have no specific new methodologies for measuring modernism to offer. Several reasonable starts have been made, and all but one or two of them have resulted in genuinely cautious instruments and were developed as exploratory rather than final devices. We do join others, however, in advising that measurement in this broad area is fraught with difficulties, the chief one being the assumption that a traditional-modern continuum is unidimensional and that an implied cross-culturally invariant definition of modernism is clear.

## Summary

The chapter began with a mild exhortation that cross-cultural psychologists should concentrate on global theoretical issues of recurring importance rather than taking a random probe approach in studying cross-culturally the various domains of psychology. An attempt was made to describe what may be involved in "thinking cross-culturally"; likewise, an attempt was made to explain what that term may mean. This is especially important with respect to research strategies and questions and data interpretation. The latter point was stressed by using the argument that hypothesis testing in the social sciences is fundamentally different from hypothesis testing in physics. The former aims for probable differences, while the latter is concerned with point values among variables. Thus it is very easy in the social sciences to find significant differences merely by increasing sample sizes or by devising "cute" or "clever" experiments. One way to avoid making specious interpretations of statistically significant findings is to use multiple methods which will serve as means to corroborate findings.

A general introduction to several repositories of ethnographic material was given. The Human Relations Area Files, including their development, availability, and general use were introduced first, followed by various HRAF-related procedures for sampling societies and by a brief discussion of the Societal Research Archives System. HRAF and the other library systems have been designed to help answer questions likely to be formulated by anthropologists, but certain questions (not all!) of interest to other social scientists can also be pursued. The researcher would start with a question; for instance: What is the relation between culture stress and incidents such as drunken brawling? The files would then be searched, the researcher looking for ethnographies from hundreds of cultures that report the presence or absence of both traits. Immediately, two methodological questions arise and they have received explicit attention, especially by Naroll (see Naroll and Cohen, 1970). The first deals with sampling, since an association between two traits can be due to functional relations or to the fact that the two have remained together while ancestral cultures diffused. The problem, then, is one of independence of observations, and Naroll has suggested different sampling techniques to be used in drawing information from HRAF. The other problem concerns the quality of the data. Information is reported, after all, by anthropologists who have had different types of training, have spent different amounts of time in the culture, and whose knowledge of the local vernacular differs. A "data quality control" index has been developed to approach a solution to this problem.

None of the frames of reference that we chose to outline and summarize has received as much cross-cultural attention as HRAF. Nevertheless, a major conclusion of the reviews of others is that HRAF should be a starting point to be complemented by other information, perhaps other ethnographies or other forms of data.

Three ways of conceptualizing behavior sampling problems were presented. These included: the *cultunit*, which is an anthropological technique to define discrete cultural units; the differential impact that *behavior settings* can have on the behavior of individuals who are part of differing psychological ecologies; and the *emic-etic-theoric* distinction. The latter approach concerns the truly unique aspects of culture (emic), the pancultural (etic), and the typologies of etic and emic systems (theorics). Cross-cultural psychologists are familiar with emics and etics, but only recently has the anthropological term "theorics" been advanced for possible use in this area.

A large portion of the chapter was devoted to fairly extensive summaries of four established frames of reference which will be of continuing importance to cross-cultural psychology. These frames of reference were chosen for one or more of the following reasons: (1) they have been widely used, (2) their generalizability should be great, (3) robust methodological techniques have been developed, (4) they will probably receive widespread attention in future years.

*Piaget's Theories.* Some major theories of child development are those of Jean Piaget. His suggestion is that thought and intellectual functioning develop in stages, and this hypothesis has received considerable cross-cultural attention resulting in valuable additions to his theory. The specific principle that has received most attention is conservation, for example, the amount of water remains the same regardless of the container's shape. At least twelve distinct research strategies using Piaget's concepts can be identified, and these include the effects of: degree of urban contact; degree of Western influence; cultural enrichment; schooling; magic and superstition. An advantage of Piagetian methods of measuring cognitive development is that they can usually be adapted so that they are familiar to members of a given culture.

*The Need for Achievement.* The concept of the individual's need to achieve and its consequent effects on society has been intensively studied by David McClelland and his colleagues. They have documented that members of various societies have different mean levels of a need to achieve, and this correlates with the growth of a country as measured by gross national product and other economic indicators. The role of the mother and father are especially important in individual development, and the presence or absence of the father has been found to be very critical. Methods of measuring *n* Ach include responses to cards from the Thematic Aperception Test and content analyses of children's school primers from different cultures.

*Bio-social Theory.* The purpose of the bio-social approach, a developing tactic is to examine behavior as a function of environment and socialization practices which lead to the survival of groups. Extreme environments are often studied, and Witkin's work (see Chapter 8), as well as other points of view, are freely used. It is an ecological system, and is amenable to tight laboratory experimentation with both animals and humans. A scale designed to measure traditional versus modern attitudes has been developed to serve the system. Other ways to measure modernism have also been developed, and the recommended approach is to use several in any one investigation.

*Measures of Modernism.* Most of those who have developed such scales have combined their conceptions of modernism with those found in the literature, after which they empirically check modernity scores as they relate to social indices related to modernity. Smith and Inkeles (1966) were especially deft at this approach in developing a series of scales. Kahl (1968) generally adopted the same approach as Smith and Inkeles, while Guthrie and his associates (1970) developed, for use in the Philippines, an interview schedule which included items from sources important to Filipinos. Doob (1967) let local African leaders define what appeared to be important dimensions of modernism, and from these definitions he developed scales that are indigeneously useful. Stephenson (1968) took somewhat the same approach in constructing a scale for use in rural Appalachia. Stephenson also triggered a debate concerning the essential nature of modernism and traditionism and what the ingredients of a good scale might be. This area is fraught with definitional problems which must be solved before the existing scales, or new ones, will be endorsed by all researchers.

An unfortunate but unavoidable consequence of summarizing the frames of reference we chose to use as "generalizing agents" is that so many other equally important research areas were scarcely mentioned, or were not mentioned at all. In an earlier draft of this book we included detailed summaries of two additional frames of reference: The Freudian tradition and subjective culture. Space limitations dictated their extraction, but not because we considered them to be less important than the ones we retained. Treatments of Freudian orientations abound, especially from an anthropological perspective, and subjective culture is fully explained in the second book in this series (Triandis et al., 1972).

Very brief sketches of numerous other popular or promising cross-cultural research areas are to be found throughout this book. But despite that, the true scope of cross-cultural research has not been fully outlined by any means. Conspicuous by their absence are such profoundly broad and important areas as psycholinguistics, mental health issues, proxemics and social schemas, criminality and delinquency, cultural strategies in coping behavior, and national character. The list could go on. Those who wish to get a glimpse of the entire range of research in cross-cultural psychology during the past decade are directed to very brief synopses of research abstracted by Pelto (1967) and Triandis, Malpass, and Davidson (1971). Finally, at least these five books of readings cover a fairly wide range of research topics: Wickert (1967), Price-Williams (1969), Al-Issa and Dennis (1970), Lambert and Weisbrod (1971), and Berry and Dasen (1972).

# CHAPTER SEVEN

# *Conclusions*

There has been a great deal of cross-cultural research in the last twenty-five years, but much of it is diffuse, unorganized, and uninspired. By "diffuse" we mean that the literature is scattered throughout dozens of journals, and so is extremely hard to find. A glance through our bibliography will show the vast number of places in which cross-cultural research is located. "Unorganized" refers to the discipline's lack of focus and lack of agreement on a set of worthwhile problems for investigation. There are literally hundreds of isolated studies which have received no attention and no follow-up. This shotgun approach has given cross-cultural psychology very few replicated findings. "Uninspired" refers to the regrettable fact that too many researchers undertake studies with *no* plan for discovering anything important. Publication has been done for publication's sake. We still occasionally receive letters from researchers who, before traveling abroad, report that they will give such-and-such a test to such-and-such a group. "This ought to be worth an article in the . . . journal," they inform us.

We would like to suggest some possible solutions to these problems. We will organize our efforts around three themes: (1) the use of paper-and-pencil data gathering techniques; (2) integration of findings; (3) collaboration among social scientists. These themes may seem like strange bedfellows, but they are alike in that they are central to the future of cross-cultural research.

## *The Gathering of Objective Paper-and-Pencil Data—Key Points*

A significant proportion of cross-cultural research is of the correlational type, where responses to tests, questionnaires, and inventories are coded and analyzed. While we hold the general view that paper-and-pencil measures should be used only when experimenters cannot be present to control the approaches to data gathering, the distance between the researcher and potential samples in cross-cultural psychology probably means that paper-and-pencil tactics will be used indefinitely. Moreover, the standardized nature of the printed word or the printed stimulus reduces an important source of unwanted variance, and well-conceived paper-and-pencil instruments offer the cross-cultural researcher certain advantages.

204

A central factor to continually keep in mind is that an impeccable translation or adaptation of an instrument is a necessary but not sufficient condition for use in the target culture in the same way it was used in the originating culture. Psychologists from test- and questionnaire-oriented Western cultures have been guilty of imposing on other cultures the Western attitudes toward such instruments; that is, the basic Western rationale for using paper-and-pencil devices is not clearly understood in many cultures. Hence the "perfect" adaptation of an objective instrument may yield responses that are rendered useless by such factors as unusual response sets. The common Yes,?, No format of many devices is a case in point. For instance, the neutral (?) category may be strictly avoided by subjects from some cultures if the directions suggest that they avoid it, while such avoidance instructions may be completely ignored by people from other cultures. Or, acquiescent response set (agreeing with anything) could be a mode of response in some cultures. Whatever type of instrument is used, the researcher should verify that: (1) style of item or device is reasonably familiar to all subjects, and (2) response styles or sets are similar, so that extreme differences in this area do not invalidate any meaningful comparisons.

Since paper-and-pencil tests will always be with us, problems like the above deserve attention. Another problem is the large number of tests now available, inviting a little data on a large number of tests rather than a great deal of data on a small number of tests. Everyone who uses paper-and-pencil devices seems to have a pet instrument, and it is difficult to dislodge preferences. However, it may now be critical to keep the number of such devices to a minimum. Surely among the 35 or 40 popular cross-culturally viable tests and the dozen or so basic shapes and forms which questionnaires may take can be found a suitable instrument for any purpose. Fancy innovations will probably not fare too well cross-culturally.

Many cross-cultural projects involving psychometric devices attempt to combine quasi-empiricism with speculation, and this poses another problem for the future. For instance, researcher A gives instrument B to subjects from cultures C and D. He thus has "data" and, of course, the statistical techniques to hunt for similarities and differences across groups. The researcher may then feel obligated to append a series of ad hoc armchair analyses to explain that prized creature, the significant difference, calling upon anthropological lore to help him out of tight spots. Perhaps the scores themselves (or the specific statistically significant differences) could be made more scientifically valuable by relating them to specific, concrete, factual data from reliable sources. As Lindzey (1961) pointed out in his analysis of the cross-cultural use of projective techniques, projectives and other open-ended techniques are especially conducive to armchair analyses. If speculations were to be briefly summarized first, and then followed by specific *point* predictions (Meehl, 1967), there would be a substantial decrease in idle musings or attempts to explain away whatever seems messy.

## The Integration of Findings

Cross-cultural psychology may well adopt the position that its sole *raison d'etre* is to make itself obsolete. Its major goal is to explicate a finite number of basic psychological processes as they are modified by cultural conditions. Once these permutations are understood and integrated with the "mainstream" of psychological fact and theory, the term "cross-cultural" will have become vestigial. Thus at this point in the development of psychology, it may be anachronistic, or at least redundant, to speak of the development of cross-cultural *theories*. That is, the modifier "cross-cultural" merely adds an important dimension for all of psychology to consider; the cross-cultural method would by definition be guided by a superordinate theory.

As mentioned earlier, one of the chief difficulties in the development of cross-cultural frames of reference is the scattered nature of cross-cultural research. "Potshot" cross-cultural articles that are of immediate interest seem to be warmly welcomed by nearly all appropriate professional publications. Some of the better psychological journals in the social and personality area even give immediate publication priority to cross-cultural research. Such diversity of implicit keen interest in the field is encouraging to cross-cultural researchers. However, literature reviews that integrate a large number of findings have been rare. The enormously diversified publication system which has immediately rewarded cross-cultural efforts also has unknowingly aided and abetted the proliferation of unrelated and poorly integrated studies. This is no one's fault. Who is to blame journal editors for being excited about an exotic cross-cultural report after they have seen dozens of variations of the same traditional theme from one culture? The situation has been somewhat analogous to a circularity of minor scientific revolutions—with the exception of those who keep abreast of the developments, the wheel is invented and re-invented two or three times a year. Cross-cultural researchers would benefit by commissioning a few among their members to prepare annual in-depth reviews of major substantive areas, and these reviews should guide research. This may be one of the major tasks of the new organizations mentioned below.

When a psychologist initiates a cross-cultural project he usually goes about his business in a reasonably well-informed way, hoping to avoid many of the pitfalls that are omnipresent. If the researcher is a cross-cultural psychologist, he is more than likely engaged in parsimonious and integrated research. If he is not at all familiar with the area, either he will not make a contribution of substance or he will make a number of methodological mistakes, or both. We pointed out in Chapter 6 that cross-cultural psychology means more than taking potshots at theory. Thus we recommend that research orientations be developed which will at once guard against avoidable redundancy, making a contribution to what is already known cross-culturally in the domain being studied. For instance, studies of child-rearing practices should be preceded by a thorough investigation of previous work done in both the culture being investigated and similar cultures. If the same general pattern of findings has occurred in, say, twenty previous studies, perhaps the basic design used in those studies should not be replicated. It should be remembered that any cross-cultural study can use material from previous investigations, and with good benefit. Most studies can be integrated with a significant body of data from such widely studied focal points as Piaget's or Bruner's developmental psychology, or McClelland's work in achievement motivation, and cultural thematics. Likewise, a growing number of people are becoming intrigued with the bio-social framework, also discussed in Chapter 6.

## Collaboration, with Cautions

In the future, there will be many more multiculture studies than exist today, and these will replace the common two-culture comparisons. There are several organizations devoted to encouraging collaboration among social scientists (for example, the International Association for Cross-Cultural Psychology, the International Studies Association, and the Society for Cross-Cultural Research); thus researchers will have the opportunity to meet and work with others who hold similar interests. One researcher might administer a questionnaire or run experiments in a culture to which he has access, in exchange for the same service by another social scientist. Campbell (1968) has suggested more specific methods for such a procedure. The goal is, of course, to have data from a large number of cultures since there will be fewer plausible rival hypotheses than if data from only two cultures are gathered.

Note that the key word is "multiple." In the near future, journal editors will probably not accept articles unless there is some form of replication in terms of a number of experiments on the same hypothesis, a series of studies in various cultures, and so forth. Such a practice will obviate the current policy of submitting related articles to scattered journals in order to build up a large list of publications. A shorter, quality list will replace quantity. This practice will also lessen the pressure always to work in new areas, since replication will be a desired commodity. We are reminded of a professional meeting held in 1970. A series of presentations was being given using Campbell and Fiske's (1959) framework for doing exactly the kind of multiple method and multiple study approach recommended here. One person in the audience whispered in a derogatory tone, "The basis of this framework was thought out 15 years ago!" The audience member was correct, but we disagree that old is bad, and that good existing frameworks should be discarded for anything new that comes along in the 1970's.

Something should be said about the negative aspects of collaborative efforts and interdisciplinary approaches to cross-cultural research. While collaborative, multination and longitudinal designs are obviously best on paper, such as the one involving Campbell, LeVine and others in a massive ethnocentrism study (see page 90), reality militates against expecting too much from collaborative efforts. Grand schemes can be planned, but unless funding is adequate and the same high level of interest (in that order) among collaborators in various cultures is sustained, the project may gradually fade away for any number of reasons. For instance, a key researcher may move, another may not do his share of the work, another may have trouble finding facilities or subjects, and another may "sit" on the data, keeping them unpublished. Because these difficulties were anticipated, some of the better collaborative efforts have been done under highly specific experimental conditions *after* the collaborators had worked together under one roof on a common project. One such project is the series of cognitive conflict studies done by Hammond et al. (1968) and Brehmer et al. (1970).

Difficulties notwithstanding, studies involving more than two cultures are on the increase, and as methodology improves and more people see the immense value of multicultural studies, successful colloborative efforts will likely increase even more. Our hunch is, however, that fruitful efforts will be possible only if collaborators meet face-to-face to plan the strategy; direction by mail may be too complicated, especially with experimental studies.

Interdisciplinary efforts are in double jeopardy at the outset simply because they involve collaborators representing disciplines which use different jargon and paradigms. On paper one could design an imaginative study to compare levels of aggression as a function of types of government. Neither psychologists nor political scientists are likely to agree immediately on reciprocal definitions of aggression and types of government, for example.

However, future hopes cancel out past failures. Certain signs suggest that cross-cultural researchers who represent various social sciences are developing similar research strategies, or at least are recognizing some of the same problems. It is especially encouraging when one reads an account of projective testing "accurately" written by a political scientist, or when psychologists pose hypotheses about governments which can be tested outside the laboratory with the blessings of political scientists. It is also encouraging to see so many highly related books appear within a period of about five years. Several books of readings were mentioned in the closing paragraph of Chapter 6. A number of new books which address specific themes from a cross-cultural perspective are also available. These include one on intelligence (Vernon, 1969), the measurement of subjective culture (Triandis et. al., 1972), and drinking behavior (McClelland et al., 1972). Political scientists have contributed a number of important recent books on comparative methodology. Examples are Przeworski and Teune (1970) and Holt and Turner (1970), as well as a number of new titles which are appearing in the series of which this book is a part. Of course, important contributions by anthropologists are always evident. The recent extensive volume by Naroll and Cohen (1970) on methodology will continue to be valuable.

PART TWO

# Specific Techniques

# CHAPTER EIGHT

## *Cross-Cultural Assessment: An Inventory of Specific Instruments*

In the past those who have written about cross-cultural testing problems have discussed general methodological issues, sometimes mentioning specific tests to illustrate certain points. This is certainly a reasonable way to approach the topic, and it is essentially the approach we used in Chapter 5 on the cross-cultural use of tests. However, one advantage of giving brief descriptions of specific tests, along with numerous cross-cultural projects which have employed them, is that the unique characteristics of the tests will not be taken out of context and become lost or obscured in generalities. Therefore, presented in this chapter are abbreviated descriptions of some thirty tests and psychometric devices that by both deed and theory appear to be well-suited for cross-cultural research on a more or less continuing experimental basis. Some of them were designed specifically for cross-cultural applications, some appear to be reasonably appropriate for such use, while others, because of their fame, qualify for inclusion under a universal psychometric grandfather clause. Moreover, most of them are rather ubiquitous, inexpensive, and readily available, and nearly all of them can boast long research bibliographies. This latter point may give their contemporary use at least the benefit of prolific research perspective. At the end of the chapter the names and addresses of the publishers of each test are given.

It is an ethnocentric list, paralleling the ethnocentrism which has characterized most psychological research, since most bear United States or British copyrights. No pretense is made that this is *the* definitive list of cross-culturally appropriate tests, nor does their inclusion necessarily imply our unequivocal endorsement of any or all of them. Scores of other tests could legitimately qualify for inclusion here, many of them indigenous to countries other than the United States and Great Britain, and therefore not well known because of limited distribution. These chosen few tests should be viewed as a relatively complete representation of devices which, when prudently selected and properly used, may enable the cross-cultural researcher to give both quantitative and qualitative dimensions to a host of constructs and concepts.

211

One scarcely needs to be reminded that the series of *Mental Measurement Yearbooks* by O. K. Buros is the most appropriate place to search for thorough reviews and bibliographies, as well as for prices and other information, of virtually all tests in print. Buros' most recent publication, *Personality Tests and Reviews* (Buros, 1970) is basically a compendium of what has appeared by way of research and review in the domain of personality tests over the last several decades.

There are literally thousands of tests in the world today, and one could defend the cross-cultural adaptation and use of nearly all of them. But the line must be drawn somewhere; otherwise we could easily witness an endless proliferation of scattered test-related data that would themselves be more difficult to interrelate than the dimensions that they have been designed to measure. Cross-cultural research may benefit if we declared a moratorium for a decade on the development of new tests.  Doob (1967) has made a similar point reminding us that a medical study is not dismissed just because the researcher used a simple, standard thermometer. That line of reasoning guided us in selecting the following instruments. We feel that if other tests are used they should at least match the credentials that those in our selected list possess.

The tests are grouped into two sections: (1) cognitive-intellectual, and (2) personality-interest. Following this simple division, the following devices, alphabetically ordered, are discussed:

### *Cognitive-Intellectual*[1]

"Cognitive Style" tests of Witkin and his associates, including:
  Rod-and-Frame Test
  Room Adjustment Test and Body Adjustment Test
  Embedded Figures Test
  Children's Embedded Figures Test
  Group Embedded Figures Test
  Articulation of Body Concept Scale
Concept formation, classification, and object-sorting techniques
Culture Fair Intelligence Test
D48
Goodenough-Harris Drawing Test
Kohs Blocks
Leiter International Performance Scale
Perceptual Acuity Test
Pictorial Depth Precision Test ("Hudson's Test")

[1] The reader is reminded that a test designed to measure the Piagetian principle of conservation, has been developed by Goldschmid and Bentler (1968), and is a valuable new cross-cultural instrument (see p. 170).

The PIR and Queensland Tests
Porteus Maze Test
Ravens Progressive Matrices

### *Personality-Interest*

Adjective Check List
California Personality Inventory
Eysenck Personality Inventory
Minnesota Multiphasic Personality Inventory
Rotter's Internal versus External Locus of Control Scale
Semantic Differential Technique
Sixteen P-F Test
Strong Vocational Interest Blank
Study of Values
Survey of Personal Values
Ways to Live Questionnaire

## *Cognitive-Intellectual*

### *"Cognitive Style" Tests of Witkin and Associates.*

The relatively crisp dichotomy of field-dependent versus field-independent ways of perceiving has generated much research, some of it cross-cultural, under the basic paradigm of "cognitive style." The tests and procedures that have been developed by Herman A. Witkin and his associates to measure these ways of perceiving include the Embedded Figure Test (EFT) [which also has Group (GEFT) and Children's (CEFT) versions], and Rod-and-Frame Test (RFT), the Body Adjustment Test (BAT) and its companion, the Room Adjustment Test (RAT), and the Articulation of Body Concept Scale (ABC), which uses a figure-drawing approach. These tests are briefly described below.

The two major sources of information concerning these measures are by Witkin, Lewis, Hertzman, Machover, Meissner, and Wapner (1954) and Witkin, Dyk, Faterson, Goodenough, and Karp (1962). The latter book, *Psychological Differentiation,* focuses on the basic differentiation hypothesis, which

". . . proposes an association among the characteristics of greater or more limited differentiation, identified in the comparison of early and later functioning in each of several psychological areas: degree of articulation of experience of the world; degree of articulation of experience of the self, reflected particularly in nature of the body concept and extent of development of a sense of separate identity; and extent of development of specialized, structured controls and defenses. Implicit in this hypothesis is the view that greater inner differentiation is associated with greater articulation of experience of the world" (p. 16).

Table 8.1 presents a sample of some of the areas which have been investigated along the field-dependent—field-independent continuum. Support for most or all of them has been given, but in the cross-cultural realm they should be viewed as hypotheses or questions suggestive of interesting research possibilities.

Table 8-1

| Field-Independent (Parts of the field are experienced as discrete from organized ground) | Field-Dependent (Perception dominated by organization of surrounding field, and parts of field are experienced as fused) |
| --- | --- |
| "Fluid" or analytic ability | "Crystallized" or trained ability |
| More differentiated perception | Less differentiated perception |
| Males tend to be higher | Females tend to be higher |
| Increases with age plateau in young adulthood | Geriatrics "return to field dependence" |
| "Articulated" cognitive style | "Global" cognitive style |
| "Articulated" body concept (body has definite limits) | "Global" body concept (body is less separated from environment) |
| Sense of separate identity high | Low sense of separate identity |
| Nonconforming, less easily influenced socially | Conforming, more easily influenced socially |
| Isolation as a major defense | Massive repression and primitive denial as major defenses |
| Pathologically, delusions and other means to struggle for maintenance of identity | Pathologically, tend to show severe identity problems |
| Permissively raised | Strictly raised |

Some now-classic cross-cultural studies in this area give the basic research strategy involved. The primary hypothesis tested in these studies was that child-rearing practices or environmental conditions (or both) will lead to different modes of perceiving or thinking. Berry (1966) and Dawson (1967a,b) selected groups differing in socialization practices and/or ecological (subsistance) requirements. Thus, Berry contrasted Eskimos of Baffin Bay, with their extremely permissive child-rearing practices *and* the Eskimo's need to place great importance during development of fostering the articulation of the environment, with the Temne of Sierra Leone. The Temne are much stricter in child-rearing than the Eskimo, and their already highly articulated and agricultural (non-hunting, as is the case with the Eskimo) environment does not demand investment in developing articulation. Berry's data showed that the Eskimo are much more field-independent than the Temne. Dawson strikingly supported Berry's findings by comparing two tribal groups in Sierra Leone, the Temne and the Mende. The Mende have much less harsh socialization and punishment practices, with the result that they are more field-independent. Earlier, Dawson (1963) showed that field-dependent Sierra Leone men had mothers who exerted strict control in raising them, compared with field-independent men. Witkin (1967) discusses these and other aspects of psychological differentiation in the framework of cross-cultural research.

Berry (1969) has reiterated a caveat given by Wober (1966, 1967), who pointed out that individuals in different cultures may have an orientation to receive most of their sensory information in different modalities. Thus, differentiation is likely a function of various cultural and ecological parameters, and modalities of sensing may be more complex internationally than these earlier studies suggest.

Finally, we wish to direct the reader to a doctorial dissertation on the topic (Irving, 1970). Irving investigated the differentiation hypothesis using subjects from two Dutch villages, two Mexican villages, and a Negro ghetto in southern United States. He tentatively suggests that (1) the patterns of abilities develop in response to social role prescriptions for behavior, and (2) general intelligence and intellectual development can account for the communality (factor analytic) attributed to psychological differentiation dimensions more "precisely and parsimoniously" than can the differentiation hypothesis as originally stated. Additionally, Irving's study describes more devices than we shall present which can also be used to measure personality and cognitive dimensions postulated by the differentiation hypothesis.

With these summary comments as a backdrop, several tests designed to assess psychological differentiation will now be presented.

*The Rod-and-Frame Test (RFT).* A full description of this apparatus, which is the primary procedure to assess field-dependence-independence, and most of the other Witkin tests can be found in Witkin et al. (1954, 1962). The RFT consists of a luminous square frame and a luminous rod mounted within it. Both are pivoted centrally and can be tilted independently of each other. The subject sits in a completely darkened room in a high-back chair and can see only the rod and the frame. His job is to adjust the rod to a position he perceives as vertical. Various combinations of "tilt" are used in the testing: frame left, chair left; frame right, chair right, and so forth, and these combinations are used in three series of tests, each consisting of eight trials.

The score is the mean absolute error in degrees from the true upright for the eight trials in each of the three series. Using appropriate age-group means and standard deviations, the raw scores are converted to standard scores. The total RFT score is the mean of the standard score for each of the series. Positive scores reflect relatively field-dependent, while negative scores relatively field-independent performance.

Since a 6 by 6 by 6-foot room is standard for the RFT, it is impractical to depend on such an apparatus in many cross-cultural research settings. Oltman (1968) has developed a portable rod-and-frame (PRFT) apparatus which can conveniently be used in a variety of settings. The subject views the rod and frame, which can be titled 28° left or right and are at the opposite end of an otherwise darkened rectangular enclosure. His field of vision is restricted to the interior of the enclosure by means of a curved shield attached to a headrest.

PRFT scores for 163 college students (83 females, 80 males) correlated .89 with scores on the standard version. Generally, the PRFT may be a valid substitute for the standard apparatus, but since the chair cannot be tilted as in the standard RFT, it has obvious diminished flexibility. Also, one wonders if the headrest, with which the subject is in continuous contact, allows unwanted proprioceptive cues to affect performance. Such cues, however, are not unlike the cues one would normally have contact with in non-artificial settings, so this argument is likely not important.

*The Room-Adjustment Test (RAT) and Body-Adjustment Test (BAT).* These "tilting-room-tilting-chair" tests evaluate the subjects perception of the position of his body and of the entire surrounding field in relation to the upright. This apparatus is also in a 6 by 6 by 6- room that can be tilted by any amount left or right. Inside the room is a chair which can be tilted left or right independently of the room. Standard procedures exist to determine if the subject brings himself to the upright by his position in terms of his apparent relation to the field or if, on the other hand, he resists the influence of the field and adjusts himself according to bodily sensations. (In aviation jargon, this is called "flying by the seat of your pants." A pilot flying by instruments is trained to disregard bodily sensations, imposing on himself, as it were, a momentary state of field-dependence.)

The standard test for both the RAT and BAT consists of two series of tests with chair-and-room-tilt permutations similar to those given for the RFT. Raw scores are mean absolute errors in degrees from the true upright. Each series is converted to a standard score, using means and standard deviations of the subject's age groups. Separate RAT and BAT indexes are thus obtained, and positive and negative scores are designated field-dependent or field-independent, respectively.

*The Embedded Figures Test (EFT).* Two sets of 12 cards with Complex Figures (Forms A and B) and a set of 8 cards with Simple Forms, designated by letter A to H, are the essential materials. This and the other tests developed by Witkin et al. are described in the manual (Witkin, Oltman, Raskin and Karp, 1971). A practice Complex Figure card and an accompanying card with a practice Simple Form, as well as a stylus to be used by the subject to trace the outline of the Simple Form are also provided. A stopwatch that can be stopped and restarted without resetting the second hand at zero is necessary.

The subject is required to "disembed" one of the Simple Forms from a predesignated Complex Figure (see Figure 8.1). The Simple Form, exposed for 10 seconds, and Complex Figure are never shown simultaneously, although the Simple Form may be shown for another 10 seconds as often as requested.

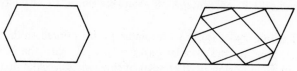

**Figure 8.1.** Simple Figure (left) which is embedded in Complex Figure (right).

A maximum of 3 minutes for each of the 12 "solutions" is allowed. Thus, an outer limit of about 45 minutes of testing time is needed, but normally 20-25 minutes should be sufficient. The time in seconds for solution is recorded for each of the Complex Figures. A subject's score is his mean solution time in seconds.

Norms and reliability data are provided in the manual for groups in the United States ranging in age from 10 to 39 years. Reliability coefficients range from .61 to .92. Numerous validity data are presented, relative to correlational and factor analytic studies. Construct validation studies, studies relating EFT performance to social behavior, body concept, nature of defenses, forms of pathology, and family and cultural experiences are also discussed.

*The Children's Embedded Figures Test (CEFT).* Because experience with the EFT showed that it was too difficult for ost children below the age of 9, the CEFT was designed chiefly to investigate differentiation during development.

Two 25-item forms of the test are available. Unlike the EFT, the CEFT is currently untimed, although the value of using a time limit is under investigation. It consists of two Simple Forms (a Tent and a House) which are embedded in the Complex Figures, 11 of which have the simple Tent figure embedded and 14 of which have the House figure embedded. A discrimination series, demonstration series, and practice series are used prior to actual testing. Responses are scored 1 or 0. A score of 1 is given only when the first choice is correct and verified.

Norms and reliability data, again United States-based, are presented for 160 boys and girls ranging in age from 5 to 12 years. Internal consistency reliability coefficients ranging from .83 to .90 are reported. Some validity data are given in the manual. Correlations with the EFT (among older children who can understand the EFT) are given as .41 for 40 children age 9-10, and .85 for 40 children age 11-12. The test developers have recommended that the CEFT be used for research purposes only since current validity data are sparse and incomplete.

*The Group Embedded Figures Test (GEFT)* Although still experimental and to be used only when the EFT is not practicable, the GEFT can be given to many individuals in a single 20-minute testing session. It is modelled as closely as possible after the EFT and contains 18 complex figures, 17 of which are taken from the EFT.

The GEFT is in booklet form, with Simple Forms printed on the back cover and Complex Forms on the booklet pages so that, as with the EFT, subjects cannot see both simultaneously. It consists of three sections: the first section (7 items) is essentially for practice and the second and third sections, considered alternate or parallel forms, each contain 9 items.

Subjects are required to trace with a soft black pencil the Simple Figures embedded in each of the Complex Figures. Five minutes each are allowed for the 9 figures in both sections two and three. The score is the total number of Simple Forms correctly traced in the second and third sections.

Norms, again, are based on men and women from a United States college. Separate Spearman-Brown reliability coefficients between second and third sections scores for 80 males and 97 females were both .82, similar to values found for the EFT. Correlations comparing the GEFT with EFT are high, but are fairly low when it is compared with the Portable Rod-and-Frame test. Moderately high correlations with the Articulation of Body Concept scale (see below) are reported.

*The Articulation of Body Concept Scale (ABC).* Earlier called the sophistica-tion-of-body-concept scale (Witkin et al., 1962) the ABC Scale uses figure drawings to determine the extent to which the subject's body concept is articulated (field-independent) or global (field-dependent). The subject is required to draw a person, following which he draws a person of the opposite sex. The 5-point ABC Scale covers "most articulated drawings" (5) to "most primitive and infantile drawings" (1). Interjudge reliability coefficients ranging from .79 to .99 have been obtained for this scale (e.g., see Burton and Sjoberg, 1964; Corah, 1965; Fuller and Lunney, 1965; Witkin et al., 1962).

In a longitudinal study, Faterson and Witkin (1970) give evidence that the articulation of body concept increases during growth years and shows relative stability after that period. They also report that sex differences in ABC performance are in the opposite direction from that consistently found for field-dependence—field-independence using other techniques, those differences being that females show a consistent and slight tendency to be more field dependent than men. They note that this unexpected reversal is very likely a function of stylistic differences that females show in drawing the fully clothed and adorned human figure.

The ABC Scale offers some interesting cross-cultural research possibilities, since, like most of the Witkin-type procedures, it does not depend to any degree on language. Further, this technique can be coordinated with the Goodenough-Harris method of measuring intelligence through the drawing of human figures (see below).

## Concept Formation, Classification, and Object-Sorting Techniques

Cross-cultural researchers may occasionally find that the nature of cultural groups or conditions precludes the reliance on one or more of the appropriate "standard" intelligence tests described in this section. When this is the case, a variety of techniques are at their disposal to "get at" intelligence, ability, cognitive functioning, or problem-solving ability in a rather oblique manner. Tests or techniques of this kind demand qualitative rather than quantitative interpretation. The emphasis is on how a subject *approaches* a problem rather than on an end result.

Two tests, now somewhat old but still widely used clinically, are among the pioneers in this area. The Concept Formation Test was adapted from an earlier test (the Vigotsky) by Hanfmann and Kasanin (1936). The test materials are 22 blocks varying in size, shape, color, and height. Printed on the underside of each is a category name (nonsense syllables) that the subject cannot initially see. The subject is to sort the blocks into four groups according to some meaningful principle, using the category names as a guide. Early errors in grouping are pointed out by the examiner, and the subject works until he arrives at the correct solution. His next step is to resort the blocks according to the discovered principle.

Goldstein and Scheerer (1941) introduced their series of tests to assess abstract and concrete thinking in brain damaged patients. The series of five tests is sensitive to inability to abstract common properties from objects, to grasp the basic elements of a given whole, to break up a whole into constituent parts, or to shift from one aspect of a given task to another. A Cube Test (a modification of the Kohs Blocks), a Color-Form Sorting Test, a Stick Test, a Color Sorting Test and an Object Sorting Test are individually administered.

Standardization of the series is poor, but this is not necessarily critical from a cross-cultural standpoint, since the primary utility of such tests is in the observational opportunities they make possible and in the analysis of within-culture qualitative responses. However, a basic cross-cultural shortcoming is that at least one of the tests (Object Sorting) contains many objects that would be unfamiliar to people in many cultures. The tests have shown high correlations with scores on verbal intelligence tests.

Some researchers have adapted previously devised tests for studying concept formation or classificatory ability. For example, de Lacey (1970) used the techniques of Inhelder and Piaget (1964) in studying the classificatory ability of two groups of Aborigines who had high and low contact with European ways, showing the marked effect that cultural enrichment has on the ability to classify. Others (cf. Price-Williams, 1962; Kellaghan, 1965) have used indigenous objects to study classificatory ability, generally showing that the use of appropriate test materials narrows or closes the gap in abstract ability traditionally found to be considerable between Western and remote non-Western groups. Okonji (1971) has followed their lead, and the lead of Inhelder and Piaget, by comparing the effects that familiar objects have on classificatory ability.

These and similar approaches can be useful in studying development and cognitive or conceptual differences in problem-solving ability, but should not be assumed as measures of intelligence, conventionally defined, without supporting data.

## Culture Fair Intelligence Test

The Culture Fair (nee Culture-Free) Intelligence Test was introduced in 1940 (Cattell, 1940; Cattell, Feingold, and Sarason, 1941). As mentioned earlier (Chapter 5, p. 112), no small contribution to its evolvement was Cattell's discontent with researchers for "years of neglect in regard to the real problems of intelligence testing" (Cattell, 1940, p. 162) and his subsequent search for common objects and common processes.

Like the Raven Matrices, the Culture Fair is nonverbal and is supposed to be a test of "g." More precisely, it is primarily a test of "fluid" ability (spatial and inductive reasoning) as opposed to "crystallized" ability (skills that have been acquired by cultural experience, for example, vocabulary size, memory, habits of logical thinking). Its evolution has covered the better part of forty years, and since the 1950's, all forms of it have been published by the Institute for Personality and Ability Testing. Three scales are available:

Scale 1—for ages 4-8 and adult retardates or defectives.

Scale 2—(equivalent forms A and B) for ages 8-13 and average unselected adults.

Scale 3—(equivalent forms A and B) for high school ages and adults of superior intelligence.

Scale 3 is identical in form but more difficult than Scale 2. Forms A and B of both scales each require 12 1/2 minutes actual testing time, to which should be added about 15 minutes for administration preliminaries. The scales can be administered individually or in groups.

In addition to the test (with optional answer sheets) and stopwatch needed for Scales 2 and 3, parts of Scale 1 require several other items (coins, books, a table and two extra chairs, for example), making it unattractive for those who would rather travel with little luggage. About an hour is recommended for a testing session.

Scale 1 is not completely figural, making it admittedly not culture fair, and four of its eight subtests have to be administered individually. Each scale consists of the following four subtests, sample items of which are shown in Figure 8.2.

1. *Series.* Selecting items that complete the series.

2. *Classification.* Marking one item in each row that does not belong with the others.

3. *Matrices.* Marking items that complete the given pattern, or matrix.

4. *Conditions.* Inserting dots in one of the alternative designs so as to meet the same conditions indicated in the sample design.

The manuals and their supplements report reliability coefficients of total test scores to be in the .80's and .90's, while subtest reliabilities are somewhat lower. Validity coefficients have covered a very wide range. Correlations with the Raven are generally between .50 and .60, while correlations with other intelligence measures have ranged from .49 (Otis Beta) to .72 with Full Scale WISC I.Q. Domino (1964) found a correlation of .51 between the Culture Fair and the D 48, another test of considerable merit for cross-cultural work (see below). Other validity data reported by Krug (1967) indicate that the test's lack of sensitivity in discriminating between widely differing cultural groups gives evidence for the validity of the scales. MacArthur and Elley (1963) have testified in favor of the test's "culture-reducing" aspects, noting that their computed correlations of .24 between social status and Culture Fair scores reduces the traditionally great influence that social status has had on intelligence tests scores.

The manuals provide tables allowing scores to be reported as percentiles and "classical" (Binet-type), as well as normalized standard score, I.Q.'s. Norms are provided for the test when administered without a time limit. All standardization data given in the manuals are based on the testing of American and British subjects.

Marquardt and Bailey (1955) have argued that if the Culture Fair approaches its goal, the difference in average scores between socioeconomic classes should be greater on the Stanford-Binet than on the Culture Fair. Upper- and middle-class children should make relatively higher scores on the S-B, while lower-class children should score higher on the Culture Fair. Their study showed that Scale 1 was influenced by culture (social status) as much as was the S-B, while Scale 2 was influenced relatively less by sociocultural factors.

Kidd (1962) investigated the culture fair aspects of Scale 2 using four groups of male and female children between the ages of 10 and 11, selected on the basis of socioeconomic status and ethnicity (Mexican-American). For comparative purposes, the 1937 S-B (Form L) was used. She found a definite positive relationship between scores obtained on the S-B and on the Culture Fair.

Of particular interest is Kidd's finding that 22 of the 46 items did not differentiate between the subcultural groups or economic levels. She concluded from this that the 22 items can be considered culture fair. A factor analysis of these items indicated that four reference vectors were operating:

1. Ability to overcome appropriate set (to "disembed") one obvious element while overlooking other important elements.
2. Ability to localize the elements of an item (awareness of the placement of major elements of items and use the correct placement to select the answer).
3. Awareness of size or of progressive change in size (called "magnitude").
4. Ability to understand the essential change in a progressive series.

A second-order factor analysis indicated that two general reference vectors were operating: (1) recognition of total figure-ground relationships, and (2) set, or the tendency to note one obvious element to the exclusion of other important elements.

Kidd concluded that "future culture fair tests can be based on perception if future research demonstrates that norms for perceptual development are valid in all countries and among all cultures" (p. 359).

Kidd and Rivoire (1965) analyzed the items that appear to be culture fair, giving data to support the hypothesis that they are "based upon the most elementary spatial concepts and that it is the basic topological properties that are untouched by cultural processes or are found in a majority of known cultures" (p. 109). They note that their data could support theories claiming that perception is learned, but that they could also support theories holding that perceptual organization is at least partially innate. The possible universality of the topological properties of the 20-odd items of the 46 that have been identified as "culture fair" is given further credibility by anthropological accounts of the relative invariability of the forms depicted in the items.

It is thus a valuable, if unsurprising, finding that more than half the items on Scale 2 (the one most likely to receive continued cross-cultural use) favor some cultural groups over others. It is especially important to recognize that many items are perceptually unfair. Many of the items are weird, and perhaps to people unaccustomed to the mental gymnastics necessary for the correct solution, all items are baffling. Items such as those found on the Culture Fair have been constructed by Western psychologists who are adept at transformational or abstract thinking. To assign primitive, unacculturated, or uninitiated people the strange task of unraveling their creations without the benefit of even reasonably similar familiarity with the mode of thinking required to do well is obviously unfair.

## The D 48

A distinct European development, the D 48 (D for dominoes, 48 for the number of items) is another test of "g," and it is receiving increasing

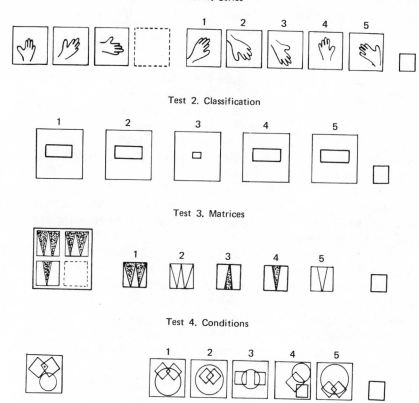

**Figure 8.2.** Practice items from the Culture Free Intelligence Test, Scale 2, Form B.

international attention. British researchers developed the method of testing in the 1940's, and a French adaptation of one of four British forms was published and copyrighted in 1948 by the *Centre de Psychologie Appliquee* in Paris under the name D 48. It was brought out in the United States in 1961 by Consulting Psychologists Press, Inc. The manual, which was revised and adapted from the French manual by John D. Black (Consulting Psychologists Press, undated), carries the notice that in the United States the test is for experimental use only, since adequate normative and validity data on United State populations are not available.

Dominoes, or games similar to it, may contain stimuli so equally familiar to all literate civilizations that the D 48 has an advantage over other cross-culturally appropriate ability tests that attempt to present stimuli of equal *un*familiarity to all. Gough and Domino (1963) have written of the apparent international and historical ubiquity of the domino, noting, for example, that the game of dominoes has been played in China for at least 1000 years. The D 48 does not, however, have anything to do with the game itself or the skill necessary to play it; only the simple stimuli are used.

The test contains 44 problems (and 4 practice items) of increasing difficulty, each consisting of a series of dominoes defining a principle of progression. The subject is required to write in each half of one blank domino the number of dots that will complete or sustain the progression (see Figure 8.3). The solutions to the progressions involve simple addition and subtraction, addition and subtraction with progression, double progression, and so forth.

Similar in some respects to the Raven Matrices, the D 48 has the same basic goals: to minimize language handicaps, to obtain a nonverbal measure of intelligence, and to use test material free of cultural influences. Unlike the matrices, it uses absolutely homogeneous stimuli, and its format almost completely eliminates chance, since subjects must determine which numbers go into each half of the blank domino. The Matrices gives 6 or 8 alternatives, only one of which is correct.

The D 48 can be administered either individually or in groups, and either under timed (25 minutes plus administrative details) or power conditions. Testing material consists of a reusable test booklet, separate answer sheets, and a scoring template. The United States manual is minimally adequate and, at this time, necessarily brief, especially with respect to normative data. Research reviews (Ferracuti and Rizzo, 1959, Pasquasy and Doutrepont, 1956; Pichot, Rennes, and Taver, 1953) can be consulted for more extensive data.

Vernon (1950) gives evidence that the D 48 is more highly saturated with "g" (.87) than is the Raven Matrices (.79) and that it is virtually free of loadings on

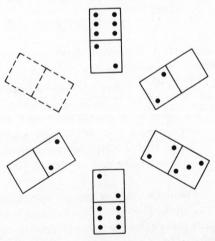

**Figure 8.3.** Sample item from the D 48 of about average difficulty.

other factors. Gough and Domino (1963) display illustrative norms for the D 48, and they suggest that "average scores for subjects of similar age and educational level in different countries will be about the same" (p. 346). There are also data suggesting that sex differences on the D 48 may be inconsequential.

Domino (1964) found that for a college sample in the United States the D 48 had slightly more predictive validity than the Cattell Culture Fair or the Army Beta (one of the earlier group intelligence tests) and that it is similar to other measures of ability. He found a correlation of +.51 with the Culture Fair, +.41 with the Army Beta, and +.22 with grade point average. Later, Domino found similar results when 108 foreign students from 21 countries attending a California state college took the D 48, the Revised Beta examination, the Cattell Culture Fair, and the Progressive Matrices (Domino, 1968). The tests were correlated with grade point average, and only the D 48 ($r = .28, p < .01$) and the Culture Fair ($r = .23, p < .05$) achieved statistical significance. Administrative differences were virtually nonexistent with the D 48 and the Progressive Matrices, while several foreign students reported difficulties in understanding and following directions for the other two tests.

Gough and Domino (1963) found that with a fifth-grade United States class ($N = 34$) the D 48 correlated +.58 with grades, and that it correlated from .25 to .51 with four subtests of the Stanford Achievement Tests. Kagitcibasi (1972) administered the D 48 to groups of Turkish sixth and seventh grade students, with the result that in most cases its correlations with grades in separate courses (.15 to .70), as well as with overall grade point averages (.31 to .62),were at least as high as those reported by Gough and Domino. Kagitcibasi also showed that the relative difficulty level of the 44 items was essentially the same for Turkish and United States children.

Cross-cultural comparisons of the D 48, the Culture Fair, Raven's Matrices and other tests vying for the limelight in cross-cultural intelligence testing would be welcome indeed.

## Goodenough-Harris Drawing Test

Florence Goodenough developed her Draw-a-Man Test in 1926 as a means to measure intelligence through scoring qualitative features of the drawings (Goodenough, 1926a,b). Its metamorphasis included changes of format, but the current form (Harris, 1963) retains as a basic purpose the measurement of intelligence, or intellectual maturity. Its attractiveness to many cross-cultural researchers is obvious, if for no other reasons than its reliance on simply drawing the human form and its essentially nonverbal method of administration.

Early cross-cultural work with the original Goodenough Test was done by Peterson and Telford (1930) and Menzel (1935). These studies are of historical interest only, for they are a cariacture of what would be done today cross-culturally in terms of methodology and interpretation of results. Also of historical interest is the series of reports by Haward and Roland (1954a,b; 1955), and Haward (1956) concerning the application of the technique in Africa. Armstrong's (1954) bitingly incisive criticism of the African reports (e.g., "Certainly no anthropologist with serious experience in Nigeria would have drawn the conclusions that the authors . . . draw" (p. 147) is generally on-target.

Dennis (1942, 1957, 1970) has given us the most thorough and guarded analyses of the Goodenough and Goodenough-Harris techniques. Much more profound than any real value it offers as a "culture fair" intelligence test is Dennis' conclusion that the technique may be a useful index of "degrees of acculturation, Westernization, modernization, and social change" (Dennis, 1970, p. 151). In comparing 40 groups of 6-year-olds differing widely in culture and degree of modernization, Dennis convincingly argues that the independent variable most directly related to Goodenough scores is the amount of experience with representational art, stimulated by indigenous forms of encouragement. At the same time Dennis denounced four possible alternative or rival hypotheses (hereditary factors, schooling differences, urban-rural differences, and parental literacy) that could account for the diversity of group means.

Thus, the future use of drawing techniques used cross-culturally will likely be focused on their ability to assess non-cognitive functions, since a number of other procedures are much better suited to give estimates of intelligence. This line of reasoning, however, is seriously damaged by Adler (1970). In a psychiatric setting, Adler studied the factorial composition of scores derived from drawing the human figure, using scoring categories suggested by the literature. He found the figure drawing procedure to be essentially a one-factor test, that factor clearly being a cognitive one (specifically, the maturity of the body image representation). This is consistent with Goodenough and Harris' original intent to measure intellectual maturity. Adler suggests that "It is probable that whatever usefulness drawings might have in contributing to judgments about personality, diagnosis, adjustment, and the like, is only to the extent that these variables are related to cognitive maturity in any one particular population" (pp. 56-57).

## Kohs Blocks

The Kohs Block Design Test was originated in 1923 by S. C. Kohs, a clinical psychologist (Kohs, 1923). As Cronbach (1970, p. 48) has pointed out, the Kohs Test was but one of a large number of tests devised during the 1920's when mental testing and applied psychology first came into prominence. The block designs were used in a large number of the tests developed in that era, and they are still found in many of the most widely used tests. The Wechsler Scales (WISC, WAIS) use them as one of their performance subtests, as do the Arthur Point

Scale, the Leiter International Performance Scale, and the Queensland Test (see below), among others.

The subject's task is to construct designs out of colored one-inch cubes, copying the designs from cards. In some tests the cubes are of only two colors, while others use multicolored cubes. Verbal instructions can be kept to a minimum when the blocks are used alone.

The Kohs Blocks or modifications of them are diagnostically flexible. The Block Design subtest of the Wechsler scales, together with the Vocabulary subtest (a one-two Western punch of nonverbal-verbal measured intelligence) is the best two-subtest combination of the eleven standard Wechsler subtests. Wechsler (1958) described a clinically useful *deterioration index* using "Hold" tests (little or no decline with age, such as vocabulary) and "Don't Hold" tests (relatively steep decline with age; the Block Design subtest is included here) to check on abnormal age decline. Ample evidence says that the various block design tests are all related to field dependence (cf. Goodenough and Karp, 1961). Witkin and his colleagues (1962) maintain that the extent of field dependence and performance on standard intelligence tests has as its base a common cognitive style.

To test the blind, one modification of the Kohs Blocks has surfaces with different textures (see Dauterman and Suinn, 1966), and there is no reason why such a tactile (with or without colors) approach cannot be tried cross-culturally.

## Leiter International Performance Scale

The Leiter is an individually administered test which was originally designed to assess the ability of those with hearing, speech, or language handicaps. Because of its simple materials, and because it can be administered without instructions, the test has enjoyed considerable cross-cultural use. It is a nonverbal mental age scale (similar to but not patterned after the Binet) for use between the ages of 2-18. It has gone through a series of revisions during the last 35 years, starting with the testing of different ethnic groups in Hawaii, later by Porteus' application to various African groups, and later still with American children, Army recruits in World War II, and various subcultural groups in the United States.

The scale in its latest (1948) form consists of fifty-six standardized tests. Materials include a response frame with an adjustable card holder (see Figure 8.4). The appropriate card, containing the printed pictures which define each task, is attached to the frame. The subject selects the blocks which will correctly complete the task and inserts them into the frame. The beginning frames in each test are easy, but they get successively more difficult. The tests include a wide range of functions: color and form matching, analogies, copying block designs, series completion, spatial relations, footprint recognition, similarities, memory for series, animal classification, recognition of facial expression, matching items on the basis of use, plus many other types which cannot be adequately described with a short phrase.

Scores are in terms of ratio I.Q. The Manual (Leiter, 1966) reports a great amount of reliability and validity data, including comparisons with other tests and with teacher's ratings. There is considerable fluctuation in standard deviations for the different age levels and for different classifications of ethnicity. The 1948 Revision and the Arthur Adaptation (Arthur, 1949), a point scale, are identical through the twelve year level, although norms for the Arthur do not go beyond 7.99 years.

## Perceptual Acuity Test (PAT)

This test concentrates primarily on the well-documented susceptibility (or lack of it) to various illusions, and measures ability to perceive them and geometric forms (Gough and McGurk, 1967). It contains 5 non-illusion items (judgment of size, length, or area of geometric forms) and 25 illusion items drawn from illusions such as the vertical-horizontal, Mueller-Lyer, Poggendorf, Ponzo, Baldwin, Delbouf, and the circle of Titchener (see Chapter 4 for a discussion of illusions). Presented by means of a 35-mm slide projector to

**Figure 8.4.** An item from the Leiter, *Analogous Designs.* Procedure: Place the test material before the subject with the blocks in random order. Give no help.

individuals or groups of 75 to 100, it is easy to administer (with minimum written or verbal directions) in 20 to 25 minutes. Certain minimum viewing requirements, including angle and distance from projected slides, are necessary. Five options are given for each item, as exemplified in Figure 8.5.

Three scores are recorded: (1) the number of correct responses to the 5 non-illusion items; (2) the number of correct responses to the 25 illusions; and (3) a weighted total score giving 1 point for each correct response to a non-illusion item, 2 points for each correct response to an illusion item, and 1 point for designated *incorrect* choices on 12 of the illusion items. The assignment of points for the latter category is based on their positive correlations with the number of correct responses in the initial standardization of the test.

The test reflects Gough's penchant for items in cross-cultural tests that can meet universal standards of applicability. As Gough and McGurk (1967) suggested, the PAT opens up a number of areas worthy of investigation cross-culturally. For example, in the area of development, can reliable and equivalent year-by-year increments in scores be demonstrated among children from different cultures? Piaget (1961), it should be noted, distinguished between primary illusions—those yielding systematic errors which decrease with age—and secondary—those for which errors either remain constant or increase with age. The PAT can be useful here. Its relation to the Witkin tests of field-dependence and to other viable cross-cultural tests, such as the D 48, matrices tests, and the Porteus Mazes, should be determined, and investigations in the area of ego functioning, personological study, and clinical inquiry would also be valuable.

Some of the above questions have already been partially answered. In a series of studies (Gough and Hug, 1968; Gough and Delcourt, 1969; Gough and Meschieri, 1971), PAT performance of French, Swiss, and Italian children was compared with American children, of ages between 8 and 16 years. Age-related developmental functions were the focus of all these studies. Scores correlated +.33 with age in the French, +.21 in the Swiss, +.31 in the Italian, and +.22 in the American samples. With minor variations, age norms across all groups were similar. In the Italian study (Gough and Meschieri, 1971) PAT scores for Italian children and adults were also compared. Adults scored higher than children, although the two distributions overlapped considerably.

With respect to its ability to assess field-dependence—field-independence (discussed earlier), Gough and Olton (1972) have shown that of five groups administered nonverbal tests the PAT had the highest correlation with field dependence (−.41), the latter being measured by the Portable Rod-and-Frame Test. The four other group tests, taken by 309 California college students, were the D 48, Gottschaldt Hidden Figures (the forerunner of the Embedded Figures Test, discussed earlier), Survey of Space Relations, and the Street Gestalt, all thought to be relevant to field-independence.

A multiple correlation of .52 was found between the PRFT and a 4-test

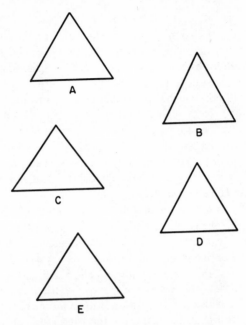

**Figure 8.5.** Problem 5 of the Perceptual Acuity Test. Instructions: "Choose the figure in which all three sides are equal in length."

combination of the PAT, Gottschaldt, SSR, and Street Gestalt. However, this coefficient is no higher than many correlations reported between the RFT and the EFT, itself a non-apparatus measure of field-dependence. Nonetheless, it may be concluded that this brief visual test (the PAT) has promise as a tool for use in cross-cultural testing and research.

## Pictorial Depth Perception Test ("Hudson's Test")

This test was designed to study the perception of three dimensions represented by pictorial material. It was first reported by Hudson (1960) and has since been used by a number of researchers, all studying pictorial perception difficulties among unacculterated groups, generally in Africa. Excellent examples of its use, in addition to Hudson's original application, can be found in Deregowski (1968a, b), Deregowski and Byth (1970), Holmes (1963), Hudson (1962, 1967), and Mundy-Castle (1966).

The test materials include eleven outline (two-dimensional) drawings and one photograph of modelled objects. Six of the drawings are designed to give subjects depth cues of size, overlap, and perspective in horizontal pictorial space (side-to-side scanning) and five are designed to give the same depth cues in vertical space (bottom-to-top scanning). Objects familiar to the originally tested subjects (hunter, elephant, antelope, and tree) are used. The drawings in Figure 8.6 are examples of the horizontal pictorial space represented by the drawings. The photograph of modelled objects is one of the "hunting scenes" depicted in the horizontal pictures.

Subjects are asked a few simple questions while viewing each picture; the pictures are presented separately. Answers to such questions (which is nearer the man—elephant or antelope? What do you see?) are scored according to preceived two- or three-dimensionality.

In Hudson's original study, it was proven that cultural isolation was effective in preventing or retarding the process of learning to perceive depicted three-dimensionality.

## The PIR and Queensland Tests

The PIR (Pacific Islands Regiment) test was developed during the late 1950's and 1960's as a result of a need to classify and place illiterate military recruits from Papua and New Guinea. Since the Regiment is associated with the Australian Army, a team of Australian researchers, led by Major I. G. Ord, was given the task of developing a test for this purpose. The development of the test and its reliability and validity data and norms are given in Ord (1970). McElwain and Kearney (1970) have used all but one of the subtests of the PIR battery in adapting and extending it for use with other South Pacific groups, notably Papuans and New Guineans and Australian Aborigines, for the purpose of training and educational placement. This version is known as the Queensland Test.

In developing the PIR battery, Ord tried about a dozen tests in combination (e.g., several of the Binet subtests, the Goodenough Draw-a-Man, Porteus Mazes, Kohs Blocks, and other performance-type tests). His efforts resulted in the final selection of six subtests which constitute the current PIR. The five tests common to it and the Queensland Test are:

1. *An adaptation of the Knox Cube Imitation Test.* The subject's task is to imitate the examiner's sequence of tapping the sides of cubes that are affixed to a board.

2. *A Binet-type Bead Threading Test.* The subject threads beads of various shapes according to a predesignated plan.

3. *The Passalong Test.* The subject must slide colored tile squares in a tray, attempting to match diagrams presented individually by the examiner.

4. *A Form Assembly Test.* The subject is required, over a number of trials, to point to which of several irregular shapes will complete a square.

5. *The Pattern Matching Test.* This is an adaptation of the Kohs Blocks. Fifteen different patterns are presented, and the subject is to reproduce the

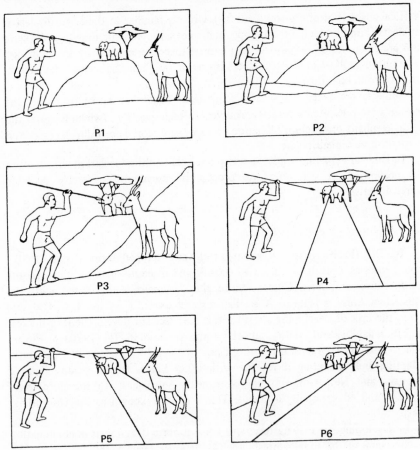

**Figure 8.6.** Horizontal pictorial space represented by Hudson's Test.

patterns by using tiles (rather than cubes, as in Kohs Blocks).

Since the Queensland Test will likely be used more widely than the PIR, some additional comments pertaining to it are in order. The test authors admit that it almost certainly has a culture loading which is positive for Westerners; that it is expensive to purchase and time consuming (about one hour to administer); and that a skilled psychologist must administer it. Moreover, McElwain and Kearney do not claim that the test is at all original or innovative, since they borrowed almost all the subtests from other well known tests which had made earlier "culture-free" claims. Finally, they make no claim that it itself is culture-free, preferring rather to call it culture reducing and sensitive to the measurement of contact with European groups.

## Porteus Maze Test

Stanley D. Porteus' Maze Test has been a psychological diagnostic instrument for nearly 60 years. Started in 1913, partially as an answer to observed shortcomings of the Goddard Revision of the Stanford-Binet, the Maze Test has persisted virtually unchanged. Its original purpose was for the differential diagnosis of feebleminded people, but it has enjoyed a variety of applications. It is included as one of nine subtests of the Arthur Point Scale of Performance Tests (see under the Leiter, above) which, when it was first released in 1930, included the most promising performance tests then available. It can best be described as having had more use in the clinic than in anthropological or psychological field work, although the name "Porteus" conjures up images of a man testing Australian Aborigines or the Bushmen of Kalahari.

Earlier cross-cultural work by Porteus (1933, 1937) has been incorporated in the most comprehensive review of the test and its uses (Porteus, 1965), which is at once a scholarly sourcebook and manual for administration as well as a lively travelogue through hospital wards and remote corners of the world. This book contains information concerning its many applications, for example, in studies of psychosurgery, drugs, juvenile delinquency and crime, testing in industry, as well as numerous ethnic studies.

The Porteus (it should be identified as such, since mazes are used in other tests, for example, the Wechsler Intelligence Scale for Children) has three forms: the Original or Vineland Revision, the Extension series, and the Supplement. Only the Original can be used for age 3 onwards. The series consists of a number of mazes sharply graded in difficulty (see Figure 8.7). The subject is to trace with a pencil the shortest way out of the maze without lifting the pencil from the paper. If two consecutive errors (cutting corners, entering a "blind alley") are made, a failure for that level is recorded. Crossing or touching lines and lifting the pencil are qualitative and not test age errors (see below). Scores are assigned by taking as the ceiling the highest test passed in the allowed number of trials, then deducting one-half year for every unsuccessful trial. Through the use of tables, scores are converted to Maze Test Quotients. Since it is not a general intelligence test (Porteus has also expressed doubts that there is such a thing) these quotients are not equivalent to the usual intelligence quotients (I.Q.), but scores are, of course, a function of test age and chronological age. The early standardization involved correlating it with the Stanford-Binet.

The qualitative (Q) score concerns the evaluation of errors in drawing or execution rather than in planning. Usually beginning with year VII, Q-scores take into account the crossing of lines, general neatness, and whether quantitative errors took place near the beginning or the end of the mazes. The Q-scores are based on comparative studies of delinquents, and they are supposed

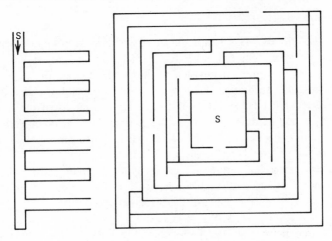

**Figure 8.7.** Two of the Porteus Mazes.

to be related to impulsivity, overconfident habits, or task absorption to the exclusion of attending to specific directions of administration.

The Porteus is often described as being intrinsically motivating. Some evidence (e.g., Porteus and Gregor, 1963) suggests that its game-like format may be completely engrossing to subjects anywhere. Researchers have stimulated motivation by equating the test with real-life familiar situations. For instance, getting out of the "monkey house" (jail) proved to be highly motivating in the testing of Australian Aborigines (Bochner, 1971).

## Raven's Progressive Matrices

Easily one of the most widely used intelligence or ability tests in cross-cultural research, Raven's Matrices appeared commercially in 1938 (Penrose and Raven, 1937). Raven, assisted by others, produced the matrices under the general supervision and influence of Cyril Burt who, along with Charles Spearman, was a proponent of the general ("g") factor theory of intelligence. Ever since British psychologists have thought in terms of a "g" factor operating in mental ability, the Raven has often been cited as a "relatively pure" measure of it. Factor loadings on "g" are usually reported in the .50 to .80 range for the test, with small loadings on other factors such as "k" and "n." Vernon and Parry (1949) described it as "an almost pure 'g' test."

Although it is identified as an intelligence test, one of its chief initial aims was for use with mental defectives. Raven regards it as "a test of a person's capacity to form comparisons, reason by analogy, and develop a logical method of thinking, regardless of previously acquired thinking" (Raven, 1948, p. 13). In Britain, the Mill Hill Vocabulary Test is often used with it, the two tests giving essentially nonverbal and verbal measures of intelligence, respectively.

Commonly called the Raven 38 or the Raven PM, the Standard Form (there are also colored matrices for use with children and advanced matrices for use with superior adults) consist of 60 matrices, each having a missing part [see Figure 8.8; see also Keir, (1949) for a discussion of the historical development of the matrix and the rationale behind "reasoning by analogy"]. The subject is required to select the missing part from six to eight alternatives. Five series of 12 matrices each, arranged with increasing difficulty but following the same principle, are included in the untimed or "power" test which, incidentally, can be timed or speeded. It can be administered individually or in groups, and a form board can be used with less mature subjects. The brief verbal directions are simple, and pantomime can be used to eliminate the verbal factor in administration. In the Standard Matrices (which can be used, according to the manual, for persons between the ages of 6 to 65), the five series of 12 items are discontinuous, that is, each series taps a slightly different type of ability. As Keir (1949) explains, the five types of patterns are (1) single continuous patterns, (2) figure analogies, (3) progressively altered patterns, (4) permutations of patterns, and (5) the resolution of figures into constituent parts.

Its nonverbal "ambiguous" content and assumed independence of special culture-bound abilities or achievement are the more obvious reasons why it has drawn such frequent use. It is often cited as an intrinsically motivating test; people seem to enjoy taking it. However, it is unsurprisingly much more valid and reliable when used in relatively advanced cultures. The routine Western ability to think abstractly or transformationally will yield higher scores. At least the Westerner will not be overwhelmed by the rather weird designs and geometric figures. In his review of the Raven 38 in Africa, Irvine(1969c) notes

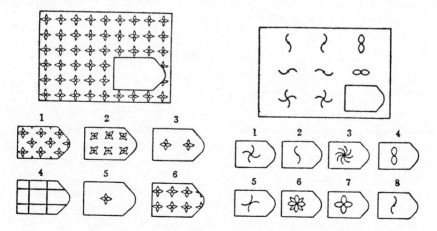

**Figure 8.8.** Sample items from Raven's Progressive Matrices.

that items are best grouped into their perceptual and reasoning components. He maintains that reasoning is initiated by the figural stimulus of each item but that it is "mediated by the ability to transfer cues and codes from previous relevant perceptual experience" (p. 225).

Strategies used in taking the test and in "solving" each matrix are undoubtedly complex. Silvey (1963) and LaRoche (1959) have described the effects of different methods of test administration, and both found vast gains in scores and reduction of variance after using introductory procedures or allowing test interpretations. To date, a good set of standard instructions is not available, and the published norms are notably inflexible for cross-cultural research. Like other tests, differences in learning opportunities and school achievement can have a significant effect on Matrices scores, as can individual strategies, cultural value systems, the degree of field-dependence (Berry, 1966; Witkin, 1962, 1966; Wober, 1967), and verbal (subvocalization) differences (Irvine, 1965).

A wealth of references concerning the test are available. Burke (1958) has provided a critical evaluation of it, giving at the same time a kaleidoscopic picture of validity and reliability information, most of which is not concerned with cross-cultural applications. Raven (1960) has also provided a bibliography. His now outdated list nevertheless gives an excellent bibliography of nearly 150 studies using his test. Court (1972) has compiled an extensive annotated bibliography of both the Raven and the Mill Hill Vocabulary Scales. Vernon (1969) has used the Raven on numerous occasions, and has developed his own matrix test. Elley and MacArthur (1962) and West and MacArthur (1964) have used it with various Canadian samples; Jamal (1965) has used it in Pakistan, as have a host of researchers in Africa (cf. Klingelhofer, 1967; Notcutt, 1949; and Irvine's 1969c review). American researchers have used it liberally. See, for example, Sperazzo and Wilkins (1959), and for a number of references amid a controversial issue, Jensen (1968).

### Personality-Interest

## Adjective Check List (ACL)

The Adjective Check List has proven to be flexible on many fronts, including the cross-cultural one. It consists of 300 adjectives (absentminded to methodical to zany) and can be a self-report inventory, or judges can rate subjects or clients. It can also be used to describe historical figures, cities, Japanese, Arabs, and indeed *anything*.

Gough (1960) discussed adjective check lists in general as personality research tools, and he and A. B. Heilbrun joined efforts to develop the current Adjective Check List and its *Manual* (Gough and Heilbrun, 1965). At present it contains 24 scales, 15 of which are based on Murray's need theory of personality (see, for example, Hall and Lindzey, 1970). It can be hand scored or machine scored, and from 1 to 24 scales can be selected for use. Its characteristics also allow one the opportunity to develop additional scales.

The *Manual* contains the essential information for United States consumption, including much comparative data with many United States tests. It contains no explicit cross-cultural data, but of course should be the first document to be consulted prior to cross-cultural use.

The Italian translation appears to account for much of the published cross-cultural work with the ACL (Gough and Abbele, 1967; Gough and Meschieri, 1967; Gough and Riva, 1967). German, French, and Spanish translations have also been prepared, and all of these plus information on current cross-cultural use of the ACL can be obtained from the University of California's Institute for Personality Assessment and Research.

## *The California Psychological Inventory (CPI).*

United States researchers have developed a number of excellent multidimensional personality measuring devices. One of these is the CPI, a very well-known paper-and-pencil personality test that has also been designed for cross-cultural use. By any reasonable cross-cultural criteria it ranks as the most well-known and prolifically used objective personality test. Furthermore, its inventor and chief advocate, Harrison Gough, a top cross-cultural personologist, continues to promote and refine its proper cross-cultural use.

The CPI contains 480 true-false items (many of them borrowed from the MMPI) contained in an eleven-page booklet. Tested singly or in groups, individuals mark true or false (agree or disagree) on a separate answer sheet.

The test is for use with "normals," that is, individuals free of pathological classification, in a broad personally and socially relevant context. Because of this and because of its explicit cross-cultural applicability, the items (concepts) on the CPI are those that arise from social interaction and occur, more or less, in everyday life. These "folk concepts," Gough writes, are". . . aspects and attributes of interpersonal behavior that are to be found in all cultures and societies, and that possess a direct and integral relationship to all forms of social interaction" (1968a, p. 57). In spite of widespread cultural validity, however, Gough insists that each item be correctly translated for mutual cultural equivalence.

The inventory can currently scale and profile 18 variables:

| | | | |
|---|---|---|---|
| Do | Dominance | To | Tolerance |
| Cs | Capacity for status | Gi | Good impression |
| Sy | Sociability | Cm | Communality |
| Sp | Social presence | Ac | Achievement via conformance |

| | | | |
|---|---|---|---|
| Sa | Self-acceptance | Ai | Achievement via independence |
| Wb | Sense of well-being | Ie | Intellectual efficiency |
| Re | Responsibility | Py | Psychological-mindedness |
| So | Socialization | Fx | Flexibility |
| Sc | Self-control | Fe | Femininity |

Each scale has its own key, or set of items, and raw scores are converted to standard scores with means of 50 and standard deviations of 10. Although many, but not all, of the scales were developed empirically, it is a mistake to assume that the CPI belongs to that genre of tests that were developed in the "dust bowl of empiricism." Gough prefers to view the set of 18 scales as an open system. Scales can be added or dropped as need arises. It is a robustly developed yet delicate instrument, and calls for true clinical interpretation. In addition to the *Manual* (Gough, 1964a), an informative and non-technical treatment (Gough, 1968a) will acquaint the reader with the CPI. An extensive CPI handbook recently became available (Megargee, 1972).

There are many published and unpublished cross-cultural studies which have used the inventory. Some of these are concerned with validating specific scales for use in other cultures. For example, Gough and Sandhu (1964) successfully validated the So scale in India, while Gough, Chun, and Chung (1968) and Levin and Karni (1971) validated the Fe scale in Korea and Israel, respectively. Gough (1966) has given a six-nation analysis of the Fe scale. In all investigations with this scale to date, mean scores for males and females in each culture are significantly different, and the level of differentiation suggested by point-biserial coefficients (.37 to .64) leads to the conclusion of moderate cross-cultural validity for this scale. In another domain, Gough (1964b, 1965) studied scholastic achievement (Ac and Ai) in Italy. The test has also been used cross-culturally in studies of asocial behavior (Gough, 1965) and delinquency (Mizushima and De Vos, 1967; Gough, 1968b). Finally, Levin and Karni (1970) have argued that high scale intercorrelations between Israeli and American samples prove essential invariance of the entire CPI between the two cultures.

Translations of the CPI are available in at least these languages: French, Spanish, Italian, German, Israeli, Norwegian, Turkish, Korean, Indian, and Japanese. Information concerning these and other translations as well as information relative to any aspect of the cross-cultural use of the CPI can be acquired from the Institute for Personality Assessment and Research, University of California, Berkeley.

## *Eysenck Personality Inventory (EPI).*

Both the EPI and its immediate predecessor, the Maudsley Personality Inventory (MPI), are designed to measure the two well-known, factor-analytic-ally-derived dimensions of personality, extraversion-introversion (E) and neuroticism-stability (N). The MPI, developed in the late 1950's and used widely in Great Britain, is by all indications being replaced by the EPI, which has been in circulation for nearly a decade. The several reasons for this, given in the preliminary manual for the EPI (Eysenck and Eysenck, 1963), are:

1. The EPI consists of parallel forms.
2. Reworded items make the EPI more understandable by subjects of low intelligence or education.
3. Item replacement has caused the small correlation between E and N on the MPI to disappear on the EPI.
4. The EPI contains a Lie Scale to detect subjects showing a desirability response set.
5. The PEI has superior retest reliability—even after several months being in excess of .85.
6. Better validity evidence is given that the EPI is a superior descriptive instrument of behavioral manifestations of personality.

Both forms of the EPI contain 57 items (e.g., "Do you often think of your past?"). Adults, for whom the test was standardized, should be able to complete either form in 15 minutes. The current manual gives English norms for E and N as well as representative scores received by select pathological and normal groups, these graphically displayed in grid form on axes depicting the assumed orthogonality of the two dimensions, E and N. No norms are given for the Lie Scale, which was patterned after the Lie Scale of the MMPI (and uses some of the MMPI items).

Due to the somewhat longer history of the MPI, more cross-cultural studies pertaining to it than to the EPI are available. Choynowski (1969) adapted the MPI for use in Poland, and cross-validated it on Polish samples. He also presents various international comparative data. Rafi (1965) used the untranslated MPI and other tests in comparing English, American and Lebanese samples. One of his conclusions was that English norms proved applicable to his Lebanese sample. Kline (1967) administered both the untranslated EPI and Cattell's 16 PF (see below) to a literate population in Ghana, and found the EPI's N scale to be suitable for comparative purposes. But he also showed that many E scale items showed low discrimination, making cross-cultural comparisons with it less acceptable. These few articles cite previous cross-cultural research with both instruments, primarily the MPI.

The "clear-cut" two dimensions of personality that the EPI measures—dimensions which Eysenck claims account for a large proportion of the total common variance found in personality studies—allow a relatively unfettered and unambiguous, if somewhat abbreviated, approach to personality measurement. Such a simple dichotomy, however, may prove to be valuable in cross-cultural research.

## Minnesota Multiphasic Personality Inventory (MMPI).

This is one of the most clinically useful objective tests ever devised. Unfortunately, cross-cultural researchers can currently reap little direct benefit from its warehouse of accumulated data that are, for the most part, singularly American. Like a finely tuned sports car, these data can give impressive and even eye-popping performance (by a few clinicians), but in the wrong hands they can be deadly.

Following the empirical footsteps of the SVIB (see below), the MMPI originated over 25 years ago in the psychiatric and psychological clinics of the University of Minnesota. Using the now defunct Kraepelinian system of psychiatric diagnosis, its originators sought to differentiate clinically diagnosed patients both from each other and from so-called normals or controls. It must be emphasized that this original nosological rationale has been replaced by much more sophisticated scoring procedures, and it is therefore incumbent upon those wishing to employ current translations of the MMPI, of which there are an estimated 30, or those wishing to start anew to become familiar with certain basic documents. These include the works of Dahlstrom and Welsh (1960), Welsh and Dahlstrom (1956), Hathaway and Meehl (1951), and Hathaway and Monachesi (1953). Hathaway (1964) and Butcher (1969) give further important information, and any thorough treatment of psychological testing (e.g., Cronbach, 1970; Anastasi, 1968) will give a good descriptive account of the test and its applications.

Only a severely brief description of the complex MMPI will be given here. It consists of 556 items covering areas such as psychosomatic complaints or symptoms, various attitudinal positions, family and marital questions, and common, stereotyped neurotic and psychotic manifestations, such as hallucinations, ideas of reference, phobias, sadism, and masochism. The subject is to respond *true, false,* or *?* to each item. There are 10 clinical scales (e.g., depression, hysteria, paranoia), three validity scales, and one scale which corrects for test-taking attitude. Scores are reported as T scores, and a number of elaborate scoring and coding procedures are available. More than 100 supplementary keys have been developed, but these are not used widely.

Cross-culturally, there are several useful studies delineating translation problems, and problems and cautions concerning the use of United States norms once the MMPI is translated. Sundberg (1956) and Spreen and Spreen (1963) have discussed the German translation, now known as the *MMPI Saarbruecken* (Spreen, 1963). They note that even if the translation is accurate (which, by strict definitions, it is not), any cultural psychiatric nosology departing from the American tradition reduces its valid interpretation.

In one study, Australian students scored similar to American students, but Australian males scored higher on the Mf (Masculinity-Femininity) scale and on several additional scales (Taft, 1957). Australian females scored lower than

American females on Mf. Rosen and Rizzo (1961) worked with an Italian standardization, but a new and presumably better translation rendered their study virtually useless. Hama (1966) used the Japanese translation to compare Japanese and American patients on the Depression scale. Kadri (1971) had 260 University of Singapore students take the untranslated MMPI (after rewording several items for religious appropriateness, for example). Kadri's scores without K corrections (a refined validity adjustment) were fairly similar to reported scores of a group of California college students, tested in 1954. Lanyon (1968) summarized several cross-cultural and United States subcultural studies, as well as other group profiles (prisoners, psychiatric disorders, and so forth). As already mentioned in Chapter 5, Glatt (1969) evaluated the French, Spanish, and German translations of the MMPI. His conclusion that the German and Spanish translations were clinically adequate, and that the French was not, must be considered along with methodological deficiencies (small samples of bilingual volunteers taking translated and untranslated forms within two days).

The cross-cultural possibilities with the MMPI continue to be intriguing, though there are many who blanch at the sight of the instrument. It would be folly and a waste to dismiss all United States and other MMPI data, suggesting that the *only* reasonable approach with the MMPI would be to develop cultural norms. It would be equally foolish to tread in this jungle of clinical and psychometric data without utmost caution. No previous MMPI translation or cross-validation study across cultures with commendable accuracy can be found in the literature. What is critically needed is a series of cross-cultural cross-validation studies with the MMPI that document empirically the measured similarities and differences of clinical diagnosis and personality assessment as a function of culture.

## Rotter's Internal versus External Locus of Control Scale

Extending the findings of social learning theory, Rotter (1966), supplemented with other material by Lefcourt (1966), has supported the hypothesis that a salient personality dimension is that people can have a belief in either *external* control or *internal* control of reinforcement, contingent upon generalized learned expectancies. One who believes in external control perceives that reinforcement is not entirely contingent upon his own action. Rather, it is the result of luck, fate, or chance. One who believes in internal control preceives that reinforcement is contingent upon his own behavior. Thus, a "locus of control" personality dimension has end points labeled internal and external. A complete discussion of this position and its theoretical background can be found in Rotter (1966).

The I-E Scale as currently used consists of 23 items (plus six "filler" items to disguise the purpose of the test), each containing two statements, one of which is suggestive of external control and the other being suggestive of internal control. The subject is "forced" to select one statement per item, and his score is the number of "external" choices. The items are similar to the following:

a. *The average college student can do little to select the instructors and courses he wants.* (external)

b. *With enough effort a student can select exactly the instructors and courses he wants.* (internal)

Other measures of the concept have also been devised. These include the Children's Picture Test of Internal Control (Battle and Rotter, 1963), the Children's Internal-External Control Scale (Morrison, 1966), and the Intellectual Achievement Responsibility Scale (Crandall, Katkovsky, and Crandall, 1965). These and the basic I-E scale have been used to study risk-taking, academic achievement, aspirations, goal-related behavior, involvement with social issues, student activism, Black militancy, the Protestant Ethic, readiness to seek abortions, and so forth.

This I-E scale has stimulated a great deal of research, some of it cross-cultural. On the theoretical level, Hersch and Scheibe (1967) present data which suggest that internal scorers are a more homogeneous group than external scorers. They suggest that the concept of externality should be differentiated. Mirels (1970) factor analyzed item responses of United States college males and females. He identified two factors: (1) a belief concerning felt mastery over the course of one's life, and (2) a belief concerning the extent to which the individual citizen is deemed capable of exerting an impact on political institutions.

In another factorial approach, Gurin, Gurin, Lao, and Beattie (1969) factor analyzed United States Negro responses to the original I-E items which were presented along with several other items relevant to the concept. Like Mirels, they also found two major factors: (1) a *personal control* factor which included nearly all the items which were phrased in the first person, and (2) a *control ideology* factor which included items generally containing a third-person referent. One who endorses items which loaded on the personal control factor believes he has control over what happens in his *own* life, while one who endorses control ideology items rejects luck or the "right breaks," believing rather that hard work, effort, skill, and ability are the ingredients for a successful life. To study Black militancy, Forward and Williams (1970) used the Gurin et al. revised and adapted I-E scale, as well as other measures, and found that Black high school students who scored high on the personal control items reacted positively to the 1967 Detroit riots, while those who scored low reacted negatively. No clear relationship between riot evaluation and control ideology items was found.

Cross-culturally, Tin-Yee Hsieh, Shybut, and Lotsof (1969) confirmed a relationship between internal and external control and ethnic group membership. The "individual-centered" American personality scored toward the internal control pole, while the "situation-centered" Hong Kong Chinese personality received significantly higher external control scores. Chinese-Americans scored between these two groups, giving support to the concept of marginality. Parsons, Schneider, and Hanson (1970) and Schneider and Parsons (1970) studied the I-E scores of Danish and American university students, these groups theoretically differing because of the degree to which their governments exhibit control. Danes and Americans had the same level of internality, but when each group was asked to predict I-E responses of students from other countries, there were differences in ascribed internality-externality. The Danes ascribed greater internality to American and West German students, and American students ascribed greater externality to West German, Japanese and other United States students. Schneider and Parsons also analyzed categories on the scale (luck or fate, politics, respect, academics, and leadership and success) rather than unidimensionality, and suggest that the scale can be used in the study of national stereotypes.

In studying African supernatural beliefs, Jahoda (1970b) administered the I-E scale and other measures to university students in Ghana. Higher externality was related to Jahoda's Index of Supernatural Beliefs (consisting of 10 forced-choice items dealing with traditional beliefs), with younger Ghana students receiving higher external scores than older students. However, the mean I-E scores for his sample corresponded closely to scores received by American university students (reported in Rotter, 1966). This squelches what one may immediately expect to find—that high external scores should have a decided relationship to magic, fate, or supernatural beliefs. As Jahoda notes, ". . . this implies that the stereotype frequently voiced in the past about superstitious Africans feeling themselves constantly in the grip of malevolent external forces is unfounded" (p. 127).

No bifurcated dimension in psychology retains a respectable degree of linearity. It is now clear that the concept of internal-external is not as simple or unitary as was once hoped it might be. A variety of conditions and measures can alter the dimensions it seems to tap. Nevertheless, the concept—control from "within" or from "not within"—is obviously a fetching one for cross-cultural research.

## Semantic Differential Technique (SD)

Not a test as traditionally defined, Osgood's Semantic Differential Technique and its various modifications are easily the most common single method of measurement to be found in published cross-cultural research. Since its debut two decades ago (Osgood, 1952; Osgood, Suci, and Tannenbaum, 1957), the technique has generated a staggering amount of research in many countries in such areas as meanings, values, attitudes, and feelings.

The technique is deceptively simple. *Concepts* (e.g., mother, war, peace) are rated on *scales* of bipolar adjectives (e.g., good-bad, warm-cold, loud-silent) by *subjects*. What results from factor analysis of concept/scale interaction is the location of each concept in semantic space—a space with an unknown number of dimensions but which has a common origin or zero-point for all scales. The further a concept is from the origin [analogous to its communality in a three-factor semantic space (see Chapter 9, p. 269).] the more "meaningful" the concept. An example of a concept, Mother, and three pairs of bipolar adjectives is:

Mother

good :___:___:___:___:___:___:___:bad
warm :___:___:___:___:___:___:___:cold
loud :___:___:___:___:___:___:___:silent

Three dominant, orthogonal factors have consistently appeared: an *evaluative* factor (good-bad), a *potency* factor (strong-weak), and an *activity* factor (fast-slow). Together they account for about 50-60 percent of concept "meanings," with the evaluative factor usually being the most powerful or salient. After the less salient factors of potency and activity come an apparently large number of other factors of decreasing importance and increasing rarity.

In a rigorous cross-cultural pilot project (but after numerous less rigorous cross-cultural applications), Osgood and his associates studied the rankings of 100 "culture fair" concepts (e.g., man, sky, future) using indigeneously developed adjectives (see Snider and Osgood, 1969). Subjects from several language/culture communities were included in the project. Among the more impressive results were that great similarities of meaning were attributed to the concepts and that evaluation, potency, and activity emerged as the first three factors in magnitude across language/culture groups.

The SD can be a powerful tool both in capturing the correct common "evaluative feeling tone" (Osgood, 1965, p. 102) between linguistic/culture groups and in sharpening the focus of translated words and phrases. For example, below are four sets of French adjectives and their approximate English equivalents. While the first French and the first English set gives the approximate reciprocal meaning, adding the other three (or more) sets gives considerably more certainty that the correct feeling tone is being tapped, since they serve as checks and balances.

| *French* | *English* |
|---|---|
| sympathique-antipathique | likeable-repugnant |
| rassurant-effrayant | calm-frightened |
| gai-triste | happy-sad |
| gentil-méchant | nice-awful |

Once concept and scale translation problems, solved within each language/ culture community, are proven to be minimal, the SD can be used to help answer an unlimited number of questions, such as: "How do people view political leaders?" "How is 'self' viewed internationally?" "What are attitudes toward war?" Of great value here is the immense amount of ongoing work at the University of Illinois' Center for Comparative Psycholinquistics. This work will appear indefinitely into the future under such likely titles as *The Generality of Affective Meaning Systems, The Atlas of Affective Meaning,* and *The Affective Dimension of Subjective Culture.* All these documents will have as a major purpose the analysis of scale/concept interaction across cultural groups, allowing one to select, for any pancultural concept, the modifiers (bipolar adjectives) which have been empirically derived and scaled within each culture. This would in turn allow cross-cultural comparisons to rest on a more systematic, equivalent basis.

Readers may wish to become well-grounded in the technique by selecting any number of basic sources. Good starters would include a book devoted to a variety of applications (Snider and Osgood, 1969), a basic discussion of its rationale and methodology for cross-cultural use, expanding upon what has been presented here (Osgood, 1965), affective meaning systems (Osgood, Archer, and Miron, 1963; Tanaka and Osgood, 1965), and its use in the study of subjective culture (Tanaka, 1972; Triandis et al., 1972).

The technique does not necessarily demand the use of written words, nor is it restricted for use with literate peoples. For example, Schensul (1969) constructed a wooden board with seven rectangular cut-outs corresponding to the seven-point scale. Then, studying the definitions of the "rural-urban continuum," he had rural subjects in Uganda and Northern Minnesota respond to concepts like "myself," "the city," "the market," and so on, after each subject was given instructions about the bipolar adjectives that the ends of the board represented (for example, "clean-dirty," "hospitable-inhospitable"). Schensul discovered many similarities in the way that rural people in both cultures rated in semantic space certain geographic and social concepts.

## Sixteen Personality Factor Questionnaire (16 PF Test)

The 16 PF Test is one of several personality tests developed by Raymond B. Cattell and his associates of the Institute for Personality and Ability Testing (IPAT). Through factor analysis they have purportedly identified 16 primary source traits (factors A through Q4) accounting for nearly all aspects of personality. A small number of the total number of items in equivalent forms A and B measure each of the factors, identified for reporting and interpretive purposes as 16 sets of bipolar adjectives (see Table 8.2). Each of the factors is associated with a Universal Index (U.I.), a proposed universal system for coding personality and ability factors (Cattell, 1957).

In its approximately 25-year history, the test can claim one of the lengthiest research bibliographies of all self-report personality inventories. Cross-culturally, it ranks near the top in use, and there are many translations available, some with standardization. Typically, however, cross-cultural applications have amounted to testing different cultural groups with or without translated forms and then making comparisons with American norms. Similarities and differences always result, of course, and the task in such research is to explicate the "findings."

Table 8.2    Technical and Popular Labels for Personality Factors A to $Q_4$

| Low Score Description | Factor | | Factor | High Score Description |
|---|---|---|---|---|
| Reserved (Sizothymia) | A− | vs. | A+ | Outgoing (Affectothymia) |
| Less intelligent (Low 'g') | B− | vs. | B+ | More intelligent (High 'g') |
| Emotional (Low ego strength) | C− | vs. | C+ | Stable (High ego strength) |
| Humble (Submissiveness) | E− | vs. | E+ | Assertive (Dominance) |
| Sober (Desurgency) | F− | vs. | F+ | Happy-go-lucky (Surgency) |
| Expedient (Low super-ego) | G− | vs. | G+ | Conscientious (High super-ego) |
| Shy (Threctia) | H− | vs. | H+ | Venturesome (Parmia) |
| Tough-minded (Harria) | I − | vs. | I+ | Tender-minded (Premsia) |
| Trusting (Alaxia) | L− | vs. | L+ | Suspicious (Protension) |
| Practical (Praxernia) | M− | vs. | M+ | Imaginative (Autia) |
| Forthright (Artlessness) | N− | vs. | N+ | Shrewd (Shrewdness) |
| Placid (Assurance) | O− | vs. | O+ | Apprehensive (Guilt-proneness) |
| Conservative (Conservatism) | $Q_1$ − | vs. | $Q_1$ + | Experimenting (Radicalism) |
| Group-tied (Group adherence) | $Q_2$ − | vs. | $Q_2$ + | Self-sufficient (Self-sufficiency) |
| Casual (Low integration) | $Q_3$ − | vs. | $Q_3$ + | Controlled (High self-concept) |
| Relaxed (Low ergic tension) | $Q_4$ − | vs. | $Q_4$ + | Tense (Ergic tension) |

Scale reliabilities are low, and the authors recommend using Forms A and B together to increase reliability. Levonian (1961) has questioned both the factorial homogeneity of items within each scale and the factorial independence of scales.

Sampling some of the cross-cultural studies we find a variety of approaches. Anderson (1960) discussed the similarities and differences of scores between Australian and American male and female students. Cattell and Warburton (1961) found American students to have a higher level of anxiety, to be more extraverted, more conservative and less emotionally sensitive than British students, who had higher ego strength and self-sentiment scores. McQuaid (1967) applied American norms to eight samples of Scottish subjects, partially confirming Cattell and Warburton's findings. No mention was made concerning the equivalence of item meaning for these samples. Kapoor (1965) cross-validated a Hindi version, and Tsujioka and Cattell (1965a,b) made extensive Japanese and American comparisons, finding excellent similarity of simple structure (source traits), but on factor *levels* very many significant differences, partly due, they say, to Japanese being more introverted. Meredith and Meredith (1966) is one of several investigations of the acculturation of Japanese-Americans in Hawaii using the test. Kline (1967) used it with the Eysenck Personality Inventory on educated, literate Ghanaians.

Its factorial structure seems simple and clear enough, but the great number of applications its authors have advanced actually make it a very complex instrument. This is especially true when its continued cross-cultural use is contemplated. Like similar multidimensional personality tests of considerable popularity, one would have little trouble finding numerous examples of previous cross-cultural applications, but caution against the blind repetition of "other cultures versus American norms" type of research is urged.

## Strong Vocational Interest Blanks (SVIB)

These interest inventories can claim nearly half a century of research and cautious development. This unusually long history, together with the frank atheoretical approach that is customarily used with them, make them candidates for cross-cultural research among the more advanced societies. No sterile or Western theory need be injected or imposed. However, the originator of the method, Edward K. Strong, Jr., did not direct their development in any substantial way toward cross-cultural applications. (See Strong, 1943, for empirical antecedents and procedures, and Campbell, 1968, for an informal history of the technique.)

The underlying assumption, essentially long-confirmed, is that "birds of a feather flock together." Groups of men and women in a particular occupation who are successful in their work, and who like their work, have basically the same interests. In advanced Western countries this seems to be true of all discrete occupational groups, and the SVIB can identify the characteristic and configural ways that successful men and women in a variety of occupations respond to the items. In this way, students and people in general can get a basic idea or confirmation of their interests. Other scores on the Blanks can supply information more related to general personality characteristics rather than to interests, if there is a real distinction between the two.

In the men's form there are 399 items (398 in the women's) grouped according to activities, amusements, school subjects, and five other categories. (A combined male-female "neuter" form has recently been developed.) The subject responds "Like," "Indifferent," or "Dislike" to each item. Responses are then compared with "scales," or groups of items that have previously empirically differentiated each single occupational group from all others. Raw scores are converted to standard scores (means of 50, standard deviations of 10), and one's profile of interests gives him an indication of how his interests compare with those of men in about 70 separate occupations. Nonoccupational scales (e.g., extraversion-introversion, masculinity-femininity) as well as Basic Scales (related to general occupational areas rather than to specific occupations) give data related to other dimensions of personality. The two main sources of information and application for all forms of the SVIB are to be found in Campbell (1966, 1971).

Various attempts to translate and adapt it for use in other countries have been made. The most concerted effort to date, however, was with the German translation (Lonner, 1967, 1968). In that study, German, Austrian, and Swiss psychologists and accountants were given the translated SVIB (Lonner and Stauffer, 1967), and their responses were compared with the respective scales for the anchoring United States data. The European psychologists scored very similarly to their United States counterparts, while comparisons among accountants were less similar. Using a Dutch translation, Meijman (1968) found less similarity of interests between United States and Dutch psychologists and psychology students, but the basic features of the interest profile were compellingly similar to the United States and the other European data.

In a study using the untranslated men's form, Lonner and Adams (1972) asked random samples of psychologists in Australia, Canada, Great Britain, New Zealand, and South Africa to complete the inventory. Again, the results closely paralleled United States data, while some minor variations between pairs of countries emerged.

To determine if the SVIB could be adapted for use in Pakistan, Shah (1970) asked samples of Pakistani physicians and engineers to complete the inventory. Like previous results from Euro-American cultures, she found great similarities, generally, between the Pakistani respondents and the parallel American groups used for comparative purposes. However, the Pakistani sample was mailed an *untranslated* blank, and those who responded (a discouraging 29% of 419 physicians and 307 engineers) may have been (1) educated in the United States, (2) fully fluent in idiomatic English and all of its cultural trappings, (3) sufficiently identified with the "American Way," or any combination of these factors to the extent the Pakastani sample was not, finally, terribly representative of their nonresponding Pakistani colleagues. Nevertheless, Shah demonstrated that the SVIB can be adapted for use in Pakistan *if* Pakistani norms are employed together with those American data that are shown to be culturally invariant.

Great caution must be used in cross-cultural use of the SVIB. Accurate translations must be used, cross-validation using the abundant United States anchoring data should be accomplished, and subjects should be relatively sophisticated (perhaps college-bound) and at least 16 years of "United States" age, or the maturational equivalent. With regard to the latter point, a similar technique used to measure the interests of those aiming for blue-collar careers is embodied in the Minnesota Vocational Interest Inventory (Clark and Campbell, 1965). The MVII may, in many instances, be better suited than the SVIB for use in developing countries since educators and psychologists in many countries must attend to large numbers of students who are necessarily destined for "lower level" occupations.

Two chief reasons, mentioned above, do make the SVIB a legitimate candidate for continued cross-cultural use: (1) the vast amount of data accumulated over many years give a very ample but culturally restricted foundation, and (2) the empirical technique it uses, unfettered by theory, allows researchers the recommended option of gathering clearcut norms in the other cultures being studied.

Finally, the SVIB may be an indirect way to measure modernization or the degree of Westernization that a person possesses (see Chapter 6). Presumably, the more understandable the heavily Western-based items are to those from emerging countries (or the nearer scale scores are to established Western norms) then the more likely it may be that the respondent has been influenced both cognitively and attitudinally by the Western style. Or, one may consider using it as a means to help train people in less developed countries who desire to be transformed into Western-type thinkers. McClelland and his colleagues (see Chapter 6) essentially experimented with such behavior modification in their attempts to stimulate entrepreneurial behavior in Indians by, for example, having them respond in characteristically high need achievement ways to the Thematic Apperception Test.

An important alternative to these empirical techniques is the interest measurement device advanced by Geist (1959; 1969). His *Picture Interest Inventory*, which requires minimal verbal sophistication on the part of the subject, has enjoyed considerable success in many Latin American countries, and forms have been prepared for use in about a dozen countries. The Geist is especially valuable as an alternative to the Strong since, unlike the Strong, it is designed to assess interests over the entire occupational spectrum. This makes it a logical candidate for use in countries where higher level occupations are either few or virtually closed to most people.

## Study of Values

The Allport-Vernon-Lindzey Study of Values is designed to give *relative* scores on six basic motives or themes in personality:

1. *Theoretical.* Characterized by a dominant interest in the discovery of truth and by an empirical, critical, rational, "intellectual" approach.

2. *Economic.* Emphasizing useful and practical values; conforming closely to the prevailing stereotype of the "average American businessman."

3. *Aesthetic.* Placing the highest value on form and harmony; judging and

enjoying each unique experience from the standpoint of its grace, symmetry, or fitness.

4. *Social.* Originally defined as love of people, this category has been more narrowly limited in later revisions of the test to cover only altruism and philanthropy.

5. *Political.* Primarily interested in personal power, influence, and renown; not necessarily limited to the field of politics.

6. *Religious.* Mystical, concerned with the unity of all experience, and seeking to comprehend the cosmos as a whole.

The classification is based on Spranger's *Types of Men* (1928), a classification that the developers of the *Study of Values* admit is a flattering view of human nature. The instrument has been in use since 1931, predominantly in the United States, and its third and latest revision (Allport, Vernon, and Lindzey, 1960) includes several modifications of older forms bearing 1931 and 1951 copyright dates.

The test really compares the extent to which each value competes with other values in person A as contrasted with the corresponding extents in person B, rather than the strength of values in A versus their strength in B. The scale is thus an example of ipsative scoring—the true frame of reference is the individual and not the normative group. However, norms are available and, ipsative scores notwithstanding, it is possible to determine a person's relative standing within a group (or a group's standing in relation to other groups) for any or all the values.

Cross-cultural use of it may have to make a broad, general assumption that Spranger's *Types* are culturally invariant and, if so, that the six categories take on the same or similar interpretative meanings in all cultures. This would be a very dubious assumption. To date, cross-cultural use of the *Study of Values* has been limited largely to a few Asian studies, and these with older forms. In one study, Nobechi and Kimura (1957) compared Japanese males and females in various academic fields both with each other and with American students. Rodd (1959) compared scores from Taiwan, Japanese, and Chinese samples with United States norms for both males and females. He discussed a large number of differences in view of sex, cultural, and acculturation differences. In an earlier study, Mohsin (1950) used an Indian translation, but it is of historical significance only.

## Survey of Personal Values (SPV)

The Survey of Personal Values is a brief forced-choice test consisting of 30 blocks of three statements each. As summarized by Kikuchi and Gordon (1970), "In each block, or triad, three different values are represented and the respondent is to specify the one statement that reflects what is most important to him and the one that represents what is least important to him" (p. 184).

Those familiar with the Kuder Preference Record, Form CH, will note the similarity of format. The author of the SPV, Leonard V. Gordon, notes that the use of such a forced-choice format will eliminate the type of response sets often found with Likert scales (see, for example, Gordon and Kikuchi, 1970a).

The SPV measures six ways in which an individual can cope with his non-interpersonal environment and, in this respect similar to the Study of Values, is designed to "force" the individual to rate himself on the relative importance of each of the values. The six values are

P (Practical Mindedness) — to do things that will pay off.
A (Achievement) — to have a challenging job.
V (Variety) — to have a variety of experiences.
D (Decisiveness) — to make decisions quickly.
O (Orderliness) — to be systematic, orderly.
G (Goal Orientation) — to stick to a problem until completion.

The reader may wish to compare the SPV with its immediate predecessor, the Survey of Interpersonal Values (SIV) which measures six different values: Support, Conformity, Recognition, Independence, Benevolence, and Leadership (cf. Kikuchi and Gordon, 1966).

Few cross-cultural studies using the SPV have yet appeared. Gordon and Kikuchi (1970b) assessed bureaucratic orientation in Japan by means of another test (the Work Environment Preference Schedule), correlating its scores with scores on both the SIV and the SPV. Kikuchi and Gordon (1970) present evidence that Western value constructs are highly meaningful in Japanese culture.

## Ways to Live Questionnaire

In its original form, the subject is asked to rate the extent to which he would personally *like* to live each of 13 "ways to live" (Morris and Jones, 1955; Morris, 1956). The ways to live basically represent the conceptions of life as embodied in the major ethical and religious traditions. The ways are summarized in Table 8.3.

Table 8.3    Brief Contents of Value Scale "Ways to Live" of Morris[a]

| | |
|---|---|
| Way 1: | preserve the best that man has attained |
| Way 2: | cultivate independence of persons and things |
| Way 3: | show sympathetic concern for others |
| Way 4: | experience festivity and solitude in alternation |
| Way 5: | act and enjoy life through group participation |
| Way 6: | constantly master changing conditions |
| Way 7: | integrate action, enjoyment, and contemplation |

[a]This is cited from Morris (1955, p. 1).

Table 8.3  Continued

| | |
|---|---|
| Way 8: | live with wholesome, carefree enjoyment |
| Way 9: | wait in quiet receptivity |
| Way 10: | control the self stoically |
| Way 11: | meditate on the inner life |
| Way 12: | changing adventuresome deeds |
| Way 13: | obey the cosmic purposes |

The subject reads an approximately 150-word statement describing each "way" and rates them separately on a 7-point scale (1 = dislike it very much, 4 = indifferent, 7 = like it very much).

The scaling procedures, evidence for the existence of a value structure holding across cultures, and factorial approaches in their evaluation can be found in Morris and Jones (1955). Jones and Bock (1960) have applied multiple discriminant analysis to the scales, noting that while factor analysis is appropriate for analysis of value structures within cultures, it is not quite appropriate for between culture analysis. They studied responses of groups from the United States, India, Japan, China, and Norway. Others giving accounts of its application include studies with Arabs (Prothro, 1958), Americans, Indians, and Chinese (Singh, Huang, and Thompson, 1962), seven cultural groups (Ando, 1965), "diachronic" Japanese (Misumi and Ando, 1964), in which war-torn 1949 Japanese were compared with more adequate samples some 15 years later, and with Hungarian and other students from five countries (Varga, 1970).

Because of what Kilby (1963, 1970) considered to be limitations of the early scale—lengthiness of statements, multiple emphases in some statements, and a generally heavy stress on what the given way was *against* rather than *for*—a Ways to Live II was prepared. This was followed by a Ways to Live III which incorporated the above changes as well as a response form adapted from the Semantic Differential, discussed earlier in this section. The latter addition allows the subject to react to each of the Ways by marking a set of 10 bipolar adjectives, five of which are evaluative (e.g., interesting-uninteresting, important-unimportant), and five of which are nonevaluative (e.g., slow-fast, new-old). Each pair of adjectives is scaled as before (1 to 7) covering the range, for example, of from very interesting to very uninteresting. Ways to Live II and III, however, should be viewed as research forms only at this time, since Kilby's (1970) unpublished study comparing the values of Indian, American and Japanese students is to our knowledge the only one to date exploring its usefulness.

Below are the names and addresses, when applicable, of the publishers of the tests presented in this chapter. The tests appear alphabetically. Prices will be found in the latest test publisher catalog or, less officially, in Buros' *Mental Measurements Yearbook*.

| *Name of Test* | *Publisher* |
|---|---|
| Adjective Check List | Consulting Psychologists Press, 577 College Avenue, Palo Alto, California 94306 |
| California Psychological Inventory | Consulting Psychologists Press (see above) |
| "Cognitive Style" Tests | Herman A. Witkin, State University College of Medicine, 450 Clarkson Avenue, Brooklyn, New York 11203. The Embedded Figures Test is available from Consulting Psychologists Press (see above) |
| Concept Formation Test | C. H. Stoelting Co., 424 North Homan Avenue, Chicago, Illinois 60624 |
| Culture Fair Intelligence Test | Institute for Personality and Ability Testing, 1602 Coronado Drive, Champaign, Illinois 61822 |
| D 48 | Consulting Psychologists Press (see above) |
| Eysenck Personality Inventory | Educational and Industrial Testing Service, P. O. Box 7234, San Diego, California 92107 |
| Geist Picture Interest Inventory | Western Psychological Services, 12035 Wilshire Boulevard, Los Angeles, California 90025 |
| Goodenough-Harris Drawing Test | Harcourt, Brace, Jovanovich, 757 Third Avenue, New York, N.Y. 10017 |
| Goldstein-Scheerer Tests of Abstract and Concrete Thinking | Psychological Corporation, 304 E. 45th Street, New York, N. Y. 10017 |
| Kohs Blocks | Not applicable |
| Leiter International Performance Scale | C. H. Stoelting Co. (see above) |

| *Name of Test* | *Publisher* |
|---|---|
| Minnesota Multiphasic Personality Inventory | Psychological Corporation (see above) |
| Perceptual Acuity Test | Consulting Psychologists Press (see above) |
| Pictorial Depth Perception (Hudson's Test) | Not applicable |
| The PIR and Queensland Tests | Educational and Industrial Testing Service (see above) |
| Porteus Maze Test | Psychological Corporation (see above) |
| Raven Progressive Matrices | Psychological Corporation (see above) Also available in Great Britain from H. K. Lewis and Co., Ltd. |
| Rotter's Internal/External Control Scale | Not applicable |
| Semantic Differential Technique | Not applicable |
| Sixteen Personality Factor Questionnaire | Institute for Personality and Ability Testing (see above) |
| Strong Vocational Interest Blanks | Stanford University Press, Stanford, California 94305 |
| Study of Values | Houghton Mifflin Co., 110 Tremont Street, Boston, Massachusetts 02107 |
| Survey of Personal Values | Science Research Associates, Inc., 259 East Erie Street, Chicago, Illinois 60611 |
| Ways to Live Questionnaire | Not applicable |

# CHAPTER NINE

## *Factor Analysis*

Previous chapters in this book have dealt with problems of instrument construction and data collection in cross-cultural research. Once the data have been collected, it is necessary to distill them in some way so that regularities can be identified and, perhaps, causal chains of events proposed. Statistics provides a means of effecting this distillation and a language for communicating the results in a concise form. In this chapter the logic of correlations and factor analysis is presented in an intuitive, non-mathematical way. The following chapter presents a similar treatment of other multivariate techniques of potential use for researchers in cross-cultural psychology.

It is important when designing a study of variables in different cultures to know what techniques of data analysis are likely to be available. Most of the methods described in this and the following chapter require access to a computer or many hours of hand labor. This fact should be taken into account when planning for the number of variables and subjects to be included in the study so that the investigator will not find himself with masses of data which he cannot analyze. Such specific analysis plans are also valuable in the selection of variables. Many multivariate techniques rest on assumptions about the scaling properties of the variables to be analyzed. If the data do not meet these assumptions, the results of analyses based on such data may be distorted in unknown ways.

In these chapters we do not treat statistical inference for two reasons. First, this branch of statistics generally receives a much more complete treatment in graduate programs, so that most researchers have some sophistication in the area. Second, there are several readable texts (e.g., Hays, 1963; Walker and Lev, 1969; Winer, 1962) to which the researcher can refer. Such books for multivariate correlational analysis are conspicuous by their absence, and hence these two chapters.

## Bivariate Relationships and Linearity

The concept of correlation in its most general form concerns the relationships among sets of variables. The simplest case of this generality exists when each of two sets contains a single variable. Suppose that we have a variable, $X$, which can take on several values depending upon the degree to which a culture may be described as patrilineal, and another variable, $Y$, which is essentially continuous, such as average age of marriage. The numbers which we assign to $X$ form an ordinal series while those of $Y$ are ratio.

Figure 9.1 was contrived to present a problem which cannot be handled well by conventional correlation because the relationship is not linear. Since a product-moment correlation, for example, between these two variables assumes linearity of relationship, it is important to first inspect the bivariate (i.e., two variables at a time) plots among the variables to determine whether additional analyses can be performed free of danger of distortion due to nonlinearity.

Another important benefit may be gained by investigating the relationships between variables in the above manner. In the example given in Figure 9.1 the variance of each $Y$ distribution within a category of $X$ is smaller than the variance of the distribution of all $Y$ scores. The formula for the correlation ratio (eta)

$$\eta^2 = 1 - \frac{S_y^2(x)}{S_y^2} \qquad (1)$$

indicates the extent of this tendency. $S_y^2(x)$ in formula (1) is the average variance of $Y$ scores within each of the categories of $X$. $\eta^2$ indicates the proportion of the variance in $Y$ which can be accounted for by knowing $X$. We shall see shortly that $\eta^2$ is closely related to one interpretation of the correlation coefficient [see

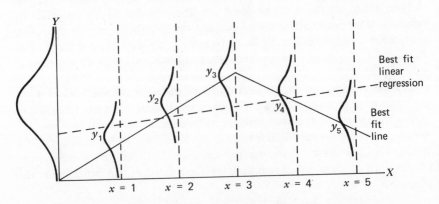

**Figure 9.1.** One continuous ($Y$) and one discrete ($X$) variable nonlinear relationship.

McNemar (1969, p. 231) for a more complete development]. Eta can be used to test the linearity of a relationship by comparing it with the correlation coefficient. If eta is substantially larger than the correlation, there is significant nonlinearity in the relationship.

In the example given in Figure 9.1, the $X$ variable was assumed to take on discrete values and the relationship was given as curvilinear. In many cases we find both variables to be essentially continuous. In cases such as this, a bivariate scatter plot such as that shown in Figure 9.2 can be prepared and inspected. If the relationship is found to be nonlinear, categories of the independent variable should be formed and an eta-analysis carried out to indicate the degree of bivariate relationship, but no further multivariate analyses should be performed. When the relationship is essentially linear, it becomes possible to employ other statistical techniques. Bivariate regression analysis may be used when the investigator wishes to work with raw scores. The product-moment correlation coefficient, $r$, may be used to analyze linear relationships between variables in standard score form. (A good discussion of many types of regression and correlation analysis may be found in Ezekial and Fox, 1959).

## Interpretations of Product-Moment Correlations

There are several different interpretations of the product-moment correlation coefficient, most of which are treated in introductory statistics texts and will only be mentioned briefly here. Each of these ways of interpreting correlations has its place in understanding factor analysis and getting maximum information from the results of factor analytic research.

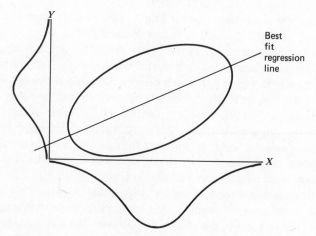

**Figure 9.2.** Two continuous variables, linear relationship.

The definitional formula for the product-moment correlation coefficient states that it is the mean cross-product of standardized scores on two variables. Thus, the numerical value of $r$ indicates the degree to which each individual retains the same relative position within his group on the two variables. By squaring $r$, we can tell what proportion of the variation in one variable is accounted for by (or related to) variation in the other variable ($r^2$ will equal $\eta^2$ when the relationship is linear). Since the raw scores for the variable have been standardized in the process of computing $r$, its value also gives us the slope of the best-fit regression line relating the two variables. [See McNemar (1969) or Ezekiel and Fox (1959) for more detail.]

The most important interpretation of the correlation coefficient for understanding factor analysis is that it is equal to the cosine of the angle formed by two variables when they are represented as vectors. Since this is not a common way of viewing $r$, we will go into it in more detail.

If we represent people as lines which form right angles with each other, we can form a geometry of people in which each person is independent of every other person from a mathematical point of view. This has been done in Figure 9.3 for three people. It is possible to represent mathematically, although not graphically, a space with as many dimensions as people. If we were to do this, we could represent each variable as a point defined by the score obtained by each person on the variable. For example, in Figure 9.3 the point representing variable $X$ is plotted as though Persons 1, 2, and 3 obtained deviation scores of -2, +2, and +1, respectively, while the point marked $Y$ indicates that these same individuals obtained deviation scores of 0, +3, and +1 on variable $Y$. If we draw lines (vectors) from the origin to each of these points to represent our variables, then the cosine of the angle between the lines gives us the correlation between the variables when standard scores are used.

By making the assumption that the length of each vector is unity (that is, the variables have been standardized to have a variance of 1.0) we can also say that the proportion of variance which two tests have in common is equal to the square of the projection of one test vector on the other. This relationship is shown graphically in Figure 9.4, which demonstrates that as two test vectors ($A$ and $B$) tend to coincide in space the angle between them approaches 0 and the cosine of that angle (the correlation) approaches unity. Vectors $A$ and $C$ (at right angles) show no relationship (cosine $90° = 0$) and no projection of either vector on the other. Vectors $A$ and $D$ demonstrate the case of a negative correlation. (A more complete and mathematically elegant demonstration of the validity of this interpretation of correlation may be found in Harman, 1967.)

The ability to see variables as vectors in space and to picture correlations as angles and projections is essential to a conceptual understanding of factor analysis as it is laid out in the rest of this chapter. The task becomes difficult when we are dealing with a space of 20 dimensions, but it is generally possible to

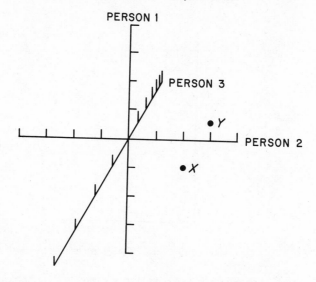

**Figure 9.3.** Two variables represented in a space of 3 persons.

work with two or three dimensional subspaces to permit graphic presentation and understanding.

## The General Factor Analysis Model

Simply stated in geometric terms, factor analysis is a means for finding a set of dimensions which account for the relationship among the variables under study. We will need to put some additional restrictions on our definition shortly, but first we must define some terms.

In virtually all cases where factor analysis will be used, the investigator is interested in more than three variables. With the exception of rare cases where one or more of the variables add no information beyond that conveyed by the rest of the set (i.e., they are linearly dependent upon and perfectly correlated with some subset of the other variables), we will need as many dimensions as there are variables to completely describe the relationships. If we have $n$ variables, we are generally dealing with an $n$-dimensional space (an $n$-space) which is called a hyperspace. Within this hyperspace are an infinite number of spaces of smaller dimensionality which are called subspaces of the hyperspace. In a three-dimensional example there would be an infinite number of planes existing in a sphere. Figure 9.5a illustrates some of the possible planes in such a three- space.

In Figure 9.5b a line (A) has been drawn through the spherical three-space. This is exactly what happens when we find a factor in a space defined by tests.

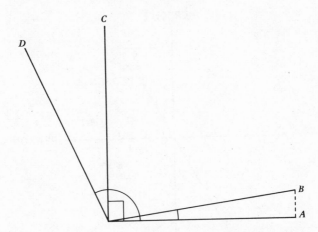

**Figure 9.4.** Variables having positive, zero, and negative relationship with variable *A*.

There is one plane (*P*) which is orthogonal to the line (at right angles with it) and passes through the center of the space (the origin). When a factor is found in a hyperspace, there is one hyperplane of $n - 1$ dimensions (analogous to our plane in three- space) which is orthogonal to the factor and passes through the origin.

After we have found the first factor in our *n*-space, we can look for another factor in the $n - 1$ dimensional subspace or hyperplane which is left over after we take out our factor. This has been done in Figure 9.5*b* resulting in line *B* in plane *P*. When this second factor has been found, there remains an $n - 2$ dimensional hyperplane which is orthogonal to both of the factors and passes through the origin. In our example this is a one-dimensional subspace, line *C*. If we had started with a four-space, we would have a two-dimensional plane (like *P*) left at this point and could continue defining lines. Precisely the same principle would hold true if we had started with a space of 100 dimensions. (A more complete discussion of the general factor analysis model may be found in Harman, 1967.)

At this point we must introduce some practical restrictions on the basic definition. These are of two kinds and they constitute the two major areas of controversy in the theory of factor analysis. The first deals with the placement of the lines (which will be called axes or factors for the remainder of this chapter). The second deals with the number of dimensions necessary to describe the relationships among the variables. For the present we will provide arbitrary answers for these problems, deferring a complete discussion until we have a better understanding of the mathematical nature of factors.

We return now to our graphic illustrations. Figure 9.6*a* depicts three variables represented in two dimensions. The lines in the figure represent the projections

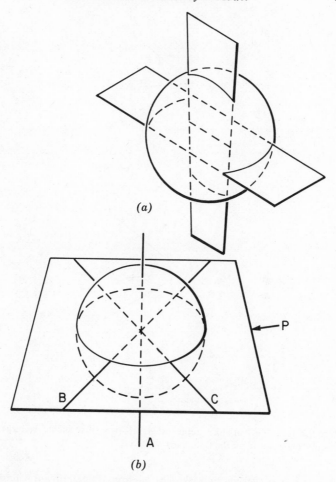

(a)

(b)

**Figure 9.5.**(a): Two of the possible planes in a space of three dimensions; (b): Successive restrictions put on a three dimensional space. Line *A* restricts the position of plane *B*.

of the variables in the plane of the paper and are of different lengths because this particular plane is not equally related to all of the variables. That is, not all variables lie in the plane. In a space of three dimensions, all the lines would have unit length; however, this plane was chosen so that variables 1 and 3 lie in it. Their vectors have unit length, while the line representing variable 2 is necessarily shorter because it does not lie in the plane and is represented by its projection onto the plane. In fact, line 2 would lie at a 45° angle to the paper in a space of 3 dimensions. It would have been possible to choose a plane containing any pair of lines, a single line, or none of them.

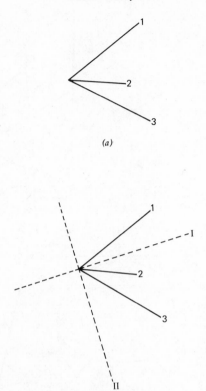

Figure 9.6.(*a*): The variables represented in two dimensions, and (*b*): An arbitrary reference frame placed on the three variables.

We can now define two axes or factors to describe the positions of our variables in this plane. The choice is arbitrary. One pair of orthogonal axes in the plane will serve as well as any other. In Figure 9.6*b* one of the possible pairs of axes has been chosen. However, axis I was chosen to fulfill a particular condition, that the sum of squared projections of the vectors on that axis be a maximum, thus accounting for the greatest possible proportion of the variance of the set because we have maximized the correlation of the factor with each variable. This axis is unique in fulfilling condition for this set of variables this and hence is not arbitrary. Once the first axis was chosen, the second could only have one position within the plane due to the restriction of orthogonality. When the *N* dimensions of a hyperspace of *N* variables have been chosen to meet this condition, the result is called a *principal components analysis*. The first axis in a principal components analysis accounts for the maximum possible amount of linear variation and covariation in the set of variables and each succeeding axis accounts the maximum possible linear amount of variance which is left over.

The factors resulting from any factor analysis have no independent existence apart from the variables which they describe. In fact, the factors are defined by their relationships with the variables. They are linear composites of the variables, their variance being composed of portions of the variance of the original variables. The mathematics of composites will be discussed shortly, but for the reader to follow the remainder of this chapter and much of the next it is essential that he be able to think of abstract variables (such as factors), which are composed of parts of other, real variables.

*The Mathematics of Factor Analysis.* As we mentioned earlier, factor analysis requires far too much computation for the researcher to undertake most analyses without the aid of a computer. Most computer centers provide factor analysis programs sufficient for the needs of most users, so it is not necessary for the investigator to know the mathematics by which factors are computed. (Those who are interested in the details of factor analysis should consult Harman, 1967, or Horst, 1965). However, the results of a factor analysis are reported in numerical rather than graphical form, and so an understanding of what the entries in a factor table represent is necessary. A small example will be used to illustrate the various points.

Table 9.1 contains the correlations among the five variables of Figure 9.7 and the results of a principal components analysis of these five variables. The variables define a five-dimensional space and the columns labeled $P_1$, $P_2$ etc. refer to the axes chosen to represent those five dimensions. The values in each column of the factor matrix are the correlations between the variables and that axis (factor) and are called factor loadings. Thus, variable 4 has a loading of .93 on factor I, which means that the composite is made up of variance largely attributable to variation on whatever trait is being measured by variable 4. The interpretation of a factor loading is the same as for a correlation, except that the latter is a measure of the relationship between *two* observed variables while the former reflects the relationship between an observed variable and a mathematical composite of variables.

The entries in the body of Table 9.1 are all factor loadings and are subject to the above type of interpretation. The first row at the bottom of the table, which may be labelled "variance" or "eigenvalue," contains the sum of squared loadings in each of the columns. These values give the amount of variance from the original correlation matrix which is accounted for by each successive factor. In our sample, 2.87 units of variance (out of 5.00) were accounted for by the first axis, 1.80 by the second, and so on. The last row of Table 9.1 gives the percent of variance accounted for by each factor (the variance entry divided by the total variance). The entries in the last column of Table 9.1 give the

Table 9-1.   Correlation and Principal Components Matrices for Five Variables[a]

| Variable | | | | | |
|---|---|---|---|---|---|
| 1 | 1.00000 | .00975 | .97245 | .43887 | .02241 |
| 2 | .00975 | 1.00000 | .15428 | .69141 | .86307 |
| 3 | .97245 | .15428 | 1.00000 | .51472 | .12193 |
| 4 | .43887 | .69141 | .51472 | 1.00000 | .77765 |
| 5 | .02241 | .86307 | .12193 | .77765 | 1.00000 |

*Principal Components*

| Variable | $P_1$ | $P_2$ | $P_3$ | $P_4$ | $P_5$ | Variable Variance ($h^2$) |
|---|---|---|---|---|---|---|
| 1 | .5810 | .8064 | .0276 | -.0645 | -.0852 | 1.0000 |
| 2 | .7671 | -.5448 | .3193 | .1118 | -.0216 | 1.0002 |
| 3 | .6724 | .7260 | .1149 | -.0072 | .0862 | .9999 |
| 4 | .9324 | -.1043 | -.3078 | .1582 | .0000 | 1.0000 |
| 5 | .7911 | -.5582 | -.0647 | -.2413 | .0102 | .9999 |
| Factor Variance (Eigenvalue) | 2.8733 | 1.7966 | .2148 | .1000 | .0153 | 5.0000 |
| Percent total variance | 57.2 | 35.9 | 4.3 | 2.0 | 0.3 | 100.00 |

[a]From Harman, 1967, Table 2.2 and Table 8.1.

proportion of the variance of each variable which is accounted for by the factors. In this case, as might be expected, all of the variance of each variable was accounted for by the five factors.

Now that we have an example before us, we can consider the complete factor analysis model in some detail. One form of the general model consists of $n$ (the number of variables) equations of the form

$$Z_{il} = a_{i1}F_{1l} + a_{i2}F_{2l} + \ldots a_{ik}F_k + \ldots a_{im}F_m \tag{2}$$

where $Z_{il}$ is the standard score of individual $l$ on variable $i$, $a_{i1}$, $a_{i2}$, etc. are the coefficients associated with each of the $m$ factors for variable $i$, and $F_1$, $F_2$, and so forth are the values of individual $l$ on the $m$ independent factors. For our example, a partial statement (the dots signify omitted values) of the equations would be

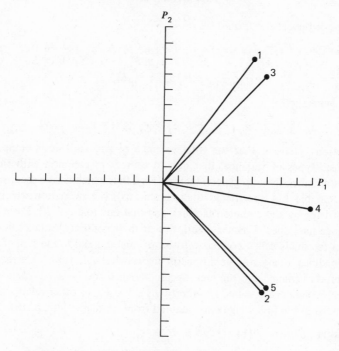

**Figure 9.7.** Principal components of five variables.

$$Z_1 = .58\,P_1 + .81\,P_2 + .03\,P_3 + (-)\,.06\,P_4 + (-)\,.09\,P_5$$
$$Z_2 = .77\,P_1 \;\cdots\;\cdots\;\cdots\;\cdots\; + (-)\,.02\,P_5 \qquad (3)$$
$$\vdots$$
$$Z_5 = .79\,P_1 + (-)\,.56\,P_2 + \;\ldots\;\ldots\; + .01\,P_5$$

Note that in our example we have kept as many factors as we have variables. But the last three factors account for such a small amount of variance that we may not want to bother having them in our analysis. One of the purposes of factor analysis is to explain the relationships among many variables by a small number of composites. If we retain all of the factors, we might just as well keep our original variables. We have gained nothing in parsimony.

A complete factor analytic model must account in some way for all of the variance of the variables analyzed. In the above example this was accomplished using as many factors as variables. But when there may be a substantial amount of error of measurement affecting the correlations, as is often the case in cross-cultural research, we may feel that the smaller factors represent variance due to the specific character of individual variables or chance covariance of errors. The complete form of the factor analysis model acknowledges these sources of variance by adding some terms to equation (2). The result is a set of $n$

equations of the general form

$$Z_1 = a_{11} F_1 + a_{12} F_2 + \ldots + a_{1m} F_m + b_1 S_1 + e_1 E_1$$
$$Z_2 = a_{21} F_1 + \ldots\ldots\ldots + a_{2m} F_m + b_2 S_2 + e_2 E_2$$
$$Z_n = a_{n_1} F_1 \cdots a_{nm} F_m + b_n S_n + e_n E_n$$

or more generally

$$Z_j = a_{jj} F_1 + \ldots a_{jm} F_m + b_j S_j + e_j E_j \quad (j = 1, 2, \ldots N) \tag{4}$$

Equation 3 tells us that the total variance of any variable is composed of three basic types of variance, that due to sources in common with the other variables and measured by general factors ($F$'s), that which is true score variation on the variable but specific to that variable ($S$), (i.e., variation which is not accounted for by the common factors), and that due to error ($E$). These sources of variance have special names descriptive of their content. Variance due to the common factors is called *communality* or $h^2$ and is equal to the sum of squares of the loadings in any row of the factor matrix. Reliable variance is the sum of the common variance and the real specific variance and is called *reliability*. The real specific variance is called *specificity* ($b_j^2$). These and other relationships are summarized in the following table (adapted from Harman, 1967, p. 19).

| | | | | |
|---|---|---|---|---|
| Total variance | (1) | $= h_j^2 + b_j^2 + e_j^2$ | | |
| Reliability | ($r_{jj}$) | $= h_j^2 + b_j^2$ | $= 1 - e_j^2$ | |
| | | | $= m$ | |
| Communality | ($h_j^2$) $= h_j^2$ | | $\sum_{i=1}^{m} a_{ij}^2$ | |
| Uniqueness | ($u_j^2$) $=$ | $b_j^2 + e_j^2$ | $= 1 - h_j^2$ | |
| Specificity | ($b_j^2$) $=$ | $b_j^2$ | $= 1 - (h_j^2 + e_j^2)$ | |
| Error variance | ($e_j^2$) $=$ | | $e_j^2 = 1 - r_{jj}$ | |

The value of $h^2$ will depend to a certain extent on the number of factors which the investigator chooses to consider common factors. In our previous example, all factors were considered to be common. But, if we had chosen to retain only the first two of these, the values in the last column of our revised factor matrix (Table 9.2) would all be less than unity. Our factor analysis would then be accounting for less than the total variance. The sum of the communalities indicates the total amount of variance from all of the variables which is accounted for by our analysis.

When we show the results of a factor analysis graphically, as we have done in Figure 9.7 for the data in Table 9.2, another interpretation of $h^2$ becomes apparent. The communality of a variable (its common variance) is equal to the square of the length of the vector (because the length of a test vector is in standard deviation units) representing that variable in the space defined by the

Table 9.2 First 2 Principal Components with Communalities

| Variable | Principal Components | | |
|---|---|---|---|
| | $P_1$ | $P_2$ | $h^2$ |
| 1 | .5810 | .8064 | .9878 |
| 2 | .7671 | -.5448 | .8852 |
| 3 | .6724 | .7260 | .9792 |
| 4 | .9324 | -.1043 | .8802 |
| 5 | .7911 | -.5582 | .9375 |
| Variance | 2.8733 | 1.7966 | 4.6700 |
| Percent Common | 61.5 | 38.5 | 100.00 |
| Percent Total | 57.5 | 35.9 | 93.4 |

common factors. The length of a test vector in the common factor space equals $\sqrt{h^2}$ or $h$. Remember that the variables have been standardized and that the variances accounted for by the complete principal components analysis (its $h^2$'s) are all equal to unity. This interpretation of communality provides a useful piece of information for interpreting graphic reports of factor analyses (factor plots), particularly when there are more than two factors so that the complete results cannot be presented on a single pair of axes.

A comparison of Table 9.2 with Figure 9.7 illustrates how the information contained in a matrix of factor loadings is the same as that from a graphic plot of the factors. From the values in Table 9.2 we would expect variable 4 to lie quite near factor 1 ($P_1$) because the loading is very high. We would expect this same variable to be essentially orthogonal to factor 2 ($P_2$) because of its low loading on that factor. Using the same approach, we would expect variables 1 and 3 to be close to each other in the upper right quadrant and slightly closer to factor 2 than to factor 1 because both variables have positive loadings on both factors and the loadings on factor 2 are somewhat larger than those on factor 1 for both variables. By exactly the same line of reasoning, i.e., sign and relative magnitude of loadings, we would expect variables 2 and 5 to fall in the lower right quadrant, close together, and closer to factor 1 than to factor 2. Inspection of Figure 9.7 shows that each of these predictions is confirmed.

The communalities of these variables are all fairly high, indicating that our two factors account for most of the variance in each variable. At this point we can make some predictions about the correlations among the variables. Although we already have these correlations (Table 9.1) and used them to determine our factors, it is often valuable to attempt to reproduce them from our factors as an index of how well the factors fit the original data. From the factor plot we can suggest that variables 1 and 3 will be highly correlated with each other, 2 and 5 will be even more highly correlated with each other (but largely independent of 1 and 3), and that variable 4 should correlate at a moderate level with the other four, (but higher with 2 and 5). Referring to Table 9-1, we find our predictions confirmed.

A more exact estimate of the correlation between any two variables may be obtained from the factor matrix by multiplying the loadings of one variable by those of the other and summing across the rows. For example, our estimate of the correlation between variables 1 and 2 by this method would be

$$r_{12} = \sum_{i=1}^{m} a_{i_1} a_{i2} = .58 \ (.77) + .81 \ (-.54) = (.45) - (.44) = .01$$

The value of the original correlation was .00975, yielding an error of .00025 in our estimate.

The difference between the original correlation and our estimate of it from the factor loadings is called the residual correlation. The theory of multiple factor analysis proposed by Thurstone (1947) was based largely on the idea that the residual correlations should be near zero. If they are not, more factors should be extracted from the data to account for them. Harman (1967) has developed a method of factor analysis called Minres (minimum residual) factor analysis which finds the best possible factors according to this criterion. Minimizing residual correlations is one of several goals which a factor analysis can have and is an important one because small residuals indicate that the factors account for most of the variance of the original variables. The various types of factor analysis and the goals of each are discussed later in this chapter under "choice of a model."

## Special Problems in Factor Analysis

Up to this point we have been discussing factor analysis as a mathematical model rather than as a technique for research. Whenever we leave the realm of theoretical models and attempt to apply our technique to problems of the real world, real cultures, and real data, certain compromises must be made. In factor analysis these compromises raise four difficult questions which the researcher must answer. These questions are the basis for many controversies in the area. The issues are number of factors, communality estimates, choice of factor model, and selection of axis location (rotation), and although they are closely interrelated, they will each be treated somewhat separately below.

*How Many Factors?* In Table 9.1 on page 264 we showed the results of a principal components analysis of five variables. By using five factors we were able to account for all of the variance in the five variables. But one of the chief uses to which factor analysis has been put is the description of many variables in terms of a few composites of those variables. That is, factor analysis is a means of achieving a parsimonious description of the data. When we use five factors to describe five variables, we have gained nothing in parsimony. But how many factors do we need to describe our variables? A general but not very useful answer to this question is that we should keep enough so that we have not lost much information but have maximum parsimony of description.

Several people have suggested rules to follow in deciding what constitutes a useful factor. One of the most popular and intuitively most satisfying decision rules has been proposed by Kaiser (1960). He reasoned that since each of the variables in the analysis has a variance of 1.0, we should keep only those factors from a principal components solution which account for at least as much variance as a single variable. This "Kaiser criterion" has enjoyed such wide popularity that it is included as an option in many computer programs.

The Kaiser criterion has been criticized by Cattell (1966b) because it keeps too few factors in small studies (less than 20 variables) and keeps too many factors in large studies (more than 50 variables). To replace it, Cattell (1966a) has suggested what he calls the "Scree test." This criterion involves plotting the variance contributions of all the factors and retaining those that appear to account for enough variance to be meaningful. The plot of these variances will form a curve like that in Figure 9.8, where we have plotted the variances of our five principal components from Table 9.1. Cattell suggests that factors lying beyond the somewhat flattened out curve should not be interpreted. In the case of our example, both the "Scree test" and the Kaiser criterion suggest that the proper number of factors is 2. (The interested reader should consult Cattell, 1966a, for a more complete statement of the Scree criterion).

There are several other criteria for the number of factors to keep in factor analytic investigations. Some of these are statistical tests associated with particular methods of factor analysis. For example, Harman (1967) has provided statistical tests to indicate when a sufficient number of factors have been

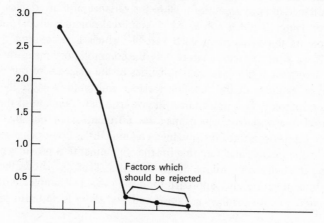

**Figure 9.8.** Plot showing the "Scree" for five variable examples.

obtained by his minimum residuals method. Rao (1955) and Jöreskog (1967) have also provided statistical tests in association with their special factoring methods. However, the general user of factor analysis as a research tool does not need to concern himself with the subtle distinctions which occupy the factor specialist. He need only remember that there is no single true number of factors for any set of data. The Kaiser criterion generally provides a good starting point, but the researcher is free to add or subtract factors if his knowledge of the domain he is studying and his personal judgment warrant the change. Probably the best strategy is to try several different values for the number of factors and choose the one which seems to fit the data. We will have another word or two to say on this topic after we have discussed the other three issues.

*Communalities.* The general model for factor analysis which we discussed above dealt with all of the variance of each variable. That is, the correlation matrix in its usual form (Table 9.1) contains all of the variance terms in equation 3 [the correlation matrix contains the variance of standardized variables (1.0's) in its diagonal and the correlations off the diagonal are the covariances among these variables.][1] But equation 3 states that there is some error of measurement and some specific variance in each variable. This variance cannot meaningfully contribute to our description of the common dimensions in our set of variables. Therefore, it might be better if we subtracted some estimate of this non-common variance from our correlation matrix before we perform our factor analysis so that it does not distort our factors. Estimating the (unknown) proportion of common variance of each variable is the second problem which has confronted the users of factor analysis.

One possible solution to the problem can be seen from Table 9.2. When we kept fewer factors than variables (in this case, 2 factors from 5 variables), the factors retained did not account for all of the variance of the variables. The sums of squared factor loadings (obtained or empirical communalities) indicate the proportion of the variance of each variable which is accounted for by the factors. If we wish to factor analyze only the common portions of the variables, we may insert these obtained communalities in the diagonal of our correlation matrix as an estimate of the common variance and factor analyze the "reduced correlation matrix." This procedure will give us a new estimate of the common portions of the variables which may be different from our first estimate. Repeating this process until the obtained communalities do not change from one analysis to the next (called iterating for the communalities) provides one way of estimating the common portions of the variables. Table 9.3 shows the results of applying this direct iterative approach for our 5-variable example. Note that the changes in the factor loadings are small and that there is no uniform tendency

---

[1] Correlations are covariances among standardized variables.

for the final communalities to be higher or lower for the iterative solution. However, the factor variances will always be lower when a reduced correlation matrix is analyzed.

Communalities obtained in this way are in part dependent upon the number of factors which the investigator chooses to keep. In fact, this will be true of all obtained communalities. There have been several methods proposed for estimating communalities before factoring which are independent of the number of factors (we will call them theoretical communalities). Two of these have seen fairly wide use and are based on the logic that a variable cannot have a lower communality than its correlations with other variables in the set being analyzed. The first estimate, advocated by Thurstone (1938), is that the communality of a variable should be about equal to its highest correlation with some one other variable in the set. The problem is that this estimate is based on only a small fraction of the information in the correlation matrix and may be distorted through the sampling of variables. [This reasoning assumes that we have taken a sample of all of the variables in which we might be interested and have, by chance, included variables very similar to (or dissimilar from) the variable whose communality we are trying to estimate.]

A better estimate of the communality of a variable, and one that makes use of more of the information in our correlation matrix, is the squared multiple correlation[2] (SMC) of the variable with all the other variables in the set. Guttman (1954a) has shown that this value provides a lower bound estimate for the communality of a variable, that is, the "true" communality of the variable, will not be less than its SMC with the other variables of the set.

Just as we could offer no definitive answers to the question of number of

Table 9.3    Iteration for Communalities with 2 Factors[a]

| Variable | Common Factors | | Communality |
| | $P_1$ | $P_2$ | ($h^2$) |
| --- | --- | --- | --- |
| 1 | .622 | .785 | 1.000 |
| 2 | .702 | −.524 | .767 |
| 3 | .701 | .681 | .956 |
| 4 | .882 | −.145 | .798 |
| 5 | .779 | −.604 | .971 |
| Factor Variance | 2.756 | 1.740 | 4.492 |
| Percent Common | 61.3 | 38.7 | 100.0 |

[a]From Harman, 1967, Table 8.14.

[2] See Chapter 10 for a discussion of multiple correlation.

factors, we can offer no pat solutions to the communality problem. The two problems are closely related to one another and their answers in any particular research situation must be left to the judgment of the investigator. If an accurate estimate of common variance is not crucial to the problem under investigation, as is the case in most exploratory studies, then analyzing the full correlation matrix should provide a satisfactory solution. Otherwise, some reduced form of the correlation matrix, perhaps dependent upon the type of solution chosen (see the next section) will provide an adequate analysis. The decision should be based on the degree of accuracy required in estimating the factors. The greater the accuracy desired, the better the communality estimate must be.

We have noted that the obtained communalities are always dependent to a certain extent on the number of factors retained. This fact indicates one potentially dangerous error which an investigator might make — retaining too few factors. An error of this type can cause severe distortion of a factor analysis in two ways. One of these is its potential effect on the rotation of factors (see below) and the other is its effect on the magnitude of the communalities. If there are factors on which some of the variables would have high loadings, but these factors are not kept in the analysis, the communalities of the variables involved may be substantially lower than they should be, resulting in inaccurate statements about their involvement in the factor solution.

*Choice of Factor Model.* Our development of the general factor model with $N$ factors used to describe $N$ variables was referred to as a *principal components solution*. The same name may be applied when fewer than $N$ factors are used to account for the relations among our variables as long as an unreduced correlation matrix is being analyzed (i.e., the diagonal entries of the matrix are 1.0's, not communalities) and the factors are determined subject to the restriction that each succeeding factor account for the maximum amount of variance remaining in the set independent of previously extracted factors. When the diagonal entries of the original matrix are replaced by some estimate of the communalities of the variables, but the second condition is still met, we refer to the resulting factor matrix as a *principal factor solution* (Kendall, 1954). In the next section we shall discuss altering an original solution to maximize interpretability by rotating the factors in the space they define while keeping the positions of the variables constant. These factors, which no longer meet the restrictions of accounting for maximum successive amounts of variance, we will call a rotated factor solution, regardless of whether the original dimensions were obtained from an original or a reduced correlation matrix.

Many different opinions have been offered regarding the best way to obtain factors. Historically, the first practical method for analyzing large numbers of variables was Thurstone's centroid method (see Thurstone, 1947), which provides an approximation to the principal axis (either component or factor) solution derived by Hotelling (1933). Before computers became available, the centroid solution was widely used as a shortcut approximation to the mathematically rigorous but laborious principal axis solution. The current wide availability of computers has made the centroid solution much less desirable than it was 20 years ago, and most researchers with access to computers should probably avoid it.

Virtually all of the widely used factor analytic procedures presently available use a basic principal axis solution to obtain the factors. The differences between methods arise from the way in which the reductions of the original correlation matrix are obtained (i.e., the method for getting initial estimates of the communalities). Two of these methods, direct iteration and squared multiple correlations, were described in the previous section. The other methods are generally less direct, but the investigator should be aware of their general properties so that he may make a decision about the most appropriate method for his research problem.

Guttman (1953, 1954 a,b) extended the logic of using SMC's as estimate of common variance to the entire matrix of correlations. He reasoned that it might be appropriate to estimate the proportion of the variance of each variable which is predictable from the other variables in the set being analyzed and include only that predictable variance in calculating the correlations. Using this logic, the SMC of each variable becomes its variance (in the diagonal). However, reducing the amount of variance for each variable also reduces the correlations of that variable with other, also-reduced variables. Guttman (1953) calls the predictable variance of a variable its *image* and the analysis of the covariances among images is known as image analysis. This method assumes that the investigator has obtained his data for a *population of variables* from a *population of subjects.* These assumptions are seldom met in practice. Also, image analysis may not give as interpretable results as some other methods and may not give a solution at all (see Thorndike, 1970). It should, therefore, probably be avoided by most researchers unless its restrictive assumptions can be met. Where the assumptions are met, it gives good estimates of the common dimensions in a set of data where only the common variance is to be analyzed. The major advantage of image analysis is that the communalities are defined rather than estimated. The method has been further developed by Harris (1962) and Jöreskog (1969a).

A similar method, but one with more intuitive appeal and fewer mathematical problems, has been proposed by Kaiser and Caffrey (1965). Again, the variables are rescaled in terms of their common parts, but the reduction is not so severe as in image analysis. The authors have called their method "alpha factor analysis" because "the principle upon which alpha factor analysis is based is that *common factors are to be determined* which have maximum correlations with correspond- ing universe common factors" and these correlations are alpha coefficients of generalizability (Kaiser and Caffrey, 1965, p. 5). Alpha factor analysis also differs from image analysis in that it assumes that variables have been sampled for a population of subjects, and it seems to be less affected by failure to meet these assumptions than image analysis is.

Alpha analysis has been called a *psychometric* factoring method (Kaiser and Caffrey, 1965) because it is concerned with samples of variables and the estimation of factors for a population of variables. Another class of factoring methods has been called *statistical* because they assume that the variables being studied constitute a population and the subjects are a sample. The goal of these methods is to estimate the factors in the population of individuals from the sample data.

Several statistical factoring procedures have been proposed, but few have found wide application due to the computational labor involved (see Lawley, 1940, and Rao, 1955). The most promising method of this type appears to be Jöreskog's (1967) maximum likelihood solution, which can be performed on a computer within reasonable time allowances (Harris, personal communication). Methods of this (statistical) type generally have severe mathematical restrictions, which may mean that no solution is possible for a given set of data. Unless the investigator can be reasonably sure that his data have the required mathematical properties,[3] it is unlikely that statistical factoring methods will be worth the trouble except for one specific application, the confirmation of a previously obtained set of factors (see below). Jöreskog's method does have the advantage of providing a statistical test to indicate when a sufficient number of factors have been obtained.

The final factoring method which we will consider is quite close to the direct iterative approach discussed above and cannot be really classified as either psychometric or statistical. Earlier we said that it was possible to estimate the original correlations from the factors by multiplying the factor loadings of pairs of variables on the factors and summing across factors. The differences between the correlations reproduced in this way and the original correlations are called residuals. Cattell (1958) has stated that "the only final, available test for goodness of a particular factor resolution. . .is the precision with which it *restores the original correlation* matrix" (p. 810). Thurstone (1947) has voiced a similar opinion.

A method of factor analysis has been developed by Harman (Harman and Jones, 1966; Harman and Fukuda, 1966; Harman, 1967) which obtains factors to maximally satisfy this criterion. The method, mentioned earlier, which is called minimum residual factor analysis (minres), computes factors which will give the best possible reproduction of the original correlations while using less than all possible factors. A complete principal components solution ($N$ factors

---

[3] Maximum likelihood and image analysis require a positive definite correaltion matrix, and alpha requires that the matrix be positive semi-definite (see Horst, 1963).

for $N$ variables) will perfectly reproduce the original correlations. Minres gives a best approximation to this ideal by analyzing a reduced correlation matrix where the diagonal elements (communalities) have been determined to optimize this reproduction for a given number of factors.

Aside from the fact that it is a best approach to one of the criteria for good factors, the minres solution has several advantages and a problem. The problem is that, being an iterative procedure, it may require a very long time to reach a solution for large sets of data and is completely out of reach for researchers with large problems and small computers. Given the necessary computing facilities, the method has two advantages. First, there is a statistical test which indicates when to stop factoring. In a statistical sense, the number of factors to retain is fairly well defined for the minres procedure . Second, the method is not affected by the mathematical restrictions which limit the applicability of the image, alpha, and maximum likelihood methods. Minres shares this property with the principal components and direct iteration procedure.

As a final comment on different factoring procedures we would like to bring to the reader's attention a new method of factor analysis which has been proposed by Joreskog (1969b) called *confirmatory maximum likelihood factor analysis*. The goal of this procedure is to confirm the existence of factors found in one sample on data from a second sample. Joreskog's approach extracts from one correlation matrix factors which are maximally similar to those which were found in another correlation matrix and provides a statistical test for the adequacy of the approximation. This, for the first time, makes it possible to cross validate factors directly, rather than by judgment.[4]

One potential application of Joreskog's procedure which could make it a particularly useful form of analysis in cross-cultural research is that it would make possible direct comparisons of factors obtained in different societies. For example, an investigator might be interested in determining whether the factors found by Irvine (1969b) are unique to sub-Saharan Africa. With Joreskog's procedure it would be possible to "confirm" or "disconfirm" the same factors in other societies, depending on whether or not they could be extracted. Irvine's factors would be fed into the computer as the target, and the analysis would give the best possible match to the target from new data, obtained, perhaps, from a Melanesian or Arabian society. Obviously, a factor analysis of this type could be of great benefit in answering some of the very difficult questions in cross-cultural research.

*Interpretation of Factors (Rotation).* In some of his early factor analyses

---

[4] The interested reader should consult Joreskog (1969b) for details. Alternative approaches to this problem have been offered by Ahmavaara (1954) and Cliff (1966), but theirs are rotational procedures.

Thurstone (1938) found the interpretation of factors to be a difficult matter. He found that almost all of the variables in a given study loaded heavily on the first factor and that the remaining factors tended to be bipolar, that is, had some high positive loadings and some high negative loadings. Thurstone was working with ability tests which were generally positively correlated with each other, and he felt that bipolar factors might be a statistical artifact. Figure 9.7 on page 265 is an example of this kind of finding.

Since the location of factors is arbitrary from an interpretive point of view,[5] Thurstone devised a method of relocating the factors (called rotation) to maximize their interpretability. The relocation was made on the basis of two criteria, psychological meaningfulness and simple structure. That is, Thurstone attempted to alter the positions of factors to make interpretation most easy and direct (simple structure) and of greatest scientific value (meaningfulness). In Figure 9.9 we have shown one of the possible rotations which might make the factors from Figure 9.7 more interpretable. The original positions of the factors are designated by $P$'s and the rotated positions are called $A$'s. Note that the factors are still at right angles to each other. Thurstone's method of rotation permitted the angles between the factors to become oblique (less than $90°$, resulting in correlated factors), but this procedure is more complicated and we will not deal with it.

The reader will recall that the cosine of the angle between the vector representing a variable and the line representing a factor is equal to the factor loading of that variable on that factor. Obviously, the angles between the five variables in Figure 9.9 and the two rotated factors ($A$'s) are different from the angles for the unrotated factors ($P$'s), but the angles (correlations) between the variables have remained unchanged. Rotation affects the factor loadings, but not the communalities or correlations among the variables themselves. The loadings for the rotated factors, which are given in Table 9.4, are quite different. The original loadings indicate a general first factor with positive loadings on all the variables and a bipolar second factor with positive loadings for variables 1 and 3, negative loadings for variables 2 and 5, and an essentially zero loading for variable 4. The matrix of rotated factor loadings shows factor $A_1$, with very high positive loadings for variables 2 and 5, a high positive loading for variable 4, and essentially zero-loadings for variables 1 and 3. Factor $A_2$ shows high positive loadings for variables 1 and 3, a low positive loading for variable 4, and essentially zero loadings for variables 2 and 5.

The rotation of factors has been a source of much disagreement among psychologists. It can be justifiably argued that the researcher can use rotation to find anything he wants to find in the results of a factor analysis. It is quite

[5] One must distinguish between interpretation and the purely mathematical restriction placed on the location of factors by the principal components method of extraction.

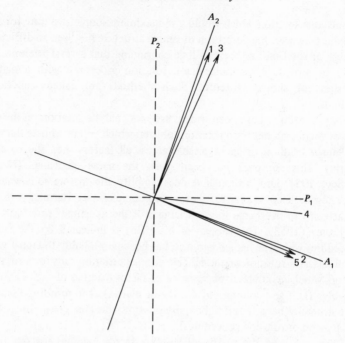

**Figure 9.9.** Results of a varimax rotation of five variables.

possible for two different researchers to come to quite different conclusions about the structure of a scientific domain from the same data by rotating the factors to different positions (or by one of them not rotating at all). Thurstone's (see Thurstone, 1947) proposal to seek simple structure was an attempt to provide guidelines to make rotations more uniform because he felt there could

Table 9.4    Varimax Rotation of 2 Factors[a]

| Variable | Rotated Factors | | Communality |
| | $A_1$ | $A_2$ | $(h^2)$ |
|---|---|---|---|
| 1 | .01602 | .99377 | .98783 |
| 2 | .94079 | −.00883 | .88515 |
| 3 | .13702 | .98006 | .97930 |
| 4 | .82479 | .44714 | .88022 |
| 5 | .96821 | −.00604 | .93747 |
| | | | |
| Variance | 2.52182 | 2.14815 | 4.66997 |
| Percent of Total | 50.4 | 43.0 | 93.4 |
| Percent of Common | 54.0 | 46.0 | 100.0 |

[a]From Harman, 1967, Table 14.6.

be only one solution which would give maximum simple structure for a given set of data. However, the definition of simple structure has been so difficult and the process of rotation has been so time-consuming that several attempts have been made to provide a computer-based rotation procedure with a mathematical criterion for simple structure. Such methods are called analytic rotation methods.

Two procedures have been widely used for analytic rotation on the computer. One of them searches for a rotation solution which will maximize the variance of the factor loadings of each variable across all factors (i.e., the rows of factor matrix). This approach has been given the name quartimax (Neuhaus and Wrigley, 1954) and, although it does simplify the factors somewhat, it has a tendency to keep the largest factors too complex (see Harman, 1967, p. 304). An attempt to overcome the deficiencies of the quartimax procedure was made by Kaiser (1958). The success of his effort is indicated by the fact that his procedure, which he named varimax, has become probably the most widely used of all analytic rotation methods. The varimax criterion calls for a rotation of the factors which maximizes the variance of factor loadings of each factor across all variables (i.e., the columns of the factor matrix). The resulting factor loadings have generally been found to be quite interpretable (see Zimmerman, 1964, for a comparison of rotation procedures).

Table 9.4 gave the matrix of varimax factor loadings for our five-variable example. The interpretation of these factors would be quite clear and the simple structure of the factors according to Thurstone's (1947, p. 335) five criteria is quite good.

Many other analytic rotation procedures have been proposed, generally resulting in factors which are correlated with each other. The interpretation and use of such factors can become quite messy. For the reader who wishes to delve deeply into the intricacies of factor analysis with a view to using the more complex solutions, we recommend Harman (1967) for a balanced overview. A rotation technique with potential has been proposed by Cattell and Muerle (1960) and refined by Eber (1966, 1968).

*Factor Scores.* Early in our discussion of factor analysis we pointed out that a factor is a linear composite of the variables under study. That is, variation on the factor is made up of parts of the variances of several variables. Although we do not have direct measures of the factors themselves, there are ways by which we can estimate what each individual would have received (scored) on a measure of the factor if we had it. These estimates are called factor scores (for computational details see Harman, 1967, Chapter 16).

Factor scores can serve several useful functions in a research program. For example, the researcher might wish to know how his subjects would be ordered by his factors. From the factor scores he could obtain such an ordering for the subjects on each factor. As a second example, he might wish to know the correlations between the factors and some new variables which had not been included in the original factor analysis (remember that the factor loadings give the correlations between the factors and the variables which were factor analyzed). The factor scores would permit such an an analysis.

Computing factor scores is only one of the possible ways of getting scores for linear combinations of variables. In this case the factor scores are developed in such a way as to provide the best estimate of the factors themselves. In the next chapter we will explore some of the other uses of linear composites and scores on such composites.

## Applying the Factor Analytic Model

Factor analysis is a tool of great potential power in cross-cultural research. However, like any tool, it must be used properly or the results will be of little value. The only real drawback to the rise of computers in factor analytic research has been that factor analyses have become so easy to obtain that some researchers have published elaborate factor analytic studies without knowing what they were doing. Although most such errors are of the interpretive sort (and therefore easily corrected), other kinds of difficulties do arise. As our closing comments on factor analysis, we offer some suggestions which should constitute minimum methodological caution. We feel that these guidelines are something which the investigator should try to meet, but we do not offer them as the *sine qua non* of factor analysis. There is no substitute for scientific skill and human insight.

The first requirement for any correlational study is adequate sample size, and this is particularly true where large numbers of variables are involved. The data collected in cross-cultural research usually contain liberal amounts of unavoidable measurement error. The best guard against sampling error is a large and representative sample from the population of interest. A rough guide to necessary sample size is to square the number of variables and add 50. Thus, for a factor analysis of twenty variables, an appropriate sample size would be 450 subjects. A bare minimum sample should include 10 times as many subjects as variables. For example, data from 200 people would be necessary for a factor analysis of 20 variables.

Cross-cultural research, which is still largely in an exploratory stage and seeking to define relevant variables, may be an exception to the above guidelines on sample size. In exploratory research it is often necessary to examine a large number of variables to find out which ones are relevant. Under these exploratory circumstances large samples may be too costly to obtain in terms of time and money. Pilot studies of this type can be carried out with relatively small samples (2 or 3 times as many individuals or variables) to provide guides for more definitive, large-sample research with the instruments finally selected. However, we would caution the reader that multivariate research *requires* large samples before confidence can be placed in the results because errors of measurement and sampling bias can severely distort results in multivariate studies and these effects are much more likely where small samples are used. If a promising result is obtained with a small sample, check it out on a large sample *before* publishing the study.

Once a sample of sufficient size has been obtained, the relationships among the variables should be checked for linearity, either by making scatter plots or by comparing the product-moment correlations with etas. If $r^2$ and $\eta^2$ are approximately equal, the relationship is approximately linear. If some of the relationships depart substantially from linearity a factor analysis may give distorted results because the product-moment correlations will underestimate the nonlinear relationships.

After the linearity of relationships in the sample is established, the factoring can begin. Some decision about communalities and number of factors must be made at this point, as well as choosing the factoring method if more than one is available. For most purposes the principal factor direct iteration method will give as good results as any method at less expenditure in time. Choosing this method means that a decision will have to be made only about the number of factors. The minimum residual method gives excellent results, but it has the disadvantage of requiring much more time for larger problems.

As we said before, the decision of how many factors to extract will affect the size of the obtained communalities. It is generally better to extract more factors than the number suggested by the Kaiser criterion. The reason for this is twofold. First, underestimating the communalities throws away information which should be kept in the factor solution. Second, when it is time to rotate the factors, if a rotation is desired, an underestimate of the number of factors will prevent clear definition of the factors. There won't be enough room to spread the variance out properly (see Levonian and Comrey, 1966).

One solution which has been proposed (Thorndike, 1970) is to postpone a decision about the number of factors to retain until after an initial rotation. The logic of this suggestion is that it is the rotated factors, which are to be interpreted. If one obtains a principal components solution and then rotates (probably by varimax) different numbers of factors, starting with the Kaiser criterion and increasing the number of factors by one for each successive rotation, he will be able to get a good idea of what the final solution will look like for different numbers of factors. Once a satisfactory number of factors is found, direct iteration for the communalities can be undertaken. When the communalities have stabilized, the matrix can be rotated again and the Kaiser criterion applied to the rotated matrix as a final decision for the number of factors to retain. It is then up to the investigator to exercise his scientific judgment in the interpretation of the factors.

Obviously, we view factor analysis as a process requiring successive approximation. There is no prescribed correct procedure for performing a factor analysis and what we have proposed is a set of decision rules which seem to us to be generally applicable in most factor analytic investigations. Where the investigator can postulate specific factors and wishes to confirm their existence, Jöreskog's procedure would definitely be in order. However, by following our guidelines in attacking a new area, the investigator may avoid many of the methodological weaknesses which have occurred in other factor analytic studies in cross-cultural research.

The last stage of a factor analysis is the interpretation of the factors. Here the investigator is completely on his own and any decisions he makes are between him and the data. We would add one note of caution. There is a tendency, even among experienced factor analysts, to overlook loadings which are not in line with one's hypotheses and favorite interpretations. It is *not* appropriate to ignore a loading of .50 and interpret a loading of .30 if the latter fits one's hypothesis and the former does not. Instead, both loadings should be considered and a qualification should be placed on the interpretation.

## Empirical Examples of Factor Analysis

Factor analysis has been used by many researchers in the area of cross-cultural research. Up to this point our discussion of factor analytic methodology has been largely abstract in nature. In this section we shall present several empirical studies in which factor analysis has been used in order to illustrate some of the points of good methodology and to indicate some potential pitfalls which the researcher may encounter.

Our first study is one by Irvine (1969b) in which he examined the patterns of abilities in five African groups from three nationalities. This study was selected because it is one of the most adequate applications of factor analysis to the study of cross-cultural stability of patterns of ability. Tests were given to 1615 Rhodesian eight-graders, 684 Zambian eighth-graders, 72 Zambian mine youth, 442 Zambian tenth-graders, and 185 Kenyan secondary school students. In some cases different tests were given to the different groups, but there was enough overlap in the batteries to permit comparison of the factors obtained. Note that, with the exception of the Zambian mine youth group, the sample sizes are all large enough to permit interpretation of the results with confidence. Since the one small group can be considered a replication of the other results, its size is not a problem.

Irvine obtained the principal components from each group separately and rotated the matrices independently to varimax solutions. This use of identical factoring procedures in the five independent samples means that the factor patterns which appeared in all samples can be considered to be either characteristic of all of the groups or a function of the particular method of analysis chosen. The nature of the factors indicates that they reflect truly common elements of mental functioning because they can be identified as highly similar to factors found by many other investigators using similar tests but other factoring methods in other cultures. However, Irvine's conclusions would receive some additional support if his results could be replicated using other factoring procedures on his data, as has been suggested by Harris (1967). It would be a worthwhile addition to his study to show that such similar results could be found for the different groups not only using the same method of factoring but also different methods. Such a finding would be strong evidence that the cross-cultural similarities observed were not due to the similarity of method.

It should be pointed out that both approaches to the analysis provide valuable information in this case. If differences were found using different factor procedures, it would be possible to interpret those differences as being due to variation in analysis or variation in the samples. By using the same factoring procedure, one of those interpretations could be ruled out. Likewise, finding a high degree of similarity among the factors from different samples could be interpreted as arising from the use of a common factoring method (and therefore a methodological artifact) or from the existence of similar factors in the different groups. Use of several different factoring methods would make clear which is the appropriate interpretation. If the necessary programs and computer time are available, this approach can provide confirmation of interesting and suggestive results. However, results such as those obtained by Irvine are valuable as he has presented them. Our suggestions would only serve to bolster his conclusions but could be important additions in studies where the variables have been less well researched.

Our second example of the use of factor analysis in cross-cultural research comes from the work of Triandis, Vassiliou, and Nassiakou (1968) on role perception in the United States and Greece. The authors used facet theory (see next chapter) to set up a classification system of social behaviors. Their procedure produced 100 roles and two sets of 60 social behaviors each from a United States group for use in the main part of their study. The same procedure was applied in Greece resulting in 120 behaviors and 92 roles.

After determining that their instrument was sufficiently reliable, the authors found the principal components of the correlations among behaviors and of the correlations among roles. These principal components analyses were carried out separately in the two cultures and separately for the two sets of behaviors within each culture. Thus for the American group, factor analyses were performed on the 100 roles and on the two sets of behaviors (60 in each set). The same procedure was carried out for the 92 Greek roles and the two sets (60 in each set) of Greek behaviors. The four resulting behavior factor matrices were rotated to maximize the varimax criterion.

The first three role factors were found to exhibit high similarity between the two cultures before rotation, each of the factors from one culture having a parallel factor in the other. In the behavior domain, the authors compared the factors found in one set of behaviors with those found in the second set within one culture after varimax rotation and found parallel factors in the two sets within cultures. This is further evidence that they have done a good job in sampling the behavior domain within each culture. Across cultures the degree of correspondence among the factors was somewhat lower, indicating that the behavior domains in the two cultures are different.

This latter finding illustrates an important point in factor analytic methodology. If the authors had used only a single sample of behaviors from each culture and found some differences between the factor structures obtained in the two cultures, there would remain a question about the origin of the differences. They could have been due either to real differences in the behavior domain between the two cultures or to imperfect and non-parallel sampling from the behavior domain in either or both cultures. By taking two samples from the domain in each culture and demonstrating parallelism within culture, the authors have ruled out the latter explanation for the differences they obtained.

After performing the conventional factor analyses, Triandis et al. extended their research by using a type of factor analysis which we have not discussed. They wished to determine the factor structure simultaneously for both behaviors and roles. To do this they used a technique called *two-mode factor analysis* in which they extracted factors from the behavior domain and then computed factor scores for roles. This procedure expressed the roles in terms of the behavior factors and permitted the authors to identify clusters of roles which were associated with clusters of behaviors. After discussing their interpretation of the two-mode factors, the authors made a point which is very important in cross-cultural applications of factor analysis. "The interpretation of factor patterns requires intimate knowledge of the culture" (Triandis et al., 1968). As the authors point out, specific aspects of factors found in data from different cultures may reflect identifiable differences in the cultures or temporally specific situations (such as the tensions in Greece when their data were collected).

A study by Triandis and Lambert (1961) provided the data for our third example. The authors were interested in the dimensions of socialization practices shown by six dissimilar cultures. Using trained interviewers, they obtained answers to 21 classes of questions from 133 mothers. Attempts were made to counterbalance the group for age and sex of child so that 4-6 mothers of children from each group were interviewed. Each culture was represented by 16-24 mothers and the mothers were categorized as to whether their child was male or female and 3-6 or 7-10 years of age. The interviews were then coded by raters on 26 content variables and these variables, along with age and sex, were factor analyzed by the centroid method and rotated according to the varimax criterion.

This study illustrates several potential problems which the user of factor analysis may encounter. The first is sample size and character. Triandis and Lambert made an effort to counterbalance two potentially important variables, age and sex of children. Since their procedure for data collection made use of large samples difficult, their counterbalancing was particularly important to assure that their results were not contaminated by an unmeasured variable. The fact that sex of child did not have a substantial effect on the factor analysis does not mean that controlling for it was unnecessary, but does add to the generality of their findings. Where large samples cannot be used, it is best to control explicitly for the effects of demographic variables such as age and sex. Such controls may be less necessary, although still desirable, where large samples can be obtained.

Small sample size created another methodological problem for Triandis and Lambert. It would have been valuable if they had been able to examine the factor structure of each culture independently, as Irvine did. However, even in those cultures where they had the largest numbers of subjects, they were faced with the problem of having more variables than individuals. Consequently, they had to disregard the cultural dimension and factor analyze the data from all cultures together. This procedure cannot provide information about specific similarities and differences between cultures. Instead, it provides factors descriptive of some average culture which may not be representative of any of the specific cultures studied. The authors do present some indirect evidence from an analysis of variance that their factors represent dimensions with some cross-cultural implications, but their evidence of comparable factor structures is not as strong as that presented in two previous examples. They have done as much as possible with the samples available, but they could have done more with larger samples.

The Triandis and Lambert study illustrates another area of difficulty for factor analytic research with interview data, the coding and scaling of responses. The authors had the interviews translated into English and analyzed by trained personnel. They report reliability coefficients for this procedure which indicate moderate reliability for the scales. They report that a nine-point rating scale was used for three of the variables and a seven-point scale was used for 15 of the variables, but no justification is given for this change in scaling procedure. Since the data were standardized by computing correlation coefficients, the issue is not particularly important for this case. However, if the relative variability in responses is to be retained (and therefore the covariances or cross-products analyzed, as Triandis, Vassiliou, and Nassiakou did for their two-mode factor analysis in the second example) the scaling problem becomes real and requires attention. Answers to questions about the scaling of data should be provided explicitly by the investigator; they should not result from default or convenience.

The authors reported reliability coefficients for their scales, which is something that should be done whenever it is possible to obtain the information. They also iterated for the communalities, but they did not report the final value which they used in their analysis. When reliability information is available, this is often the best estimate of communality because the reliabilities of the variables provide upper limits for the communalities. It makes no sense to include unreliable error variance in a factor analysis. Therefore, if communalities are obtained by iteration and reliability information is available, the communalities used in the factor analysis should not exceed the reliabilities of the variables. It is also good practice to report the communalities whenever the analysis is not a principal components analysis (where the communalities are, by definition, 1.0).

The problem of scaling variables for use in factor analysis arose in a somewhat different form in a study by Sawyer and LeVine (1966). These authors factor analyzed 30 cultural characteristics for the World Ethnographic Sample (see Chapter 6) to determine universal dimensions of culture. The 30 characteristics had originally been tabulated in nominal (verbally labelled) categories so that there was no quantitative information in the variables. New quantitative variables were developed from the nominal categories by imposing a new verbal label on each set of categories according to its relative position on the characteristic. Finally, numerical values were assigned to the groupings to represent different amounts of the variable in question. This procedure appears to have produced ordinal scales for the new variables.

The intercorrelations of the thirty ordinal variables which resulted from the scaling procedure were computed. The authors state that product-moment correlations were computed, but it is not clear from their statement whether Pearson product-moment coefficients or Spearman rank-order correlations were used. Use of the former requires an assumption that interval scaling has been achieved, and this assumption would be unwarranted in the present case. Spearman's procedure provides an approximation to the Pearson coefficient when the data have only ordinal properties and would be the proper statistic in this case. It is unlikely that use of the wrong coefficient would seriously affect the resulting factors, but it is generally methodologically better to use a statistic which requires fewer assumptions when one is unsure of the scaling properties of his data. Such caution would seem particularly appropriate where the scaling is as coarse as that achieved by Sawyer and LeVine. In any case, it should be made clear exactly what form of correlation coefficient has been computed.

The correlation matrix (which is provided in the paper — a desirable practice) was factor analyzed by the principal components method. The authors note that this procedure provides an exact solution, which is true. However, it also analyzes all of the variance of each variable, including error variance. In studies where there is likely to be substantial measurement error, such as Sawyer and LeVine's, it is generally better to use some estimate of the common or reliable variance in the main diagonal, rather than unities. This practice may have less appeal for the investigator and may be harder to interpret, but it has the advantage of excluding error variance from the analysis.

Sawyer and LeVine's interpretation of their factors is generally clear and appropriate. However, they are guilty of a practice which is all too common in factor analysis and which should be avoided in the interpretation of factors. This is the tendency on the part of investigators to interpret moderate loadings which fi⁺ preconceptions their while ignoring larger loadings of the same variable on other factors. Two variables exemplify this practice in this example. The variable of "bride price" is included in the group of variables defining a factor of "patrilineality," where it had a loading of .35. "Bride price" should have been placed in the cluster of variables defining the factor of "animal husbandry" because its loading on that factor is .50. Concessions are made to this fact in the interpretations of the factors, but group membership was determined by theory rather than empirical evidence. The same criticisms may be applied to the interpretation of the variable called "polygyny," which loads about equally on four factors but is included in the factor on which it has its second highest loading. This practice does not create confidence in the authors' interpretations of their factors.

The four studies which we have reviewed in this section were chosen because they illustrated specific points of factor analytic methodology applied to cross-cultural research. Other studies could have been selected, but these four cover many of the problems and decisions which arise in multivariate research. We hope that these illustrations will lead to a general improvement in factor analytic methodology and its wider use by cross-cultural investigators.

## Summary

We chose to present factor analysis in an intuitive, non-mathematical way because so few non-technical explanations of this technique exist. Since the presentation was as concise as we could make it, this summary assumes a basic understanding of the main presentation. We defined factor analysis as a means for finding a set of dimensions which account for the relationships among the variables under study. In this section we bring together procedural advice for those wishing to use factor analysis in cross-cultural research.

First, the investigator should have plans regarding the number of variables and subjects he wants to study so that he will not find himself with masses of data that he cannot analyze. Even with the presence of high speed computers, proper analysis can take many months. A major requirement is adequate sample size, others as prediction strategies. Factor analysis describes the given set of variab[...] and nothing more. The techniques of this chapter can be used to predict th[...] external variable(s) from the set being analyzed. Thus, multiple correlation can be viewed as a technique either for describing the component of a set of variables that has maximum relationship with an external variable (external factor analysis) or for obtaining a set of weights that will give the best possible estimates of a dependent variable from a set of independent variables (prediction). The results of such an analysis may be used for either purpose.

## Multiple Correlation

In a prediction situation the simplest case is when we have a single variable to predict, which we will call the *criterion*, and two variables from which to make our prediction. What we wish to find is the best possible combination of our two predictors for predicting our criterion. From our product-moment correlations we already know the relationship between each of the predictors taken separately and the criterion. We also know the amount of relationship between our two predictors. Assuming that each of the three variables has a non-zero relationship with the other two, some additive combination of the two predictors should give better results than either of them alone.

In correlational analysis we are dealing with standardized variables, so each has unit variance (i.e., 1.0). But if our two predictors are correlated with each other, they have some proportion of their variance in common. This common variance can only be used once in our prediction equation. Therefore, we require a method for determining the correlation of each of our predictors with the criterion when the variance in common with the third variable has been removed.

*Part and Partial Correlation.* There are two approaches we could take to remove the effect of variation on a third variable from the relationship between the other two. Both of these approaches result in a description of a bivariate relationship and are therefore not actually part of the multiple correlation type of analysis, but they are closely related to multiple correlation and will be useful in understanding it.

Occasionally, situations arise where we would like to know the degree of relationship between variable $A$ and variable $B$ which exists independently of the effect of variable $C$. Such a situation might exist, for example, where we have a measure of aptitude ($A$), a measure of achievement ($B$), and a measure of interest ($C$). We may feel that variation in aptitude and interest combine to produce the variation we observe in achievement. We could ask two kinds of questions about these relationships which typify the two approaches to removing variance from a relationship. First, what is the degree of relationship

and this is especially true where large numbers of variables are involved. Since measurement error is likely to be high in cross-cultural research, a conservative approach is called for. A rough guide to sample size is to square the number of variables and add 50. Since the expense of cross-cultrual research is usually greater than that of unicultrual research, small samples are proper in preliminary work but not for the final published report. The investigator should also have plans for the selection of variables since the scaling properties of the variables will determine many of the options open to him within the factor analytic framework. It is also very important to determine if the relation between any two variables is linear or nonlinear. Distributions should be plotted and mathematical tests performed when there is a doubt.

After these preliminaries are solved, the specific factoring procedure must be chosen. One procedure may have specific cross-cultural application. Jöreskog (1969) has developed confirmatory maximum likelihood factor analysis which has the goal of confirming the existence of factors from one sample on data from a second sample. For instance, Irvine, (1969b) found certain factors after administering a series of mental abilities tests in sub-Saharan Africa. Using the Jöreskog procedure another researcher could administer the same tests in another culture and could obtain the best possible "match" to the target culture, thus confirming or disconfirming the existence of the same factors in the second culture.

The purpose of rotating factors is to increase interpretability, and much disagreement exists as to the exact rotation that should be used. It can be justifiably argued that the researcher can find anything he wants in a set of data by using a rotation that suits him. It is possible to program computers in a certain way so as to achieve a mathematical criterion, and these programs should be considered since they keep the investigator's feelings out of the analysis. Another possibility is to analyze the same data using two or more rotations, thus determining whether the exact factors that emerge are a function of method (the rotation chosen) or process (actual underlying structure). A major conclusion: if the researcher is comparing factors between cultures, he should anticipate the possibility of interpreting the meaning of both similar and different factors. He should realize that the factors can be based on instrumentation, rotation techniques, actual content, and so forth.

Other guidelines can be gathered from the published literature. As already mentioned, Irvine (1969b) measured mental abilities in sub-Saharan Africia using the same factor analytic techniques in the five groups under study. The sample sizes were large enough so that factors across groups could be compared. Since he used the same techniques, results across groups could be interpreted as due to substantive similarities rather than methodological artifacts. The study could have been even better, however, if different methods were used on the same data in addition to the technique used in the primary analysis.

In a study of role perception in Greece and the United States, Triandis, Vassiliou, and Nassiakou (1968) employed a sophisticated factor analysis. They devised instruments to measure perception of roles and social behaviors, and they divided the behaviors into two sets (60 in each of the two sets). The different sets of behaviors yielded the same underlying factors within each culture, showing that the researchers had done a good job in sampling the behavior domains. Between-culture similarities were of lower magnitude. If the two sets of behaviors had not been analyzed, interpretation would have been difficult since the *between*-culture differences could have been due to definitional problems *within* each culture. As always, instruments and analyses that allow replication are desirable. The researchers also made the important point that interpretation of the factor patterns demands intimate knowledge of the cultures. The Greek results, for instance, may have been due to identifiable cultural differences or to the tensions at the time of data collection. Awareness of such variables makes intelligent interpretation possible.

In the Triandis and Lambert (1961) study of socialization practices, issues arose that were based on the use of small samples. When small samples are used, counterbalancing on demographic variables such as age and sex of children are necessary, and the authors did so in their study. Since the samples in the different cultures were so small, however, factor structures within samples could not be compared. In addition, the exact scaling procedures used in the research were not reported, so interpretation by the reader is difficult. The problem of scaling also arose in the Sawyer and LeVine (1966) study of cultural universals. The authors factor analyzed 30 cultural characteristics obtained from the World Ethnographic Sample to determine universal dimensions. It is likely that ordinal variables resulted from ratings of ethnographies, but this is left implicit. The reader thus does not know if the subsequent statistical procedures were warranted. The general lessons to be learned are (1) explicit reporting of scaling procedures and (2) use of a statistic which requires few assumptions if the data so warrant. In the actual analysis, Sawyer and LeVine should have reported the common and reliable variance since the concepts under study were likely to carry a large error variance. Finally, the authors made the common mistake of noting factor loadings that supported their framework and ignoring others that didn't.

# CHAPTER TEN

## *Other Multivariate Techniques*

In the preceding chapter we discussed factor analysis at some length. As a technique for data reduction, factor analysis is unique among the multivariate methods in that it attempts to explain the variance *within* a set of variables. That is, the analysis is performed on the variables of interest without regard to anything that is not in the set. Often in cross-cultural research we are interested in analyzing the variance in one set of variables with respect to one or more additional variables which are not in the set being analyzed. Such a situation would arise, for example, when a battery of ability tests has been given to samples from two or more societies with a view to determining whether the patterns of abilities are the same in the different cultures. In such a case there are at least two possible courses of analysis. One, which is typified in the work of Irvine (1969b, see p. 285), is to factor analyze the ability battery separately for the different groups and attempt to match the factors afterward. A second course of analysis would be to consider the different societies to constitute a nominally scaled dependent variable and use the ability tests to predict to which group each individual belongs.

These two approaches have one major difference in the logic underlying their use. In the first case each separate analysis determines the structure of the variables internally and independently. In the second approach the goal is to maximize differences in structure with reference to the external variable. Those strategies of analysis which utilize only internal structure have been called "internal factor analysis," while strategies which determine composites of variables with reference to another variable or set of variables may be called "external factor analysis" (Bartlett, 1948). In this chapter we will be concerned primarily with external factor analytic strategies. These strategies go under many different names, but generally they may all be considered members of this group.

Another way to view the differences between the topics of this section and factor analysis is to consider factor analysis as a descriptive strategy and the

between aptitude and achievement with the effect of variation in interest removed from achievement *only*? This type of analysis is called *part correlation*. Second, what degree of relationship remains between aptitude and achievement with the effect of interest variation removed from *both* aptitude and achievement. The name *partial correlation* has been given to this procedure.

Perhaps the best way to view part and partial correlation is to consider the situation in which we have a large number of people from whom we have information on all three variables. If we categorize people in terms of their level on the variable whose effect is to be removed (variable *C* or interest) we can find the means for one or both of the other variables for the several groups which we have formed in this categorization. By subtracting his group's mean from each person's score, we get a deviation score within the group for one (part correlation) or both (partial correlation) cf the other two variables. The correlation between these deviation scores is what we are looking for.

To carry our example through, we first form categories of level of interest. If we wish to remove the effect of interest from achievement scores only (part correlation), we find the deviation scores for achievement within the levels of interest and correlate these deviation scores with the *original* scores for aptitude. If we wish to do a partial correlation and remove the effect of interest from both aptitude and achievement we find the deviation scores for achievement and the deviation scores for aptitude within interest levels. The correlation between these two sets of deviation scores is our partial correlation. Notice that we could find two different part correlations (interest removed from achievement *or* aptitude) but only one partial correlation. The decision of which part correlation to use, of course, depends upon the research question at hand.

In practice, it is not necessary to form categories of the third variable to determine part and partial correlations. The formula for the partial correlation between variables *A* and *B* with the effect of *C* removed is

$$r_{ab.c} = \frac{r_{ab} - r_{ac} \cdot r_{bc}}{\sqrt{1 - r_{ac}^2}\sqrt{1 - r_{bc}^2}}$$

Where $r_{ab}$, $r_{ac}$, and $r_{bc}$ are the bivariate correlations between variables *A* and *B*, *A* and *C*, and *B* and *C*. The formula for the part correlation of *A* and *B* with *C* removed from *B* is

$$r_{a(b.c)} = \frac{r_{ab} - r_{ac} \cdot r_{bc}}{\sqrt{1 - r_{bc}^2}}$$

To find the part correlation of *A* and *B* with *C* removed from *A*, the formula is

$$r_{b(a.c)} = \frac{r_{ab} - r_{bc} \cdot r_{ac}}{\sqrt{1 - r_{ac}^2}}$$

For a more complete treatment of part and partial correlation, see McNemar (1969, Chapter 10).

*Logic of Multiple Correlation.* There are many research situations in which one wishes to predict the status of individuals on one variable from their positions on several other variables. We might, for example, wish to predict status on achievement from *both* aptitude and interest, rather than determine the part or partial relationships. Research problems of this type are called multiple correlation (or regression) problems, and the logic used in their solution is a combination of the logic of simple correlation and factor analysis. Multiple correlation is the simplest case of what Bartlett (1948) has called "external factor analysis."

The reader will recall that we placed a restriction on our factors in Chapter 9 which required that each successive factor account for as much linear variance as possible in the *set of variables being analyzed*. In multiple correlation we are also determining a linear composite of our set of predictor variables. However, in this case we place a slightly different restriction on our composite, that it be determined in such a way as to account for the maximum possible amount of variance *in the variable which we are trying to predict*. Bartlett (1948) noted this basic difference in logic of the two types of analysis and coined the term "internal factor analysis" to identify situations in which interest centers on the internal structure of a set of variables (traditional factor analysis as described in the previous chapter). The term "external factor analysis" is used to refer to cases where the structure of one set of variables is being determined with reference to a variable (multiple correlation) or set of variables (canonical correlation) external to the set being analyzed. This distinction is fruitful for understanding the applications of various multivariate analysis approaches.

Returning to our example, we would like to know what composite of our two independent variables is most highly related to (i.e., accounts for the greatest proportion of variance of) our third or dependent variable.[1] The task before us is to find a "factor" in the set of independent variables which has the greatest correlation with the dependent variable. In geometric terms this is analogous to finding an axis of the independent set which has the smallest angle with the vector representing the dependent variable. This situation is shown in Figure 10.1 for our three-variable example. Lines *A* (aptitude) and *C* (interest) lie in a plane while line *B* (achievement) lies in a third dimension above the plane. If we were to hold a flashlight directly over the plane and perpendicular to it, line *B* would cast a shadow (its projection) on the plane. The shadow (line *B'*) would

---

[1] In prediction situations it is customary to call independent variables "predictors" and the variable being predicted the "criterion." However, the terms "independent" and "dependent" variables are more general and are appropriate in cases where description is the goal, as well as in the more common prediction case.

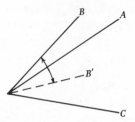

**Figure 10.1.** Composite of variables $A$ and $C$ which has maximum correlation with variable $B$.

be the line in the plane which forms the smallest angle with $B$ and would be the line we want. Since any line going through the origin and lying in the plane can be expressed as a linear combination of $A$ and $C$, $B'$ is the linear composite we seek. The correlation between $B$ and $B'$ is the multiple correlation of $B$ with $A$ and $C$.

*Mathematics of Multiple Correlation.*, In factor analysis we were using the variance of the variables to describe the internal structure of the set of variables. The factors could be used to predict the variables if we wished to do so, but this is seldom done. In multiple correlation the situation is somewhat different. The factors of Chapter 9 were independent (orthogonal) and therefore would make independent contributions in predicting the variables. That is, the contribution of factor I in predicting variable 1 would be independent of the contribution of factor II in predicting variable 1. In multiple correlation the independent variables are usually correlated with one another, as well as with the dependent variable. The shared variance between the independent variables (due to their correlation) is redundant variance and therefore cannot be used in determining the linear composite for predicting the dependent variable. The composite must be made up of independent contributions from the independent variables. We must therefore determine the proportion of variance in each independent variable which is related to the dependent variable and is independent of all other independent variables. By weighting each independent variable by this proportion, we get a linear composite which has no redundant information and has maximum correlation with the dependent variable.

At this point the reader should have begun to realize that there is a connection between the weight given each independent variable and the part correlation between the independent variable and the dependent variable with the effect of the other independent variables held constant. For our three-variable example, the weight of variable $A$ in predicting variable $B$ will be the proportion of variance in $B$ accounted for by $A$ with the effect of $C$ held constant in $A$. This is very much like the part correlation $r_{b(a.c)}$. It can be shown that, in the case of two independent variables, the weight of $A$ for determining the linear composite is given by

$$\beta_{b(a.c)} = \frac{r_{ab} - r_{bc}\, r_{ac}}{1 - r_{ac}^2} \quad ,$$

and the weight for $C$ is given by

$$\beta_{b(c.a)} = \frac{r_{bc} - r_{ab}\, r_{ac}}{1 = r_{ac}^2} \quad .$$

Both of these formulas differ from the respective part correlation formulas only in the absence of the square root sign in the denominator. In view of the logic of part correlation, this seems very reasonable.[2]

When dealing with more than two independent variables, the algebra for expressing the weights which define the linear composite becomes very complicated and is more easily phrased in the terminology of matrix algebra. Such a treatment is beyond the scope of this book. However, the logic underlying these weights remains the same and, with modern computer technology, the researcher can get answers to his research questions without needing to know how to work out the mathematical details.

*Raw Score Regression.* Up to this point in our discussion there has been an implicit assumption that we have standard scores for individuals on our variables because the scores are standardized in the process of computing bivariate correlation coefficients. For describing the relationships between variables this is often the best way to proceed. However, when we wish to predict scores on a dependent variable from scores on a set of independent variables it is often more convenient to work with raw scores. When this is the case, we must adjust our weights to reflect differences in the standard deviations of our variables.

An individual's score on the composite for standard scores is the simple linear sum of his standard score for each variable multiplied by the weight for that variable. That is, his predicted score, $\hat{Z}_{yi}$, is found by

$$\hat{Z}_{yi} = \beta_{x_1} Z_{x_1 i} + \beta_{x_2} Z_{x_2 i} + \ldots + \beta_{x_n} Z_{x_n i}$$

When the scores have not been standardized, the $\beta$-weights must be adjusted by the ratio of each independent variable's standard deviation to the dependent

[2] The reader who is interested in the derivation of these relationships should consult McNemar (1969, Chapter 11).

variable's standard deviation, and are called *b*-weights. For example.

$$b_{x_1} = \frac{S_{x_1}}{S_y} \beta_{x_1}$$

After this adjustment has been made, the equation for the composite will reflect the relative magnitude of variability in each of the independent variables.

One final adjustment in the equation must still be made. In bivariate regression equations there is a term called the intercept, or $A$, which takes into account the means of the variables and adjusts the elevation of the regression line above or below the origin. A similar correction which takes into account the means of all of the variables must be made in multiple regression. The output from a computer program will generally give the *b*-weights and intercept as well as the standard score weights. Using the formula

$$\hat{Y}_i = b_{x_1} X_{1i} + b_{x_2} X_{2i} + \ldots + b_{x_n} X_{ni} + A$$

it is possible to predict a person's raw score on the dependent variable from his raw scores on the independent variables. (For a further discussion of these aspects of multiple correlation and regression the reader should consult such sources as Ezekiel and Fox, 1959, or McNemar, 1969.)

*Interpreting Composites.* It has been common practice for many years for researchers to attempt to interpret the composites resulting from an internal factor analysis. Recently the suggestion has been made that the researcher may wish to interpret the composites resulting from an external factor analysis (Cooley and Lohnes, 1971). That is, the researcher may wish to attach a name to his composite which reflects the various sources of variance of which it is composed. This may be a concern in both multiple and canonical correlation.

The task of interpreting composities requires that we know the proportion of variance which each variable has in common with the composite. It would seem at first glance that the $\beta$-weights should give us this information, but such is not the case. The $\beta$-weights are standard *partial* regression coefficients, which means that they reflect the proportion of each variable's variance which is common with the composite and independent of all other independent variables. This means that an independent variable which is highly correlated with other independent variables cannot receive a large $\beta$-weight even if it is almost perfectly related to the composite. Therefore, what is needed for interpretation of the composite is the correlation of each independent variable with the composite. The most conceptually simple way to do this is to compute each individual's score on the composite and calculate the correlations between composite scores and independent variable scores. A procedure which provides the necessary correlations without the labor of calculating the composite scores is given by Cooley and Lohnes (1971).

Once we have the correlation of each variable with the composite, interpretation follows the same process as that used in standard (internal) factor analysis. The composite is most similar in content to those variables which are most highly correlated with it. Factors and composites should be given names which reflect the content of the variables which they resemble and are as descriptive of that content as possible. If we had used in our three-variable example a measure of mechanical aptitude, a measure of mechanical interest, and a measure of achievement in mechanics, and we had found both independent variables to be substantially correlated with the composite, we might interpret the composite as "interest in and aptitude for mechanical work." This example verges on the trivial, but may be taken to illustrate the process involved.

*Stepwise Analysis.* When prediction of a dependent variable is the goal of a multiple regression analysis, we sometimes find that a few variables will yield as good prediction as a much larger set due to the common variance among the independent variables. If the independent variables are to be used for prediction with many individuals over a substantial period of time, considerable saving in cost and effort can be realized by using a small number of variables which do the work of many. To achieve the best prediction it is often necessary to start with a large number of variables and drop out those which do not contribute significantly to the prediction of the dependent variable. The process of doing this is called *stepwise regression analysis* (see Draper and Smith, 1966, Chapter 6, for computational details).

If the object of a regression analysis is description and the researcher wishes to name the resulting composite, a stepwise procedure may also be called for. If one is looking for the structure of a set of variables under the restriction of maximum relationship to the external variable, it would be inappropriate to eliminate variables from the set. On the other hand, the investigator may wish to simplify his description of the composite as much as possible to facilitate its interpretation. Then, a stepwise procedure in regression can serve a function analogous to that of rotation in traditional factor analysis. By eliminating variables which are unnecessary to fix the location of the composite, it may be possible to clarify the interpretation at the same time. We know of no cases where this has actually been tried, but the idea is inviting.

*Cross-Validation.* Whenever we are dealing with a group of individuals (a sample) who are representatives of a larger group (a population) and we wish to make statements about the population based on the evidence from our sample, we are faced with two problems. The first of these deals with the accuracy of our measurements. This problem exists regardless of whether we are measuring an individual, a sample, or a population, and it must be solved before we can draw any conclusions at all. The second problem concerns the specific case of drawing inferences about a population from a sample. In the area of statistical inference, we use tests of statistical significance to determine the probability that the result we obtained occurred by chance and we can place confidence limits on the statements which we make about the population based on our sample data. Tests of statistical significance are available for most of the procedures described in this chapter (see McNemar, 1969; or Cooley and Lohnes, 1971, for the appropriate tests). However, these significance tests give us only very limited information. We can test the statistical significance of a multiple correlation, for example, but all this tells us is that the multiple correlation in the population is probably not zero. Whenever we are dealing with a group of variables that will have different relationships with our composite (as in multiple correlation), we need to know how stable the contribution of each variable to the composite will be. The technique which permits us to determine the stability of each variable's contribution (and thus the stability of the resulting composite's relationship to other, external variables) is known as cross-validation.

Cross-validation is a fairly simple procedure compared to the techniques used to calculate initial values in multivariate statistics. It involves applying the results of a multivariate analysis obtained from one sample to the data from a new sample to determine whether the results obtained initially can be reproduced. It might seem that all that it would be necessary for an investigator to do would be to perform similar analyses on two independent samples and see that the same magnitude of relationship between the composite and the external variable is obtained (a procedure called replication), but such is not the case. When many variables are analyzed simultaneously, the statistical procedures will capitalize upon small chance variations in the relationships between them to maximize their relationship with the external variable in ways which cannot be detected. These chance variations are due to characteristics of the specific sample being studied and are therefore errors. If the data from two samples are analyzed independently, there is no way to separate error variance due to sample characteristics from true variance due to population characteristics. However, if the results from one sample are applied to the data from another sample, relationships due to sample-specific characteristics will disappear because the two samples share only population characteristics. Thus, the results of a cross-validation are a better estimate of population values than are the results from either sample.

The procedures involved in a cross-validation are relatively simple. Obtaining two samples can be handled in either of two ways: by gathering data from one large sample and randomly assigning individuals to either the development or the cross-validation group, or by gathering the data from the two samples independently. The latter method is likely to give more conservative results because there may be minor variations in testing procedure or sample characteristics on variables not being studied. These factors are likely to be randomized in the former method. The choice of which method to use must be left to the judgment of the investigator.

When the results of the first analysis have been obtained, the weights developed in that group are applied to the scores of the second group. This gives a score for each person in the second group on the composite which was developed in the first group. The correlation between the composite score and the external variable in the second group is a cross-validation multiple correlation. The correlation between composite score and each of the variables contributing to the composite is a cross-validation of the description of the composite. This procedure can also be used with canonical analysis and discriminant function analysis. The need for cross-validation in multivariate research has been discussed by Thorndike and Weiss (1973).

## Discriminant Function Analysis

There is a special application of multiple correlation logic which may be of particular interest to those working on cross-cultural problems. Suppose that we have measures of several variables on people from two different cultures and we wish to determine how these two groups differ in terms of their patterns of scores on the several variables. One way to approach this problem is to consider group membership to be the dependent variable and attempt to determine the linear composite of our several independent variables which will enable us to predict group membership most accurately. This is obviously a case of multiple regression, but when the dependent variable is categorical rather than continuous it is called discriminant function analysis. The composite which we seek is the one that will show the greatest differences between group means and the least overlap in group distributions for composite scores.

A simple graphic example may help clarify the logic of discriminant function. Suppose we have data on need achievement (NA) and strength of father image (FI) for individuals from two cultures and we wish to determine whether our two cultures differ in the combination of these variables. We can prepare a scatter plot of the relationship between NA and FI for each culture separately on the same set of coordinate axes. This has been done in Figure 10.2. Notice that culture 1 is shown as having the higher mean on NA and culture 2 has the higher mean on FI, but that the effect of these differences would cancel out if we took a straight sum of scores on the two variables. The normal curves on the axes show the frequency distributions of the two cultures on the two separate independent variables.

The mathematics of discriminant function analysis determines a composite of the independent variables which maximizes the separation of the groups. In our example the line which maximally separates the two groups is shown as line I.

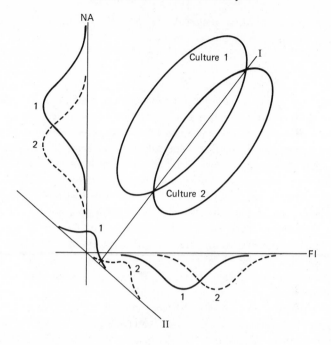

**Figure 10.2.** Bivariate distributions of scores for two cultures and distributions of discriminant function scores.

The line which is orthogonal to line I and passes through the origin (labelled line II) is the axis corresponding to scores on the composite. If we project each point in the two scatter plots perpendicularly onto line II, we get the distributions of scores for the two cultures on the composite. Obviously, the overlap of the two groups on the composite is much less than on either of the independent variables alone. It is also less than that which would be found for any other combination of the two variables.

Our example has been somewhat artificial in that we considered only two groups and two independent variables; however, the logic which we applied will hold for any number of independent variables. The case of more than two groups is somewhat more complicated. In general, we may say that, for $g$ groups and $p$ independent variables, there will be either $g - 1$ or $p$ (whichever is smaller) independent composites which could be found. These composites are similar to principal components in that they are successively determined in such a way as to maximize the separation of the groups on the available information. The first composite or discriminant function will be such as to maximize separation of the groups based on all this information. The second composite will yield maximum discrimination of the groups based on whatever information is left after the effect of the first composite is removed. This procedure continues until all of the information is exhausted by the last composite.[3]

## Canonical Analysis

In the last ten years substantial progress has been made in the methodology of a statistical technique which is a generalization of multiple correlation. This technique, which is called canonical analysis, analyzes the relationships between *sets* of variables. The mathematics of canonical analysis is so complex and laborious that its use had to await the advent of high-speed computers. It has only recently become a widely known and available technique.

The logic of canonical analysis is very similar to that of multiple correlation except that the single dependent variable is replaced by a set of variables. The goal of a canonical analysis is to find a composite of the set of independent variables which is maximally correlated with a composite of the set of dependent variables. (Actually, the distinction between independent and dependent variables is unnecessary in canonical analysis, just as it is in bivariate correlation, so we will speak of "set 1" and "set 2" variables.)

The fact that we are dealing with two *sets* of variables in canonical analysis makes interpretation of the results of such an analysis more complex than is the case with the other types of external factor analysis. For example, there is not just one canonical correlation between set 1 and set 2; there are as many of these correlations as there are variables in the smaller set. The reader will recall that we had a similar situation in the case of factor analysis, where it was necessary to have as many principal components as variables to *completely* describe the relationships among the variables. We are in a similar position here. If there are $m$ variables in set 1 and $n$ variables in set 2 ($m > n$), there are $n$ independent components in set 2 for which we can find $n$ matching components in set 1. However, in canonical analysis the components are ordered not by the amount of variance they extract from their own set but by the magnitude of their correlation with a component in the other set. It is important that the reader keep this distinction in mind because, as we shall see shortly, it is quite possible for a pair of components to be highly correlated (and thus be the first pair extracted) and yet account for a very small proportion of the variance in their respective sets.

A canonical analysis results in a set of weights (which are analogous to multiple correlation β-weights) *for each set of variables for each canonical correlation.* Each set of weights defines a *canonical variate* which is a linear

[3] The reader who is interested in using discriminant function analysis should consult Cooley and Lohnes (1971) for a detailed description of the procedure and a computer program. An excellent example of the use of discriminant function analysis is cross-cultural research is a study by Jones and Bock (1960).

combination of the variables in the set and a *canonical correlation* is the product-moment correlation between a pair of variates. Or, looking at the problem in another way, multiplying each person's score[4] on each variable by the weight for that variable will yield two *variate scores* for each person. The product-moment correlation between the two sets of variate scores (summing across people) is the canonical correlation between that pair of variates.

There are generally two possible goals of a canonical analysis, prediction and description. Where the results of the analysis are to be used in prediction, the canonical variates are used to develop predicted variate (or composite) scores for the dependent or criterion set. Cross-validation to demonstrate the stability of the weights is necessary here just as it is for prediction in the multiple correlation case.

Most canonical analyses undertaken to date have had description of the linear composites as their objective rather than prediction of one set from the other. When description is the goal, the weights which define the variate are not satisfactory because they are partial weights which depict the *independent* contribution of each variable to the composite. What are needed here are the correlations of the individual variables in each set with the canonical variates of that set. These correlations are essentially the same as the loadings in a principal components analysis and are called the *canonical component loadings*. The linear composites which are described by these loadings are called the *canonical components*.

By now the terminology of canonical analysis may have become somewhat confusing and a few words of clarification may be necessary. The terms *canonical variate* and *canonical component* both refer to the same linear composite. However, when that composite is described by the relative *independent* contributions of variance of the several variables in its set (i.e., by the weights) it is called a canonical variate. When the description of the composite is in terms of the *relationships* between it and the variables in the set (i.e., the correlations between the variables and the composite, or the loadings), it is called a canonical component and the correlations of the variables with the composite are called component loadings.[5] To the extent that the variables in either set correlate highly among themselves, these two ways of describing the composites will yield quite different pictures of the nature of the composites. Where the composites are to be interpreted, the component loadings are the

---

[4]When the canonical analysis is performed on the correlations among the variables, as is usually the case, the resulting weights are standardized and must be applied to standard scores. Equations for analyzing a covariance matrix, yielding weights which can be applied to deviation scores, are given by Morrison (1967).

[5]Cooley and Lohnes (1971) call these correlations "factor loadings." For a discussion and justification of the present terminology, see Thorndike and Weiss (1973).

appropriate indices to use and the components are interpreted by identifying the variables to which they are most similar.

Earlier we said that the canonical correlation was an index of the relationship between pairs of composites rather than between the sets of variables themselves. This means that *the square of the canonical correlation is the proportion of variance of a composite of set 1 which is accounted for by a composite in set 2* (and vice versa) *rather than the proportion of the variance of set 1 which is accounted for by set 2.* The canonical component loadings, when squared, give the proportion of variance of each variable which is accounted for by each canonical component. By summing the squared loadings of the variables in a set for a given component of that set and dividing by the number of variables in the set we obtain the proportion of variance of the set which is accounted for by the component. When this has been done it becomes possible to determine the proportion of variance in one set which is accounted for by a given canonical component, and is common to the other set, by multiplying the obtained proportion of variance for the component in that set by the squared canonical correlation. The resulting value has been given the name *"redundancy"* or $R_d$ Stewart and Love (1968) because it indicates the proportion of variance in one set which is redundant with variance in the other set for a given pair of canonical components.

For any given canonical correlation there are actually two redundancy indices, one for the proportion of variance in set 1 accounted for by set 2 and one for the proportion of variance in set 2 accounted for by set 1. These two indices, $R_{d_{1.2}}$ and $R_{d_{2.1}}$, will generally not be equal. It should be obvious that this will be true because the number of variables in the two sets will often be different. Also, it is quite possible for the component of one set to be defined almost entirely by a single variable which has high correlations with the variables of the other set (say set 2) and low correlations with the variables of its own set (set 1). Then the component in set 1 would account for only a small proportion of the total variance in set 1, but the component in set 2 would account for a large proportion of the set 2 variance. The redundancy indices would then reveal that the component of set 2 is redundant with only a small proportion of the set 1 variance because the set 1 component accounts for little variance in its own set, but that the set 1 component has substantial redundant variance with set 2 because the set 2 component accounts for a large proportion of the set 2 variance.

The concept of redundancy can be viewed in another way which may make its meaning more clear. If we look first at the variables in set 2 we can ask what proportion of the variance of each variable is accounted for by the first component of set 1. Obviously, this information is given by the squares of the correlations of the variables in set 2 with the component in set 1. The redundancy of the component of set 1 with the variables of set 2 is then simply the average squared correlation between the variables of set 2 and the variate scores for the component of interest in set 1. Of course, the procedure can be reversed to obtain redundancy values for the components of set 2.

There are as many pairs of components as there are variables in the smaller set, and within each set each component is independent of all the others. This means that no two components within a set account for the same portions of variance of the variables in the set. Therefore, if we wish to know what proportion of the variance of one *entire* set of variables is redundant with the other *entire* set of variables we must consider all of the pairs of canonical components. The index of total set redundancy, $\overline{R}_d$, is the sum of the individual redundancies for the several pairs of canonical components. In general it will again be the case that $\overline{R}_{d_{1.2}}$ will not be equal to $\overline{R}_{d_{2.1}}$.

When we perform a canonical analysis, we generally wish to interpret only a few of the canonical relationships. In this case the answer to the problem of which of the canonical components to retain for interpretation is more clear cut than was the case in factor analysis. There is a test for the statistical significance of a canonical correlation (given by Cooley and Lohnes, 1971, p. 175) which indicates when a canonical relationship may be due to chance. We may then interpret those pairs of canonical components found to be significantly related and determine the total redundancy of the set of canonical relationships retained. To justify any claims of generality for our interpretations, however, it is necessary to cross-validate the relationships on a new sample (see Thorndike and Weiss, 1973, for a discussion of cross-validation in canonical analysis).

When one is doing research in the cross-cultural area the general paradigm of cross-validation offers some very interesting research possibilities. In general, cross-validation involves applying a set of weights developed in one sample to the data from a different sample to determine whether the relationships found in the first sample can be generalized to other samples. In multiple correlation and canonical analyses it is particularly important to satisfy oneself that the obtained relationships did not arise from sample-specific characteristics because these analysis procedures will capitalize on any sample-specific covariation. But it is also possible to use the paradigm for another purpose in cross-cultural research. Suppose we have found a particular relationship in culture A, say, for example, a relationship between attitudes and interests using a canonical analysis. Our results indicate that attitudes Q, V, X, and Z are related to interests 3, 7, and 10. Does this same relationship hold to the same degree in cultures B, C, and D? We may attempt to answer this question by applying the weights developed on the data from culture A to the data from cultures B, C, and D. There is research evidence (Thorndike and Weiss, 1973) which indicates that the canonical components will not change substantially in such an analysis but that the canonical correlations may drop to zero. Such an analysis would then answer the question of whether the relationship *between the components* is specific to one culture or exists in several cultures. In using such an approach it would be a good idea to cross-validate the weights from culture A within the culture (i.e., on data from other individuals in culture A) before working cross-culturally so that one may be assured that the obtained relationship was not sample-specific.

## Facet Theory

Recently some researchers have been working with a family of analysis techniques, developed by Guttman (1954, 1959, 1966) and described by Foa (1965), which is known as facet theory. There are two aspects of this approach: (1) facet design, which deals with a logic for the construction of psychological and sociological measuring instruments according to a particular model, and (2) facet analysis, which determines whether the logic of facet design fits a given set of data, whether or not that logic was used to develop the instruments.

When an investigator has two or more dimensions which he wishes to include in a measuring instrument, he can use the principles of facet design to insure includsion of the appropriate elements of each dimension in his final product. (If he has an idea about the nature of the domain under study, then facet design can guide him in the way he puts the elements of each dimension together.)

The fundamental idea in facet theory is a set of dimensions which are relevant to the trait being studied. For the purpose of our discussion we will construct a hypothetical example using the Diadic Silhouette Test (DST) (Knapp, 1964). The DST is composed of bust silhouettes of a male and female facing each other. The figures vary only in terms of relative elevation and inclination of the head. Thus, there are three dimensions which can be used in the facet design: elevation, with three levels (male higher, equal, female higher), relative position of the male head (looking up, straight ahead, or down), and relative position of the female head (looking up, ahead, or down). We will call these facets A, B, and C, each with three levels: $a_1$ $a_2$, $a_3$, $b_1$, and so forth. An element is the Cartesian product of a level on each dimension. For example, the element $a_1$ $b_2$ $c_1$ is the case where the male head is higher and looking straight ahead and the female is looking up.

In our example there are 27 possible elements which can be formed from the three levels of the three facets. If we wish to examine the effect of each of these facets of posture on the perception of social acceptance of the female by the male for several cultures, we may run an experiment in which we ask individuals to make judgments on a seven-point scale of the degree of acceptance of the female. From such a study we could obtain information about the degree of relationship (i.e., correlation) among the elements and arrive at an ordering of the elements in terms of perceived acceptance in the relationship.

By means of facet analysis we can determine empirically the order among our variables. However, we may wish to make some predictions about the type of ordering we will find. Suppose we assume that Facet A is the most important of our dimensions, Facet B is second most important, and Facet C is least important in determining acceptance. Let us also predict that elements which have more facet levels in common will be closer in the order than elements with fewer common facet levels. This is the principle of contiguity proposed by Foa (1965). These assumptions might lead to the following predicted order among the elements:

| | | |
|---|---|---|
| 1. $a_1 b_1 c_1$ | 10. $a_2 b_1 c_1$ | 19. $a_3 b_1 c_1$ |
| 2. $a_1 b_1 c_2$ | 11. $a_2 b_1 c_2$ | 20. $a_3 b_1 c_2$ |
| 3. $a_1 b_1 c_3$ | 12. $a_2 b_1 c_3$ | 21. $a_3 b_1 c_3$ |
| 4. $a_1 b_2 c_1$ | 13. $a_2 b_2 c_1$ | 22. $a_3 b_2 c_1$ |
| 5. $a_1 b_2 c_2$ | 14. $a_2 b_2 c_2$ | 23. $a_3 b_2 c_2$ |
| 6. $a_1 b_2 c_3$ | 15. $a_2 b_2 c_3$ | 24. $a_3 b_2 c_3$ |
| 7. $a_1 b_3 c_1$ | 16. $a_2 b_3 c_1$ | 25. $a_3 b_3 c_2$ |
| 8. $a_1 b_3 c_2$ | 17. $a_2 b_3 c_2$ | 26. $a_3 b_3 c_2$ |
| 9. $a_1 b_3 c_3$ | 18. $a_2 b_3 c_3$ | 27. $a_3 b_3 c_3$ |

A straight-line ordering of this type has been called a simplex and may be identified from the matrix of correlation among the elements because, when the elements are arranged in the proper order, the correlations near the main diagonal are high and consistently decrease as you get farther away from the diagonal.

There are other assumptions which may be made about the ordering among the variables. For example, we might assume that Facets B and C are of equal strength in determining the closeness of relationships but that Facet A is still the strongest. Such an assumption might lead to an ordering of the elements as shown in the diagram on the following page.

A complex ordering such as this does not have a specific name, but each of the orderings within a level of A resembles an ordering called a circumplex. Such an ordering can be identified by a pattern of correlations where the correlations near the main diagonal are high, decrease and then increase again as one moves away from the main diagonal.

Our example has shown only two of the many possible orderings which data may have. We have also overlooked one of the important applications of facet theory, the construction of measuring devices. A good example of this application is given by Foa (1965), showing how the levels of facets can be combined to form statements for an attitude questionnaire. In this type of application facet theory provides a mapping sentence which gives the various facets and their levels. The investigator combines these elements into sentences with particular strengths of the attitudes being measured and can be reasonably sure that he has achieved a good representation of levels of intensity of the

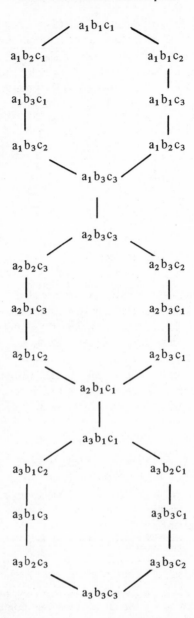

attitude. He can then collect data to test his predictions. These data result in a scaling of the statements and can be used to test hypotheses about the relative strengths of the different facets.

## Summary

We have given descriptions of only a few of the many techniques of multivariate analysis available to the cross-cultural researcher. Our selection has been made on the basis of our own preferences for certain types of analysis and on the basis of probable applicability to cross-cultural problems. With the exception of factor analysis, our goal has been merely to provide brief descriptions of the different types of analysis so that individual investigators will be aware of some of the less common multivariate techniques which may be useful to them. If there are more tools available, we can ask more questions of our data and get more answers.

# Bibliography

Abel, T. M. (1948), The Rorschach test in the study of culture. *Rorschach Research Exchange*, **12**, 79-93.

Adcock, C. J., and Ritchie, J. E. (1958), Intercultural use of the Rorschach. *American Anthropologist*, **60**, 881-892.

Adler, P. T. (1970), Evaluation of the figure drawing technique: reliability, factorial structure, and diagnostic usefulness. *Journal of Consulting and Clinical Psychology*, **35**, 52-57.

Ahmavaara, Y. (1954), Transformation analysis of factorial data. Helsinki: *Annals of the Finnish Academy of Science*, 888, 2.

Alexander, T., and Anderson, R. (1957), Children in a society under stress. *Behavioral Science*, **2**, 46-55.

Al-Issa, I., and Dennis, W. (Eds.) (1970), *Cross-cultural studies of behavior*. New York: Holt, Rinehart and Winston.

Allport, G., and Pettigrew, T. (1957), Cultural influence on the perception of movement: the trapezoidal illusion among Zulus. *Journal of Abnormal and Social Psychology*, **55**, 104-113.

Allport, G. W., Vernon, P. E., and Lindzey, G. (1960), *Study of Values: a scale for measuring the dominant interests in personality*, 3rd ed. New York: Houghton Mifflin.

Almond, G., and Verba, S. (1963), *The civic culture: political attitudes and democracy in five nations*. Princeton: Princeton University Press.

Anastasi, Anne (1968), *Psychological testing*, 3rd ed. New York: Macmillan.

Anderson A. W. (1960), Personality traits of Western Australia University freshmen, *Journal of Social Psychology*, **51**, 87-91.

Anderson, R. (1967), On the comparability of meaningful stimuli in cross-cultural research. *Sociometry*, **30**, 124-136.

Ando, N. (1965), A cross-cultural study on value patterns of seven cultural samples. *Psychologia*, **8**, 177-186.

Angelini, A. L. (1966), Measuring the achievement motive in Brazil. *Journal of Social Psychology*, **68**, 35-40.

Armstrong, L. (No date), Technical survey difficulties in India. Cited in F. Frey (1970), Cross-cultural survey research in political science. In R. Holt and J. Turner (Eds.),

*The methodology of comparative research* , New York: The Free Press, pp. 173-294.

Armstrong, R. G. (1954), The Draw-a-Man Test and the African, letter to the editor, *Man*, pp. 147-148.

Aronson, E., and Carlsmith, J. (1968), Experimentation in social psychology. In Lindzey, G., and Aronson, E., (Eds.), *Handbook of Social Psychology*, 2nd ed., Vol. 2, Reading, Mass.: Addison-Wesley, pp. 1-79.

Arthur, Grace (1949), The Arthur adaptation of the Leiter International Performance Scale. *Journal of Clinical Psychology*, 5, 345-349.

Asch, S. (1952), *Social psychology*, Englewood Cliffs, N.J.: Prentice-Hall.

Asch, S. (1966), Personal communication. Discussed in Whittaker, J., and Meade, R. (1967), Social pressure in the modification and distortion of judgment: a cross-cultural study. *International Journal of Psychology*, 2, 110-113.

Askenasy, A. (1966), The multinational comparative research corporation. *American Behavioral Scientist*, 10, Whole No. 4.

Atkinson, J. W. (Ed.) (1958), *Motives in fantasy, action, and society*, Princeton, N.J.: Van Nostrand.

Atkinson, J. W., and Feather, D. G. (Eds.) (1966), *A theory of achievement motivation*, New York: John Wiley.

Bandura, A. (1969), *Principles of behavior modification*, New York: Holt, Rinehart and Winston.

Barik, H. (1971), A description of various types of omissions, additions and errors of translation encountered in simultaneous interpretation. *Meta*, 16, 199-210.

Barker, R. G. (1968), *Ecological psychology*, Stanford, Calif.: Stanford University Press.

Barker, R. G. (1971), Individual motivation and the behavior setting claim. In W. W. Lambert and Rita Weisbrod (Eds.) *Comparative perspectives on social psychology*, Boston: Little, Brown.

Barker, R. G., and Barker, Louise S. (1961), Behavior units for the comparative study of cultures. In B. Kaplan (Ed.), *Studying personality cross-culturally*, New York: Harper and Row, pp. 457-476.

Barker, R. G., and Wright, H. F. (1955), *Midwest and its children*, Evanston, Ill.: Row, Peterson.

Barrett, G., and Bass, B. (1970), Comparative surveys of managerial attitudes and behavior. University of Rochester: Management Research Center, Tech. Rep. 36.

Barrett, G. V., and Franke, R. H. (1969), Communication preference and performance: a cross-cultural comparison. *Proceedings, 77th Annual Convention, American Psychological Association*, 597-598.

Barrett, G. V., and Franke, R. H. (1970), "Psychogenic" death: a reappraisal. *Science*, 167, 304-306.

Barrioux, M. (1948), Experience in the Time international survey: techniques used in France. *Public Opinion Quarterly*, 12, 715-718.

Barry, H., Child, I., and Bacon, Margaret (1959), Relation of child training to subsistence economy. *American Anthropologist*, 61, 51-63.

Bartlett F. (1937), Psychological methods and anthropological problems. *Africa*, 10, 401-419.

Bartlett, M. S. (1948), Internal and external factor analysis. *British Journal of Psychology (Statistical Section)*, 1, 73-81.

Bass, B. (1968), Personal communication.

Battle, E. S., and Rotter, J. B. (1963), Children's feelings of personal control as related to social class and ethnic group. *Journal of Personality,* 21, 482-490.

Bayley, Nancy (1955), On the growth of intelligence. *American Psychologist,* 10, 805-818.

Becker, H. (1958), Problems of inference and proof in participant observation. *American Sociological Review,* 23, 652-666.

Bentz, V. (1955), A comparison of the Spanish and English Versions of the Sears Executive Battery. Chicago: Sears Roebuck and Company, National Personality Department (mimeo).

Bernardoni, L. C. (1964), A culture fair intelligence test for the Ugh, No and Oo-La-La cultures. *Personal and Guidance Journal,* 42, 554-557.

Berrien, F. K. (1967), Methodological and related problems in cross-cultural research. *International Journal of Psychology,* 2, 33-43.

Berrien, F. K. (1968), Cross-cultural equivalence of personality measures. *Journal of Social Psychology,* 75, 3-9.

Berrien, F. K. (1970), A super-ego for cross-cultural research. *International Journal of Psychology,* 5, 1-9.

Berry, J. W. (1966), Temne and Eskimo perceptual skills. *International Journal of Psychology,* 1, 207-229.

Berry, J. W. (1967), Independence and conformity in subsistence-level societies. *Journal of Personality and Social Psychology,* 7, 415-418.

Berry, J. W. (1968), Ecology, perceptual development and the Müller-Lyer illusion. *British Journal of Psychology,* 59, 205-210.

Berry, J. W. (1969), On cross-cultural comparability. *International Journal of Psychology,* 4, 119-128.

Berry, J. W. (1970), Marginality, stress, and ethnic identification in an acculturated Aboriginal community. *Journal of Cross-Cultural Psychology,* 1, 239-252.

Berry, J. W. (1971), Ecological and cultural factors in spatial perceptual development. *Canadian Journal of Behavioral Science,* 3, 324-336.

Berry, J. W., and Dasen, P. R. (1972), *Culture and cognition: readings in cross-cultural psychology.* London: Methuen.

Beveridge, W. (1939), Some racial differences in perception. *British Journal of Psychology,* 30, 57-64.

Bickman, L., and Henchy, T. (Eds.) (1972), *Beyond the laboratory: field research in social psychology.* New York: McGraw-Hill.

Biesheuvel, S. (1949), Psychological tests and their application to non-European peoples. In G. B. Jeffrey (Ed.), *The Yearbook of Education.* London: Evans.

Biesheuvel, S. (1958), Methodology in the study of attitudes of Africans. *Journal of Social Psychology,* 47, 169-184.

Biesheuvel, S. (1972), The measurement of adaptability and its determinants. In L. J. Cronbach and P. J. D. Drenth (Eds.), *Mental tests and cultural adaptation.* The Hague: Mouton.

Birney, R. C. (1968), Research on the achievement motive. In E. F. Borgatta and W. W. Lambert (Eds.), *Handbook of personality theory and research.* Chicago: Rand McNally.

Black, J. D. (undated), *Preliminary manual for the D 48 test.* Palo Alto, Calif.: Consulting Psychologists Press.

Blanc, H. (1956), Multilingual interviewing in Israel. *American Journal of Sociology*, **62**, 205-209.

Bleuler, M., and Bleuler, R. (1935), Rorschach's ink-blot test and racial psychology: mental peculiarities of Moroccans. *Character and Personality*, **4**, 97-114.

Bochner, S. (1971), Personal communication.

Bonilla, F. (1964), Survey techniques. In R. Ward (Ed.), *Studying politics abroad*, Boston: Little, Brown; pp. 134-152.

Bradburn, N. M. (1963), Need achievement and father dominance in Turkey, *Journal of Abnormal and Social Psychology*, **67**, 464-468.

Brehmer, B., Asuma, H., Hammond, K., Kostron, L., and Varonos, D. (1970), A cross-national comparison of cognitive conflict. *Journal of Cross-Cultural Psychology*, **1**, 5-20.

Brewer, Marilyn (1968), Determinants of social distance among East African tribal groups. *Journal of Personality and Social Psychology*, **10**, 279-289.

Brimble, A. R. (1963), The construction of a non-verbal intelligence test in Northern Rhodesia. *Rhodes-Livingstone Journal*, **34**, 23-35.

Brislin, R. W. (1968), Contact as a variable in intergroup interaction. *Journal of Social Psychology*, **76**, 149-154.

Brislin, R. W. (1970), Back-translation for cross-cultural research. *Journal of Cross-Cultural Psychology*, **1**, 185-216.

Brislin, R. W. (1971), Interaction among members of nine ethnic groups and the belief similarity hypothesis. *Journal of Social Psychology*, **85**, 171-179.

Brislin, R. W. (1972), Translation issues: multi-language versions and writing translatable English. *Proceedings of the 80th annual convention of the American Psychological Association*, Honolulu, pp. 299-300.

Brislin, R. W., and Baumgardner, S. (1971), Non-random sampling of individuals in cross-cultural research. *Journal of Cross-Cultural Psychology*, **2**, 397-400.

Brislin, R. W., and Leibowitz, H. (1970), The effect of separation between test and comparison objects on size constancy at various age levels. *American Journal of Psychology*, **83**, 372-376.

Brislin, R. W., and Leibowitz, H. (1972), Cross-cultural developmental studies of size constancy and the Ponzo illusion. Unpublished manuscript.

Brode, J. (1969), *The process of modernization: An annotated bibliography on the sociocultural aspects of development.* Cambridge, Mass.: Harvard University.

Bronfenbrenner, U. (1970), Reaction to social pressure from adults vs. peers among Soviet day school and boarding school pupils in the perspective of an American sample. *Journal of Personality and Social Psychology*, **15**, 179-189.

Brown, F. G. (1970), *Principles of educational and psychological testing.* Hinsdale, Ill. The Dryden Press.

Bruner, J. S., Olver, R., and Greenfield, Patricia, M. (1966), *Studies in cognitive growth.* New York: John Wiley.

Burke, H. R. (1958), Raven's Progressive Matrices: A review and critical evaluation. *Journal of Genetic Psychology*, **93**, 199-228.

Buros, O. K. (1970), *Personality tests and reviews.* Highland Park, N. J.: The Gryphon Press.

Burton, A., and Sjoberg, B., Jr. (1964), The diagnostic validity of human figure drawings in schizophrenia. *Journal of Psychology*, **57**, 3-18.

Butcher, J. N. (Ed.) (1969), *MMPI: Research developments and clinical applications.* New York: McGraw-Hill.

Campbell, D. P. (1966), *Manual for the Strong Vocational Interest Blank.* Stanford, Calif.: Stanford University Press.

Campbell, D. P. (1968) The Strong Vocational Interest Blank: 1927-1967. In P. McReynolds (Ed.), *Advances in psychological assessment,* Vol. I., Palo Alto, Calif.: Science and Behavior Books, Inc.

Campbell, D. P. (1971) *Handbook for the Strong Vocational Interest Blank.* Stanford, Calif.: Stanford University Press.

Campbell, D. T. (1961), The mutual methodological relevance of anthropology and psychology. In F. Hsu (Ed.), *Psychological anthropology,* Homewood, Ill.: Dorsey Press, pp. 333-352.

Campbell, D. T. (1964), Distinguishing differences of perception from failure of communication in cross-cultural studies. In F. Northop and H. Livingston (Eds.), *Cross-cultural understandings: Epistemology in anthropology.* New York: Harper and Row, pp. 308-336.

Campbell, D. T. (1968), A cooperative multinational opinion sample exchange. *Journal of Social Issues,* **24,** 245-258.

Campbell, D. T. (1969a), Reforms as experiments. *American Psychologist,* **24,** 409-429.

Campbell, D. T. (1969b), Perspective artifact and control. In R. Rosenthal and R. Rosnow (Eds.), *Artifact in behavioral research.* New York: Academic Press, pp. 351-382.

Campbell, D. T., and Clayton, K. (1961), Avoiding regression effects in panel studies of communication impact. *Studies in Public Communication,* No. 3, Summer, 1961. Department of Sociology, University of Chicago.

Campbell, D. T., and Erlebacher, A. (1970), How regression artifacts in quasi-experimental evaluations can mistakenly make compensatory education look harmful. In J. Hellmuth (Ed.), *Compensatory education: a national debate.* New York: Brunner/Mazel.

Campbell, D. T., and Fiske, D. (1959), Convergent and discriminant validity by the multitrait-multimethod matrix. *Psychological Bulletin,* **56,** 81-105.

Campbell, D. T., and LeVine, R. (1961), A proposal for cooperative cross-cultural research on ethnocentrism. *Journal of Conflict Resolution,* **5,** 82-108.

Campbell, D. T., and Stanley, J. (1966), *Experimental and quasi-experimental design for research.* Chicago: Rand-McNally.

Cannell, C., and Kahn, R. (1968), Interviewing. In G. Lindzey and E. Aronson (Eds.), *Handbook of social psychology,* 2nd ed. Vol. 5. Reading, Mass.: Addison-Wesley, pp. 526-595.

Cantril, H. (1963), A study of aspirations. *Scientific American,* **208** (2), 41-45.

Cantril, H. (1965), *The pattern of human concerns.* New Brunswick: Rutgers University Press.

Carroll, J. (1966), Quelques measures subjectives en psychologie: frequence des mots, significativite et qualite de traduction. *Bulletin de Psychologie,* **19,** 335-340.

Casagrande, J. (1954), The ends of translation. *International Journal of American Linguistics,* **20,** 335-340.

Catford, J. (1965), *A linguistic theory of translation.* London: Oxford University Press.

Cattell, R. B. (1940), A culture-free intelligence test: I. *Journal of Educational Psychology,* **31,** 161-179.

Cattell, R. B. (1957), A universal index of psychological factors. *Psychologia*, 1, 74-85.

Cattell, R. B. (1958), Extracting the correct number of factors in factor analysis. *Educational and Psychological Measurement*, 18, 791-838.

Cattell, R.B. (1963), Theory of fluid and crystallized intelligence: a critical experiment. *Journal of Educational Psychology*, 54, 1-22.

Cattell, R. B. (1966a), The scree test for the number of factors. *Multivariate Behavioral Research*, 1, 245-276.

Cattell, R. B. (1966b), The meaning and strategic use of factor analysis. In R. B. Cattell (Ed.), *Handbook of multivariate experimental psychology*. Chicago: Rand McNally and Co., pp. 174-243.

Cattell, R. B., Feingold, S. N., and Sarason, S. B. (1941), A culture-free intelligence test II: evaluation of cultural influence on test performance. *Journal of Educational Psychology*, 32, 81-100.

Cattell, R. B., and Muerle, J. L. (1960), The "maxplane" program for factor rotation to oblique simple structure. *Educational and Psychological Measurement*, 20, 569-590.

Cattell, R. B., and Warburton, F. W. (1961), A cross-cultural comparison of patterns of extraversion and anxiety. *British Journal of Psychology*, 52, 3-15.

Chapanis, A. (1965), *Man-machine engineering*. Belmont, Calif.: Wadsworth.

Choynowski, M. (1969), The development of the Polish adaptation of the Eysenck 'Maudsley Personality Inventory.' *Acta Psychologica*, 31, 45-65.

Clark, K. E., and Campbell, D. P. (1965), *Minnesota Vocational Interest Inventory*. New York: Psychological Corporation.

Cliff, N. (1966), Orthogonal rotation to congruence. *Psychometrika*, 31, 33-42.

Cole, M., Gay, J., and Glick, J. (1968), Some experimental studies of Kpelle quantitative behavior. Psychonomic Monograph Supplements, 2, Whole No. 26.

Cole, M., Gay, J., Glick, J., and Sharp, D. (1971), *The cultural context of learning and thinking*. New York: Basic Books.

Converse, P. (1964), New dimensions of meaning for cross-section sample surveys in politics. *International Social Science Journal*, 16, 19-34.

Cooley, W. W., and Lohnes, P. R. (1971), *Multivariate data analysis*. New York: John Wiley.

Corah, N. L. (1965), Differentiation in children and their parents. *Journal of Personality*, 33, 300-308.

Court, J. H. (1972), *Researcher's bibliography for Raven's Progressive Matrices and Mill Hill Vocabulary Scales*. Bedford Park, South Australia: Flinders University School of Social Sciences. (mimeo.)

Crandall, V. C., Katkovsky, W., and Crandall, V. J. (1965), Children's beliefs in their control of reinforcement in intellectual-academic achievement situations. *Child Development*, 36, 91-109.

Cronbach, L. J. (1949), Statistical methods applied to Rorschach scores: a review. *Psychological Bulletin*, 46, 393-429.

Cronbach, L. J. (1957), The two disciplines of scientific psychology. *American Psychologist*, 12, 671-684.

Cronbach, L. J. (1970), *Essentials of psychological testing*, 3rd ed. New York: Harper and Row.

Cronbach, L. J., and Drenth, P. J. D. (Eds.), (1972), *Mental tests and cultural adaptation*. The Hague: Mouton.

Cronbach L. J., and Meehl, P. E. (1955), Construct validity in psychological tests. *Psychological Bulletin*, 53, 281-302.

Crowne, D., and Marlowe, D. (1964), *The approval motive.* New York: John Wiley.

Cryns, A. G. J. (1962), African intelligence: A critical survey of cross-culture intelligence research in Africa south of the Sahara. *Journal of Social Psychology*, 57, 283-301.

Dahlstrom, W. G., and Welsh, G. S. (1960), *An MMPI handbook.* Minneapolis: University of Minnesota Press.

Dasen, P. R. (1970), Cognitive development in Aborigines of Central Australia: concrete operations and perceptual activities. Unpublished doctoral dissertation, Australia National University, Canberra.

Dasen, P. R. (1972), Cross-cultural Piagetian research: a summary *Journal of Cross-Cultural Psychology*, 3, 23-39.

Dauterman, W. L., and Suinn, R. M. (1966), Stanford-Ohwaki-Kohs Tactile Block Design Intelligence Test for the blind: Final report. Washington, D.C.: Vocational Rehabilitation Administration.

Davis, C., and Carlson, J. (1970), A cross-cultural study of the strength of the Müller-Lyer illusion as a function of attentional factors. *Journal of Personality and Social Psychology*, 16, 403-410.

Dawson, J. L. M. (1963), Psychological effects of social change in a West African community, Doctoral dissertation, University of Oxford.

Dawson, J. L. M. (1967a), Cultural and physiological influences on spatial-perceptual processes in West Africa, Part 1. *International Journal of Psychology*, 2, 115-125.

Dawson, J. L. M. (1967b), Cultural and physiological influences on spatial and perceptual processes in West Africa, Part II. *International Journal of Psychology*, 2, 171-185.

Dawson, J. L. M. (1967c), Traditional versus Western attitudes in West Africa: the construction, validation, and application of a measuring device. *The British Journal of Social and Clinical Psychology*, 6, 81-96.

Dawson, J. L. M. (1969a), Research and theoretical bases of bio-social psychology. Inaugural Lecture from the Chair of Psychology, University of Hong Kong, Supplement to the *Gazette*, 16, (2), 1-10.

Dawson, J. L. M. (1969b), Exchange theory and comparison level changes among Australian Aborigines. *British Journal of Social and Clinical Psychology*, 8, 133-140.

Dawson, J. L. M. (1972a), Effects of sex hormones on cognitive style in rats and men. *Behavior Genetics*, 2, 20-41.

Dawson, J. L. M., and Whitney, R. E. (1972), Attitudinal conflict, GSR, and attitude change in Hong Kong Chinese. *British Journal of Social and Clinical Psychology* (in press).

Dawson, J. L. M., Law, H., Leung, A., and Whitney, R. E. (1971), Scaling Chinese traditional-modern attitudes and the GSR measurement of "important" versus "unimportant" Chinese concepts. *Journal of Cross-Cultural Psychology*, 2, 1-27.

de Lacey, P. R. (1970), A cross-cultural study of classificatory ability in Australia. *Journal of Cross-Cultural Psychology*, 1, 293-304.

de Lemos, Marion M. (1966), The development of the concept of conservation in Australian Aboriginal children. Unpublished doctoral dissertation, Australian National University, Canberra.

de Lemos, Marion M. (1969a), Conceptual development in Aboriginal children: implications for Aboriginal education. In S. S. Dunn and C. M. Tatz (Eds.) *Aborigines and education.* Melbourne: Sun Books.

de Lemos, Marion M. (1969b), The development of conservation in Aboriginal children. *International Journal of Psychology,* **4**, 255-269.

Dennis, W. (1942), The performance of Hopi children on the Goodenough Draw-a-Man Test. *Journal of Comparative Psychology,* **34**, 341-348.

Dennis, W. (1957), Performance of Near Eastern children on the Draw-a-Man Test. *Child Development,* **28**, 427-430.

Dennis, W. (1966b), Goodenough scores, art, experience, and modernization. *Journal of Social Psychology,* **68**, 211-228.

Dennis, W. (1970), Goodenough scores, art experience, and modernization. In W. Dennis and I. Al-Issa (Eds.), *Cross-Cultural studies of behavior.* New York: Holt, Rinehart and Winston.

Dent, G. R. (1937), An investigation into the applicability of certain performance and other mental tests to Zulu children: educational adaptations in a changing society. In E. G. Malherbe (Ed.) *Report of New Educational Fellowship Conference,* Capetown.

Deregowski, J. B. (1967), The horizontal-vertical illusion and the ecological hypothesis. *International Journal of Psychology,* **2**, 269-273.

Deregowski, J. B. (1968a), Difficulties in pictorial depth perception in Africa. *British Journal of Psychology,* **59**, 195-204.

Deregowski, J. B. (1968b), Pictorial recognition in subjects from a relatively pictureless environment. *African Social Research,* **5**, 356-364.

Deregowski, J. B., and Byth, W. (1970), Hudson's Pictures in Pandora's Box. *Journal of Cross-Cultural Psychology,* **1**, 315-323.

de Ridder, J. C. (1961), *The personality of the urban African in South Africa.* London: Routledge and Kegan Paul.

Dershowitz, Z. (1966), Influences of cultural patterns on the thinking of children in certain ethnic groups: A study of the effect of Jewish subcultures on the field-dependence-independence dimension of cognition. Unpublished doctoral dissertation, New York University.

Deutscher, I. (1968), Asking questions cross-culturally: some problems of linguistic comparability. In H. Becker et al. (Eds.), *Institutions and the person.* Chicago: Aldine, pp. 318-341.

Domino, G. (1964), Comparison of the D 48, Cattell Culture Fair, and Army Beta Tests in a sample of college males. *Journal of Consulting Psychology,* **28** (5), 469-472.

Domino, G. (1968), Culture-free tests and the academic achievement of foreign students. *Journal of Consulting and Clinical Psychology,* **32**, 102.

Doob, L. W. (1960), *Becoming more civilized:* A psychological exploration. New Haven, Conn.: Yale University Press.

Doob, L. W. (1967), Scales for assaying psychological modernization in Africa. *Public Opinion Quarterly,* **31**, 414-421.

Draper, N., and Smith, H. (1966), *Applied regression analysis.* New York: John Wiley.

Duijker, H. (1955), Comparative research in social science with special reference to attitude research. *International Social Science Bulletin,* **7**, 555-566.

Dunnette, M. (1963), A note on *The* criterion *Journal of Applied Psychology,* **47**, 251-254.

Eber, H. W. (1966), Toward oblique simple structure: Maxplane. *Multivariate Behavioral Research,* **1**, 112-125.

Eber, H. W. (1968), Maxplane meets Thurstone's "factorially invariant" box problem. *Multivariate Behavioral Research,* **3**, 249-254.

Edwards, A. (1957), *The social desirability variable in personality assessment and research.* New York: Dryden.

Elley, W. B., and MacArthur, R. S. (1962), The Standard Progressive Matrices as a culture-reducing measure of general intellectual ability. *Alberta Journal of Educational Research,* 8, 54-65.

Ervin, Susan (1964), Language and TAT content in French-English bilinguals. *Journal of Abnormal and Social Psychology,* 68, 500-507.

Ervin, S., and Bower, R. (1952), Translation problems in international surveys. *Public Opinion Quarterly,* 16, 595-604.

Eysenck, H. J., and Eysenck, Sybil, B. G. (1963), *Manual for the Eysenck Personality Inventory: Preliminary Edition.* San Diego, Calif.: Educational and Industrial Testing Service.

Ezekiel, M., and Fox, K. A. (1959), *Methods of Correlation and Regression Analysis,* 3rd ed. New York: John Wiley.

Faterson, H. F., and Witkin, H. A. (1970), Longitudinal study of development of the body concept. *Developmental Psychology,* 2, 429-438.

Feldman, R. (1968), Response to compatriot and foreigner who seek assistance. *Journal of Personality and Social Psychology,* 10, 202-214.

Ferracuti, F., and Rizzo, G. B. (1959), Studio sul test D 48 applicato ad una populazione italiana di livello scolastico superiore. *Bull. Psicol. Sociol. Appl.,* No. 31-36, 77-83.

Festinger, L. (1957), *A theory of cognitive dissonance.* Evanston, Ill.: Row, Peterson.

Fink, R. (1963), Interviewer training and supervision in a survey of Laos. *International Social Science Journal,* 15, 21-34.

Flavell, J. H. (1963), *The developmental psychology of Jean Piaget.* Princeton: D. Van Nostrand.

Foa, U. G. (1965), New developments in facet design and analysis. *Psychological Review,* 72, 262-274.

Ford, C. S. (Ed.) (1967), *Cross-cultural approaches: Readings in comparative research.* New Haven: HRAF Press.

Forward, J. R., and Williams, J. R. (1970), Internal-external control and Black militancy. *Journal of Social Issues,* 26, 75-92.

Frager, R. (1970), Conformity and anticonformity in Japan. *Journal of Personality and Social Psychology,* 15, 203-210.

Freeman, F. S. (1962), *Theory and practice of psychological testing,* 3rd ed. New York: Holt, Rinehart and Winston.

Freud, S. (1911), Psychoanalytic notes on an autobiographical account of paranoia (dementia paranoides). In J. Strachey (Ed.), *The complete psychological works of Sigmund Freud,* Vol. 12. London: Hogarth, 1958, pp. 9-82.

Freud, S. (1913), Totem and taboo. In J. Strachey (Ed.), *The complete psychological works of Sigmund Freud,* Vol. 13. London: Hogarth for Routledge and Kegan Paul, 1955, pp. 1-161.

Frey, F. (1970), Cross-cultural survey research in political science. in R. Holt and J. Turner (Eds.), *The methodology of comparative research.* New York: The Free Press, pp. 173-264.

Frijda, N., and Jahoda, G. (1966), On the scope and methods of cross-cultural research. *International Journal of Psychology,* 1, 109-127.

Fuller, G. B., and Lunney, G. H. (1965), Relationships between preception and body image among emotionally disturbed children. *Perceptual and Motor Skills,* 21, 530.

Furby, Lita (1971), A theoretical analysis of cross-cultural research in cognitive development: Piaget's conservation task. *Journal of Cross-Cultural Psychology,* 2, 241-255.

Furth, H. G. (1969), *Piaget and knowledge.* New Jersey: Prentice-Hall.

Gay, J., and Cole, M. (1967), *The new mathematics and an old culture.* New York: Holt, Rinehart and Winston.

Geist, H. (1959), *The Geist Picture Interest Inventory: Male and Female.* Beverly Hills, Calif.: Western Psychological Services.

Geist, H. (1969), A comparison of vocation interests in various countries in Latin America. *Revista Interamericana de Psicologia,* 3, (3), 169-176.

Georgas, J. G., and Vassilion, Vasso (1967), A normative Rorschach study of Athenians. *Journal of Projective Techniques,* 31, 31-38.

Georgie-Hyde, D. M. G. (1970), *Piaget and conceptual development.* London: Holt, Rinehart and Winston.

Gillespie, J., and Allport, G. (1955), *Youth's outlook on the future.* New York: Doubleday Papers in Psychology.

Ginsburg, H., and Opper, S. (1969), *Piaget's theory of intellectual development: an introduction.* Englewood Cliffs, N.J.: Prentice-Hall.

Girard, A. (1963), Introduction. *International Social Science Journal,* 15, 7-20.

Glatt, K. M. (1969), An evaluation of the French, Spanish, and German translations of the MMPI. *Acta Psychologica,* 29, 65-84.

Goldschmid, M. L., and Bentler, P. M. (1968), *Concept Assessment Kit – Conservation* (Manual). San Diego, California: Educational and Industrial Testing Service.

Goldschmid, M. L., Bentler, P. M., et al. (1973), A cross-cultural investigation of conservation. *Journal of Cross-Cultural Psychology,* 4, (in press).

Goldschmidt, W. (1966), *Comparative functionalism.* Berkeley: University of California Press.

Goldschmidt, W. (1971), Areté – motivation and models for behavior. In. I. Galdston (Ed.), *The interface between psychiatry and anthropology.* New York: Brunner/Mazel.

Goldstein, K., and Scheerer, M. (1941), Abstract and concrete behavior: an experimental study with special tests. *Psychological Monographs,* 54, No. 2

Goodenough, D. R., and Karp, S. A. (1961), Field dependence and intellectual functioning. *Journal of Abnormal and Social Psychology,* 63, 241-246.

Goodenough, F. L. (1926a), Racial differences in the intelligence of school children. *Journal of Experimental Psychology,* 9, 388-397.

Goodenough, F. L. (1926b), *The measurement of intelligence by drawings.* Yonkers-on-Hudson, New York: World Book.

Goodenough, W. H. (1970), *Description and comparison in cultural anthropology.* Chicago:Aldine.

Goodnow, J. (1969), Cultural variation in cognitive skills. In D. R. Price-Williams (Ed.), *Cross-cultural studies.* Baltimore, Penguin.

Gordon, L. V. (1968), Comments on "Cross-cultural equivalence of personality measures." *Journal of Social Psychology,* 75, 11-19.

Gordon, L. V., and Kikuchi, A. (1966), American personality tests in cross-cultural research: a caution. *Journal of Social Psychology,* 69,179-183.

Gordon, L. V., and Kikuchi, A. (1970a), Response sets of Japanese and American students. *Journal of Social Psychology,* 82, 143-148.

Gordon, L. V., and Kikuchi, A. (1970b), The measurement of bureaucratic orientation in Japan. *International Review of Applied Psychology,* 19, 133-140.

Gough, H. G. (1960), The Adjective Check List as a personality assessment research technique. *Psychological Reports,* 6, 107-122.

Gough, H. G., (1964a), *Manual for the California Psychological Inventory.* Palo Alto, California: Consulting Psychologists Press.

Gough, H. G. (1964b), A cross-cultural study of achievement motivation, *Journal of Applied Psychology,* 48, 191-196.

Gough, H. G. (1965a), Cross-cultural validation of a measure of asocial behavior. *Psychological Reports,* 17, 379-387.

Gough, H. G. (1965b), La predizione del successo scolastico attraverso il California Psychological Inventory. *Bollettino di psicologia Applicata,* No. 67-68, 29-38.

Gough, H. G. (1966), A cross-cultural analysis of the CPI Femininity scale. *Journal of Consulting Psychology,* 30, 136-141.

Gough, H. G. (1968a), An interpreter's syllabus for the California Psychological Inventory, In P. McReynolds (Ed.), *Advances in psychological assessment,* Palo Alto, California: Science and Behavior Books, pp. 55-79.

Gough, H. G. (1968b), Cross-cultural approaches to the study of delinquency. Paper presented at the meeting of the American Psychological Association, San Francisco.

Gough, H. G. (1968c), Personal communication.

Gough, H. G. (1970), Personal communication.

Gough, H. G., and Abbele, F. M. (1967), Una edizione Italiana del "Adjective Check List." *Bollettino di Psicologia Applicata,* N. 79-82, 3-27.

Gough, H. G., and Delcourt, M. J. (1969), Developmental increments in perceptual acuity among Swiss and American school children. *Developmental Psychology,* 1, 260-264.

Gough, H. G., and DiPalma, G. (1965), Attitudes toward colonialism, political dependence, and independence. *The Journal of Psychology,* 60, 155-163.

Gough, H. G., and Domino, G. (1963), The D 48 Test as a measure of general ability among grade school children. *Journal of Consulting Psychology,* 27 (4), 344-349.

Gough, H. G., and Heilburn, A. B., Jr. (1965), *The Adjective Check List manual.* Palo Alto, California: Consulting Psychologists Press.

Gough, H. G., and Hug, C. (1968), Perception de formes geometriques et d'illusions chez des enfants Francais et Americains. *Journal International de Psychologie,* 3, 183-190.

Gough, H. G., and McGurk, E. (1967), A group test of perceptual acuity. *Perceptual and Motor Skills,* 24, 1107-1115.

Gough, H. G., and Meschieri, L. (1967), Applicazioni de el' Adjective Check List allo studio di fenomeni economici e politici. *Bollettino di Psicologia Applicata,* N. 79-82, 29-45.

Gough, H. G. and Meschieri, L. (1971), A cross-cultural study of age-related differences in perceptual acuity. *Journal of Consulting and Clinical Psychology,* 37, 135-140.

Gough, H. G., and Olton, R. M. (1972), Field independence as related to nonverbal measures of perceptual performance. *Journal of Consulting and Clinical Psychology,* 38, 338-342.

Gough, H. G., and Riva, Anna (1967), L'applicazione dell'Adjective Check List all studio del successo scolastico. *Bollettino di Psicologia Applicata,* N. 79-82, 47-55.

Gough, H. G., and Sandhu, H. S. (1964), Validation of the CPI socilization scale in India. *Journal of Abnormal and Social Psychology,* **68**, 544-547.

Gough, H. G., Chun, K., and Chung, Y, (1968), Validation of the CPI Femininity scale in Korea. *Psychological Reports,* **22**, 155-160.

Green, D. R., Ford, Marguerite P., and Flammer, G. B. (1971), *Measurement and Piaget.* New York: McGraw-Hill.

Greenfield, P. (1966), On culture and conservation. In Bruner, J., Olver, R., and Greenfield, P., (Eds.), *Studies in cognitive growth.* New York: John Wiley, pp. 225-256.

Griffith, R. (1953), *The world of Robert Flaherty.* New York: Duell, Sloan, and Pearce.

Gruen, A. (1955), Dancing experience and personality in relation to perception. *Psychological Monographs,* **69** (14), Whole number 399.

Guilford, J. P. (1967), *The nature of human intelligence.* New York: McGraw-Hill.

Guilford, J. P., and Hoepfner, R. (1971), *The analysis of intelligence.* New York: McGraw-Hill.

Gurin, Patricia, Gurin, G., Lao, Rosina C., and Beattie, Muriel (1969)   Internal-external control in the motivation dynamics of Negro youth. *Journal of Social Issues,* **25** 29-52.

Gusfield, J. R. (1967), Tradition and modernity: misplaced polarities in the study of social change. *American Journal of Sociology,* **72**, 351-362.

Gusfield, J. R. (Ed.) (1968), Tradition and modernity: conflict and congruence. *Journal of Social Issues,* **24** (4), 1-158.

Guthrie, G. M. (1971), Unexpected correlations and the cross-cultural method. *Journal of Cross-Cultural Psychology,* **2**, 315-323.

Guthrie, G. W., Brislin, R. W., and Sinaiko, H. (1970), Some aptitudes and abilities of Vietnamese technicians: implications for training. Research paper P-659, Arlington, Virginia. Institute for Defense Analysis. Also in *Journal of Social Psychology*, 1971, **84**, 183-190.

Guthrie, G. M. et al. (1970), *The psychology of modernization in the Philippines.* Quezon City, the Philippines: Manila University Press.

Guttman, L. (1953), Image theory for the structure of quantitative variates. *Psychometrika,* **18**, 277-296.

Guttman, L. (1954a), Some necessary conditions for common-factor analysis. *Psychometrika,* **19**, 149-161.

Guttman L. (1954b), A new approach to factor analysis: the Radex. In P. F. Lazarsfeld (Ed.), *Mathematical Thinking in the Social Sciences.* Glencoe, Ill.: Free Press, pp. 216-348.

Guttman, L. (1959), A structural theory for intergroup beliefs and action. *American Sociological Review,* **24**, 318-328.

Guttman, L. (1965), A faceted definition of intelligence. *Scripts Hierosolymitana,* **14**, 166-181.

Guttman, L. (1966), Order analysis of correlation matrices. In R. B. Cattell (Ed.), *Handbook of Multivariate Experimental Psychology.* Chicago, Ill.: Rand-McNally, pp. 439-458.

Haire, M., Ghiselli, E., and Porter, L. (1966), *Managerial thinking: an international study.* New York: John Wiley.

Hall, C. A., and Lindzey, G. (1970), *Theories of personality,* 2nd ed. New York: John Wiley.

Hallowell, A. I. (1945), The Rorschach technique in the study of personality and culture. *American Anthropologist,* 47, 195-210.

Hama, H. (1966), Evaluation of clinical depression by means of a Japanese translation of the Minnesota Multiphasic Personality Inventory. *Psychologia,* 9, 165-176.

Hamburg, D. A. (1965), Forward. In P. H. Leiderman and D. Shapiro (Eds.) *Psychobiological approaches to social behavior.* London: Tavistock Publications.

Hammond, K., Bonaiuto, G., Faucheux, C., Moscovici, S., Frohlich, W., Joyce, C., and DiMajo, G. (1968), A comparison of cognitive conflict between persons in Western Europe and the United States. *International Journal of Psychology,* 3, 1-12.

Hanfmann, E., and Kasanin, J. (1936), A method for the study of concept formation. *Journal of Psychology,* 3, 521-554.

Hanna, W., and Hanna, J. (1966), The problem of ethnicity and factionalism in Africa survey research. *Public Opinion Quarterly,* 30, 290-294.

Harman, H. H. (1967), *Modern factor analysis,* 2nd ed. Chicago: University of Chicago Press.

Harman, H. H., and Fukuda, Y. (1966), Resolution of the Heywood case in the minres solution. *Psychometrika,* 31, 563-571.

Harman, H. H., and Jones, W. H. (1966), Factor analysis by minimizing residuals (Minres). *Psychometrika,* 31, 351-368.

Harris, C. W. (1962), Some Rao-Cuttman relationships. *Psychometrika,* 27, 247-263.

Harris, C. W. (1967), On factors and factor scales. *Psychometrika,* 32, 363-379.

Harris, D. B. (1963), *Children's drawings as measures of intellectual ability.* New York: Harcourt, Brace Jovanovich.

Hathaway, S. R. (1964), MMPI: Professional use by professional people. *American Psychologist,* 19, 204-210.

Hathaway, S. R., and Meehl, P. E. (1951), *An atlas for the clinical use of the MMPI.* Minneapolis: University of Minnesota Press.

Hathaway, S. R., and Monachesi, E. D. (Eds.) (1953), *Analyzing and predicting juvenile delinquency with the MMPI.* Minneapolis: University of Minnesota Press.

Haward, L. R. C. (1956), Extra-cultural differences in drawings of the human figure by African children. *Ethnos,* 3-4, 220-230.

Haward, L. R. C., and Roland, W. A. (1954a), Some intercultural differences on the Draw-a-Man test: Goodenough scores. *Man,* 54, 86-88.

Haward, L. R. C., and Roland, W. A. (1954b), Some intercultural differences on the Draw-a-Man test: Part II, Machover scores. *Man,* 55, 27-29.

Haward, L. R. C., and Roland, W. A. (1955), Some intercultural differences on the Draw-a-Man test: Part III, Conclusion. *Man,* 55, 40-42.

Hayes, K. J. (1962), Genes, drives, and intellect. *Psychological Reports,* 10, 299-342.

Hays, W. L. (1963), *Statistics for psychologists.* New York: Holt, Rinehart and Winston.

Hebb, D. O. (1949), *The organization of behavior.* New York: John Wiley.

Heckhausen, H. (1967), *The anatomy of achievement motivation.* New York: Academic Press.

Heider, F. (1958), *The psychology of interpersonal relations.* New York: John Wiley.

Henry, J. (1955), Symposium: Projective testing in ethnography. *American Anthropologist,* 57, 245-247, 264-269.

Henry, W. E. (1947), The Thematic Apperception Technique in the study of culture-personality relations. *Genetic Psychology Monographs,* 35, 1-34.

Heron, A. (1971), Concrete operations, "g", and achievement in Zambian children. *Journal of Cross-Cultural Psychology,* 2, 325-336.

Hersch, P. D., and Scheibe, K. E. (1967), Reliability and validity of internal-external control as a personality dimension. *Journal of Consulting Psychology,* 31, 609-613.

Hicks, R. E. (1969), Some comments on test developments in emerging countries: with special reference to Papua and New Guinea. *Papua and New Guinea Journal of Education,* pp. 29-43.

Hoffman, M. (1963), Research on opinions and attitudes in West Africa. *International Social Science Journal,* 15, 59-69.

Hollander, E., and Willis, R. (1967), Some current issues in the psychology of conformity and nonconformity. *Psychological Bulletin,* 68, 62-76.

Holmes, A. C. (1963), *A study of understanding of visual symbols in Kenya.* London: Overseas Visual Aids Centre.

Holt, R. T. (1971), Comparative studies look outward. In F. W. Riggs (Ed.), *International studies: present status and future prospects.* Philadelphia: The American Academy of Political and Social Science (Monograph 12).

Holt, R., and Turner, J. (Eds.) (1970), *The methodology of comparative research.* New York: Free Press.

Holtzman, W. H. (1968), The Holtzman Inkblot Technique. In A. I. Rabin (Ed.), *Projective techniques in personality assessment.* New York: Springer. pp. 136-170.

Holtzman, W. H., Thorpe, J. S., Swartz, J. D., and Herron, E. W. (1961), *Inkblot perception and personality.* Austin: University of Texas Press.

Horrocks, J. E. (1964), *Assessment of behavior.* Columbus, Ohio: Charles E. Merrill.

Horst, P. (1963), *Matrix algebra for social scientists.* New York: Holt, Rinehart and Winston.

Horst, P. (1965), *Factor analysis of data matrices.* New York: Holt, Rinehart and Winston.

Hotelling, H. (1933) Analysis of a complex of statistical variables into principal components. *Journal of Educational Psychology,* 24, 417-441, 498-520.

Hsu, F. L. K. (Ed.) (1961), *Psychological anthropology.* Homewood, Illinois: Dorsey Press.

Hubbert, H. B. (1915), The effect of age on habit formation in the albino rat. *Behavior Monograph,* 2, 1-55.

Hudson, B., Barakat, B., and Laforge, R. (1959), Problems and methods of cross-cultural research. *Journal of Social Issues,* 15, 5-19.

Hudson, W. (1960), Pictorial depth perception in sub-cultural groups in Africa. *Journal of Social Psychology,* 52, 183-208.

Hudson, W. (1962), Pictorial perception and educational adaptation in Africa. *Psychologia Africana,* 9, 226-239.

Hudson, W. (1967), The study of the problem of pictorial perception among unacculturated groups. *International Journal of Psychology,* 2, 90-107.

Human Relations Area Files (1967), The HRAF quality control sample universe. *Behavior Science Notes,* 2, 81-88.

Human Relations Area Files (ca. 1969), *Research guide.* New Haven, Conn.: HRAF Press.

Hunt, W., Crane, W., and Wahlke, J. (1964), Interviewing political elites in cross-cultural comparative research. *American Journal of Sociology,* 70, 59-68.

Hyman, H. (1964), Research design, In R. Ward (Ed.), *Studying politics abroad.* Boston: Little, Brown, pp. 153-188.

Hyman, H., et al. (1954), *Interviewing in social research.* Chicago: University of Chicago Press.

Hyman, H., Levine, G., and Wright, C. (1967), Studying expert informants by survey methods: a cross-cultural inquiry. *Public Opinion Quarterly,* 31, 9-26.

Hymes, D. (1970), Linguistic aspects of comparative political research. In R. Holt and J. Turner, (Eds.), *The methodology of comparative reresearch.* New York: The Free Press, pp. 295-341.

Inhelder, Bärbel, and Piaget, J. (1964), *The early growth of logic in the child: classification and seriation.* New York: Harper and Row. (Original French edition, 1959.)

Inkeles, A. (1966), The modernization of man. In M. Weiner (Ed.), *Modernization: the dynamics of growth.* New York: Basic Books.

Inkeles, A. (1969a), Making men modern: on the causes and consequences of individual change in six developing countries. *American Journal of Sociology,* 75, 208-225.

Inkeles, A. (1969b), Comments on John Stephenson's "Is everyone going modern?" *American Journal of Sociology,* 75, 146-151.

Inkeles, A. (1971), Continuity and change in the interaction of the personal and the sociocultural systems. In B. Barber and A. Inkeles(Eds.), *Stability and social change.* Boston: Little, Brown.

I.N.S.E.E. (1967), Training in survey research techniques. In F. Wickert, (Ed.), *Readings in African Psychology from French Language sources.* Michigan State University: African Studies Center, 178-189.

Irvine, S. H. (1965), Adapting tests to the cultural setting: a comment. *Occupational Psychology,* 39, 13-23.

Irvine, S. H. (1968), Human behavior in Africa: some research problems noted while compiling source materials. Paper presented to the East Africa Institute of Social Research Workshop in Social Psychology in Africa, New York City.

Irvine, S. H. (1969a), Contributions of ability and attainment testing in Africa to a general theory of intellect. *Journal of Biosocial Science,* Supplement 1, 91-102.

Irvine, S. H. (1969b), Factor analysis of African abilities and attainments: constructs across cultures. *Psychological Bulletin,* 71, 20-32.

Irvine, S. H. (1969c), Figural tests of reasoning in Africa: studies in the use of Raven's Progressive Matrices across cultures. *International Journal of Psychology,* 4, 217-228.

Irvine, S. H. (1970), Affect and construct: a cross-cultural check on theories of intelligence. *Journal of Social Psychology,* 80, 23-30.

Irving, D. D. (1970), The field-dependence hypothesis in cross-cultural perspective. Unpublished doctoral dissertation, Rice University, Houston, Texas.

Iwawaki, S., and Lynn, R. (1972), Measuring achievement motivation in Japan and Great Britain. *Journal of Cross-Cultural Psychology,* 3, 219-220.

Jacobsen, E. (1954), Methods used for producing comparable data in the OSCR seven-nation attitude survey. *Journal of Social Issues,* 10 (4), 40-51.

Jacobsen, E. (1968), Personal communication.

Jacobsen, E., Kumata, H., and Gullahorn, J. (1960), Cross-cultural contributions to attitude research. *Public Opinion Quarterly,* **24,** 205-223.

Jahoda, G. (1958), Child animism: I: a critical survey of cross-cultural research. *Journal of Social Psychology,* 47, 197-212.

Jahoda, G. (1961), *White man.* London: Oxford University Press.

Jahoda, G. (1966), Geometric illusions and environment: a study in Ghana. *British Journal of Psychology,* **57,** 193-199.

Jahoda, G. (1968), Some research problems in African education. *Journal of Social Issues,* **24**(2), 161-175.

Jahoda, G. (1970a), A cross-cultural perspective in psychology. *The Advancement of Science,* **27,** 1-14.

Jahoda, G. (1970b), Supernatural beliefs and changing cognitive structures among Ghanaian university students. *Journal of Cross-Cultural Psychology,* **1,** 115-130.

Jahoda, G. (1971), Retinal pigmentation, illusion susceptibility and space perception. *International Journal of Psychology,* **6,** 199-208.

Jahoda, G., and Stacey, B. (1970), Susceptibility to geometrical illusions according to culture and professional training. *Perception and Psychophysics,* 7, 179-184.

Jamal, S. (1965), The validity of Raven's Coloured Progessive Matrices Test and Otis Quick scoring Mental Ability Test for Pakistani children. *Bulletin of Education and Research* (*University of the Junjab*), 4, 25-41.

Jensen, A. R. (1969), How much can we boost IQ and scholastic achievement? *Harvard Educational Review,* **39.** 1-123.

Jones, E. (1963), The courtesy bias in South-East Asian surveys. *International Social Science Journal,* **15,** (1), 70-76.

Jones, L. V., and Bock, R. D. (1960), Multiple discriminant analysis applied to "Ways to Live" ratings from six cultural groups. *Sociometry,* **23,** 162-176.

Jones, L. V., and Bock, R. D. (1965), Personal goals of Indian and American university students. *Journal of Humanistic Psychology,* **5,** 122-146.

Jöreskog, K. G. (1967), Some contributions to maximum likelihood factor analysis. *Psychometrika,* **32,** 443-482.

Jöreskog, K. G. (1969a), Efficient estimation in image factor analysis. *Psychometrika,* **34,** 51-75.

Jöreskog, K. G. (1969b), A general approach to confirmatory maximum likelihood factor analysis. *Psychometrika,* **34,** 183-202.

Kadri, Z. N. (1971), The use of the MMPI for personality study of Singapore students. *British Journal of Social and Clinical Psychology,* **10,** 90-91.

Kagitcibasi, C. (1972), Application of the D 48 Test of General Intellectual Ability in Turkey. *Journal of Cross-Cultural Psychology,* **3,** 169-176.

Kahl, J. A. (1965), Some measurement of achievement orientation. *American Journal of Sociology,* **70,** 669-681.

Kahl, J. A. (1968), *The measurement of modernism.* Austin, Texas: University of Texas Press.

Kaiser, H. F. (1958), The varimax criterion for analytic rotation in factor analysis. *Psychometrika,* **23,** 187-200.

Kaiser, H. F. (1960), The application of electronic computers to factor analysis. *Educational and Psychological Measurement,* **20,** 141-151.

Kaiser, H.F., and Caffrey, J. (1965), Alpha factor analysis. *Psychometrika*, 30, 1-14.

Kandel, D., Lesser, G., Robert, G., and Weiss, R. (1968), Adolescents in two societies: peer, school, and family in the United States and Denmark, Final report, project No. 2139, contract No. OE-4-10-069, U. S. Department of Health, Education, and Welfare.

Kaplan, B. (Ed.) (1961), *Studying personality cross-culturally*. New York: Harper and Row.

Kapoor, S. D. (1965), Cross-validation of the Hindi version of the 16 PF Test. *Indian Journal of Psychology*, 40, 115-120.

Keesing, F., and Keesing, M. (1956), *Elite communication in Samoa: A study of leadership*. Stanford: Stanford University Press.

Keir, Gertrude (1949), The Progressive Matrices as applied to school children. *British Journal of Psychology Statistical Section*, 2, 140-150.

Kellaghan, T.P. (1965), The study of cognition in a non-Western society with special reference to the Yoruba of South Nigeria. Unpublished doctoral thesis, University of Belfast.

Kellaghan, T. P. (1968), Abstraction and categorization in African children. *International Journal of Psychology*, 3, 115-120.

Kelly, H. et al. (1970), A comparative experimental study of negotiation behavior. *Journal of Personality and Social Psychology*, 16, 411-438.

Kendall, M. G. (1954), Review of the Uppsala Symposium. *Journal of the Royal Statistical Society* (Series B), 16, 482-484.

Kahn, T. (1965), Experimental study of group influence upon individual judgment. *Journal of Psychology* (Lahore, Pakistan), 2, 133-144.

Kidd, A. (1962), The culture-fair aspects of Cattell's Test of g: Culture-Free. *Journal of Genetic Psychology*, 101, 343-362.

Kidd, A. H., and Rivoire, Jeanne L. (1965), The culture-fair aspects of the development of spatial perception. *Journal of Genetic Psychology*, 106, 101-111.

Kiesler, C., and Kiesler, S. (1969), *Conformity*. Reading, Mass.: Addison-Wesley.

Kikuchi, A., and Gordon, L. V. (1966), Evaluation and cross-cultural application of a Japanese form of the survey of interpersonal values. *Journal of Social Psychology*, 69, 185-195.

Kikuchi, A., and Gordon, L. V. (1970), Japanese and American personal values. Some cross-cultural findings. *International Journal of Psychology*, 5, 183-187.

Kilby, R. W. (1963), Personal values of Indian and American university students. *Journal of Humanistic Psychology*, 3, 108-145.

Kilby, R. W. (1970), Values of Indian, American, and Japanese university students. Unpublished manuscript.

Kimmel, P. R., and Perlman, D. (1970), Psychosocial modernity and the initial accommodation of foreigners visiting the United States. *Journal of Social Psychology*, 81, 121-123.

Kleinmuntz, B. (1969), Personality test interpretation by computer and clinician. In J. Butcher (Ed.), *MMPI: Research developments and clinical applications.* New York: McGraw-Hill, pp. 67-104.

Kline, P. (1967), The use of the Cattell 16 PF Test and Eysenck's EPI with a literate population in Ghana. *British Journal of Social and Clinical Psychology*, 6, 92-107.

Klingelhofer, E. L. (1967), Performance of Tanzania secondary school pupils on the Raven Standard Progressive Matrices Test. *Journal of Social Psychology*, 72, 205-215.

Kluckhohn, F. (1960), A method for eliciting value orientations. *Anthropological Linguistics,* 2 (2), 1-23.

Kluckhohn, F., and Strodtbeck, F. (1961), *Variation in value orientations.* New York: Harper and Row.

Knapp, R. R. (1960), The effects of time limits on the intelligence test performance of Mexican and American subjects. *Journal of Educational Psychology,* 51, 14-20.

Knapp, R. (1964), Perceptual interpretations of the diad: I. judgments of acceptance *Journal of Social Psychology,* 63, 169-177.

Kohs, C. S. (1923), *Intelligence measurement.* New York: MacMillan.

Kroeber, A. L. (1909), Classificatory systems of relationships. *Journal of the Royal Anthropological Institute,* 39, 77-84.

Kroeber, A., and Kluckhohn, C. (1952), *Culture.* Papers of the Peabody Museum, 47, No. 1.

Krug, S. E. (1967), Psychometric properties of the Culture Fair scales: reliability and validity. Institute for Personality and Ability Testing, Bulletin No. 14.

Kubany, E. S., Gallimore, R., and Buell, Judith (1970), The effects of extrinsic factors on achievement-oriented behavior: a non-Western case. *Journal of Cross-Cultural Psychology,* 1, 77-84.

Labov, W. (1970), The logic of nonstandard English. In F. Williams (Ed.), *Language and poverty.* Chicago: Markham.

Lambert, W., and Klineberg, O. (1967), *Children's views of foreign peoples.* New York: Appleton-Century-Crofts.

Lambert, W., and Weisbrod, Rita (Eds.) (1971), *Comparative perspectives on social psychology.* Boston: Little, Brown.

Lantz, H. (1948), Rorschach testing in pre-literate cultures. *American Journal of Orthopsychiatry,* 18, 287-291.

Lanyon, R. I. (1968), *A handbook of MMPI group profiles.* Minneapolis: University of Minnesota Press.

La Roche, J. L. (1959), Effets de repetition du Matrix 38 sur les resultats d'enfants katangais. *Bulletin du Centre d'Estudes et de Recherches Psychotechniques,* 8, 85-89.

Lawley, D. N. (1940), The estimation of factor loadings by the method of maximum likelihood. *Proceedings of the Royal Society of Edinburgh,* 60, 64-82.

Lee, S. G. (1953), *Manual of a Thematic Apperception Test for African subjects.* Pietermaritzburg, South Africa: University of Natal Press.

Lefcourt, H. M. (1966), Internal vs. external control of reinforcement: a review. *Psychological Bulletin,* 65, 206-220.

Leibowitz, H., and Judisch, J. (1967), The relation between age and magnitude of the Ponzo illusion. *American Journal of Psychology,* 80, 105-109.

Leibowitz, H. and Pick, H. (1972), Cross-cultural and educational aspects of the Ponzo illusion. *Proceedings of the XXth International Congress of Psychology* p. 326.

Leibowitz, H., Brislin, R., Perlmutter, L., and Hennessy, R. (1969), Ponzo perspective illusion as a manifestation of space perception. *Science,* 166, 1174-1176.

Leiter, R. G. (1966), *Manual for the Leiter International Performance Scale: Parts I and II.* Beverly Hills, California: Western Psychological Services.

Lessa, W., and Spiegelman, M. (1954), Ulithian personality as seen through ethnological materials and thematic test analysis. *University of California publications in culture and society,* 2, 243-301.

Lesser, G., and Kandel, D. (1968), Cross-cultural research: advantages and problems. Unpublished paper.

Levin, J., and Karni, E. (1970), Demonstration of cross-cultural invariance of the California Psychological Inventory in America and Israel by the Guttman-Lingoes Smallest Space Analysis. *Journal of Cross-Cultural Psychology,* 1, 253-260.

Levin, J., and Karni, E. (1971), A comparative study of the CPI Femininity scale: validation in Israel. *Journal of Cross-Cultural Psychology,* 2, 387-391.

LeVine, R. A. (1966), *Dreams and deeds: achievement motivation in Nigeria.* Chicago: University of Chicago Press.

LeVine, R. A. (1970), Cross-cultural study in child psychology. In Mussen, P., (Ed.), *Carmichael's Manual of child psychology,* Vol. 2. New York: John Wiley, pp. 559-612.

LeVine, R. A., and Campbell, D. T. (1972), *Ethnocentrism.* New York: John Wiley.

Levonian, E. (1961), A statistical analysis of the 16 Personality Factor Questionnaire. *Education and Psychological Measurement,* 21, 589-596.

Levonian, E., and Comrey, A. L. (1966), Factorial stability as a function of the number of orthogonally-rotated factors. *Behavioral Science,* 11, 400-404.

Lewis, O. (1953), Controls and experiments in field work. In Kroeber, A. (Ed.), *Anthropology today.* Chicago: University of Chicago Press, pp. 452-475.

Lincoln, J. (1935), *The dream in primitive cultures.* Baltimore: Williams and Wilkins.

Lindzey, G. (1961), *Projective techniques and cross-cultural research.* New York: Appleton-Century-Crofts.

Littig, L. W. (1971), Motives of Negro Americans who aspire to traditionally open and closed occupations. *Journal of Cross-Cultural Psychology,* 2, 77-86.

Lloyd, F., and Pidgeon, D. D. (1961), An investigation into the effects of coaching on nonverbal test material with European, Indian, and African children. *British Journal of Educational Psychology,* 31, 145-151.

Loh, W. D., and Triandis, H. C. (1968), Role perceptions in Peru. *International Journal of Psychology,* 3, 175-182.

Longacre, R. (1958), Items in context—their bearing on translation theory. *Language,* 34, 482-491.

Lonner, W. J. (1967), Cross-cultural measurement of vocational interests. Unpublished doctoral dissertation, University of Minnesota.

Lonner, W. J. (1968), The SVIB visits German, Austrian, and Swiss psychologists. *American Psychologist* 23, 164-179.

Lonner, W. J., and Adams, H. L. (1972), Interest patterns of psychologists in nine western nations. *Journal of Applied Psychology,* 56, 146-151.

Lonner, W. J., and Stauffer, E. (1967), Strong's Berufsinteressentest feur Maenner (SMTM), deutsche fassung des Strong Vocational Interest Blank for Men. Göttinger, Germany: Verlag Hogrefe.

Lovegrove, M. N. (1968), Problems of educational selection and assessment in developing countries. In Proceedings of XVIth International Congress of Psychology, Amsterdam.

Lubin, B., Wallis, R. R., and Paine, C. (1971), Patterns of psychological test usage in the United States: 1935-1969. *Professional Psychology,* 2, 70-74.

Lykken, D. T. (1968), Statistical significance in psychological research. *Psychological Bulletin,* 70, 151-159.

Lynn, R. (1969), An achievement motivation questionnaire. *British Journal of Psychology,* 60, 529-534.

MacArthur, R. S. (1967), Sex differences in field dependence for the Eskimo: replication of Berry's findings. *International Journal of Psychology,* 2, 139-140.

MacArthur, R. S., and Elley, W. B. (1963), The reduction of socioeconomic bias in intelligence testing. *British Journal of Educational Psychology,* 33, 107-119.

McArthur, R. S., Irvine, S. H., and Brimble, A. R. (1964), *The Northern Rhodesian mental ability survey, 1963.* Lusaka: Rhodes- Livingstone Institute.

McClelland, D. C. (1961), *The achieving society.* Princeton, New Jersey: Van Nostrand.

McClelland, D. C. (1970), Personal communication.

McClelland, D. C., and Winter, D. (1969), *Motivating economic achievement.* New York: Free Press.

McClelland, D. C., Atkinson, J. W., Clark, R. A., and Lowell, E. L. (1953), *The achievement motive.* New York: Appleton-Century-Crofts.

McClelland, D. C., Davis, W. N., Kalin, R., and Wanner, E. (1972), *The drinking man: cross-cultural research on alcohol and human motivation,* Riverside, New Jersey: The Free Press.

McElwain, D. W., and Kearney, G. E. (1970), *Handbook: The Queensland Test.* Victoria, Australia: The Australian Council for Educational Research.

Macnamara, J. (1967), The bilingual's linguistic performance—a psychological overview. *The Journal of Social Issues,* 23, (2), 58-77.

McNemar, Q. (1969), *Psychological statistics,* 4th ed. New York: John Wiley.

McNemar, Q., and Stone, C. P. (1932), The set difference in rats on three learning tasks. *Journal of Comparative Psychology,* 14, 171-180.

McQuaid, J. (1967), A note on trends and answers to Cattell personality questionnaires by Scottish subjects. *British Journal of Psychology,* 58, 455-458.

McReynolds, P. (Ed.) (1968), *Advances in psychological assessment,* Vol. 1. Palo Alto: Science and Behavior Books.

Marquart, Dorothy I., and Bailey, Lois L. (1955), An evaluation of the Culture Free Test of Intelligence. *Journal of Genetic Psychology,* 86, 353-358.

Marsh, R. (1967), *Comparative sociology: toward a codification of cross-societal analysis.* New York: Harcourt, Brace and World.

Marwick, M. (1958), An experiment in public opinion polling among preliterate people. *Africa,* 26, 149-159.

Meade, R. (1967), An experimental study of leadership in India. *Journal of Social Psychology,* 72, 35-43.

Meade, R. (1968), Psychological time in India and America, *Journal of Social Psychology,* 76, 169-174.

Meade, R. (1970), Leadership studies of Chinese and Chinese-Americans. *Journal of Cross-Cultural Psychology,* 1, 325-332.

Meade, R., and Barnard, W., Conformity and anticonformity among Americans and Chinese. *Journal of Social Psychology,* 89, 15-24.

Meehl, P. E. (1954), *Clinical vs. statistical prediction.* Minneapolis: University of Minnesota Press.

Meehl, P. E. (1967), Theory-testing in psychology and physics: A methodological paradox. *Philosophy of Science,* 34, 103-115.

Megargee, E. I. (1972), *The California Psychological Inventory handbook*, San Francisco: Jossey-Bass.

Meijman, T. F. (1968), Onderzoek naar de beroepsinteresse van Nederlandse psychologen en studenten psychologie met behulp van de Strong Vocational Interest Blank, Amsterdam: University of Amsterdam Psychology Laboratory (mimeo).

Melikian, L. (1964), The use of selected TAT cards among Arab university students: a cross-cultural study. *Journal of Social Psychology, 62*, 12-19.

Melikian, L., Ginsberg, A., Cuceloglu, D., and Lynn, R. (1971), Achievement motivation in Afghanistan, Brazil, Saudi Arabia, and Turkey, *Journal of Social Psychology, 83*, 183-184.

Mensh, I., and Henry, J. (1953), Direct observation and psychological tests in anthropological field work. *American Anthropologist, 55*, 461-480.

Menzel, E. W. (1935), The Goodenough intelligence test in India. *Journal of Applied Psychology, 19*, 615-624.

Meredith, G. M., and Meredith, C. W. (1966), Acculturation and personality among Japanese-American college students in Hawaii. *Journal of Social Psychology, 68*, 175-182.

Milgram, S. (1961), Nationality and conformity. *Scientific American, 205*, (6) 45-52.

Miller, G. (1953), What is information measurement? *American Psychologist, 9*, 3-11.

Miller, G., and Beebe-Center, J. (1956), Some psychological methods for evaluating the quality of translation. *Mechanical Translation, 3*, 73-80.

Minturn, Leigh, Lambert, W. W., et al. (1964), *Mothers of six cultures: Antecedents of child rearing*. New York: John Wiley.

Mirels, H. L. (1970), Dimensions of internal versus external control. *Journal of Consulting and Clinical Psychology, 34*, 226-228.

Mischel, W. (1961), Delay of gratification, need for achievement, and acquiescence in another culture. *Journal of Abnormal and Social Psychological, 62*, 543-552.

Misumi, J., and Ando, N. (1964), A cross-cultural and dia-chronical study on Japanese college student's responses to the Morris Value Scale. *Psychologia, 7*, 175-184.

Mitchell, R. (1966), The problems and possibilities of measuring social attitudes in African social surveys. Paper presented at the ninth annual meeting of the African Studies Association, Bloomington, Indiana.

Mitchell, R. (1968), Survey materials collected in the developing countries: obstacles to comparisons. In S. Rokkan (Ed.), *Comparative research across cultures and nations*. Paris: Mouton, pp. 210-238.

Mizushima, K., and De Vos, G. (1967), An application of the California Psychological Inventory in a study of Japanese delinquency. *Journal of Social Psychology, 71*, 45-51.

Mohsin, S. M. (1950), A study of the relationship of evaluative attitudes to sex difference, intellectual level, expressed occupational interest and hobbies. *Indian Journal of Psychology, 25*, 59-70.

Moore, F. W. (Ed.) (1961), *Readings in cross-cultural methodology*. New Haven, Conn.: HRAF Press.

Morris, C. (1956), *Varities of human value*. Chicago: University of Chicago Press.

Morris, C., and Jones, L. V. (1955), Value scales and dimensions. *Journal of Abnormal and Social Psychology, 51*, 523-535.

Morrison, B. M. (1966), The reactions of external and internal pupils to patterns of teaching behavior. Unpublished doctoral dissertation, University of Michigan, Ann Arbor.

Morrison, D. E., and Henkel, R. E. (Eds.) (1970), *The significance test controversy.* Chicago: Aldine.

Morrison, D. F. (1967), *Multivariate statistical methods.* New York: McGraw-Hill.

Mundy-Castle, A. C. (1966), Pictorial depth perception in Ghanaian children. *International Journal of Psychology,* 1, 289-300.

Murdock, G. P. (1969), *Outline of world cultures* 3rd ed., revised (third printing, corrected). New Haven, Conn.: HRAF Press.

Murdock, G. P. et al. (1967), *Outline of cultural materials,* fourth revised edition (third printing, with modifications). New Haven, Conn.: HRAF Press.

Murphy, G. (1947), *Personality: A biosocial approach to origins and structure.* New York: Harper.

Murphy, J., Saumer, M., and Vachon-Spilka, I. (1968), The comparability of psychiatric assessments in different languages and cultures. Final report on Federal-Provincial Mental Health project No. 604-7-550, 1966-67.

Naroll, R. (1962), *Data quality control—a new research technique.* New York: Macmillan.

Naroll, R. (1964), On ethnic unit classification. *Current Anthropology,* 5, 283-312.

Naroll, R. (1970a), Cross-cultural sampling, In R. Naroll and R. Cohen (Eds.), *A handbook of method in cultural anthropology.* New York: Natural History Press, pp. 889-926.

Naroll, R. (1970b), What have we learned from cross-cultural surveys? *American Anthropologist,* 72, 1227-1288.

Naroll, R. (1970c), Galton's problem. In R. Naroll and R. Cohen (Eds.), *A handbook of method in cultural anthropology.* New York: Natural History Press, pp. 974-989.

Naroll, R. (1970d), The culture-bearing unit in cross-cultural surveys. In R. Naroll and R. Cohen (Eds.), *A handbook of method in cultural anthropology.* New York: Natural History Press, pp. 721-765.

Naroll, R. (1971), "Conceptualizing the Problem" as seen by an anthropologist. Paper presented at the Annual Meeting of the American Political Science Association, Chicago, Illinois.

Naroll, R. and Cohen, R. (Eds.) (1970), *A handbook of method in cultural anthropology.* New York: Natural History Press.

Naroll, R., Alnot, W., Caplan, Janet, Hansen, Judith F., Maxant, Jeanne, and Schmidt, Nancy (1970), Standard ethnographic sample. *Current Anthropology,* 11, 235-248.

Nath, R. (1968), A methodological review of cross-cultural management research. *International Social Science Journal,* 20, 35-62.

Neuhaus, J. O., and Wrigley, C. (1954), The quartimax method: An analytic approach to orthogonal simple structure. *British Journal of Statistical Psychology,* 7, 81-91.

Nida, E. (1964), *Toward a science of translating.* Leiden, Netherlands: E. J. Brill.

Niyekawa-Howard, A. (1968), A study of second language learning. U. S. Department of Health, Education, and Welfare. Final Report, Project No. 3260, Contract No. OE-6-10-308.

Nobechi, M., and Kimura, T. (1957), *Study of Values* applied to Japanese students. *Psychologia,* 1, 120-122.

Norbeck, E. Price-Williams, D. R., McCord, W. M. (Eds.) (1968), *The study of personality: an interdisciplinary appraisal.* New York: Holt, Rinehart and Winston.

Notcutt, B. (1949), The distribution of scores on Raven's Progressive Matrices Test. *British Journal of Psychology,* **40**, 68-70.

Nowak, S. (1962), Correlational approach to the control of meaning of attitudinal variables in cross-cultural surveys. *Polish Sociological Bulletin,* **5-6**, 15-27.

Nutall, R. L. (1964), Some correlates of high need for achievement among urban Northern Negroes. *Journal of Abnormal and Social Psychology,* **68**, 593-600.

Okonji, O. M. (1971), A cross-cultural study of the effects of familiarity on classificatory behavior. *Journal of Cross-Cultural Psychology,* **2**, 34-49.

O'leary, T. J. (1969), Concordance of the Ethnographic Atlas with the Outline of World Cultures. *Behavior Science Notes,* **4**, 165-207.

Oltman, P.K. (1968), A portable rod-and-frame apparatus. *Perceptual and Motor Skills,* **26**, 503-506.

Ord, I. G. (1970), *Mental tests for pre-literates.* London: Ginn and Company.

Orne, M. (1962), On the social psychology of the psychological experiment: with particular reference to demand characteristics and their implications. *American Psychologist,* **17**, 776-783.

Ortar, Gina R. (1963), The transfer of psychological diagnostic measures from one culture to another. *Acta Psychologica,* **21**, 218-230.

OSCR Survey (1952), Collation of item translations. CO/29A, Oslo, Norway.

Osgood, C. E. (1952), The nature and measurement of meaning. *Psychological Bulletin,* **49**, 197-237.

Osgood, C. E. (1960), The cross-cultural generality of visual-verbal synesthetic tendencies. *Behavioral Science,* **5**, 146-169.

Osgood, C. E. (1962), Studies on the generality of affective meaning systems. *American Psychologist,* **17**, 10-28.

Osgood, C. E. (1965), Cross-cultural comparability in attitude measurement via multilingual semantic differentials. In I.. Steiner and M. Fishbein (Eds.), *Current studies in social psychology.* New York: Holt, Rinehart and Winston, pp.. 95-106.

Osgood, C. E., and Tannenbaum, P. H. (1955), The principle of congruity in the prediction of attitude change. *Psychological Review,* **62**, 42-55.

Osgood, C. E., Archer, W. K., and Miron, M. S. (1963), The cross-cultural generality of meaning systems. Urbana, Illinois: University of Illinois, Institute of Communications Research (mimeo.).

Osgood, C. E., Suci, G. J., and Tannenbaum P. H. (1957), *The measurement of meaning.* Urbana, Illinois: University of Illinois Press.

Parsons, O. A., Schneider, J. M., and Hansen, A. S. (1970), Internal-external locus of control and national stereotypes in Denmark and the United States. *Journal of Consulting and Clinical Psychology,* **35**, 30-37.

Pasquasy, R., and Doutrepont, G. (1956), Le test des dominos (d.48). *Bull. Orient. Scol. Profess.,* **5**, 20-34.

Pastor, Leslie E. (1970), Differential effects of pictorial cues on need achievement in American Indian and Caucasian adolescents. Unpublished Master's thesis, Western Washington State College, Bellingham, Washington.

Payne, S. (1951), *The art of asking questions.* Princeton: Princeton University Press.

Pearlin, L., & Kohn, M. (1966), Social class, occupation, and parental values: a cross-national study. *American Sociological Review,* **31**, 466-479.

Pelto, P. J. (1967), Psychological anthropology. In B. J. Siegel and A. R. Beals (Eds.), *Biennial review of anthropology*, 141-208.

Pelto, P. J. (1970), *Anthropological research.* New York: Harper and Row.

Penrose, L. S., and Raven, J. C. (1937), A new series of perceptual tests. *British Journal of Medical Psychology,* 16, 97-104.

Peshkin, A., and Cohen, R. (1967), The values of modernization. *Journal of Developing Areas,* 2, 7-22.

Peterson, J., and Telford, C. W. (1930), Results of group and individual tests applied to practically pure-blood Negro children on St. Helena Island. *Journal of Comparative Psychology,* 11, 115-134.

Phillips, H. (1959), Problems of meaning and translation in field work. *Human Organization,* 18, 184-192.

Phillips, J. L., Jr. (1969), *The origins of intellect: Piaget's theory.* San Francisco: W. H. Freeman.

Piaget, J. (1961), Les mecanismes perceptifs: modeles probabilisties, analyse genetique, relations avec l'intelligence. Paris: Presses Universitaires de France.

Pichot, P., Rennes, P., and Taver, G. (1953), Quelques considerations á propos des tests D 48 et vocabulaire. *Rev. Psychol. Appl.,* 4, 395-405.

Pike, K. L. (1966), *Language in relation to a unified theory of the structure of human behavior.* The Hague: Mouton.

Porteus, S. D. (1933), *The Maze Test and mental differences.* Vineland, New Jersey: Smith Printing and Publishing House.

Porteus, S. D. (1937), *Primitive intelligence and environment.* New York: Macmillan.

Porteus, S. D., (1950), *The Porteus maze test and intelligence.* Palo Alto, California: Pacific Books.

Porteus, S. D. (1965), *Porteus maze test-fifty years application.* Palo Alto, California: Pacific Books.

Porteus, S. D., and Gregor, A. J. (1963), Studies in intercultural testing. *Perceptual and Motor Skills,* 16, 705-724. Monograph Supplement 7-V16.

Preston, Caroline E. (1964), Psychological testing with Northwest coast Alaskan Eskimos. *Genetic Psychology Monographs,* 69, 323-419.

Price-Williams, D. R. (1961), A study concerning concepts of conservation of quanties among primitive children. *Acta Psychologica,* 18, 297-305.

Price-Williams, D. R. (1962), Abstract and concrete modes of classification in a primitive society. *British Journal of Educational psychology,* 32, 50-61.

Price-Williams, D. R. (Ed.) (1969), *Cross-cultural studies.* Baltimore: Penguin.

Price-Williams, D. R., Gordon, W., and Ramirez, M. (1969), Skill and conservation. *Developmental Psychology,* 1, 769.

Prince, R., and Mombour, W. (1967), A technique for improving linguistic equivalence in cross-cultural surveys. *International Journal of Social Psychiatry,* 13, 229-237.

Proshansky, H. M., Ittelson, W. H., and Rivlin, L. G. (Eds.) (1970), *Environmental psychology: man and his physical setting.* New York: Holt, Rinehart and Winston.

Prothro, E. T. (1958), Arab students' choices of ways to live. *Journal of Social Psychology,* 47, 3-7.

Przeworski, A., and Teune, H. (1966), Equivalence in cross-national research. *Public Opinion Quarterly,* 30, 33-43.

Przeworski, A., and Teune, H. (1970), *The logic of comparative social inquiry*. New York: John Wiley.

*Psychology Today*, (1970), "Tie Line," **22**, August.

Rabin, A. I. (1968), *Projective techniques in personality assessment*. New York: Springer.

Rafi, A. A. (1965), The Maudsley Personality Inventory: a cross-cultural study. *British Journal of Social and Clinical Psychology*, **4**, 266-268.

Rao, C. R. (1955), Estimation and tests of significance in factor analysis, *Psychometrika*, **20**, 93-111.

Rappaport, R. A. (1969), *Pigs for the ancestors*. New Haven: Yale University Press.

Raven, J. C. (1948), *Guide to using Progressive Matrices*. London: Lewis and Company.

Raven J. C. (1960), *Guide to the standard progressive matrices*. London: Lewis and Company.

Reboussin, R., and Goldstein, J. W. (1966), Achievement motivation in Navajo and White students. *American Anthropologist*, **68**, 740-744.

Reiss, B. F., Schwartz E. K., and Cottingham, Alice (1950), An experimental critique of assumptions underlying the Negro version of the TAT. *Journal of Abnormal and Social Psychology*, **45**, 700-709.

Riggs, F. (1970), The comparison of whole political systems. In R. Holt and J. Turner (Eds.), *The methodology of comparative research*. New York: The Free Press, pp. 73-121.

Rivers, W. (1901), Introduction and vision. In A. Haddon (Ed.), *Reports of the Cambridge anthropological expedition to the Torres Straights*, Vol. 2, Pt. 1. Cambridge: University Press.

Robertson, J. P. S., and Batcheldor, K. L. (1956), Cultural aspects of the Wechsler Adult Intelligence Scale in relation to British mental patients. *Journal of Mental Science*, **102**, 612-618.

Rodd, W. G. (1959), Cross-cultural use of the "Study of Values." *Psychologia*, **2**, 157-164.

Rorschach, H. (1942), *Psychodiagnostics: A diagnostic test based on perception* 4th ed. New York: Grune and Stratton. (Originally published in 1921).

Rosen, B. C. (1962), Socialization and achievement motivation in Brazil. *American Sociological Review*, **27**, 612-623.

Rosen, B. C. & D'Andrade, R. G. (1959), The psychosocial origins of achievement motivation. *Sociometry*, **22**, 185-218.

Rosen, E., and Rizzo, G. B. (1961), Preliminary standardization of the MMPI for use in Italy: a case study in intercultural and intracultural differences. *Educational and Psychological Measurement*, **21**, 629-636.

Rosenthal, R. (1966), *Experimenter effects in behavioral research*. New York: Appleton-Century-Crofts.

Rotter, J. B. (1966), Generalized expectancies for internal versus external control of reinforcement. *Psychological Monographs*, **80**, Whole No. 609.

Rudin, S. A. (1968), National motives predict psychogenic deaths 25 years later. *Science*, **160**, 901-903.

Rulon, P. J., and Schweiker, R. F. (1953), *Validation of a nonverbal test of military trainability*. Harvard University: Graduate School of Education.

Ryterband, E., and Barrett, G. (1970), Managers and their relationship to the management of tasks: a cross-cultural comparison. In Bass, B., Cooper, R., & Haas, J., (Eds.),

*Managing for accomplishment.* Lexington, Mass.: Heath Lexington, pp. 226-261.

Sawyer, J., and LeVine, R. A. (1966), Cultural dimensions: a factor analysis of the World Ethnographic Sample. *American Anthropologist,* 68, 708-731.

Schachter, S. (1954), Interpretative and methodological problems of replicated research. *Journal of Social Issues,* 10 (4), 52-60.

Schachter, S. (1955), Cross-cultural experimental research: methodological problems and factor findings in an international study in group behavior. *Acta Psychologica,* 11, 208-210.

Schachter, S., et al. (1954), Cross-cultural experiments on threat and rejection. *Human Relations,* 7, 413-439.

Schensul, S. (1969), Marginal rural peoples: behavior and cognitive models among Northern Minnesotans and Western Ugandans. Unpublished doctoral dissertation, University of Minnesota.

Scheuch, E. (1968), The cross-cultural use of sample surveys: problems of comparability. In S. Rokkan (Ed.), *Comparative research across cultures and nations.* Paris: Mouton, pp. 179-209.

Schneider, J. M., and Parsons, O. A. (1970), Categories on the locus of control scale and cross-cultural comparisons in Denmark and the United States. *Journal of Cross-Cultural Psychology,* 1, 131-138.

Schuman, H. (1966), The random probe: a technique for evaluating the quality of closed questions. *American Sociological Review,* 31, 218-222.

Schwartz, P. A. (1961), Aptitude tests for use in developing nations. Pittsburgh: American Institutes for Research.

Schwartz, P. A. (1963), Adapting tests to the cultural setting.*Educational and Psychological Measurement,* 23, 673-686.

Scott, G. C. (1950), Measuring Sudanese intelligence. *British Journal of Educational Psychology,* 20, 43-54.

Segall, M. (1965), Anthropology and psychology. In O. Klineberg and R. Christie (Eds.), *Perspectives in social psychology.* New York: Holt, Rinehart and Winston pp. 53-74.

Segall, M., Campbell, D., and Herskovits, M. (1966), *The influence of culture on visual perception.* Indianapolis: Bobbs-Merrill.

Shah, Iffat (1970), A cross-cultural study of vocational interests. Unpublished doctoral dissertation, University of Minnesota.

Sheatsley, P. (1951), The art of interviewing and a guide to interviewer selection and training. In M. Jahoda, M. Deutsch, and S. Cook, (Eds.), *Research methods in social relations.* New York: Dryden, pp. 463-492.

Sherif, M., Harvey, O., White, B., Hood, W., and Sherif, C. (1961), *Intergroup conflict and cooperation: the Robbers Cave experiment.* Norman: Institute of Group Relations, University of Oklahoma.

Sherwood, E. T. (1957), On the designing of TAT pictures, with special reference to a set for an African people assimilating Western culture. *Journal of Social Psychology,* 45, 161-190.

Silvey, J. (1963), Aptitude testing and educational selection in Africa. *Rhodes-Livingstone Journal,* 34, 9-22.

Sinaiko, H. (1963), Teleconferencing: preliminary experiments, Research paper P-108, Arlington, Virginia: Institute for Defense Analyses.

Sinaiko, H., and Brislin, R. (1970), Experiments in language translation: technical English to

Vietnamese. Research paper P-634, Arlington, Virginia: Institute for Defense Analyses. Also *Journal of Applied Psychology* (in press).

Singh, A. K., and Inkeles, A. (1968), A cross-cultural measure of modernity and some popular Indian images. *Journal of General and Applied Psychology,* 1, Ranchi/Patna, India.

Singh, N. (1969), *N* Ach among successful-unsuccessful and traditional-progressive agricultural entrepreneurs of Delhi. *Journal of Social Psychology,* 79, 271-272.

Singh, N. (1970), *N* Ach among agricultural and business entrepreneurs of Delhi. *Journal of Social Psychology,* 81, 145-150.

Singh, P. N., Huang, Sophia, C., and Thompson, G. G. (1962), A comparative study of selected attitudes, values, and personality characteristics of American, Chinese and Indian students. *Journal of Social Psychology,* 57, 123-132.

Sinha, J. (1968), The n-Ach/n-Cooperation under limited/unlimited resource conditions. *Journal of Experimental Social Psychology,* 4, 223-246.

Sloggett, Barbara B., Gallimore, R., and Kubany, E. S. (1970), A comparative analysis of fantasy need achievement among high and low achieving male Hawaiian-Americans. *Journal of Cross-Cultural Psychology,* 1, 53-61.

Smith, D. H., and Inkeles, A. (1966), The OM Scale: A comparative sociopsychological measure of individual modernity. *Sociometry,* 39, 353-377.

Smith, F. J., and Crano, W. D. (1971), Concerning the possibility of cross-cultural research: A reexamination of Galton's Problem. Paper presented at the meeting of the American Psychological Association, Washington, D. C.

Snider, J. G., and Osgood, C. E. (Eds.) (1969), *Semantic differential technique: a sourcebook.* Chicago: Aldine Publishing Co.

Spain, D. H. (1972), On the use of projective techniques for psychological anthropology. In F. L. K. Hsu (Ed.), *Psychological anthropology* (new edition). Cambridge, Mass.: Schenkman.

Spearman, C. (1904), "General Intelligence" objectively determined and measured. *American Journal of Psychology,* 15, 201-293.

Spearman, C. (1927), *The abilities of man.* New York: Macmillan.

Sperrazo, G., and Wilkins, W. L. (1959), Racial differences on Progressive Matrices. *Journal of Consulting Psychology,* 23, 273-274.

Spilka, I. (1968), On translating the Mental Status Schedule. *Meta,* 13, (1), 4-20.

Spranger, E. (1928), *Types of men* (translated by P. J. W. Pigors). Halle: Niemeyer.

Spreen, O. (1961), Problems of translation and re-validation of questionnaires for cross-cultural and clinical purposes. *Acta Psychologica,* 19, 1-2.

Spreen, O. (1963), *MMPI Saarbruecken. Handbuch.* Bern: Huber.

Spreen, O., and Spreen, Georgia (1963), The MMPI in a German-speaking population. Standardization report and methological problems of cross-cultural interpretations. *Acta Psychologica,* 21, 265-273.

Stephenson, J. B. (1968), Is everyone going modern? A critique and a suggestion for measuring modernism. *American Journal of Sociology,* 74, 265-275.

Stephenson, J. B. (1969), The author replies to Alex Inkeles' comments. *American Journal of Sociology,* 75, 151-156.

Stern, E., and d'Epinay, R. (1947), Some polling experiences in Switzerland. *Public Opinion Quarterly,* 11, 553-557.

Stewart, D., and Love, W. (1968), A general canonical correlation index. *Psychological Bulletin*, **70**, 160-163.

Strodtbeck, F. (1964), Considerations of meta-method in cross-cultural studies. *American Anthropologist*, **66**, 223-229.

Strong, E. K., Jr. (1943), *Vocational interests of men and women.* Stanford, California: Stanford University Press.

Stycos, J. (1955), *Family and fertility in Puerto Rico: a study of the lower income group.* New York: Columbia University Press.

Stycos, J. (1960), Sample surveys for social science in underdeveloped areas. In R. Adams and J. Preiss (Eds.), *Human Organization Research.* Homewood, Ill.: Dorsey Press, pp. 375-388.

Sundberg, N. (1956), The use of the MMPI for cross-cultural personality study: a preliminary report of the German translation. *Journal of Abnormal and Social Psychology,* **52,** 281-283.

Sundberg, N. (1961), The practice of psychological testing in clinical services in the United States. *American Psychologist,* **16,** 79-83.

Taft, R. (1957), A cross-cultural comparison of the MMPI. *Journal of Consulting Psychology,* **21,** 161-164.

Tanaka, Y. (1972), Values in the subjective culture: a social psychological view. *Journal of Cross-Cultural Psychology,* **3,** 57-69.

Tanaka, Y., and Osgood, C. (1965), Cross-culture, cross-concept, and cross-subject generality of affective meaning systems. *Journal of Personality and Social Psychology,* **2,** 143-153.

Taylor, A., and Bradshaw, G. D. (1965), Secondary school selection: the development of an intelligence test for use in Nigeria. *West African Journal of Education,* **9,** 6-12.

Tedeschi, J. T., and Kian, M. (1962), Cross-cultural study of the TAT assessment for achievement motivation: Americans and Persians. *Journal of Social Psychology,* **58,** 227-234.

Teitelbaum, P. (1967), *Physiological psychology.* Englewood Cliffs, New Jersey: Prentice-Hall.

Tessler, M. (1971), Interviewer biasing effects in a Tunisian survey. *Journal of Social Psychology,* **84,** 153-154.

Textor, R. B. (1967), *A cross-cultural summary.* New Haven, Conn.: HRAF Press.

Thompson, C. E. (1949a), The Thompson modification of the Thematic Apperception Test. *Journal of Projective Techniques,* **13,** 469-478.

Thompson, C. E. (1949b), *Thompson modification of the Thematic Apperception Test.* Cambridge, Mass.: Harvard University Press.

Thorndike, E., and Lorge, I. (1944), *The teacher's word book of 30,000 words.* New York: Bureau of Publications, Teachers College, Columbia University.

Thorndike, R. L. (1971), Concepts of culture-fairness. *Journal of Educational Measurement,* **8,** 63-70.

Thorndike, R. M. (1970), Method of extraction, type of data, and adequacy of solutions in factor analysis. *Dissertation Abstracts,* 2970-B.

Thorndike, R. M., and Weiss, D. J. (in press, 1973), A study of the stability of canonical correlations and canonical components. *Educational and Psychological Measurement.*

Thurstone, L. L. (1938), Primary mental abilities. *Psychometric Monographs,* No. 1.

Thurstone, L. L. (1947), *Multiple factor analysis.* Chicago: University of Chicago Press.

Timaeus, E. (1968), Untersuchunger zum sugenannten konformen verhalten. *Zeitschrift fur Experimentelle and Angewandte Psychologie,* 15, 176-194.

Tin-Yee Hsieh, T., Shybut, J., and Lotsof, E. J. (1969), Internal versus external control and ethnic group membership: a cross-cultural comparison. *Journal of Consulting and Clinical Psychology,* 33, 122-124.

Topping, D. (1969), *Spoken Chamorro.* Honolulu: University of Hawaii Press.

Treisman, A. (1965), The effects of redundancy and familiarity on translating and repeating back a foreign and a native language. *British Journal of Psychology,* 56, 363-379.

Triandis, H. C. (1970), Cited in D. Georgie-Hyde, *Piaget and conceptual development.* London: Holt, Rinehart and Winston.

Triandis, H. C., and Davis, E. (1965), Some methodological problems concerning research on negotiations between monolinguals. Technical Report No. 28, Group Effectiveness Research Laboratory, Urbana, Illinois.

Triandis, H. C., Vassiliou, V., and Nassiakou, M. (1968), Three cross-cultural studies of subjective culture. *Journal of Personality and Social Psychology, Monograph Supplement,* Vol. 8, No. 4, Part 2, pp. 1-42.

Triandis, H. C., Malpass, R. and Davidson, A. (1971), Cross-cultural psychology. *Biennial Review of Anthropology.* Palo Alto: Annual Reviews, Inc.

Triandis, H.C., with Vassilious, V., Vassiliou, G. Tanaka, Y., and Shanmugam, A. V. (Eds.) (1972), *The analysis of subjective culture.* New York: John Wiley.

Triandis, H.C., Kilty, I., Shanmugam, A., Tanaka, Y., and Vassiliou, V. (1968), Cultural influences upon the perception of implicative relationships among concepts and the analysis of values. Technical report No. 56, Group Effectiveness Research Laboratory, Urbana, Illinois.

Triandis, L. M. and Lambert, W. W. (1961), Pancultural factor analysis of reported socialization practices. *Journal of Abnormal and Social Psychology,* 62, 631-639.

Tsujioka, B., and Cattell, R. B. (1965a), Constancy and differences in personality structure and mean profiles, in the questionnaire medium, from applying the 16 PF Test in America and Japan. *British Journal of Social and Clinical Psychology,* 4, 287-297.

Tsujioka, B., and Cattell, R. B. (1965b), A cross-cultural comparison of second-stratum questionnaire personality factor structures—anxiety and extraversion—in American and Japan. *Journal of Social Psychology,* 65, 205-219.

Tyler, S. A. (1969), *Cognitive anthropology.* New York: Holt, Rinehart and Winston.

Tyron, R. C. (1931), Studies in individual differences in maze ability II. The determination of individual differences by age, weight, sex and pigmentation. *Journal of Comparative Physiology,* 12, 1-22.

Varga, K. (1970), The view of life of Hungarian students: an international comparison. *Journal of Cross-Cultural Psychology,* 1, 169-176.

Vayda, P. (Ed.), (1969), *Environment and cultural behavior.* Garden City, New Jersey: Natural History Press.

Vernon, P. E. (1950), *The structure of human abilities.* London: Methuen.

Vernon, P. E. (1969), *Intelligence and cultural environment.* London: Methuen.

Vernon, P. E., and Parry, J. B. (1949), *Personnel selection in the British forces.* London: University of London Press.

Vroom, V. (1964), *Work and motivation.* New York: John Wiley.

Walker, H. M., and Lev, J. (1969), *Elementary statistical methods.* New York: Holt, Rinehart and Winston.

Webb, E., Campbell, D., Schwartz, R., and Sechrest, L. (1966), *Unobtrusive measures: nonreactive research in the social sciences.* Chicago: Rand McNally.

Weber, M. (1904), *The Protestant ethic and the spirit of capitalism.* (Transl. by T. Parsons.) New York: Scribner, 1930.

Wechsler, D. (1958), *The measurement and appraisal of adult intelligence,* 4th ed. Baltimore: Williams and Wilkins.

Weiner, M. (1964), Political interviewing. In R. Ward (Ed.), *Studying politics abroad.* Boston: Little, Brown and Company, pp. 103-133.

Weiner, M. (ed.) (1966), *Modernization.* New York: Basic Books.

Welsh, G. S., and Dahlstrom, W. G. (Eds.) (1956), *Basic readings on the MMPI in psychology and medicine.* Minneapolis: University of Minnesota Press.

Werner, Emmy E., and Muralidharan, R. (1970), Nutrition, cognitive status, and achievement motivation of New Delhi nursery school children. *Journal of Cross-Cultural Psychology,* **1**, 271-281.

Werner, O., and Campbell, D. (1970), Translating, working through interpreters, and the problem of decentering. In R. Naroll and Cohen, R. (Eds.), *A handbook of method in cultural anthropology.* New York: American Museum of Natural History, pp. 398-420.

Wesley, F., and Karr, C. (1966), Problems in establishing norms for cross-cultural comparisons. *International Journal of Psychology,* **1**, 257-262.

West, L. W., and MacArthur, R. S. (1964), An evaluation of selected intelligence tests for two samples of Metis and Indian children. *Alberta Journal of Educational Research,* **10**, 17-27.

White, D. R. (1970), Societal research archives system: retrieval, quality control and analysis of comparative data. In R. Naroll and R. Naroll and R. Cohen (Eds.), *of method in cultural anthropology.* New York: Natural History Press, pp. 676-685.

Whiting, B. (Ed.) (1963), *Six cultures-studies of child rearing.* New York: John Wiley.

Whiting, J. (1954), The cross-cultural method. In G. Lindzey (Ed.), *Handbook of social psychology.* Vol. 1 Reading, Mass.: Addison–Wesley, pp. 523-531.

Whiting, J. (1968), Methods and problems in cross-cultural research. In G. Lindzey and E. Aronson (Eds.), *Handbook of Social Psychology,* Vol. 2, 2nd ed. Reading, Mass.: Addison-Wesley, pp. 693-728.

Whiting, J., and Child, I. L. (1953), *Child training and personality.* New Haven, Conn.: Yale University Press.

Whittaker, J., and Meade, R. (1967), Social pressure in the modification and distortion of judgment: A cross-cultural study. *International Journal of Psychology,* **2**, 110-113.

Wickert, F., (Ed.) (1967), *Readings in African psychology from French language sources.* Michigan State University: African Studies Center.

Wilson, E. (1958), Problems of survey research in modernizing areas. *Public Opinion Quarterly,* **22**, 230-234.

Wilson, E., and Armstrong, L. (1963), Interviewers and interviewing in India. *International Social Science Journal,* **15**, 48-58.

Winch, R., and Campbell, D. (1969), Proof? no. evidence? yes. The significance of tests of significance. *The American Sociologist,* **4**, 140-143.

Winer, B. (1962), *Statistical principles in experimental design.* New York: McGraw-Hill.

Winterbottom, Marian R. (1953), The relation of childhood training in independence to achievement motivation. Unpublished doctoral dissertation, University of Michigan.

Winterbottom, Marian R. (1958), The relation of need for achievement to learning experiences in independence and mastery. In J. W. Atkinson (Ed.), *Motives in fantasy, action, and society.* Princeton, New Jersey: Van Nostrand.

Witkin, H. (1967), A cognitive-style approach to cross-cultural research. *International Journal of Psychology, 2,* 233-250.

Witkin, H., Oltman, P. K., Raskin, E., and Karp, S. A. (1971), *A manual for the Embedded Figures Test.* Palo Alto, California: Consulting Psychologists Press.

Witkin, H., Dyk, R. B., Faterson, H. F., Goodenough, D. R., and Karp, S. A. (1962), *Psychological differentiation.* New York: John Wiley.

Witkin, H., Lewis, H. B., Hertzman, M., Machover, K., Meissner, P. B., and Wapner, S. (1954), *Personality through perception.* New York: Harper.

Wober, M. (1966), Sensotypes. *Journal of Social Psychology, 70,* 181-189.

Wober, M. (1967), Adapting Witkin's field independence theory to accommodate new information from Africa. *British Journal of Psychology, 58,* 29-38.

Wober, M. (1969), Distinguishing centri-cultural from cross-cultural tests and research. *Perceptual and Motor Skills, 28,* 488.

Wohlwill, J. F. (1966), The physical environment: a problem for the psychology of stimulation. *Journal of Social Issues, 22,* 29-38.

Wohlwill, J. F. (1970), The emerging discipline of environmental psychology. *American Psychologist, 25,* 303-312.

Wuebben, P. (1968), Experimental design, measurement, and human subjects: a neglected problem of control. *Sociometry, 31,* 89-101.

Zajonc, R., and Wahi, N. (1961), Conformity and need achievement under cross-cultural norm conflict. *Human Relations, 14,* 241-250.

Za'rour, G. I. (1971), The conservation of number and liquid by Lebanese school children in Beirut. *Journal of Cross-Cultural Psychology, 2,* 165-172.

Zimmerman, W. K. (1964), Ten methods in factor analysis: A comparison. Paper presented at the 72nd annual meeting of the American Psychological Association, Los Angeles.

# Author Index

# Subject Index